Plain And Pleasant Talk About Fruits, Flowers, And Farming

PLAIN AND PLEASANT TALK

ABOUT

Fruits, Flowers and Farming.

BY HENRY WARD BEECHER.

―――――◆―――――

NEW YORK:

DERBY & JACKSON 119 NASSAU STREET.

1859.

W. H. TINSON,
Stereotyper.

GEO. RUSSELL & Co.,
Printers.

SOMERVILLE & BROTHER,
Binders.

PREFATORY.

No one of our readers will be half so curious to know what this book contains as the author himself. For it is more than twelve years since these pieces were begun, and it is more than ten years since we have looked at them. The publishers have taken the trouble to dig them out from what we supposed to be their lasting burial-place, in the columns of the *Western Farmer and Gardener*, and they have gone through the press without our own revision.

It is now twenty years since we settled at Indianapolis, the capital of Indiana, a place then of *four*, and now of *twenty-five* thousand inhabitants. At that time, and for years afterward, there was not, within our knowledge, any other than political newspapers in the State—no educational journals, no agricultural or family papers. The *Indiana Journal* at length proposed to introduce an agricultural department, the matter of which should every month be printed, in magazine form, under the title, *Indiana Farmer and Gardener*, which was afterward changed to the more comprehensive title, *Western Farmer and Gardener*.

It may be of some service to the young, as showing how valuable the fragments of time may become, if mention is made of the way in which we became prepared to edit this journal.

The continued taxation of daily preaching, extending through months, and once through eighteen consecutive months, without the exception of a single day, began to wear upon the nerves, and made it necessary for us to seek some relaxation. Accordingly we used, after each week-night's preaching, to drive the sermon out of our heads by some alterative reading.

In the State Library were Loudon's works—his encyclopedias of Horticulture, of Agriculture, and of Architecture. We fell upon them, and, for years, almost monopolized them.

In our little one-story cottage, after the day's work was done, we pored over these monuments of an almost incredible industry, and read, we suppose, not only every line, but much of it, many times over; until, at length, we had a topographical knowledge of many of the fine English estates —quite as intimate, we dare say, as was possessed by many of their truant owners. There was something exceedingly pleasant, and is yet, in the studying over mere catalogues of flowers, trees, fruits, etc.

A seedsman's list, a nurseryman's catalogue, are more fascinating to us than any story. In this way, through several years, we gradually accumulated materials and became familiar with facts and principles, which paved the way for our editorial labors. Lindley's Horticulture and Gray's Structural Botany came in as constant companions. And when, at length, through a friend's liberality, we became the recipients of the *London Gardener's Chronicle*, edited by Prof. Lindley, our treasures were inestimable. Many hundred times have we lain awake for hours, unable to throw off the excitement of preaching, and beguiling the time with imaginary visits to the Chiswick Garden, to the more than oriental magnificence of the Duke of Devonshire's grounds at Chatsworth. We have had long discussions, in that little bedroom at Indianapolis, with Van Mons about pears, with Vibert about roses, with Thompson and Knight of fruits and theories of vegetable life, and with London about everything under the heavens in the horticultural world.

This employment of waste hours not only answered a purpose of soothing excited nerves then, but brought us into such relations to the material world, that, we speak with entire moderation, when we say that all the estates of the richest duke in England could not have given us half the pleasure which we have derived from pastures, waysides, and unoccupied prairies.

If, when the readers of this book shall have finished it, they shall say, that these papers, well enough for the circumstances in which they originally appeared, have no such merit as to justify their republication in a book form, we beg leave to tell them that their judgment is not original. It is just what we thought ourselves! But Publishers are willful, and must be obeyed!

HENRY WARD BEECHER.

BROOKLYN, *June* 1, 1859.

CONTENTS.

PLAIN AND PLEASANT TALK

ABOUT

FRUIT, FLOWERS AND FARMING.

---◆---

PRELIMINARY.

WE understand very well that every region must fashion its *system* of agriculture upon the nature of its soil, its climate, etc. The *principles* of agriculture may be alike in every zone, but the *processes* depend upon circumstances. It would be folly for a new country, without commerce, to imitate an old country with an active commerce; it would be folly, where land is cheap, abundant, and naturally fertile, to adopt the habits of those who are stinted in lands, who have a redundant population, and who find a market for even the weeds which are indigenous to the soil. The husbandry of Holland is suited to a wet soil, and of England to a humid atmosphere and a very even annual temperature. But our soil is subject to extreme wet in spring and dryness in summer, to severe cold and intense heat. A farm whose bottom-lands are reinvigorated by yearly inundations, may thrive under an exacting husbandry that would exhaust an upland farm in a few years. Modes of agriculture must be suited to circumstances. Nevertheless, the experiments and discoveries and practices of every land are worth our careful attention. We do not import *clothes—*

but we do *cloth*, to be *made up* to suit our own habits and wants.

The two extremes of husbandry are, the *adoption* of every novelty and every experiment indiscriminately, and the *rejection* of every new thing and every improvement, as indiscriminately. Wisdom consists in "proving all things and holding fast that which is *good*." We do not advocate large outlays for expensive machines—for fancy cattle, for every new thing that turns up. But when, after full trial, it is ascertained what are the best farm horses, the best breed of cattle, the best milch cows, the most profitable breed of hogs and sheep, and the most skillful routine of cultivation, we think our farmers ought to profit by the knowledge. It is never a good economy to have poor things when you can just as well have the best. This, then, is

OUR CREED.

We believe in small farms and thorough cultivation.

We believe that soil loves to eat, as well as its owner, and ought, therefore, to be manured.

We believe in large crops which leave the land better than they found it—making both the farmer and the farm rich at once.

We believe in going to the bottom of things and, therefore, in deep plowing, and enough of it. All the better if with a sub-soil plow.

We believe that every farm should own a good farmer.

We believe that the best fertilizer of any soil, is a spirit of industry, enterprise, and intelligence—without this, lime and gypsum, bones and green manure, marl and guano will be of little use.

We believe in good fences, good barns, good farmhouses, good stock, good orchards, and children enough to gather the fruit.

We believe in a clean kitchen, a neat wife in it, a spinning-piano, a clean cupboard, a clean dairy, and a clean conscience.

We firmly disbelieve in farmers that will not improve; in farms that grow poorer every year; in starveling cattle; in farmers' boys turning into clerks and merchants; in farmers' daughters unwilling to work, and in all farmers ashamed of their vocation, or who drink whisky till honest people are ashamed of them.

ALMANAC FOR THE YEAR.

1. Work for January.—If you have done as you ought to have done, you have a snug ice-house, with double walls, the space between which is filled with non-conducting substances, as pulverized charcoal, or dried saw-dust, or tanbark, which are mentioned in the order of their value. Cut your blocks of ice of a size and shape with reference to close packing. Cover over thickly with clean straw when the stock of ice is all in. Look out not to lose all your chance in waiting for a better one; sometimes careful folks mean to have such glorious ice, that an open winter cheats them out of any at all.

Warmth.—The best fire in winter is made up of *exercise,* and the poorest, of *whisky.* He that keeps warm on liquor is like a man who pulls his house to pieces to feed the fire place. The prudent and temperate use of liquor is to let it alone. If you don't touch it, it certainly won't hurt you; he that says there is no danger, boasts that he is something more than other men.

The way to summer your cattle well is to winter them well; and half the secret of good wintering is *to keep them warm.* Animal heat is generated in proportion to the abundance and excellence of their food. Exposure to the cold air withdraws heat rapidly, and of course makes more food necessary to re-supply it, just as an open door makes it necessary to have more wood in the stove. If your stock run down in the winter and come out lean and feeble, all the summer will not fully bring them up again.

2. WORK FOR FEBRUARY.—Get out rails, both for present use, and for the fence which you expect to lay in March and April. Cut, haul and stack up near your house a good supply of *fire-wood ;* no matter if the forest is within ten rods of your door, your wife ought to have her wood chopped and dried ready for use. Look at every fence upon the place ; see if the corners of your rail fences are rotting down ; if some rails have not broken ; if pig-holes have not been made ; if boys and cattle have not thrown down top-rails ; and in short, put your fences into proper repair.

Of course your tools will now be overhauled ; those with steel blades should be thoroughly cleansed when laid aside in the fall, and if you rub a little oil over them and hang them up, all the better. Repair all that are out of order. These things and all your ordinary work, may be done, and still leave you leisure for *reading.* You should have good books and good papers, and read them carefully for your own sake and for your children's. A man who brings up a family of ignorant children, cheats his children of their rights, and cheats his country of its rights ; it is therefore a crime.

GARDEN WORK.—If there be no snow on the ground, the gardens may be cleared of all rubbish, manure hauled and stacked carefully ; and if you have a clay soil, and can catch the ground without frost for a few days, it will mellow and ameliorate it to spade it up, leaving it in lumps and heaps, through which the frost may thoroughly penetrate.

It is time to prepare your hot-bed, if you design having early plants in your garden.

3. WORK FOR MARCH.—Begin the year by thorough, deep plowing, where your fields are in good order for it. Depend upon it, that deep plowing is the only good plowing.

Your first crop, generally, will tell you so. But if the subsoil is such that the first crop is rather poor, a year's exposure of the land will ameliorate it so that your second crop will remunerate all expenses of time and labor laid out in deep plowing. No farmer should be without a subsoil plow who has got his lands clear of stumps and roots.

Take especial care of cows now just coming in with calf. See that those which are heavy are carefully handled, well fed, and warmly sheltered. Mares with foal should be tenderly used, exercised a little, but not put to hard or straining work. *The condition of the mother will to a great extent determine the condition of the offspring.* Cows, mares, sows, ewes, etc. etc., should be kept in a hearty condition, without being *fat*.

ORCHARD.—Do not trouble your trees with premature pruning. Let the axe, and knife, and saw alone. Loosen the dirt or sod around and beneath your trees. The best manure for your trees is fresh mold, or forest soil and lime in the proportion of about one part to ten. Take soft soap, dilute it with urine, scrub your trees with it plentifully, having first scraped off all rough bark. If you would work easily always, never let your work drive you.

4. WORK FOR APRIL.—Gather from your barn the loose hay seed, and sow it upon your wheat fields; it will give good pasturage after harvest, and make fine stuff for plowing under. Push forward your plowing, but look well to the teams; as cattle and horses are like men, unable in early spring to endure severe labor all at once. Your spring wheat should be got in; barley is a better crop, usually, than rye. The middle and last of the month will keep you in the corn-field. Plow deep—plow thoroughly; and after planting, give the plow no rest, if you wish good corn.

YOUNG ANIMALS.—You will now begin to have plenty of calves, colts, pigs, and lambs. If you mean to have profitable pork, you ought to *push* your pigs from the birth. Look carefully after your lambs; see that the mothers are well cared for; have dry and warm pens for any that are feeble. A little tenderness to the lambs will be well repaid by and by.

GARDEN.—Your lettuce may be transplanted from the hot-bed the middle and last of this month. A foot apart is none too much, if you wish head-lettuce. Sow your main supplies of radishes, cabbage, tomatoes, etc. Get your pie-plant seed in early as possible; also carrots, parsnips, and salsify or oyster-plant. Prune your gooseberries, currants, and raspberry bushes. Grapes, which were not laid in last fall should be pruned and laid in early in March; but if neglected then, let them be till the leaves are large as the palm of your hand. Look out or worms' nests, and destroy them promptly.

5. WORK FOR MAY.—Your whole force will be required in this month. If the season has been late or wet, you still have your corn to plant. Pastures will be ready for your stock; remember to salt your stock every week. Weeds will now do their best to take your crops. Your potato crop should be put in, as there will be little danger of frost. After the 15th, you may put out sweet potato slips. If you have not grass-land for pasturage, try for one season the system of *soiling*, *i. e.* keeping up your cattle in the yard or home-lot, and cutting green-fodder for them every day. An acre or two of corn, sown broad-cast, or oats and millet, should be tried. Above all other things, if you have warm, deep sandy loam, put in an acre of lucerne.

During the last of this month, and at the beginning of the next, pruning may be done. If the limbs be large, cover the stump with a coat of paint, wax, grafting clay, or anything that will exclude air and wet.

The garden will require extra labor in all this month. After the 15th, tender bulbs and tubers may be planted, dahlias, amaryllises, tuberoses, etc. Peas will require brush;

all your plants from the hot-bed should by this time be well
a growing in open air. Roses will be showing their buds.
If large roses of a favorite sort are required, more than half
the buds should be taken off, and the whole strength of the
plant be given to the remainder. The soil for this best of
all flowers, cannot be too rich, nor too deep.

6. WORK FOR JUNE.—May, June, and September are the
dairy months. The best butter and the best cheese are
usually made in these months. If you are not neat, you
do not know how to make cheese or butter. Uncleanliness
affects not only the looks, but the quality of butter. Broad,
shallow glass pans are the best, but the most expensive. In
these milk seldom turns sour in summer thunder-storms.
Tin pans are good, but unless the dairy-woman is *scrupulously* neat, the seams will be filled with residuum of milk
and become very foul, giving a flavor to each successive
panful. The principal requisites for prime butter are,
good cows, good pasture for them, clean pans, cool, airy
cellars, clean churns. Let the cream be churned before it
is sour or bitter; and when the butter comes, at least three
thorough workings will be necessary to drive out all the
butter-milk.

GARDEN.—Transplant flowers; destroy all weeds; get
out cabbages; more lettuce; get ready celery trenches;
layer favorite roses, vines, etc.; examine and remove from
the peach-tree root, the grub which is destroying them.
Sow salt under plum-trees—put on a coat two inches
thick.

Transplant flowers; bud roses with fine kinds; see that
large plants are tied neatly to frames or stakes. Every
morning examine your beds of cabbage, etc., for cut-worms,
and destroy them if found; plant succession crops of peas,
corn, radishes, lettuce, etc.

7. WORK FOR JULY.—Great difference of practice and
opinion exists as to the methods and time of harvesting.
Some cut their grass while the dew is on it; others cut it

when perfectly dry, and say that if so cut it need not be spread, but will dry in the swath in one or two days. As to the *time* of cutting grass, we should avoid both extremes of very early or very late. Just before the seed of *timothy* is ripe, is, upon the whole, the best time for this best of grasses for the scythe. Clover should be cut when in full blossom; instead of spreading, the best farmers make it into small cocks and leave it there to cure, which it will do without shrivelling or losing its color.

GARDEN WORK.—As soon as your roses are done blooming, if you wish to increase them, take the young shoots, and about eight inches from the ground, cut, below an eye, half through, and then slit upward an inch or two through the pith; put a bit of chip in to keep the slit open; bend down the branch and cover the portion thus operated on with an inch or two of earth and put a brick upon it. It will soon send out roots, and by October may be separated from the parent plant. Quinces, gooseberries, and almost all shrubs which branch near the ground, may be propagated in this way. Still keep down weeds. Sow successive crops of corn, peas and salads, for fall use. Begin to gather such seeds as ripen early. Take up tulips, hyacinths, etc., as soon as the tops wither.

8. WORK FOR AUGUST.—If during this hot month you will clear out fence corners, and cut off vexatious intruders, the sun will do all it can to help you kill them. If your wheat is troubled with the weevil, thrash it out and leave it in the chaff. It will raise a heat fatal to its enemy without injuring itself. Every farmer should have a little nursery row of apple, pear, peach and plums of his own raising. Plant the seed; when a year old, transplant into rows eight inches apart in the row and two feet between the rows. During July, August, and September, you may bud them with choice sorts, remembering that a *first-rate* fruit will live just as easily as a worthless sort. This is a good month to sow down fallow fields to grass. Plough thoroughly—harrow till the earth is fine; be liberal of seed, and cover in with a harrow and not with a bush, which drags the seeds into heaps, or carries them in hollows. The early part of the month should be improved by all who wish to put in a crop of buck-wheat or turnips. If your pastures are getting short, let your milch cows have something every night in the yard. Corn, sown broadcast, would now render admirable service.

If you have neglected to raise your bulbs, lose no time now. Take cuttings from roses and put in small pots, invert a glass over them; in two or three weeks they will take root, and by the next spring make good plants. Gather flower seeds as soon as they ripen.

9. WORK FOR SEPTEMBER.—You should finish seeding your wheat grounds in this month. If sown too early, it is liable to suffer from the fly; if too late, from rust. Those who sow acres by the hundred, must sow early and late both. But moderate fields should be seeded by the middle of this month. In preparing the land, if the surface does not naturally drain itself, it should be so plowed as to turn the water into furrows between each land. Standing water, and, yet more, ice upon it, being fatal to it. See that your cattle are brought into good condition for wintering. Fall transplanting may be performed from the middle of this month; *take off every leaf*—re-set, and stake.

By the latter part of the month, or early in October, according to the season, it will be necessary to raise and pot such plants as you intend to keep in the house; to raise and place in a dry and frost-proof room your dahlias, tube-roses, amaryllis, tigridia, gladioli, and such other tender bulbs as you may have. Let your seed be gathered, carefully put away where it will contract no moisture. Go over your grounds and examine all your *labels*, lest the storms which are approaching should destroy them. Sow in some warm and sheltered part of your garden, early in this month, for spring use, spinage, corn salad, lettuce, etc.

As soon as the leaves fall, take cuttings from currant bushes and grapes, and plant them out in rows. They will start off and grow earlier by some six weeks, the next season. Fill in your celery trenches every ten days.

10. WORK FOR OCTOBER.—Push forward your hogs as fast as possible. If they have had a good clover range in the summer, they will be ready to start off vigorously from the moment that you begin to put them upon corn. See that good paths are made in every direction from your house; and be sure to have walks through your barn-yards raised so high as never to be muddy. Your cattle-yards should slope toward the centre in such a way that horses and cattle need not wade knee deep in going in and out.

Frosts will now begin to strip your trees and stop the growth of garden shrubs, and all your preparations should be made for protecting tender trees and shrubs. For cherry and pear-trees, especially, you should provide good covering for their trunk, until they have grown quite large. A good bundle of corn-stalks set round the body so as to keep out the sun, but not the air, will answer every purpose. For beds of China and tea, and dwarf roses, we advise a covering of three inches of half-rotted manure. Cover this with leaves about six inches. Moss is better, if you will take the trouble to collect it; and straw will do if you have neither moss nor leaves. Half cover the part that remains exposed, with fine brush, or pine branches. For single plants, drive a stake by their side, and tie the plant to it; wind loosely about it a wisp of straw or roll of bass matting, or cloth, so as to exclude the sun and not the air. The *sun*, and not the *cold*, usually destroys plants.

11. WORK FOR NOVEMBER.—During this month, if the ground is not locked by frost, you may plow stiff, tenacious clay soils to great advantage. By being broken up and subjected to the keen frosts, your soil will become mellow and tender. See that every provision is made for shelter-

ing your cattle and horses; be sure that your sheep are not obliged to lie out in drenching rains.

IN THE GARDEN see that your asparagus bed is dressed if neglected last month. House all your brush, poles, stakes, frames, etc., which will be fit for use another season. If your tulips, hyacinths, etc. have not been planted, you had better reserve them for spring, as they will be liable to rot in the ground if planted so late in the year. Cover with brush, or leaves, or straw, your lettuce, spinage, and other salad plants designed for spring use. If tender plants, roses, vines, etc., have been left unprotected, cover as directed last month. If you have no cold frame for half-hardy plants, they may be *laid in by the heels*, i. e., taken up, and the roots laid into a trench, the tops sloping at an angle of about twenty degrees, and then covered with earth. The soil should cover about half the stem.

It is now a good season for cutting grafts. Take them from the outside of the middle of the tree; let them be done up in small packages, and set up endwise in the cellar, and covered with about half-dry sand. Roots may be taken from pear and apple-trees, and packed in the same way for root-grafting.

12. DECEMBER.—The year is about to close. Look back upon your toil. In what respect will your year's labor bear an approval when calmly examined? Can you honestly acquit yourself of indolence and carelessness? and as honestly take credit for enterprise, activity, and a desire for improvement? Your barns are full—your granary is heavy with grain—the year's bounty has followed a year's labor, and if you have the heart of a man you will not forget the source whence your blessings have come. You have perhaps done well by your stock, and in so far as the body is concerned, for your children; but what have you done for their education? What have you done to promote popular education? Are you doing anything to make your neighborhood better? What good newspapers do you provide for your family? Do you lay out as much money for books as you do for tobacco? In looking forward to the next year, you ought to mark out your personal course by good resolutions, and your business course by a definite plan of operations. It would be well if a farmer should know beforehand everything he means to do; and afterwards, if he has kept such an account that you can tell anything that you have done.

Sleighing for the young and gay, and warm fire-sides for the aged, are what are now most thought of. Those who are best provided with the comforts of life should remember their less favored brethren.

EDUCATED FARMERS.

It is time for those who do not believe ignorance to be a blessing, to move in behalf of common schools. Many teachers are not practised even in the rudiments of the spelling-book; and as for reading, they stumble along the sentences, like a drunken man on a rough road. Their "*hand-write*," as they felicitously style the hieroglyphics, would be a match for Champollion, even if he *did* decipher the Egyptian inscriptions. But a more detestable fact is, that sometimes their morals are bad; they are intemperate, coarse, and ill-tempered; and wholly unfit to inspire the minds of the pupils with one generous or pure sentiment. We do not mean to characterize the *body* of the common schoolmasters by these remarks; but that any considerable portion of them should be such, is a disgraceful evidence of the low state of education.

Farmers and mechanics! this is a subject which comes home to you. Crafty politicians are constantly calling you the *bone and sinew* of the land; and you may depend upon it that you will never be anything else but bone and sinew without education. There is a law of God in this matter. That class of men who make the most and best use of their *heads*, will, in *fact*, be the most influential, will stand highest, whatever the theories and speeches may say. This is a "nature of things" which cannot be dodged, nor got over. Whatever class bestow great pains upon the cultivation of their minds will stand high. If farmers and mechanics feel themselves to be as good as other people, it all may be true ; for *goodness* is one thing and *intelligence* is another. If they think that they have just as much mind as other classes, that may be true ; but can you *use it as well?*

Lawyers, and physicians, and clergymen, and literary men, make the discipline of their intellect a constant study. They read more, think more, write more than the laboring classes. The difference between the educated and uneducated portions of society is a *real* difference. Now a proud and lazy fellow, may rail and swear at this, and have his labor for his pains. There is only one way really to get over it, and that is to rear up a generation of well educated, thinking, reading farmers and mechanics. Your skill and industry are felt ; and they put you, in these respects, ahead of any other class. Just as soon as your *heads* are felt, as much as your *hands* are, that will bring you to the top.

Many of our best farmers are men of great natural shrewdness ; but when they were young they "had no chance for learning." They feel the loss, and they are giving their children the best education they can. Farmers' sons constitute three-fifths of the educated class. But the thing is, that they are not educated *as farmers*. When they begin to study they leave the farm. They do not expect to return to it. The idea of sending a boy to the school, the academy, and the college, and then let him go back to farming, is regarded as a mere waste of time and money. You see how it is even among yourselves. If a boy has an education, you expect him to be a lawyer, or a doctor, or a preacher. You tacitly admit that a farmer

does not need such an education; and if you think so, you
cannot blame others if they follow your example.

There is no reason why men of the very highest education should not go to a farm for their living. If a son of
mine were brought up on purpose to be a farmer, if that
was the calling which he preferred, I still would educate
him, if he had common sense to begin with. He would be
as much better for it as a farmer, as he would as a lawyer.
There is no reason why a thoroughly scientific education
should not be given to every farmer and to every mechanic.
A beginning must be made at the common school. Every
neighborhood ought to have one. But they do not grow
of themselves, like toad-stools. And no decent man will
teach school on wages which a canal boy, or a hostler would
turn up his nose at. You may as well put your money into
the fire as to send it to a "make-believe" teacher—a great
noodle-head, who teaches school because he is fit for nothing
else! Lay out to get a *good teacher*. Be willing to pay
enough to make it worth while for "smart" men to become
your teachers. And when your boys show an awakening
taste for books, see that they have good histories, travels,
and scientific tracts and treatises. Above all, do not let a
boy get a notion that if he is educated, he must, of course,
quit the farm. Let him get an education that he may *make
a better farmer*. I do not despair of yet seeing a generation of honest politicians. Educated farmers and educated
mechanics, who are in good circumstances, and *do not need
office for a support*, nor make politics a trade, will stand
the best chance for honesty. But the Lord deliver us from
the political honesty of tenth-rate lawyers, vagabond doc-
tors, bawling preachers, and bankrupt clerks, turned into
patriotic politicians!

AN ACRE OF WORDS ABOUT AKER.

OUR spelling *acre* according to Webster's former method*
—*aker*, has attracted no little attention, in a small way, both
far and near. It is very difficult to fix on any rule for anything in our language. Etymology is chiefly useful in
settling the primitive signification, and is, or ought to be,
scarcely at all authoritative in orthography. Where two
languages are very different, it is absurd to attempt the
forms of the one in the other. In respect to *idiom*, no one
dreams of transferring it from one to another. Oftentimes
it is equally absurd to transfer mere literation, as in the
Greek-blooded word *Phthisic* for Tisic, or as Walker would
have spelled it, Phthisic*!* Who rebels because *demesne*,
as it is written in our best authors until within a little time,
is now spelled *domain?* We see no reason why Anglicized
words should, against all our notions of sound, retain a
cumbrous foreign spelling. Words adopted into a language by the *ear*, which are spoken before they are
written, generally conform, on being written, to our modes
of spelling. But words introduced first by the eye, as they
are written, for a long time wear the original spelling.
Thus some foreign words are spelled by one method, and
some by another.

Custom is usually regarded as determinate, in the matter
of spelling, pronunciation, idiom, purity, etc. But, in
respect to spelling, custom is not long the same. If one
will examine our literature from the time of Henry VIII., he
will find a constant succession of changes in spelling, both
for good and for bad. *I* has been generally substituted for
Y, as in *Lykwyse, accordynge, beyng, certayne.* Sir
Thomas More wrote *hym, thynges, desyer, myndes.* Skel-
ton, the Poet Laureat, has *centencyously, dyd, advysynge*
hyll, etc., etc. .

---

* Two-volume edition, imperial octavo.

There has, too, and wisely, been a constant tendency to drop all *unsovnded* letters. What earthly use is there of lugging along letters which are entirely mute? In old but classic authors we have God*de* dyd*de*, now*e*, which*e*, pul*le*, best*e*, such*e*, couert*e* (court) beetwen*e*, begun*ne*, etc.

Within our own memory the final *k* is lopped off from words where it had a perfect sinecure, as in musi*ck*, etc. "*Kan't kum it,*" does not look any more odd to our eyes than our spelling would have looked to those who wrote one hundred years ago.

If it be asked why we do not spell every word by the same rule that we do some; we reply, that violent, and sudden changes in languages are *impracticable ;* and as in everything else, are not desirable. We are glad to see spelling simplified, and shall move along just as fast as we can do it with a reasonable prospect of carrying the public.

It is not a matter of conscience; we have no necessity laid upon us to reform the language ; no call to be *literal* martyrs ; it is a matter of *convenience* and *taste*, to be done or omitted as one pleases. It would be more inconvenient to stand alone with all writers against us, for the sake of spelling consistently, than to spell foolishly and superfluously in conformity to inveterate practice. Therefore, for the sake of company, we still spell quite absurdly.

It is called *inconsistent ;* and by men, too, who spell trough, cough, enough, though, through, bought, six dissimilar sounds (*ou, ow, oo, o, uf, off*), by the same combination of letters ! If consistency be the question, every English writer that ever lived, is a mere bundle of inconsistencies. Every continental living language, and the dead classic languages, have thrown in their contributions, and our tongue comprises the scraps, odds and ends, of all lands, with all the diverse peculiarities of each language more or less retained. Under such circumstances, when no man writes a sentence without spelling inconsistently, it is quite ridiculous to oppose a simplification of spelling, because we cannot do, at once, what it is only practicable to do gradually. As fast as the public is able to bear it, we shall be glad to reduce all cumbrous spelling to a consistent simplicity.

An acquaintance declares, that the derivation of AKER from the Latin and Greek, is "without the least foundation in the words as used in the Greek and Latin and in the English, and built entirely on the resemblance of sounds," etc. The facts are the other way. In the Greek, and in the Latin, it meant simply a field, an open, cultivated spot. Now, this was the meaning of the word in English, until it was by statutes limited to a particular quantity (31 Ed. III.; 5 Ed. I., 24; Henry VIII., as quoted by Webster) and this is the meaning yet, of the word in German (*acker*) Swedish (*acker*) Dutch (*akker*). There is, therefore, ample foundation in the *use* of the word; and the *sound* our friend gives up.

In almost all the languages of the Teutonic family, of which ours is one, the word is still spelled with *k ;* and so it is in the Asiatic languages, from which, probably, both the Teutonic and the Greek, alike borrowed it.

The spelling a*cre*, as also cent*re*, thea*tre* we, probably, derived from the French; to which language we owe the emasculation of many a noble Saxon word.

In the *New England Farmer* our orthographical sins are thus set in order before us:

"The *Western Farmer and Gardiner*, is an excellent journal—very. It has only one feature that we dislike, viz.—it spells ACRE *a-k-e-r !* We are somewhat surprised at Bro. Beecher, who usually evinces such good taste, as well as such good sense, should adopt such an ugly-looking substitute for an old word of so much better appearance. although supported in it by the prince of lexicographers.

"*A-k-e-r !* Wheugh! Bro. editors, *hoot* at it till it
2

shall become obselete.   In Todd's, Johnson's, and Walker's, and Worcester's dictionaries, *fuel* is spelled *fewel*, as the most correct way.   This is odd enough and bad enough— but it is hardly so unsightly as *aker*."

Nothing becomes obsolete until it has been in vogue. But pass that: what a sight will the hooting confraternity present!   I imagine Maine Farmer Holmes—a plump, short, dapper gentleman, giving a long howl, that sounds so ludicrous, that he draws back from the open window to laugh.   Our more sober Breck performs the euphonious duty with such conscientious heartiness, that up starts the man of Buckwheat from his (mis-spelled) Plou*gh*man's chair, as also does the Cultivator Cole—a trio not practiced to sing together.   The uproar reaches Albany, and surprises him of the Cultivator, who hoots supplementary, with such voice as he happens, in his surprise, to have on hand.   Next, toward the west, Dr. Lee shall give a scientific roar or hoot such as will make his laboratory jar again. Down across the lake the hooting (not *hunting*) chorus goes (what will the sailors think is to pay!) to Elliot of the yard-long-named Magazine, who, hoarse with lake fogs and winds, shall put in so bass a hoot, that Wight and Wright of the *Prairie Farmer* will howl of mere fright, if for nothing else.

Audacious men! we utterly defy you!   We shall pass by the whole crowing brood of Polands, Dorkings and what-not; and raise a breed of genuine owls, to be our champions in this dire necessity.   We say, peremptorily, that we will not bet on any match between hooting birds and hooting editors.   But our serious opinion is, that, in grave solemnity of looks, and in professional hooting, a half dozen well-trained owls will beat the whole of you. However, we are open to conviction.

FARMERS' LIBRARY.

IT is of the highest importance that farmers should possess *reading habits;* and that they should bring up their children to a love of books. Every farmer should have a library; it may, at first, be small; but it should be select. As soon as a farmer is beforehand enough to own an acre, he is prosperous enough to begin a library. It is said by many, *books won't make money.* Yes they will. To-be-sure, their best effect is the production of intelligence in the reader; but a man well informed in his own business is just the man to make money. Who ever thought of making money by buying grindstones and whetstones? But they sharpen the scythe, and sickle, and the axe, and *they* produce money. Books are grindstones and whetstones for a man's mind.

Many are unwilling to buy a treatise upon the disease of the horse, although there are several which will *prevent* most of the evils which affect this noble animal. In the West, the horse is used, in town and country, by almost every man. But very few profess to know how he should be treated! And, of those who think they are wise, how many have any knowledge except of a few nostrums for sickness? The horse, in man's service, is living in an entirely artificial state. He takes care of himself if left wild. But living in stables, laboring every month of the year in harness, and under the saddle, not selecting his own food, but fed at the will of his master, his own instincts become of little use, and he is dependent entirely on the mercy and knowledge of those whose slave he is. It ought not to be thought unreasonable to say that every man who is willing to *own* a horse, ought to be willing to know how to *manage* him, in the stable and out of it. There is no work in the English language containing more, or better instructions than * Stew-

* *A Treatise on the management of horses in relation to stabling, grooming, feeding, watering, and working:* published by A.O.Moore & Co., N. Y.

art's Stable Economy. It should be read by the farmer; and just as much by every man, of whatever calling, who uses a horse, or owns one. It is of standard authority in England. Mr. Stewart has long been a professor in veterinary institutes. Every man ought to know how to treat a sick horse. Suppose a horse to be taken sick on a journey; most frequently the driver is the only one at hand to prescribe. If you are at a tavern, of what use, generally speaking, are the bragging pretensions of those that crowd around you? Stopping for a night at a wretched hole of a tavern, one of my horses, at night fell sick. I knew no more than a child what to do; the landlord (ah me! I shall never forget him!) was equally ignorant and much more indifferent. A big, bragging, English booby was the only one pretending to know what to do; and to him I yielded the animal. After sundry manipulations—punching him in the loins; pulling at his ears, etc.—he rolled up a wad of *hair from his tail*, and crammed it down the horse's throat! presuming, I suppose, that the hair would find its way back to the place it came from, and so pilot the disease out! I inwardly resolved never to go another journey until in possession of the best remedies for the attacks common to horses on the road.

———•••———

PREPARING CUTTINGS IN THE FALL.—Cuttings of the currant, gooseberry, and grape are better if cut immediately on the fall of the leaf, plunged into moist sand two-thirds of their length, and placed in a cellar. If nature is as propitious to others as she has been to us, the cuttings will be found in the spring with the granulations completed at the lower end, and the roots just ready to push; and on being planted out, they grow off immediately, forming during the season well established plants.

NINE MISTAKES.

In so far as instruction is concerned, I esteem my mistakes to be more valuable than my successful efforts. They excite to attention and investigation with great emphasis. I will record a few.

1. One mistake, which I record once for all, as it will probably occur every year, has been the attempting of more than I could do *well*. The ardor of spring, in spite of experience, lays out a larger garden, than can be well tended all summer.

2. In selecting the *largest* lima beans for seed, I obtained most luxuriant vines, but fewer pods. If the season were longer these vines would ultimately be most profitable; but their vigor gives a growth too rampant for our latitude. If planted for a screen, however, the rankest growers are the best.

3. Of three successive plantings of corn, for table use, the first was the best, then the second, and the third very poor. I hoed and thinned the first planting myself, and thoroughly; the second, I left to a Dutchman, directing him how to do it; the third, I left to him without directions.

4. I bought a stock of roses in the *fall of the year*. All the loss of wintering came on me. If purchased in the spring, the nurserymen loses, if there is loss.

5. I planted the silver-leaved abele (*Populus alba*) in a rich sandy loam; in which it made more wood than it could ripen. The tree was top-heavy, and required constant staking. A poorer soil should have been selected.

6. I planted abundantly of flower-seeds—just before a drought. I neither covered the earth with mats, nor watered it—supposing that the seeds would come up after the first rain. But, in a cheerless and barren garden, I have learned that *heat* will kill planted seeds, and that he who will be sure of flowers should not depend upon only one planting.

7. In the fall of 1843, I took up the bulbs of tuberoses, and wintered them safely upon the top of book-cases in a warm study. Having a better and larger stock in 1844, I would fain be yet more careful, and packed them in dry sand, and put them in a closet beyond the reach of frost. On opening them in the spring all were rotted save about half a dozen. Hereafter, I shall try the book-case.

8. We are told that glazed or painted flower-pots are not desirable, because, refusing a passage to superfluous moisture, they leave the roots to become sodden. In small stove-heated parlors, the evaporation is so great that glazed or painted flower-pots are *best*, because the danger is of dryness rather than dampness in *all plants growing in sandy loams or composts*.

9. I have resolved every summer for three years, to cut pea-brush during the winter and stack it in the shed; and every summer following, not having kept the vow, I have lacked pea-brush, being too busy to get it when it was needed, I have allowed the crop to suffer.

AGRICULTURAL SOCIETIES.

MANY county· societies were formed in 1836 and for some years flourished; few of them, we believe, exist now. We hope that the day has come for them to revive; and, that the experience of the past may not be lost, it is well to record the reasons why these county societies declined.

1. Just after their birth, came on the fatal years of fictitious prosperity; when every man expected a railroad on one side of his farm and a canal on the other—and when everybody was about to be exceedingly rich; not by legitimate business; not by producing wealth; but by the *rise of property*. Now the wealth of a farming community is always to arise from the products of the farm. Whatever

withdraws attention from assiduous cultivation, or plants the hope of gain in other sources than in the herds, the dairy, the grain and the grass field, will, eventually, insure disappointment and even poverty, as many of our farmers can testify. It would be difficult for those who had not seen it, to imagine the fervent, sanguine, exulting, state of mind with which the whole community, at the time we speak of, looked for the wealth. Farms were to quadruple in value; pork was to be cashed at enormous prices; grain and grass, stock and fruit, were to swell the golden tide; and, for once, the world was to see great riches from little labor. Carelessness, waste, rashness, and incredible presumption were the result. Societies for the promotion of a careful and patient cultivation of the soil could not long be thought worthy of attention in a community which expected to be rich by a dexterous bargain, by one lucky speculation, by town lots, and shares, and that mysterious humbug—the rise of property.

2. Succeeding such days came the opposite extreme. Everybody was poor and expected to be poorer. There was no money and no market. Hogs were hardly salable, grain a drug, and all produce unavailable. Nothing was brisk but debt and debt collecting. Men were discouraged. Said they, "if one can sell nothing, there is no use in raising anything; twenty bushels an acre is as good as forty, when one can't sell or use it." Schools languished, public spirit died, business was totally deranged, and agricultural societies became extinct with the downfall of other useful institutions.

3. There were some things in the management of the societies which embarrassed them independently of these other causes. There was too much talk and pretension— wind work; the offices were taken for the honor—patient endurance of drudgery, which somebody must bear, was *shirked* off. Men took little pains *between* the meetings; everything was to be done at the time of meeting; and, of

course, half done. This led to dissatisfaction. The mistakes of carelessness were attributed to partiality or prejudice. Some dropped off; others relaxed; and, when the excitement was gone, few cared to take the dull but real and necessary business.

4. Notwithstanding all these things, the county societies did a great deal of good. A skillful farmer told me, that in the county, where he resided, there was hardly a considerable farmer who did not try a few acres, at least, to see what he *could do;* and even many renters exhibited specimens of fine cultivation. More attention was paid to every part of the farm; and, for a time, everything felt the impulse.

A few words to those who may embark again in this good cause.

1. It is best to begin as you can hold out. A great meeting, a vast roll of by-laws, a regiment of officers, a parade of speeches, these make a fine meeting, and that's all. Let a few stanch friends to improvement put their heads and hands together, without show or noise; begin at the little end, and hold fast what is gained.

2. In choosing officers, societies almost invariably steer upon one rock on which thousands have split. There is a desire to put great men into offices, to get their influence. In a mere public meeting of a day, this is well enough; but in a society which is to exist by efficient labor, it is suicide. Such men like to be puffed and published as presidents, chairmen, etc., etc., but that ends the matter. They go away and are not seen again till the next annual meeting, when, lo! a resurrection takes place; and they flame again, a whole year's zeal exhibited in one day. It is best to select officers, who are well broken, of a good strain of blood, and who pull steadily, on hard ground, in the mud, over bridging, or upon turnpikes. In this way we may not have quite so large a show, but we shall have a steadily growing and efficient society.

3. In the award of premiums, more or less of dissatisfaction will always be felt. A man who has worked a whole year for a premium cannot be expected to lose it without some pain. Premiums should be awarded with great care, with scrupulous impartiality, and every effort made by the leading, substantial farmers to soothe and keep down everything like bitterness and faction, in consequence of disappointment.

4. It is *indispensable* that agricultural papers should go hand in hand with agricultural societies. We will venture to say, that no society will long exist prosperously, which does not have a reading membership; and that a society can hardly fail to prosper if its members are regular readers of agricultural papers.

SHIFTLESS TRICKS,

To let the cattle fodder themselves at the stack; they pull out and trample more than they eat. They eat till the edge of appetite is gone, and then daintily pick the choice parts; the residue, being coarse and refuse, they will not afterwards touch.

To sell half a stack of hay and leave the lower half open to rain and snow. In feeding out, a hay knife should be used on the stack; in selling, either dispose of the whole, or remove that which is left to a shed or barn.

It is a shiftless trick to lie about stores and groceries, arguing with men that you have *no time*, in a new country, for nice farming—for making good fences; for smooth meadows without a stump; for draining wet patches which disfigure fine fields.

To raise your own frogs in your own yard; to permit, year after year, a dirty, stinking, mantled puddle to stand before your fence in the street.

2*

To plant orchards, and allow your cattle to eat the trees
up. When gnawed down, to save your money, by trying
to nurse the stubs into good trees, instead of getting fresh
ones from the nursery.

To allow an orchard to have blank spaces, where trees
have died, and when the living trees begin to bear, to wake
up and put young whips in the vacant spots.

It is very shiftless to build your barnyard so that every
rain shall *drain* it; to build your privy and dig your well
close together; to build a privy of more than seven feet
square—some shiftless folks have it of the size of the whole
yard; to set it in the most exposed spot on the premises;
to set it at the very far end of the garden, for the pleasure
of traversing mud-puddles and labyrinths of wet weeds
in rainy days.

It is a dirty trick to make bread without washing one's
hands after cleaning fish or chickens; to use an apron for a
handkerchief; to use a veteran handkerchief just from the
wars for an apron; to use milk-pans alternately for wash-
bowls and milk. To wash dishes and baby linen in the same
tub, either alternately or altogether; to chew snuff while
you are cooking, for sometimes food will chance to be too
highly spiced. We have a distinct but unutterable remembrance of a cud of tobacco in a dish of *hashed pork*—but
it was before we were married!

A lady of our acquaintance, at a boarding-house, excited
some fears among her friends, by foaming at the mouth, of
madness. In eating a hash (made, doubtless, of every scrap
from the table, not consumed the day before), she found
herself blessed with a mouthful of *hard soap*, which only
lathered the more, the more she washed at it. It is a filthy
thing to comb one's hair in a small kitchen in the intervals
of cooking the breakfast; to use the bread trough for
a cradle—a thing which we have undoubtedly seen;
to put trunks, boxes, baskets, with sundry other utensils,
under the bed where you keep the cake for company; we

have seen a dexterous housewife whip the bed-spread aside, and bring forth, not what we feared, but a loaf-cake!

It is a dirty trick to wash children's eyes in the pudding dish; not that the sore eyes, but subsequent puddings, will not be benefited; to wipe dishes and spoons on a hand-towel; to wrap warm bread in a dirty table-cloth; to make and mold bread on a table innocent of washing for weeks; to use dirty table-clothes for *sheets*, a practice of which we have had experimental knowledge, once at least in our lives.

The standing plea of all slatterns and slovens is, that " everybody must eat a peck of dirt before they die." A peck? that would be a mercy, a mere mouthful, in comparison of cooked cart-loads of dirt which is to be eaten in steamboats, canal-boats, taverns, mansions, huts and hovels.

Tobacco Tricks.—It is a filthy trick to use it at all; and it puts an end to all our affected squeamishness at the Chinese taste, in eating rats, cats, and bird's nests. It is a filthy trick to let the exquisite juice of tobacco trickle down the corners of one's mouth; or lie in splashes on one's coat, or bosom; to squirt the juice all over a clean floor, or upon a carpet, or baptismally to sprinkle a proud pair of andirons the refulgent glory of the much-scouring housewife. It is a vile economy to lay up for re-mastication a half-chewed cud; to pocket a half-smoked cigar; and finally to be-drench one's self with tobacco juice, to so be-smoke one's clothes that a man can be scented as far off as a whale-ship can be smelt at sea.

It is a shiftless trick to snuff a candle with your fingers, or your wife's best scissors, to throw the snuff on the carpet, or on the polished floor, and then to extinguish it by treading on it!

To borrow a choice book; to read it with unwashed hands, that have been used in the charcoal bin, and finally to return it daubed on every leaf with nose-blood spots, tobacco spatter, and dirty finger-marks—this is a vile trick!

It is not altogether cleanly to use one's knife to scrape boots, to cut harness, to skin cats, to cut tobacco, and then to cut apples which other people are to eat.

It is an unthrifty trick to bring in eggs from the barn in one's coat pocket, and then to sit down on them.

It is a filthy trick to borrow of or lend for others' use, a tooth-brush, or a tooth-pick; to pick one's teeth at table with a fork, or a jack-knife; to put your hat upon the dinner table among the dishes; to spit generously into the fire, or at it, while the hearth is covered with food set to warm; for sometimes a man hits what he don't aim at.

It is an unmannerly trick to neglect the scraper outside the door, but to be scrupulous in cleaning your feet after you get inside, on the carpet, rug, or andirons; to bring your drenched umbrella into the entry, where a black puddle may leave to the housewife melancholy evidence that you have been there.

It is soul-trying for a neat dairywoman to see her "man" watering the horse out of her milk-bucket; or filtering horse-medicine through her milk-strainer; or feeding his hogs with her water-pail; or, after barn-work, to set the well-bucket outside the curb and wash his hands out of it.

ELECTRO-CULTURE.

A FEW years ago, all the world was agog about electricity applied to vegetation. Sanguine persons grew red in the face with excitement, and enterprising schemers hoped to supersede all past processes of culture by this magical fluid. Things were to be made to grow not only as fast as lightning but *by* lightning. Those mischievous bolts which had played their dangerous pranks with chimneys, oaks, and towers, were to be regularly harnessed and set to work in the field like horses or oxen. Many of our readers will recollect how widely the agricultural papers copied the glowing accounts brought from over the seas; and nobody was afraid of anything except of not believing enough.

Well, the lightning has been too smart for them; and the whole pack which opened loud on the scent, are now heard just as loud on the back track. It usually takes two foolings to satisfy the public. They first swing to an extreme folly of injudicious admiration, and them vibrate to the opposite extreme of disgust. Everybody was fever-hot with morus multicaulis; and then they went into chills about it. Durham stock brought almost their weight in silver at one time, and then could hardly be sold at butchers' prices. Berkshire hogs were all the rage, and now are in great and unmerited contempt. The guano fever sent hundreds of ships a-dung-hunting all over the earth: and lucky were they who espied a precious heap of excrement. How little did the penguins and sea gulls of the Pacific imagine, that their unconscious observance of the laws of nature was one day to figure so largely on the British Exchange, and to raise such a bustle in chemical laboratories!

We believed but few of these accounts of electricity, because we perceived nothing which could be regarded as settled. And now, we are far from sympathizing with the recantations and apostasies from the electric faith. Like all other things driven to extremes, we shall by and by see it settle upon a middle point.

Editors are not without blame for these actions and reactions. Many of our best agricultural papers are connected with agricultural warehouses which deal largely in all articles for which there is an agricultural demand. Without the slightest intention of deception, nay, with a desire to act cautiously, such pecuniary interest may sensibly affect the judgment of sanguine editors. But the wish to issue a spicy paper, full of life and surprise, inclines

an editor to publish whatever is new, without a scrutiny of
its truth. With a few honorable exceptions of standard
periodicals, we scarcely take an agricultural paper which
does not contain most absurd stories gravely indited without a word of comment. Now, it seems to us that agricultural papers ought not to be the common sewers of news,
full of waste and refuse matter ; but registers of rigid facts
and scientific expositors of the principles deducible from
facts. Farmers are at fault also in the matter. An editor
who depends for his support upon the proceeds of his
paper, must be a man of rare independence if he can shield
himself from the selfish influence of those who are his best
supporters. Men that have a novelty, a new and precious
jewel of a flower, a heavy stock of nursery commodities, or
large herds of fancy stock, sheep or swine, can afford to
circulate widely and praise any paper that will circulate
widely and praise their special interest. A sanguine
editor inditing a eulogistic article, with a red-hot specula-
tor whispering at each ear, will be very likely to lead many
simple farmers astray. Such articles, copied by newspapers,
spread the infection beyond the circle of subscribers. Farmers that take, and farmers that do not take the paper will
be deceived.

Now, let husbandmen give to their agricultural papers
such a support as shall leave the editors free from temptations to listen to interested persons ; let them contribute so
freely of their observations that editors will not have to
draw upon their imagination for facts, and the agricultural
press will become sober, stable, accurate, and so, profitable.

SINGLE-CROP FARMING.

IT is extensively the practice of large farmers, to put
their whole force upon one staple article; a style of farming as full of risk, as it would be to invest a whole fortune
in one kind of property. At the South, we have cotton
plantations; nothing but cotton is raised. If the market
and the season happen to be propitious, enormous profits
are made. If markets, or the planting or picking season
are adverse, the year is lost; for it was staked on one
article; all the risks of the year, instead of being distributed,
were concentrated. Another plantation cultivates sugar
exclusively; and the ambitious planter has his pockets full
or empty, according to chances which he cannot foresee,
calculate, or overrule.

At the North, some farmers put in nothing but wheat;
others, nothing but corn. One relies on the hay crop;
another makes or loses a year's profits on cattle. In each
case, if the staple raised happens to *hit*, in every respect
profits roll in like a flood. But such operations leave no
margin for those casualties, and annual changes, which are
inevitable.

Ireland, relying upon the potato as a support for a large
mass of its poverty-stricken people, is visited with famine
if this crop is shaken. The failure of the grain crop, in England, strikes panic into the whole nation.

A perfect system of agriculture should have in itself, a
balancing power. There should be such a distribution of
crops that a farmer may have four or five chances instead
of one. To be sure, a farmer cannot drive so large a business—cut such a swath—where five small or moderate
operations take the place of a single great one. Five years
of moderate profits are better than one gaining year, and
four years to eat it up. A farmer has 160 acres—sixty are
in wood: of the one hundred cleared acres, say *twenty* are
used for home lots, pasture, corn, etc., and *eighty* are in

wheat. The fall may be bad for planting, the spring may be bad, the fly may take the crop or the rust may strike it; escaping all these, the weevil may damage it; and, after all this, it may not bring a justifying price when got to market. Is it wise for a man to put his yearly support or gains upon one crop and that one crop depending upon six or seven contingencies? If there is a large crop *and* high prices, he makes largely. Eighty acres at thirty bushels the acre yields 2,400 bushels, worth, say, seventy cents, or $1,680 gross receipts. Elated beyond measure, the lucky fellow buys some forty acres more of cleared land, reduces his pasture, shaves off a portion from his meadow, plants a few acres only of corn, and puts every inch he can command into wheat; a good operation if he can find guaranty for as good seasons and as good market as before. But there are at least ten chances against for one in favor.

A farm which depends for its profit on butter, cheese, fruit, timber, cattle, hogs, corn, wheat, potatoes, flax, etc., makes, perhaps, but a little on each crop; but the rains that come in *drops* are useful, while those that come in *torrents* and raise freshets, leave great mischief behind.

——◆◆◆——

TICKS ON SHEEP.—A clergyman, who was early in life a regular-built shepherd, after the old-fashioned style, living with his flock, requests us to call the attention of all interested in sheep, to the prevention of ticks adopted " in the place he came from." A trough, large enough to hold a sheep, was filled with a decoction of tobacco; as soon as the sheep are sheared, they are plunged all over in, except the nose and mouth (these organs being sacred to chewers and snuffers). The lambs are treated in the same way, and a world of trouble to the owner and yet more to the flock, is saved by this nauseous bath.

IMPROVED BREEDS OF HOGS AND CATTLE.

No farmer ever owns a fine animal without being proud of it. Yet, the same man will have an inveterate prejudice against what are called improved breeds. The "fancy" prices which have been extravagantly paid, the miserable failure which some have made in attempting to stock their farm with foreign breeds, together with a suspicion of whatever is new, and a lack of enterprise, have deterred many farmers from seeking a better stock than the common run. It is in this way that speculators, besides ruining themselves, which is of no great consequence, seriously retard the progress of enlightened husbandry.

Let us take a plain and practical view of the matter.

1. Every man who has had anything to do with cattle, horses and swine, knows very well what a difference there is between different animals, in respect to size, form, and aptitude to fatten. Among twenty steers there will be a few that without any reason that the owner can see, out-grow and out-fatten all the rest. A lot of fifty hogs gathered up from one neighborhood, will naturally divide itself into three sorts, those which fatten with remarkable rapidity and on little food; those that eat voraciously without taking on fat; and those that lie between these two extremes and are not remarkable in one way or the other. Every man that buys a horse knows that some horses require as much again food as others to keep them fat.

2. It is equally true that these qualities can be transmitted, by careful breeding, from parent to offspring; until the qualities become *fixed* in the breed. A particular *strain of blood*, is then said to be established. By this process, English breeders of stock, with the greatest perseverance and with admirable skill, have established several truly improved breeds. It is not mere beauty of form that has been gained, although this has been eminently attained; but also all those qualities which make an ox valuable for

the *yoke* or for the *knife*; all that makes a cow good at the pail and afterwards for the butcher; all that makes a hog valuable in flesh and fat. It is a mistake to suppose that the improved breeds have been formed to please gentlemen farmers and amateur fanciers. They have been perfected with an eye mainly to their *profitableness* to the farmer—the real farmer. Nor are they the stock for large farmers and rich proprietors alone. They are more peculiarly suited to farmers of small or moderate means than to any other; a rich farmer can afford to keep poor stock, if anybody can; but a small farmer is badly off indeed if the little that he has is poor.

3. No class of farmers are more interested in having good stock of all kinds than western farmers. Pork and beef constitute, probably, three-fifths of their exports. It is of the last importance that they should possess animals from which can be made the utmost profit. It is as much more profitable for an Indiana farmer to drive the very best cattle, as it is for a Massachusetts farmer. If improved breeds are found on the Mohawk to be vastly more profitable than common stock, they will be found to be just the same on the Wabash.

It does not follow, either, because we have more corn than we can feed, or more grass and hay than can be used, that we can make up for inferior quality by the greater quantity of cattle kept. A western farmer may winter a hundred head of cattle without positive loss, when a New York farmer would sink money by it. But that is not the question. Suppose two herds, of a hundred each, of four year olds, preparing for the shambles. They eat the same amount of grain, and hay or grass. But when weighing-time comes, one herd averages a fourth heavier than the other, and this is clear profit. With no more food, and no more labor, and no longer time in fattening, they yield the owner a fourth more profit.

Three men start a hundred hogs apiece for market.

The first lot is of the true land-shark breed, and will average, say one hundred and twenty-five pounds; the second lot are of a better breed, and will average two hundred pounds; the third hundred are of a choice breed and average three hundred pounds. If the market happen to be heavy, the first lot can hardly be sold; the second lot sells moderately well, the third lot goes promptly and at a shade higher price. Now what is the difference of profit? If pork is selling for two dollars the hundred, the first hundred hogs bring two hundred and fifty dollars. The second, four hundred dollars; and the third, six hundred dollars. That is, a difference of breeds makes a difference in profit, feeding and labor being the same in both cases, between the first and last lot, of three hundred and fifty dollars. But it will be more than this, for hogs averaging three hundred pounds will command twenty-five cents in the hundred more than those weighing a hundred and twenty-five pounds. The price which a farmer will get, then, for his hundred acres of corn, depends upon what his hogs can do for him. One sort of hogs can make up a fourth more fat than others, and another can make up still a fourth more than these. If you owned a mill, which of two millers would you choose—the one who could make forty pounds of flour to the bushel, or the one who could make forty-five—the quality being equally good? Of two acres of land, which would you choose—the one which would yield fifteen bushels of wheat, or the one which, with the same cultivation, would yield thirty? Our farmers are willing enough to hunt for good lands; but why, on the same reasons, should they not hunt for the best breeds of cows, cattle hogs, and horses?

4. As to the different varieties which are cried up, we have no interest in urging one more than another upon the public. It is all one to us whether Hereford, Devon, or Durham, prevail; Woburn, Byfield or Berkshire. All that we ask is that farmers should aim to procure *the best*. Their

own experience must determine which that is. One kind will suit one range of land better than another. Beginning with moderation, a shrewd farmer will soon be able to tell whether any particular breed will suit his farm.

We presume that all farmers work for the sake of profit: we urge an improvement of stock simply on the ground of its *profitableness*.

———•◦•———

ABSORBENT QUALITIES OF FLOUR.

It has long been known that flour gains in weight on being made up into bread. The English act of Parliament allowed 280 lbs. (a sack) of flour to make 320 lbs. of bread. But in fact it makes a much greater weight than this. The average per cent. of water, in English flour, naturally, according to Johnson, is 15 per cent. But good English and French wheat bread, according to the same author, contains 44 per cent. of water; i. e. twenty-eight pounds are absorbed in making. By this estimate, 280 lbs. would gain nearly *seventy-four pounds*, while the act of Parliament allows only *forty pounds*.

It is understood that American wheat absorbs more water than English; and that United States southern wheat, absorbs more than northern. It is also true that good wheat gains more in baking than poor wheat, and old flour, more than new. It is not good *because* it takes up water ; but good flour has that property, and poor has not; and absorption is, therefore, an evidence of quality.

This absorption of water is in part mechanical and in part chemical. The difference between these may be illustrated ; a bushel measure of shelled corn will admit a great quantity of water into its open spaces ; it stands *between* the kernels. When water is thrown upon lime, it does not exist *between* the particles, but *combines* with them. Flour absorbs water in both ways.

Absorption, mechanically, depends upon the coarseness of flour, either from the character of its growth, or from the manner of its grinding. The want of light and heat, in unfavorable climates, or in bad seasons, induces sluggish and imperfect action. The juices are but partially digested and assimilated. Many vegetable constituents exist, in consequence, in smaller quantities, or in a crude state. In such cases the texture is porous and spongy. Grinding breaks down the organized form without altering the essential nature of the texture.

It would seem, if this be true, that grain ripened under unfavorable influences would absorb *less* rather than *more* water. since the watery particles, from the want of rapid digestion and excretion, remain in the grain. But after grain is cut, and put to dry, a literal evaporation takes place; the water is, in a measure, exhaled.

We are not to suppose that a mechanical absorption predominates. By far the greatest proportion of water is supposed to *combine* with the ingredients of the flour—starch, gluten, etc.,—chemically. And as flour is rich in starch and gluten, it will have the power of taking water into combination. It has been supposed that the absorbing power of flour depended mainly upon its gluten. But Johnson holds the position in doubt. Whereas, Webster (of England) states that it is with the starch, principally, that water combines. The per cent. of starch, sugar, and gluten, etc., in wheat, depends on the soil and climate;—on the soil, because it must derive from it, originally, the elements of its existence; on climate, because these elements require a certain temperature and quantity of light for their perfect elaboration. It is on this account, that the wheat of southern Europe is better than that of England; that that of Egypt is superior to the Italian. · In each case there is a superiority of climate which produces the most perfect elaboration of all the elements of wheat.

PORTRAIT OF AN ANTI-BOOK-FARMER.

WHENEVER our anti-book-farmers can show us better crops at a less expense, better flocks, and better farms, and better owners on them, than book-farmers can, we shall become converts to their doctrines. But, as yet, we cannot see how *intelligence* in a farmer, should injure his crops. Nor what difference it makes whether a farmer gets his ideas from a sheet of paper, or from a neighbor's mouth, or from his own experience, so that he only gets good, practical, sound ideas. A farmer never objects to receive *political* information from newspapers; he is quite willing to learn the state of markets from newspapers, and as willing to gain religious notions from reading, and historical knowledge, and all sorts of information except that which relates to his business. He will go over and hear a neighbor tell how he prepares his wheat-lands, how he selects and puts in his seed, how he deals with his grounds in spring, in harvest and after harvest-time; but if that neighbor should write it all down carefully and put it into paper, it's all poison! it's *book-farming!*

> " Strange such a difference there should be
> 'Twixt tweedledum, and tweedledee."

If I raise a head of lettuce surpassing all that has been seen hereabouts, every good farmer that loves a salad would send for a little seed, and ask, as he took it, " How do you, contrive to raise such monstrous heads? you must have some secret about it." But if my way were written down and printed, he would not touch it. " Poh, it's bookish !"

Now let us inquire in what States land is the best managed, yields the most with the least cost, where are the best sheep, the best cattle, the best hogs, the best wheat? It will be found to be in those States having the most agricultural societies and the most widely-disseminated agricultural papers.

What is there in agriculture that requires a man to be
ignorant if he will be skillful? Or why may every other
class of men learn by reading except the farmer? Mechanics have their journals; commercial men have their
papers; religious men, theirs; politicians, theirs; there are
magazines and journals for the arts, for science, for education, and *why not for that grand pursuit on which all these
stand?* We really could never understand why farmers
should not wish to have their vocation on a level with
others; why they should feel proud to have *no* paper, while
every other pursuit is fond of *having* one.

Those who are prejudiced against book-farming are
either good farmers, misinformed of the design of agricultural papers, or poor farmers who only treat this subject as
they do all others, with blundering ignorance. First, the
good farmers; there are in every county many industrious,
hard-working men, who know that they cannot afford to
risk anything upon wild experiments. They have a growing
family to support, taxes to pay, lands perhaps on which
purchase money is due, or they are straining every nerve to
make their crops build a barn, that the barn may hold their
crops. They suppose an agricultural paper to be stuffed
full of wild fancies, expensive experiments, big stories made
up by men who know of no farming except parlor-farming.
They would, doubtless, be surprised to learn that ninety-
nine parts in a hundred of the contents of agricultural
papers are written by *hard-working practical farmers!*
that the editor's business is not to foist absurd stories upon
credulous readers, but to sift stories, to scrutinize accounts,
to obtain whatever has been abundantly proved to be fact,
and to reject all that is suspected to be mere fanciful theory.
Such papers are designed to prevent imposition; to kill off
pretenders by exposing them; to search out from practical
men whatever they have found out, and to publish it for the
benefit of their brethren all over the Union; to spread
before the laboring classes such sound, well-approved scien-

tific knowledge as shall throw light upon every operation of the farm, the orchard and the garden.

The other class who rail at book-farming ought to be excused, for they do not treat book-farming any worse than they do their own farming; indeed, not half so bad. They rate the paper with their tongue; but cruelly-abuse their ground, for twelve months in the year with both hands. I will draw the portrait of a genuine anti-book-farmer of this last sort.

He plows three inches deep lest he should turn up the poison that, in his estimation, lies below; his wheat-land is plowed so as to keep as much water on it as possible; he sows two bushels to the acre and reaps ten, so that it takes a fifth of his crop to seed his ground; his corn-land has never any help from him, but bears just what it pleases, which is from thirty to thirty-five bushels by measurement, though he brags that it is fifty or sixty. His hogs, if not remarkable for fattening qualities, would beat old Eclipse at a quarter-race; and were the man not prejudiced against deep plowing, his hogs would work his grounds better with their prodigious snouts than he does with his jack-knife-plow. His meadow-lands yield him from three-quarters of a ton to a whole ton of hay, which is regularly spoiled in curing, regularly left out for a month, very irregularly stacked up, and left for the cattle to pull out at their pleasure, and half-eat and half-trample underfoot. His horses would excite the avarice of an anatomist in search of osteological specimens, and returning from their range of pasture they are walking herbariums, bearing specimens in their mane and tail of every weed that bears a bur or cockle. But oh, the cows! If held up in a bright day to the sun, don't you think they would be semi-transparent? But he tells us that good milkers are always poor! His cows get what Providence sends them, and very little beside, except in winter, then they have a half-peck of corn on ears a foot long thrown to them, and they afford lively spectacles of

animated corn and cob-crushers—never mind, they yield,
on an average, three quarts of milk a-day! and that milk
yields varieties of butter quite astonishing.

His farm never grows any better, in many respects it gets
annually worse. After ten years' work on a good soil, while
his neighbors have grown rich, he is just where he started,
only his house is dirtier, his fences more tottering, his soil
poorer, his pride and his ignorance greater. And when, at
last, he sells out to a Pennsylvanian that reads the Farmers'
Cabinet, or to some New Yorker with his Cultivator packed
up carefully as if it were gold, or to a Yankee with his New
England Farmer, he goes off to Missouri, thanking Heaven
that *he's* not a book-farmer!

Unquestionably, there are two sides to this question, and
both of them *extremes*, and therefore both of them deficient
in science and in common sense. If men were made according to our notions, there should not be a silly one alive;
but it is otherwise ordered, and there is no department of
human life in which we do not find weak and foolish men.
This is true of farming as much as of any other calling.
But no one dreams of setting down the vocation of agriculture because, like every other, it has its proportion of
stupid men.

Why then should agricultural *writers*, as a class, be sum-
marily rejected because some of them are visionary? Are
we not to be allowed our share of fools as well as every
other department of life? We insist on our rights.

A book or a paper never proposes to take the place of a
farmer's *judgment*. Not to read at all is bad enough; but
to read, and swallow everything without reflection, or discrimination, this is even worse. Such a one is not a book-
headed but a block-headed farmer. Papers are designed
to *assist*. Those who read them must select, modify, and
act according to their own native judgment. So used,
papers answer a double purpose; they convey a great
amount of valuable practical information, and then they stir

3

up the reader to habits of thought; they make him more inquisitive, more observing, more reasoning, and, therefore, more reasonable.

Now, as to the contents of agricultural papers, whose fault is it if they are not *practical?* Who are the practical men? who are daily conversant with just the things a cultivator most needs to know? who is stumbling upon difficulties, or discovering some escape from them? who is it that knows so much about gardens, orchards, farms, cattle, grains and grasses? Why, the very men *who won't write a word for the paper that they read,* and then complain that there is nothing *practical in it.* Yes there is. There is practical evidence that men are more willing to be helped than to help others; and also that men sometimes blame others for things of which they themselves are chiefly blameworthy.

GOOD BREEDS OF COWS.

THERE is hardly one thing which conduces more to the comfort of a family than a good cow. A family well supplied with rich milk twice a day cannot have poor fare; for, besides the use of pure milk by itself, there is no article, except flour, which enters into so many forms of cooking. Next in importance to the family, are the relations of the cow to the dairy; we say *next* to the family, for it is more important that there should be good cows for private families than that dairies should have them. All the dairy herds might be destroyed, and if each family has its cow, the loss would be bearable. But take from families their one cow; and all the dairies in the land could not compensate.

The question of a good breed of milch cows is important, then, to the whole community; to the dairymen of course;

but yet more to the families of laborers, mechanics, merchants, etc.

Everybody knows that it costs no more to keep a good cow than a poor one. But what is the use in talking so when good ones are not to be had? or to be had only at a price which not one in fifty can afford? But so far as we are concerned, and so far as ninety-nine in a hundred are concerned, of what use are these accounts except to make us dissatisfied with our poor old cow without enabling us to get a better? It was all right to publish them, but the sight of such facts reminded us of the low estate of our milk cows, and of the woeful carelessness of farmers about improving their stock.

It is high time that farmers should endeavor to procure a good milk breed. It is well known that horses and oxen are almost bred to order; if a fore shoulder is too slight, a breeder crosses so that in the next generation it comes out right; if the animal is too small he is enlarged; if too large he is condensed; if the back is too long, the leg too heavy, the muscle too spare, the head heavily or clumsily put on, the breeder has skill, in a great measure, to remedy the evils. Why then should it not be thought both possible and worth while to breed for good milking properties?

The least trouble, not the best stock, seems to be the question with most. The discouragement of debt, the low prices of all farm products, the habits of arrant carelessness which naturally belong to large farms, of rich lands, removed from a ready market, and on which there is more than enough for home use, and much waste of the surplus because a poor sale for it; these things are the causes why but little attention is paid to good stock. To be sure, in speculating times, large prices have been paid for animals of repute. And now, if fancy prices could be realized, there are thousands who would beg, borrow, or steal enough to rush madly into the raising of improved breeds. Even from such extravagance much collateral advantage results. Many, doubtless, are disappointed, as they expected angelic cattle, and got nothing but flesh and blood ; those who are the most furious in one extreme, revolt to the other, and are as careless and neglectful this year, as they were cattle-mad the last year. But, some good, notwithstanding, remains. Good breeds have been brought in. Good blood will run longer in good stock, than perseverance, often, will in their owners. Here and there a man holds on. His stock improves. His neighbor's herds are gradually leavened. By and by particular counties grow famous for their fine stock. The farmers feel some pride in it; and now the thing begins to work rightly. When once the best stock, of any kind, is a matter of hearty personal pride with the farmer, over and above the mere price of them in market, then there will be constant and solid improvement.

These remarks, applying to stock generally, are peculiarly applicable to the subject of milch cows with which we set out.

DAHLIAS.—It is necessary to give your plants a strong support, for, in good seasons, they grow so thriftily, that rains and winds break down the branches even when the main stalk is strongly staked. Those who are willing to be at the trouble, should put three stakes so as to leave the stem in the middle. Take a pliant withe, or small hoop, and encircle the stakes at the top, the middle, and also about a foot from the ground. In this way the branches will lean on the hoops, and not be liable to split off; a few weeks' growth will cover and conceal the stakes and hoops, leaving to the eye only a mass of foliage, apparently, self-sustained.

CUTTING AND CURING GRASS.

THE question when grass ought to be cut, it seems to us, is to be answered by the purposes to which we mean to put it.

Do we wish it for the seed, or for the stem? Are we anxious to obtain the greatest weight from an acre? or are we desirous of gaining the largest amount with the least exhaustion of the soil?

1. If one, regardless of soil, wishes the greatest weight to an acre, let the grass ripen. It will have become perfectly developed; its juices will have perfected the solid matter, and less loss will ensue in curing. But the stem will be comparatively hard, and without nutriment.

2. Do we desire, without particular regard to economy, the most nutricious food for animals? The grass should ripen and *only the upper part of the stem* and the head should be fed out; for, while the buts will be hard and juiceless, the grain and husk and neighboring parts will have received, in a concentrated form, the height of the plant's juices. Chemistry has recently shown that plants prepare in themselves, the fatty matter which is afterward laid on the bones of the cattle. This fatty substance lies not in the grain, but the husk.

Johnston, the agricultural chemist, says: "This fact of the existence of more fat in the husk than in the inner part of the grain, explains what often seems inexplicable to the practical man, why bran, namely, which *appears* to contain little or no nourishing substance, should yet fatten pigs and other full grown animals when fed to them in sufficient quantity, along with their other food." If, for example, a horse is to be trained, it has long been the *practice* (though hitherto the reason was not understood) to give the racers, the hunter, etc., only the top joint and head of hay. Now the principle on which a trained horse is fed, is to give the most solid nourishment in the most compact form—

throwing as little unnutricious food as possible into the stomach consistently with a proper distension of it.

This fact also explains the value of old hay which has been well cured and well kept. It is known that freshly gathered nuts are not so oily as those which are old. All seeds perfect their oil after being thoroughly ripened by keeping. The seed of old hay will be richer in fatty matter, then, than new.

3. The most palatable hay for cattle is that which is cut before it ripens its seed. If the farmer has enough grain to feed with, he can afford to cut his grass early. Its want of nutriment will be made up by feeding grain, and his stock will relish their food better than if it had grown hard with age before cutting.

4. *But for general purposes*, grass should be cut when just out of flower. This is a compromise between the two extremes. It combines the two advantages of juiciness of stem and richness of grain more nearly than any other. The stem will be cut while yet in juice, and the seed will continue to fill and ripen *after it has been cut*. This is well known in respect to wheat, and the best farmers cut it before it is dead ripe.

The want of barns to store it, the want of markets in which to sell it, the want of profit in raising it, and lastly, the want of thrift in making it, has caused thousands of tons of hay to be most wretchedly put up—*curing* as it is sarcastically called; cured, probably, on the principle of the following story : A physician in England went out with the gamekeeper to hunt; covey after covey was started, into which the doctor fired with a strange want of professional skill, without killing anything. The gamekeeper at length lost patience, and snatching the gun, said :

" Let me take it, I'll doctor them."

" What do you mean, sir, by *doctoring* them ?"

" Why, kill them, to be sure."

Thus, we think, grass is too often doctored.

COUNTRY AND CITY.

A WORTHY friend recently said to me: "A gentlemen of observation from one of our principal cities of the West, stated to me, that in point of fact, almost all the leading men of the cities were from the country, and had been raised farmers' sons. The reasons seemed to me quite obvious. The vigorous health, patient industry, thorough economy, and hard thinking necessary to success, are the product of the country and but seldom of the town or city. A large part of the best merit and talent of the country doubtless remains upon and adorns our farms. Another portion is drawn by a spirit for enterprise of a different kind to our towns. When they enter they find an active competition that brings out their best efforts. Success on their part takes away the necessity of effort on the part of their children; and the next result is, that their children become reduced in means and merit, and every element of success, and are driven to some refuge in vice or petty employment. It is therefore the duty of the man who has been successful in town, to retire to the country again that his children, who are to succeed him, may partake, as far as possible, of his advantages."

The *facts* stated we believe are undoubted; the business men—merchants, lawyers, physicians, and clergymen of large cities are, to a large degree, drawn from the country. And there is a system of *circulation*, if the facts could be well made out, worth attention. In travelling, one day last year, the rain drove us into a country tavern, where a fat man of some fifty years of age was waiting to entertain us with a dish of philosophy (of which, considering our accommodations, we had special need). But we were led to notice one part of his remarks: "You see, sir, everything comes round in about four generations. First comes the enterprising and hard-working fellow who gets the money; then his children begin to live in style; but their parents' example and stamina keep them pretty well up; but *their* children begin to run down; in their hands the property is wasted and they die poor; and the fourth race begin in poverty, and work upward again." Now, if our fat and somewhat dogmatical friend has reasoned aright, there is a degenerating and rejuvenating process going on in society, having a period of about four or five years. We give the theory for what it may be worth.

------ •••• ------

LIME UPON WHEAT.

Lime is used either to prepare the seed for germination, or to prepare the soil for the better growth of the seed. This latter operation it does, either by adding itself as a new ingredient, or by acting chemically upon the ingredients already in the soil.

When lime is applied *to the seed* (the seed being moist) the oxygen of the water, combining with carbon of the seed, forms carbonic acid; which, having a powerful affinity for lime, unites with it, forming a carbonate of lime. The escape of a portion of its carbon constitutes the natural preparation of a seed for growth; but why, chemists have not been able to explain.

Air-slaked lime, is lime which has combined with carbonic acid existing in the atmosphere. Unburnt limestone is a carbonate of lime; air-slaked lime is the same, and they do not materially differ. Air-slaked lime, having no longer an affinity for carbonic acid, withdraws none from the grain to which it may be applied; and in nothing helps the germinating process. Our readers will therefore see the reason why wheat does not sprout any quicker when it is limed, than when it is not. Precisely the same thing is true of other substances applied to grains. Magnesia, existing naturally as a carbonate, like lime, has its carbonic acid expelled by strong heat, and in that state applied to seeds, will assist the germination. If exposed to the air it attracts carbonic acid and becomes again a carbonate, and useless to seeds.

Where lime is employed *upon the soil*, it is either as a mere article of vegetable food, or, as a chemical agent, to change the condition of other ingredients of the soil. All good soils contain lime ; of ninety-four different cultivated soils in Rhode Island, analyzed by Professor C. T. Jackson, *eighty-nine* contained lime. Ruffin, in his essay on calcareous manures, says, after a large induction of fact, "that all soils naturally poor, are certainly destitute of calcareous earth." When there exists in the soil, already, enough lime for the wants of vegetation, the addition of more will produce no effect upon the crop. New lands, and old land not run down, and naturally rich in lime, may require none. But lime is applied not alone as food directly offered to vegetation, but to act upon and change the soil itself.

It *neutralizes* free acids which exist in the soil. This is done with quick-lime or air-slaked ; the first combining directly with the acid—the second by liberating its carbonic acid and then combining with the acid of the soil, leaving the carbonic acid to be food for plants. It is very well known by those accustomed to use peaty substances for manures, and meadow mud, that they will rather injure than benefit soils, until their acid has been neutralized.

Lime *decomposes* vegetable fibre, and reduces tough ligneous substances, to a consideration in which they can be appropriated by plants. For this purpose *quick-lime* should be used and may be applied at the rate of from twenty to thirty bushels to the acre.

Lime enters into combination with sand or silex, forming a substance different from either of them. Even strong clays will be found to contain much silex ; and lime, by combining with it, makes the soil friable or crumbling.

CULTURE OF HOPS.

WE shall state such facts as are within our reach, and leave each one to make his own calculations.

THE HOP PLANT.—The hop belongs to the natural order, Urticeæ, or the nettle and hemp family. Its root is perennial; its stem annual, twining to the height of from fifteen to twenty feet. They bear male and female flowers on different plants, and the female is the only one used for planting.

SOIL.—Rich, friable clay, and hearty loams, and vegetable molds are the best soils. A wet subsoil is fatal to their health. Any rich, light, dry (but not droughty) soil suits them. A large crop may be obtained from our rich alluvions, or bottom lands; but although uplands yield a less crop, the quality is regarded as decidedly superior. A wet clay subsoil is not good.

PLANTING.—Plants are set out in rows six to eight feet apart and six to eight feet from hill to hill in the row. Rooted plants, but more frequently cuttings from old plants are employed; five or six being planted to the hill. Poles from fifteen to twenty feet in length are placed to each hill. In England from three to six and even eight are placed to each hill. But three is about the average number.

HARVEST.—No crop is more variable than this; the yield per acre ranging according to the season from 300 to 2,000 lbs. On rich bottom lands 2,000 lbs. may be not unfrequently raised; but on an average, from 700 to 1,000 lbs. may be reckoned.

The plants bloom in July and are ready for harvest by the first of September. It is necessary to gather them promptly, as they soon deteriorate if allowed to remain after they are ripe. As soon as gathered they are kiln-dried, then placed from ten days to two weeks to cool, and, finally, they are baled for market.

GENERAL CONSIDERATIONS.—A plantation will last in full

vigor for ten years, and then will decline, but gradually, for ten more, when it is to be broken up. Fifteen years, perhaps, is the average duration of the hop plantations. They exhaust the soil, withdrawing much and returning little to it. Hops vary exceedingly in price in different years, not only on account of the varying supply arising from the uncertainty of yield, but from the quality of the article in different years. The average price in the United States is not far from sixteen cents per pound. Sometimes they rise to thirty, forty, and even fifty cents per pound.

From the moment of sprouting, in the spring, until the hop is ready for the kiln, they are liable to disaster from insects or disease. Nowhere has more experience been had in their cultivation than in England. Brown says, " they are exposed to more diseases than any other plant with which we are acquainted, and the trade offers greater room for speculation than any other exercised within the British dominions." Parkinson, with a quaint play upon the word hop, says, " the *hop* is said to be a plant very properly named, as there is never any certainty in cultivating it."

If the crop is to be planted largely, it would seem plain, from the foregoing, that one should have capital enough to be able to bear some losses, at least, at first. For ordinary cultivators, if the experiment is to be made, it would be better to begin with a small plantation at first, embarking more largely as knowledge and skill increase, and as experience determines its profitableness.

———•◦•———

GRAPE VINES should be trimmed before the sap begins to rise, else they will bleed, to their great injury. If it be neglected till the sap is in motion, let the cultivator wait till the leaves are about the size of a dollar ; then cutting may be performed without injury.

WHITE CLOVER.

WE are inclined to suppose that the excellences of white clover have not been enough esteemed among our farmers; indeed, they have adopted a few grasses as special favorites upon whom all favors are lavished, and the rest are totally or very nearly rejected.

In regions where dairies abound, and where, therefore, the subject of pasturage is of vital interest, those grasses are sown which spring early in the year and continue late; which grow quickly, abundantly, and shoot again rapidly after being cropped; which are nutritious; which tend to produce milk, and impart to it high flavor. If any *one* grass possessed all these properties, it would be perfect; and, for pastures, all others might be rejected. As it is, several grasses must conspire to form a *sward* possessed of these diverse excellences. In this joint result white clover bears no mean place. It is, on congenial soils, of vigorous growth, eminently conducive to the production of milk, and milk of fine flavor. These are its peculiar virtues. Besides these, it possesses in common with other pasture plants, hardiness, tenacity of life, nutritiousness for beef-cattle. Thaër, the most eminent practical, and scientific cultivator of his day, says: "*It is certainly the most generally approved of all plants that are cultivated for this* (pasture) *purpose.*" Sinclair, whose authority in grasses will not be disputed, says: "nor does it form a good pasture when sown *by itself.* . . but, combined with other grasses, it is a valuable plant." Great quantities of seed are annually sown in England by the best farmers. Fessenden, of New England, says, "it does not contain as much nutritive matter as red clover; yet its value as a *pasture-grass is universally admitted.*" This is the experience of Germany, England, and New England. Has experience determined that these good qualities are suppressed in western pastures? Or is there such a prejudice against it on account of its prying, intrusive disposition in arable lands, that our farmers are unwilling to give it a chance?

———•◆•———

PLOWING CORN.

MANY farmers, because their fathers did so before them, plow their corn lands very shallow before planting; but make up for it in deep plowing while dressing the corn-crop. Why is corn plowed at all?

1. To DESTROY WEEDS.—In this climate if a plow is not kept lively in the early part of the season, weeds will completely take the crop. The soil is like a table full of food. Every man who sits down to it makes it less. Every weed eats up a part of the soil, and takes away, needlessly, so much from the corn. But it is not merely the nutritive ingredients which are extracted—but what, on some soils, in some seasons, is even worse—weeds drink up the moisture. There are many soils which could afford to lose much mineral and vegetable substance without lessening the supply for corn; but, in this climate, in ordinary seasons, no soil can afford to squander its moisture.

But a corn crop is often put in to act as a cleanser of the soil when it has become foul. This end can only be answered by a rigid persecution and destruction of the weeds throughout the whole growing season. Some farmers, strangely enough, will deal thoroughly with their fields, but allow the edges and fence rows to swarm with weeds that luxuriate and ripen seed which the winds scatter all over the field. This is as if a man should busy himself all day long, in driving hogs out of his field, but leave all the holes open where they broke in. The soil should be thoroughly worked.

2. To PREVENT DRYNESS.—Nothing is wider of the truth, than letting corn alone in dry weather for fear of " firing "

it. If the plow begins early, and is kept going, no drought likely to occur in our climate can do much injury; especially if the ground has been broken up deep before planting.

Where the atmosphere is very dry, very hot and windy, the evaporation of moisture from the plant, and from the surface of the soil, is excessive. A hill of corn will exhale many pounds of moisture in a day. There is no remedy for excessive exhalation from plants; but this renders it yet more necessary that a supply should be kept up at the roots. If the soil therefore, is permitted to evaporate from its surface, the double draught upon its moisture—through the plant, and from the surface—will soon exhaust its water.

Everybody knows that if a board or cloth be put upon the ground, in dry weather, the earth under it will remain moist—its aqueous particles being checked in their passage upward. If a shovelful of fine manure be laid in a heap upon a spot of ground, the same effect will be produced. Gardeners are accustomed to cover the earth about shrubs with an inch or two of fine sand; experience teaching them that it preserves the moisture of the soil. Now, if the soil, instead of being covered with sand, or light manure, be itself pulverized, the same effect will be produced—and for reasons which will appear. When the soil is compact the moisture ascends from particle to particle without obstruction. Every crevice which separates the particles of earth, checks the passage of the moisture. This may be more readily seen in an analogous case—the transmission of heat. Take two nail-rods, lay the end of one in the fire; divide the other into inch pieces and lay them in a row from the fire, each piece touching the other. The transmission of heat in the rod made up of pieces will be checked at each point of division, while the uncut rod will heat rapidly. On this principle, an iron chain two feet long, with one end thrust into fire, will not transmit heat through its length near so soon as a solid bar of the same length.

If this reasoning be true, and experience bears it out, the plow should be kept running in dry times to save a crop from drought. But if the farmer has neglected his corn, waiting for rain, and begins to plow after his ground is very dry, and plows deep, *breaking the roots* of his corn, the crop will be "fired;" for, in this case, besides the evaporation from the leaves and the dryness of the soil, he commences breaking the roots by which the crop drinks what little water there may be left for it. Of course it despairs when it is attacked on one side by the heat, and on the other by the foolish farmer, and underneath by a treacherously dry soil. Begin, then, early, and plow often, and you may defy dry summers and cram your crib with hearty crops of corn.

BREAKING THE ROOTS.—Many farmers study to break the roots of their corn. We have heard them boast of ripping them up with a big plow till they clogged it up like bundles of yarn. It is done by some because others do it; those who attempt to reason, say, that if a root be broken it immediately puts out many more from the point of breakage; and the practice of root-pruning fruit-trees is cited, to show that the fruitfulness of a plant is increased by reducing the root and checking the growth of the wood. It is not true that the fruitfulness of a tree is increased by root-pruning, but, it is made to yield its fruit *earlier*. It is a device to bring trees rapidly into bearing. A pear-tree (grafted) requires from five to eight years before it is matured enough to commence bearing. By mutilation of root, bending of branches, or by a poor gravelly soil, the tree is partially forbidden to grow, and obliged to ripen its wood and fit it for fruit-bearing. But had it grown to its natural size, it would then have borne even more fruit than when dwarfed.

No such practice is required upon annual plants, whose

ripening is not delayed through years, but which come up and ripen and die within the limits of a single season. They need no artificial treatment to accelerate the fruiting, because it ordinarily makes no difference whether the corn crop comes in September or October. It is better to select varieties of corn which ripen within the limits of the season natural to the region where it is planted. Then there will be no occasion to break roots, or to apply any other artificial and violent process to accelerate maturation.

CLEAN OUT YOUR CELLARS.

I SPEAK to those who have cellars. If not already done, thoroughly purge this subterranean story of your house. Every decayed onion, cabbage stump, potato vine or tuber, turnip, parsnip, carrot, and all the dirt they have made, all straw and rubbish, rake them up and out with them. The cellar is no place for them at any time of year. If you still retain a few potatoes for table use, let them be picked over and all decayed ones removed. One of the best housewives of our acquaintance, greeted us not long since, with an invitation to come and see her cellar: "I have swept down every cobweb, whitewashed the walls, swept up the floor, and sowed it with salt." Decayed vegetable matter is a fertile cause of disease, and there is enough of it out of doors, in this country, without heaping it up in the cellar for the special purpose, it would almost seem, of breeding fevers. Whitewash the walls, for lime purifies as well as beautifies. Rake down the cobwebs, they are the infallible marks of a *slattern*. Every spider that is allowed to peer out of his corner in a house, up-stairs or down, undisturbed, points his long black leg in thanksgiving at the house-wife, "Hurra for folks that are not too particular." Old legends represent witches as addicted to riding brooms. I wish that many women would get bewitched enough to do this, something more than they do. Down cellar, then, with your broom. Look now; the window is perfectly covered; there is a great sprawling gaunt spider in the corner and half a dozen empty bugs hung up like scalps to commemorate his triumphs; next to him is a great over-swollen potbellied fellow—for all the world he looks like a huge glutton; then there is a sharp, nimble, enterprising spider, below him, who has just opened an office and is keen for business, preparing to inherit, like many other fellows, his neighbor's custom, who, having got rich frau-dulently, will soon burst; there, too, are several pale and shadowy spiders, who look as if the cobwebs had kept them from the light until they had become quite sallow and emaciated; then there are several little round, shining-black, pestilent fellows, whose legs are so long in proportion to their bodies, that they make one think of a little potato with yard-long sprouts all over it. I say nothing of crab-spiders on the window-sill, who, like metaphysicians, run backward just as easy as forwards. Just look, too, my dear madam, at the various patterns of their webs. Here is one from point to point resembling a sheet-like shelf of dusty cotton, and running like a tunnel, into a knot hole, where stands the venomous old fellow waiting for flies, like a usu-rer waiting for customers. Another corner is filled up with a web like a skein of tangled silk; then there is a beautiful wheel, worked more beautifully than any lace-work, while there are a multitude of base and lazy little spiders who, like many of their betters, live on other folk's webs. Well, we have talked long enough; dash your brush into that spider-village, give it a dextrous twirl, and with the whole population on the end of it, run to the door and crush them! So much for spiders.

As to salt; the only advantage of salt in a cellar, that occurs to us, is its effect in destroying snails, bugs, and that

fungus vegetation called mold.   It will do this.   But it
attracts moisture from the atmosphere and renders a cellar
damp.   If your cellar is very dry and sandy, you may use
salt without detriment.   But if too damp it will make the
matter worse.

——•◦•——

WHEN IS HAYING OVER P

In a trip through the country last summer we saw several fields of timothy, out of blossom, which had become dry,
seedy, and snuff-colored.   Haying was not over, it seems.
Cattle that had been hardened to eat iron-weed stems, jimpsum stalks, and packing straw, would probably be willing to
eat this hay.

We saw another sight.   Hay which had been cut and
partly cured, was cocked up and had been left, probably for
a week or two already ; and, doubtless, was to stand thus
much longer, for there is a fashion with some to let their
hay lie about the field in little three-feet cocks, *until it is
convenient* to haul it to the stack.   This may be in August,
or September, and sometimes we have seen a farmer (so
called) with a little sled and rope hauling his hay in October.   Now, hay thus served is good for nothing but for
litter.   The bottom of each little heap molds ; the sides are,
by sun and rain, spoiled, and the little wad in the middle
does not, after subtracting the sides and bottom, amount to
much.

I'll venture my head that these are not " book farmers."
I have no doubt that "book farmers " do some foolish things,
but farmers without books do a great many more.   No
book farmer, none but a farmer utterly without books,
would think of leaving his hay in cocks for six weeks or two
months.   We see enough of such hay offered for sale every
winter, of a dingy, lack-lustre, straw-colored look, without

fragrance, or odor of any sort except a faint smell of old wood, or more pungent odor of mold.

We say, in conclusion, grass should not be left so long that it will be already dry and cured before it is cut; and, after grass is once down, it is not to be treated like flax, and left to bleach and rot, but should be got in as *soon as possible.* Farmers whose hay is on the stack or in the mow may laugh at this article; those whose hay is not stacked or in the barn had better do something besides laugh.

———•◦•———

LAYING DOWN LAND TO GRASS.

WE shall speak of the kinds and quality of seed, and of the time and manner of putting them in.

We think our farmers err in not sowing enough kinds of seed together.

The objects to be secured are very early grass in the spring, a heavy body of hay, a rapid after-growth, and the greatest amount which the soil can yield. No one grass can be found capable of meeting all these ends. Some are very early, but not heavy enough or sufficiently nutritious for the main crop; others are admirable for hay, but do not start readily again after cutting. By judiciously mixing different sorts of grasses, any one of these objects may be secured and the meadow be admirable both for the scythe and for pasturage. Nor can the soil be made to yield all of which it is capable in any other way; for a square foot of ground may be able to sustain but a certain number of roots of any *one kind* of grass, and yet many support, in addition, as much more of another kind, since different species of grass draw their nourishment from different portions of the soil—the fibrous-rooted grasses from the surface, and tap-rooted plants from the lower strata of the soil, while broad-leaved vegetation, as clovers, lucerne, etc., draw very much of their support from the air. Indeed, this is the lesson which Nature teaches us, for a dozen kinds of grass may oftentimes be found growing wild on a single square foot.

The English farmer sows from four to seven or eight kinds of grass-seed, and sometimes as high as twelve or fourteen, each one of which is destined to answer some special end, and the whole taken together constitute as it were, a perfect grass.

We subjoin the quantity and kind of seed per acre recommended by English authorities, that our readers may have an idea of the English method, and derive such benefit from it as their circumstances will admit of:

Smooth-stalked poa,	8	quarts.
Rough-stalked poa,	8	"
Meadow fescue,	12	"
Meadow fox-tail,	8	"
Crested dog's-tail,	6	"
Rib-grass,	4	"
Timothy-grass,	4	"
Yellow oat-grass,	4	"
Perennial rye-grass,	12	"
Cock's foot,	4	"
Yarrow,	4	"
Sweet-scented vernal,	2	"
White clover,	6	lbs.
Cow-grass,	4	"

and annual meadow-grass.

These seeds may, for the most part, be had of eastern dealers, though not probably in the West.

With blue grass we should join orchard grass, say a bushel to the acre—white clover five pounds, red clover ten pounds, and sweet-scented vernal (*anthoxanthum odoratum*) say three pounds.

This last grass is remarkably early in the spring, and peculiarly fragrant; indeed, it is supposed that the famous spring butter of Philadelphia derives its peculiar flavor from this grass, and we should include it in every mixture to be sown for pasturage. The orchard grass is one of our most valuable; for hay it may be inferior to timothy; but it is decidedly superior to it for pasturage. Colonel Powell, of Pennsylvania, after growing it ten years, declares that it produces more pasturage than any cultivated grass he has even seen in America. It should be spread on a floor and sprinkled with water a day or two before sowing, it being very light, not weighing more than twelve or fourteen pounds to the bushel.

The following table exhibits the quantity of seed, by *weight*, and also on the three kinds of soil:

FOR PERMANENT PASTURE, PER IMPERIAL ACRE.

	LIGHT SOIL.		MEDIUM SOIL.		HEAVY SOIL.	
	With a crop.	Without a crop.	With a crop.	Without a crop.	With a crop.	Without a crop.
	lbs.	lbs.	lbs.	lbs.	lbs.	lbs.
Perennial rye-grass..	12	24	12	24	12	24
Meadow fox-tail.....	1¼	2½	2	4	3¼	6½
Timothy-grass.....	—	—	1½	3	3¼	5½
Meadow fescue......	2½	4	2½	4	2½	4
Cock's-foot..........	5	8	3¼	6½	2½	4
Rough-stalked poa...	—	—	1¾	3¼	3¼	6½
Smooth-stalked poa..	3¼	6½	1½	3¼	—	—
White clover........	5	8	5	8	5	8
Red clover..........	1½	2½	1½	2½	1½	2½
Hop-clover, or trefoil	1½	2½	1½	2½	1½	2½
Cow-grass...	1½	2½	1½	2½	1½	2½
	33½	60½	34	63½	36¼	66

There is a very great difference of opinion respecting the quantity of seed to be sown to an acre. There can be no doubt that the question is to be settled by the character of the soil and climate. In soils and under circumstances where every seed will vegetate and grow off with unobstructed vigor, less seed is needed than where a part will be taken by frosts, a part by drenching rains which are not well drained off, and a part by severe drought. Every farmer must employ his best judgment in this matter; but, it is better to err on the side of too much than of too little seed.

TIME OF SEEDING.—We cannot pretend to decide between the conflicting opinions on this subject. The positiveness of those who prefer spring-sowing is only to be equalled by that of those who prefer fall-planting. Young says of the month of August, " this is the best season of the whole year for laying down land to grass, and no other is admissible for it on strong, wet, or heavy soils." This, however, is said of humid England. But if the character of the season toward the close of summer favors, there can be no doubt that fall-sowing will advance the crop very early the next year, in all soils where it is not liable to be thrown out by the frosts. If the winter proves severe, it will be prudent to add an additional quantity of seed in the spring. It is objected to spring sowings, that the grass is grown in the shade during the early part of the summer, and is, of course, *tender*, so that when the grain is cut, it is enfeebled by the powerful heat, to which, then, it becomes exposed. On the whole, we are inclined to prefer the month of September, if the season favors, to any other for sowing grass seed. Since writing these lines, one of our best farmers informs us that he prefers August to any other month.

METHOD OF SOWING.—The ground should be very thoroughly prepared by deep and fine plowing, and the want of labor in this respect is want of economy.

If the soil is naturally well drained, no further provision against wet will be required. But if it be flat, it may be well to lay it off into lands, strike a furrow through the centre, and then turn the furrows toward the outer on each side. This will give a slight elevation at the middle and a drain between each land sufficient to answer the purpose of moderate surface draining. The seed should be sown with the greatest *evenness* possible. The English farmer prefers to sow some of the kinds separately on this account ; for although he has to sow the whole ground several times over, experience has taught him, as it will us, that that is the cheapest which is done the best.   Let it be covered in well with a harrow, and not with a bush, which last leaves the soil dead, and tends to drag the seed into patches and hollows.   As a general rule, grass seed may be planted as deeply as grain.   Farmers lose much more seed from shallow than from deep planting.   For although shallow-planted seed vegetates sooner, they are more liable to be winter-killed, or to perish by drought than those which are deeply covered.

------•••------

THEORY OF MANURE.

It is very well known that a young orchard will not, usually, flourish on the site of an old one; for the older trees are supposed to have withdrawn from the soil certain elements necessary to their growth; and as necessary to the growth of the young tree, should it be planted there. There is no "like" or "dislike" of the soil to the tree; it is a plain case of starvation.   The tree needs, and the soil cannot supply certain elements of its wood.

But if, after a plant has abstracted from the soil certain ingredients, the whole plant is decomposed and returned to the earth, the soil repossesses itself of the lost elements, and is ready to yield them up again to a plant of the same kind. If the straw of wheat be burned upon the field, annually, the soil would yield fine crops for a thousand successive years, that is so far as the *straw is concerned*.   But if the grain is removed, and nothing resupplies the drain of phosphates which it makes from the soil, the soil will in due time, according to the original quantities in the soil, cease to yield *grain*, although the straw may be admirable.   But if both straw and kernel were every year burned upon the field, as grass and its seed is upon the prairies, wheat would grow for a thousand years in succession. The same is true of corn, of potatoes, and of any annual crop. When the annual growth is restored to the soil, it is repossessed of all its treasure which had been loaned for a season. If a part of the crop is removed, the soil is poorer by just so much as the portion removed contained within it of the elements necessary to that crop, and it must be restored artificially, *i. e. by manuring;* or by allowing the earth to prepare (by disintegration or decomposition of its minerals) a new supply; *i. e. by fallowing.* A forest will grow for ages on the same spot, for it returns annually its leaves, and, gradually, by force of accidents and the elements, its twigs, branches, trunks, etc., to the soil again. But let the whole product be gradually removed, and the soil would soon be unable to supply the trees their nourishment, except in cases where the soil was very rich in the materials of growth. The forests of Germany, like our mines, are under the management of the government. It was customary, for a time, to allow the peasants the use of the *twigs* and *smaller branches;* but analysis has shown that in these, especially, resides the large proportion of potash entering into the composition of trees; the annual removal of it debilitated the trees to an extent that obliged the Conservators to change their mode of proceeding.

On the other hand, in one of Mr. Horsford's letters from Germany, we have the question of growing plants upon their own ashes, brought, by the ablest chemist of the age, directly to the test of experiment.

"In the spring preceding my arrival in Giessen, Professor Liebig planted some grape scions under the windows of the laboratory. He fed them, if I may use such an expression, upon the ashes of the grape vine—or upon the proper inorganic food of the grape, as shown by analyses of its ashes. The growth has been enormous, and several of the vines bore large clusters of grapes in the course of the season.

Indeed, I know not but all, as my attention was drawn to them particularly only since the fruit has been gathered. The soil otherwise is little better than a pavement—a kind of fine gravel, in which scarcely anything takes root.

"I was shown pots of wheat, in different stages of their growth, that had been fed variously—some upon the inorganic matters they needed, according to the analyses of their ashes—others had merely shared the tribute of the general soil. The results in numbers I don't yet know. In appearance, no one could be at a loss to judge of what might be expected."

The fact that depopulated forest-grounds change the character of their growth, is quite familiar to all; and the reasons of it have been variously debated.

FODDER FOR CATTLE.

ALTHOUGH the practice of soiling cattle, *i. e.* of cutting their food daily and feeding it to them in a green state, would be profitable to many small farmers, it is especially to be recommended to those living in towns, where pasturage is distant and expensive. Where an immediate supply is required, corn may be sown broadcast, and cut as wanted, until it begins to tassel, when all should be cut and cured, and the ground sown again, and a third time in the same summer.

But if half that is said of lucerne is true, and we see no reason to doubt it, it is valuable far above all other kinds of green fodder. It starts very early in spring; may be cut four times in a summer, yielding from four to nine tons to the acre, acccording to the condition of the land. It is much relished by cattle, imparts no bad flavor to milk, is a very fattening food, and one sowing will last ten years.

4

One acre is sufficient for four or five cows.   It may be sown in drills, if the land is foul, and kept clean by hoeing, the first year; but on clean ground it may be sown broadcast. It is hardy under the infliction of severe frosts; and surpasses all grasses in endurance of drought, its enormously land roots affording it moisture from a great depth.   An English writer says, its roots have been found from ten to fourteen feet below the surface; and an American writer says, that it made, on his land, roots three feet long the first summer.

Where it is sown broadcast, it is difficult to get it through the first year.   But if sown in drills ten inches apart, and hoed once or twice, it may be cut twice or thrice the first season, and be entirely established before winter.

A light, sandy soil is the best; it should not be put upon heavy and non-friable soils, though it will flourish on even these, when fully established.   Ten pounds of seed to the acre is enough, if drilled; fifteen pounds, if sown broadcast.

The only reason, that we can imagine, why this plant should not be extensively cultivated, is, the disrelish which our farmers too often have to any crop requiring much care. To slash along with a plow is all well enough; but to hoe and weed is rather tedious.   But these operations are required only during the first part of the first year.

CAMPHOR FOR FLOWERS.—Two or three drops of a saturated solution of camphor in alcohol, put into half an ounce of soft water, forms a mixture which will revive flowers that have begun to droop and wilt, and give them freshness for a long time.

THE SCIENCE OF BAD BUTTER.

WE once took occasion to give our opinion of the butter which was largely brought to our market. The article was deemed severe; but if they who think so had eaten of the butter they would have regarded *that* as the more pungent of the two. We have waited a year; and are now prepared more fully to testify against that utter abomination, slanderously called butter, so unrighteously exchanged in our market for good money. Far the most part, the cream is totally depraved at the start, and churning, working, and packing are only the successive steps of an evil education by which bad inclinations are developed into overt wickedness. We determined to keep an eye upon the matter; and now give, from life, the natural history of the butter sold.

Before doing this, we will express an opinion of what is *good butter*.

Good butter is made of sweet cream, with perfect neatness; is of a high color, perfectly sweet, free from buttermilk, and possesses a fine grass flavor.

Tolerable butter, differs from this only in not having a *fine flavor*. It is devoid of all unpleasant taste, but has not a high relish.

Whatever is less than this is bad butter; the catalogue is long and the descending scale is marked with more varieties than one may imagine.

Variety 1. BUTTER-MILK BUTTER.—This has not been well worked, and has the taste of fresh buttermilk. It is not *very* disagreeable to such as love fresh buttermilk; but as it is a flavor not expected in good butter, it is usually disagreeable.

Variety 2. STRONG BUTTER.—This is one step farther along, and the buttermilk is changing and beginning to assert its right to predominate over the butteraceous flavor;

yet it may be eaten with some pleasure if done rapidly, accompanied with very good bread.

Variety 3. FROWY OR FROWSY BUTTER.—This is a second degree of strength attained by the buttermilk. It has become pungent, and too disagreeable for any but absent-minded eaters.

Variety 4. RANCID BUTTER.—This is the putrescent stage. No description will convey, to those who have not tasted it, an idea of its unearthly flavor; while those who *have*, will hardly thank us for stirring up such awful remembrances by any description.

Variety 5. BITTER BUTTER.—Bitterness is, for the most part, incident to winter-butter. When one has but little cream and is long in collecting enough for the churn, he will be very apt to have bitter butter.

Variety 6. MUSTY BUTTER.—In summer, especially in damp, unventilated cellars, cream will gather mold; Whenever this appears, the pigs should be set to churn it. But instead, if but just touched, it is quickly churned; or, if much molded, it is slightly skimmed, as if the *flavor* of mold, which has struck through the whole mass, could be removed by taking off the colored portion! The peculiar taste arising from this affection of the milk, blessed be the man who needs to be told it!

Variety 7. SOUR-MILK BUTTER.—This is made from milk which has been allowed to sour, the milk and cream being churned up together. The flavor is that of greasy, sour milk.

Variety 8. VINEGAR BUTTER.—There are some who imagine that all milk should be *soured* before it is fit to churn. When, in cool weather, it delays to change, they expedite the matter by some acid—usually vinegar. The butter strongly retains the flavor thereof.

Variety 9. CHEESY BUTTER.—Cream comes quicker by being heated. If sour cream be heated, it is very apt to separate and deposit a *whey:* if this is strained into the churn with the cream, the butter will have a strong cheesy flavor.

Variety 10. GRANULATED BUTTER.—When, in winter, sweet cream is over-heated, preparatory to churning, it produces butter full of *grains,* as if there were meal in it.

Variety 11.—In this we will comprise the two opposite kinds—*too salt* and *unsalted butter.* We have seen butter exposed for sale with such masses of salt in it that one is tempted to believe that it was put in as a make-weight. When the salt is coarse, the operation of eating this butter affords those who have good teeth, a pleasing variety of grinding.

Variety 12. LARD BUTTER.—When lard is cheap and abundant, and butter rather dear, it is thought profitable to combine the two.

Variety 13. MIXED BUTTER.—When the shrewd housewife has several separate churnings of butter on hand, some of which would hardly be able to go alone, she puts them together, and those who buy, find out that "Union is *strength!*" Such butter is pleasingly marbled; dumps of white, of yellow, and of dingy butter melting into each other, until the whole is ring-streaked and-speckled.

Variety 14. COMPOUND BUTTER.—By compound butter we mean that which has received contributions from things animate and inanimate; feathers, hairs, rags of cloth, threads, specks, chips, straws, seeds ; in short, everything is at one time or another to be found in it, going to produce the three successive degrees of dirty, filthy, nasty.

Variety 15. TOUGH BUTTER.—When butter is worked too long after the expulsion of buttermilk, it assumes a gluey, putty-like consistence, and is tough when eaten. But, oh blessed fault! we would go ten miles to pay our admiring respects to that much-to-be-praised dairy-maid whose zeal leads her to work her butter too much! We doubt, however, if a pound of such butter was ever seen in this place.

Besides all these, whose history we have correctly traced; besides butter tasting of turpentine from being made in pine churns; butter bent on travelling, in hot weather; butter dotted, like cloves on a boiled ham, with flies, which Solomon assures us causeth the ointment to stink; besides butter in rusty tin pans, and in dirty swaddling clothes; besides butter made of milk drawn from a dirty cow, by a dirtier hand, into a yet dirtier pail, and churned in a churn the dirtiest of all; besides all these sub-varieties, there are several others with which we have formed an acquaintance, but found ourselves baffled at analysis. We could not even guess the cause of their peculiarities. Oh Dr. Liebig! how we have longed for your skill in analytic chemistry! What consternation would we speedily send among the slatternly butter-makers, revealing the mysteries of their dirty doings with more than mesmeric facility!

And now, what on earth is the reason that good butter is so great a rarity? Is it a hereditary curse in some families? or is it a punishment sent upon us for our ill-deserts? A few good butter-makers in every neighborhood are a standing proof that it is nothing but bad housewifery; mere sheer carelessness which turns the luxury of the churn into an utterly nauseating abomination.

Select cows for quality and not for quantity of milk; give them sweet and sufficient pasturage; keep clean yourself; milk into a clean pail; strain into clean pans—(pans scalded, scoured, and sunned, and if tin, with every particle of milk rubbed out of the seams.) While it is yet sweet, churn it; if it delays to come, add a little saleratus; work it thoroughly, three times, salting it at the second working; put it into a cool place, and then, when, with a conscience as clean and sweet as your butter, you have dispatched your tempting rolls to market, you may sit down and thank God that you are an honest woman!

CINCINNATI, THE QUEEN CITY.

WHATEVER may have been the squealing celebrity of Porkopolis, Cincinnati seems destined to merge the glory of that name in the more agreeable title, City of Vineyards. That she is the Queen City none denies. But on account of what single excellence, it might be difficult, for some, to say. A queen of slaughter-pens might be a hearty buxom lass, but, withal, not exactly the personage for which knights (Sancho always excepted) love to break lances. A queen of foundries and stithies, she might be, and not necessarily, on that account, a ruddy brunette; inasmuch as Sir Vulcan was, once before, the husband of Venus—queen of beauty. A blushing queen of strawberry beds would be quite romantic; but yet more appropriate if her jurisdiction were extended over vines and purple clusters and vineyards and orchards. But whether it be pork, or iron, or gardens, or vineyards, or observatories, Cincinnati is acknowledged on all hands to be the Queen City.

Leaving her commercial glories out of view, we think Cincinnati has done more for horticulture than any American city, taking into the account her recent origin and her means. In all other cities horticulture has been the child of wealth and leisure. It has *followed* commercial or manufacturing prosperity. But in this city, it began with them and kept pace with them; so that one wonders which most to admire, the thrift of industry and skill, or the elegant taste which is so generally evinced in the cultivation of fruit, and shrub and flower.

The first volume of the Transactions of the Cincinnati Horticultural Society, is eminently worthy of that enterprising corporation.

The thoughts of several principal friends of horticulture seem much directed to the subject of vine culture, and the manufacture of wine. There are more than eighty-three vineyards in the vicinity of the city containing not far from 400

acres of land! From 114 acres during the season of 1845,
more than 23,000 gallons of wine were manufactured, and
there was not more than half a crop obtained in that season. The average yield of wine per acre, for five years
in succession, is stated to be from 450 to 500 gallons per
annum.

Many think the culture of the grape will be the finishing
stroke to the temperance enterprise; affording a wholesome beverage from our hills in place of " corn juice " from
our bottoms, and beer from our hop and barley fields.

The arguments urged by some with great sincerity,
are the often-quoted facts, that the inhabitants of wine-
making countries are favorably distinguished for temperance; and that a palatable and wholesome beverage—pure
wine—would supersede the use of violent liquors. If we
thought that our people would become temperate upon
such conditions, we should be glad to see a vineyard on
every hillside, and a wine-vat to every farmhouse. But
there is no reason to expect any such result. Vineyards in
Europe exist among a quiet, comparatively unenterprising
peasantry. They have been *trained* to moderation; necessity has made them temperate in all things—in food, in
dress, in expense, and in drink. The popular habits are not
so excitable as with us; business runs in quiet streams,
and politics are unknown. With us, business is boisterous,
pleasure obstreperous, and politics outrageous. Our people are anything but quiet; they are hot, hot in tongue and
blood. It is wide enough of the mark to suppose that the
same cause existing among two entirely dissimilar people,
would, of course, produce the same results. We might as
well say that vineyards would make our people eat less meat,
less corn and pork, because the residents of wine districts
were known to be addicted to a vegetable diet. The probable consequences of abundant cheap wine must be
judged, not by what would happen in France, among
abstemious peasants, nor on the Rhine, among economical

and sober Germans; but by the tastes, habits, and tendencies of our own people. In this land everything tends to excitement. Men live upon a higher key, and live faster and live much more full of exhilaration than the same classes do in foreign lands. Our people drink not for the *taste* but for the *excitement* of liquor; and, so that wine, beer, or whisky will bring them up to the right key, the question of wholesomeness is quite unimportant. Our people are free and therefore have a right to live in the violation of natural laws; and a right, constantly exercised, of having fevers on account of surfeitings, and of dying early and by thousands by reasons of gross excesses.

Pleasures and business are esteemed by the volume of blood which they can drive, the pulse they can raise, the heat of excitement which they can produce. So long as affairs are fresh and piquant they are stimulants enough. But in the inequalities and intervals and fatigues of life, something else is required to hold the spirits up to the high level upon which everything proceeds. As soon as a man resorts to alcoholic stimulants to do this, he has embarked upon a course where all experience shows that he will drink deeper and deeper to final downright intemperance.

Some people think that cheap and wholesome beverage for the "masses," for laboring people, is desirable. While it may be well enough for every gentleman of leisure, it is to be the poor man's special blessing, saving him from the swill of the brewery and the fire of the still. Facts will stand on the side of the reverse reasoning. If wine is to be harmless at all, it will be with men who are not prone to enterprising heats; but given to the relishful pleasure of sipping just for the delicate flavors, for the aroma, for the fine *bouquet* of wine—men who need to have their blood up, and kept up, and resort to wine to supply the flagging stimulus of affairs; such men will not drink for the flavor, but for the feeling.

4*

It is for the sake of being roused; it is to be stimulated; it is, in plain language, to have the first exhilarations of drunkenness that laboring men drink, will drink, and have always drank cider, beer, wine, and brandy. The result of affording wine in abundance to such people as ours, will be to prepare them for a stronger drink just as soon as wine, by frequent use, is no longer stimulating enough. Wine will play jackal to brandy for the rich, and to whisky for the poor. We have some facts on hand touching this popular wine-drinking, which, if necessary, we shall employ at another time. Meanwhile, we are glad to see grape-culture spreading for the production of table-grapes; for the manufacture of wine, in so far as a supply of pure wine is needed for medicinal purposes. Further than that, we are opposed to wine-making. And as to cheating whisky out of its authority over "the dear people" by the blandishments of hock and champagne, or redeeming our barley and cornfields from the abominable persecutions of the brew-tub and the still, by the conservative energy or evangelizations of grape juice, we shall believe it when we see it; and we shall just as soon expect to see fire putting out fire and frost melting ice, as one degree of alcoholic stimulus curing a higher one.

——•••——

To PRESERVE GARDEN STICKS.—It is desirable when one has prepared good sticks for supporting carnations, roses, dahlias, etc., to preserve them from year to year. The following preparation will make them last a man's lifetime: When they are freshly made, allow them to become thoroughly dry; then soak them in linseed oil for some time, say two or three days. When taken out let them stand to dry till the oil is perfectly soaked in; then paint with two coats of verdigris paint. No wet can then penetrate.

CARE OF ANIMALS IN WINTER.

THE wisest man has said that "the righteous man regardeth the life of his beast; but the tender mercies of the wicked are cruel." If any one is at a loss to know the meaning of the latter part, he cannot have made good use of his eyes. Lean cattle, leaner horses, anatomical specimens of cows, half fed, dirty, drenched by every rain, and pierced by every winter wind, these are an excellent comment on the passage.

It is time for every merciful man to make provision for every dumb animal which is dependent upon him.

Cows should be provided with a comfortable stable at night. No feeding will be a substitute for good shelter. Both the quantity and quality of the milk will depend upon bodily comfort in respect to warmth and nutritious food. Such as are becoming heavy with calf should be specially cared for. Many farmers let their cows shift for themselves as soon as their milk dries away. But the health of the coming calf and the ability of the cow to supply it, and her owner, copiously with milk depend on the condition in which she is kept during the period of gestation.

Cattle should have a good shed provided for them, under which they may be dry and sheltered from winds. It is the curse of western farming that cattle and fodder are so plenty that it is hardly a loss to waste both.

Where the amount of stock is too great for comfortable home-quarters, and they are wintered in a stock field, there should be places of resort for them, so high as to remain dry, well turfed with blue-grass, and sheltered with cheap sheds, or by belts of forest.

Sheep should receive special attention. They abhor wet. They should be permitted to keep their fleece dry, and to eat their food in a dry stable. The flock should be sorted. The bucks and wethers by themselves, the ewes by themselves; lambs and weak sheep in another division; and a fourth compartment should never be wanting for the sick, where they may be nursed and medically treated.

Horses are more apt to be taken care of than cattle. But even they are often more indebted for existence to a stubborn tenacity of life, than to the care of their keepers. The horse is a more dainty feeder than ruminating animals. He should be supplied with a better article of hay; his grain should never be dirty or musty.

Hardy farm-horses may even rough out the winter without blanketing or any other care than is necessary to supply good food and enough of it. But carriage horses, and those highly prized for the saddle—aristocratic horses—should be more carefully groomed. It is not wise to blanket a horse at all, unless it can be *always* done. If he is liable to change hands; to be off on journeys under circumstances in which he cannot be blanketed at night, it will be better not to begin it.

Winter is a good time to kill off spirited horses. They are easily run down by a smashing sleigh-ride pace. Boys and girls, buzzing in a double sleigh like a hive of bees, think that the horses enjoy themselves, at the exhilarating pace of six or eight miles an hour, as much as *they* do. But this is not ordinarily the worst of it. The horse stands out, after a trip of ten or fifteen miles, at a post for an hour or two until thoroughly chilled; then home he races, and goes into the stable, steaming with sweat, to stand without blankets all night. Horses catch cold as much as men do. And a horse-cold is just as bad as a human cold. As there has been some difficulty, in the construction of fanning mills, to gain a strong enough current of wind, we would advise the builders of them to study the construction of a good stable.

WINTER NIGHTS FOR READING.

As the winter is a season of comparative leisure, it is the time for farmers to study. It is a good time for them to make themselves acquainted with the nature of soils, of manures, of vegetable organization—or structural botany. Farmers are liable to rely wholly upon their own experience, and to despise science. Book-men are apt to rely on scientific theories, and nothing upon practice. If these two tendencies would only court and marry each other, what a hopeful family would they rear! How nice it would look to see in the papers:

MARRIED.—By Philosophical Wisdom, Esq., Mr. Practical Experience, to Miss Sober Science. [We will stand godfather to all the children.]

FEATHERS.

THE quality of feathers depends on their strength, elasticity and cleanness; and these, again, depend upon the condition of the bird, its health, food, and the time of plucking its feathers. *Down* is the term applied to under-feathers—most abundant in water fowl, and in those especially which live in cold latitudes, being designed to protect them from wet and cold. The eider-down, from the eider-duck, is of the most repute. It is brought from extreme northern latitudes, and is used for coverings to beds, rather than for beds themselves, as, by being slept upon, it loses its elasticity.

Poultry feathers, as those of turkeys, ducks, and chickens, if assorted and the coarse ones rejected, afford very good beds; but they are not so elastic as geese-feathers.

Everybody knows that live geese-feathers are *the* best. Every one does not think of the reason; which, as it is the key to the art of having good feathers, we shall propound.

So long as a bird is alive, the feathers are as much an object of nutrition as the flesh, the bones, or any other part of the body.

When dead, put them into hot water to make the feathers come easy. In pulling, take out large handfuls at a time, so as to have scraps of meat and shreds of skin adhere to the quill; let them lie for several days in wet heaps to ferment a little. Then dry them suddenly by violent heat, cram them into the bed-tick, and jump on, and if you have not an odorous bed, and, in a month or two, a bedful of visitors seeking food, then there is no truth in the laws of nature.

The care of beds is not understood, often, by even good housewives. When a bed is freshly made it often smells strong. Constant airing, will, if the feathers are good, and only new, remove the scent.

A bed in constant use should be invariably beaten and shaken up daily, to enable the feathers to retain their elasticity.

It should lie after it is shaken up, for two or three hours a day, in a well ventilated room. The human body is constantly giving off a perspiration; and at night more than usual, from the relaxed condition of the skin. The bed will become foul from this cause if not well aired. If the bed is in a room which cannot be spared for such a length of time, it should be put out to air two full days in the week.

In airing beds, *the sun should never shine directly upon them.* It is *air*, not *heat*, that they need. We have seen beds lying on a roof where the direct and reflected rays of the sun had full power, and the feathers, without doubt, were *stewing*, and the oil in the quill becoming rancid; so that the bed smells worse after its roasting than before. *Always air beds in the shade, and, if possible, in cool and windy days.* And now, if any of our attentive housewife-readers, and we have not a few, are disposed to reward us for all this advice, let them give us a bed to sleep on, when we next visit them, made of growing feathers, from live and healthy geese, carefully picked, well cured, daily shaken up and thoroughly aired; and if we do not dream that the owner is an angel, it will be because we are too much occupied in sound sleeping.

NAIL UP YOUR BUGS.

"The words of the wise are as goads and as nails fastened by masters of assemblies."—SOLOMON.

AFTER a great pother about canker worms, peach-tree worms, and other audacious robber-worms; after smoke, salt, tar, and tansy, bands of wool, cups of oil, lime, ashes, and surgery have been set forth as remedies, to the confusion of those who have tried them bootlessly, it now appears that we are about to *nail* the rascals. The Boston *Cultivator*, contains an article "On Destroying Insects on Trees," from which we quote:

"I did not intend to give it publicity until I had fully tested it, but as the ravages are very extensive in the West, I cannot delay giving you the experiment, hoping that some of your western readers may now give it a fair trial and report the result. I will give one case which may induce the experiment wherever the evil is felt. In conversation with a friend in Newburyport, Dr. Watson, last fall, I mentioned the experiment; he invited me to his garden, where last year a fruit-tree was infested with the

nests of caterpillar or canker-worms, as were his neighbors'
trees; he showed me a board nailed for convenience of a
clothes-line upon one of the large limbs of the tree; he said
he noticed a little while afterward that the nests on that limb
dried up, and the worms disappeared, though the cause did
not then occur to him though apparent as it will be to any
scientific mind.

"Drive carefully well home, so that the bark will heal
over a, few headless cast iron nails, say some six or eight,
size and number according to the size of the tree, in a ring
around its body, a foot or two above the ground. The
oxidation of the iron by the sap, will evolve ammonia,
which will, of course, with the rising sap, impregnate every
part of the foliage, and prove to the delicate palate of
the patient, a nostrum, which will soon become, as in
many cases of larger animals, the real panacea for the ills of
life, _via Tomb._ I think if the ladies should drive some
small iron brads into some limbs of any plant infested with
any insect, they would find it a good and safe remedy, and
I imagine in any case, instead of injury, the ammonia will be
found particularly invigorating. Let it be tried upon a
limb of any tree, where there is a vigorous nest of cater-
pillars, and watch it for a week or ten days, and I think the
result will pay for the nails."

Let our farmers take their hammers and nails and start
for the orchard; if they see a bug on the tree, drive a nail,
and he is a bug no more! If they see a worm, in with
a nail, and the "ammonia evolved" will finish his
functions!

The _Southern Planter_ is out with a backer to the Boston
Cultivator:

"A singular fact, and one worthy of being recorded, was
mentioned to us a few days since by Mr. Alexander Duke,
of Albemarle. He stated that whilst on a visit to a neighbor, his attention was called to a large peach orchard, every
tree in which had been totally destroyed by the ravages of

the worm, with the exception of three, and these three were probably the most thrifty and flourishing peach-trees he ever saw. The only cause of their superiority known to his host, was an experiment made in consequence of observing that those parts of worm-eaten timber into which nails had been driven, were generally sound; when his trees were about a year old he had selected three of them and driven a tenpenny nail through the body, as near the ground as possible; whilst the balance of his orchard has gradually failed, and finally yielded entirely to the ravages of the worms, these three trees, selected at random, treated precisely in the same manner, with the exception of the nailing, had always been vigorous and healthy, furnishing him at that very period with the greatest profusion of the most luscious fruit. It is supposed that the salts of iron afforded by the nail are offensive to the worm, whilst they are harmless, or perhaps even beneficial to the tree."

We do not wish to interrupt any experiments which the enterprising may choose to make. To be sure we regard the facts with some incredulity, and the chemical explanations with something of the mirthful superadded to unbelief. But if nails *are* an antidote to worms—a real vermifuge—let them be administered, whatever may be the explanations; whether they are an electric battery, giving the insects a little domestic, vegetable lightning, or whether they afford "salts of iron" to physic them, or "evolve ammonia" in such potent, pungent strength that vermicular nostrils are unable to endure it!

While one is fairly engaged in a campaign of experiments, we heartily hope that war will be carried to the very territory of ignorance, and we will propound several other important questions of fact and theory, which, if settled, will crown somebody's brow with laurels.

It is said that hanging a scythe in a plum-tree, or an iron hoop, or horse shoes, will insure a crop of plums. This ought to be investigated.

It is said that pear-trees that are unfruitful, may be made to bear, by digging under them, cutting the tap root, and burying a black cat there. We do not know as it makes any difference as to the sex of the cat, though we should, if trying it, rather prefer the male cat.

Lastly, that we may contribute our mite to the advancement of science, we will state that, in our youth, we were informed, that, if we would go into the wood-house once a day and rub our hands with a chip, *without thinking of red fox's tail*, the warts would all go off. We have no doubt that it would have been successful, but every time we tried the experiment, whisk came the red fox's tail into our head and spoilt the whole affair. But might this not cure warts on trees?

ASHES AND THEIR USE.

SOME soils contain already the chemical ingredients which wood ashes supply. If lime be applied to a calcareous soil, it will do no good; there was no want of lime there before; if potash be added to a soil already abounding in it, no effect will be seen in the crops. Ashes contain lime and potash (phosphate of lime and silicate of potash). If a soil is naturally rich in these, the addition of ashes would be useless. Such cases show the true benefits of a *really* scientific knowledge of soils and manures. Every plant that grows takes out of the soil certain qualities. Wheat, among other things, extracts largely of its potash; Indian corn abstracts but little; potatoes extract phosphate of magnesia, etc. A chemist would say, at once, apply that kind of manure which is rich in the peculiar property extracted by your wheat, corn, or potatoes! What manure is that' Here again science must help. It analyzes manures—gives the farmer the choice among them. The soil being known,

the properties required by different crops being known—
the farmer applies that manure which contains what the soil
lacks. Experiments have seemed to show, that, for purposes
of tillage, *leached* ashes are just as good as the *unleached*.
So that housewives may have all the use of their ashes for
soap, and then employ them in the garden. Leached ashes
become better by being exposed for some time in the air,
absorbing from the atmosphere fertilizing qualities (carbonic acid?)

So valuable are ashes regarded in Europe, that they are
frequently hauled by farmers from twenty miles' distance—
and on Long Island they bring eight cents a bushel.

The ashes of different kinds of wood are of very unequal
value—that of the oak the least, and that of beech the
most valuable. The latter wood constitutes two-thirds of
the fire-wood of this region, and the ashes are therefore the
very best.

A coat of ashes may be laid, in the spring, over the whole
garden and spaded in with the barnyard manure.

They may be dug in about gooseberry and currant
bushes.

They are excellent about the trunks of fruit-trees, spreading the old each year, and renewing the deposit.

They may be thinly spread over the grass-plat in the
dooryard, as they will give vigor and deeper color and
strength to the grass.

We have usually added about one shovelful of ashes to
every *twenty* in making a compost for flowers, roses, shrubs,
etc.

Ashes are peculiarly good for all kinds of melon, squash,
and cucumber vines. This is well known to those who
raise watermelons on burnt fields, on old charcoal pits, etc.
We have seen statements of cucumbers being planted
upon a peck of pure, leached ashes, in a hole in the ground,
and thriving with great vigor. The ashes of vines show a
great amount of potash; and as wood ashes afford this sub-

stance abundantly, its use would seem to be indicated by theory as well as confirmed by experiment.

Lastly, whenever ground is liable to suffer severely from drought, we would advise a liberal use of ashes and salt.

———•◆•———

HARD TIMES.

WHAT are called *hard times* produce very different effects on different individuals. Some are made more industrious, and some more indolent; some grow frugal and careful, others careless and desperate; some never appear so honest as when brought to the *pinch*, but many men seem honest *until* they are brought to the trial, and then give way. Hard times are gradually passing away. As a community, are we better or worse off than before? A few particulars may help us to form some judgment.

Fewer goods are bought at the store, and more are manufactured at home; spinning-wheels and looms have renewed their youth—and so have our mothers, who, after a long disuse, may now be seen working as merrily at them, as they used to do when they spun and wove their *wedding* furnishings—although they have not now any such rosy hope to quicken their aged fingers. Men have been obliged to rely more upon their own ingenuity—for want of money to pay the carpenter, the blacksmith, the shoemaker, etc. Old clothes, old tools have been made to serve an additional campaign.

The leisure of dull times has been improved extensively in setting out orchards, and we hope this practice will be continued in busy times. No one has, during the *pressure*, suffered for food, raiment, or shelter. Indeed, it is supposed that not a pound less of sugar, tea and coffee, has been used by the farmers than hitherto. Probably the quantity has increased.

Debts have been gradually contracted or discharged. Men have seen the end of speculations to be sudden disaster —and (of all things on earth) speculation-farming has received its reward. Men contented with small gains—industrious, frugal, and prudent men—have suffered almost nothing.

———◆◆◆———

GYPSUM.—"Time and practice" have ascertained the circumstances under which gypsum should be applied. As a reason why, after repeated applications, it no longer benefits, Prof. Liebig says, " when we increase the crop of hay in a meadow by means of gypsum, we remove a greater quantity of potash with the hay, than can, under ordinary circumstances, be restored. Hence it happens that, after the lapse of several years, the crops of grass on lands manured with gypsum, diminish, owing to the deficiency of potash." In such a case, if spent ashes were employed either in connection or alternately with gypsum—potash would be resupplied from the ashes.

———◆◆◆———

ACCLIMATING A PLOW.

THE other day we were riding past a large farm, and were much gratified at a device of the owner for the preservation of his tools. A good plow, apparently new in the spring, had been left in one corner of the field, standing in the furrow, just where, four months before, the boy had finished his *stint*. Probably the timber needed *seasoning*— it was certainly getting it. Perhaps it was left out for acclimation. May-be the farmer left it there to save time in the hurry of the spring-work, in dragging it from the shed. Perhaps he covered the share to keep it from the elements, and save it from rusting. Or, again, perhaps he is troubled with neighbors that *borrow*, and had left it where it would be convenient for them. He might, at least, have built a little shed over it. Can any one tell what a farmer leaves a plow out a whole season for ? It is barely possible that he was an *Irishman*, and had *planted* for a spring crop of plows.

After we got to'sleep that night, we dreamed a dream. We went into that man's barn ; boards were kicked off, partitions were half broken down, racks broken, floor a foot deep with manure, hay trampled under foot and wasted, grain squandered. The wagon had not been hauled under the shed, though it was raining. The harness was scattered about—hames in one place, the breeching in another—the lines were used for *halters*. We went to the house. A shed stood hard by, in which a family wagon was kept for wife and daughters to go to town in. The hens had appropriated it as a roost, and however plain it was *once*, it was ornamented *now*, inside and out. (Here, by the way, let it be remembered that hen-dung is the *best* manure for melons, squashes, cucumbers, etc.) We peeped into the smoke-house, but of all the "fixings" that we ever saw ! A Chinese Museum is nothing to it. Onions, soap-grease, squashes, hogs' bristles, soap, old iron, kettles, a broken spinning-wheel, a churn, a grindstone, bacon, hams, washing tubs, a barrel of salt, bones with the meat half cut off, scraps of leather, dirty bags, a chest of Indian meal, old boots, smoked sausages, the ashes and brands that remained since the last "smoke," stumps of brooms, half a barrel of rotten apples, together with rats, bacon bugs, earwigs, sowbugs, and other vermin which collect in damp dirt. We started for the house ; the window near the door had twelve lights, two of wood, two of hats, four of paper, one of a bunch of rags, one of a pillow, and the *rest* of glass. Under it stood several cooking pots, and several that were *not* for cooking. As we were meditating whether to enter, such a squall arose from a quarrelling man and woman, that we awoke—and lo! it was a dream. So that the man who left his plow out all the season, may live in the neatest house in the county, for all that we know; only, was it not strange that we should have dreamed all this from just seeing a plow left out in the furrow.

SCOUR YOUR PLOWS BRIGHT!

FARMERS may be surprised to know that their crops will depend a good deal on the color of the plows! yet so it is. Bright plows are found to produce much better crops than any other. It may be electricity, or magic for aught we know; we merely state the fact, leaving others to account for it. But very much depends upon the manner of doing it, for merely scrubbing it by hand with emery or sand is not the thing—*it must be scoured by the soil*. It is found that the subsoil scours it better for wheat, than the top soil —for a plow kept bright by very deep plowing affords better wheat than a plow brightened by the surface of the soil. It is the same with corn. In respect to this last crop, if you will keep your plow bright as a mirror until the corn is in the milk, you will find that it will have a wonderful effect. We appeal to every good farmer if he ever knew a rusty plow to be accompanied with good crops? Iron rust on a plowshare is poisonous to corn.

A young farmer of about twenty years of age said to us the other day: "If anybody wants me, he must come to my corn-field; I live there—I am at it all the time—I have harrowed my corn once, plowed five times, and gone over it with the hoe once." "Yes," said his old father, who seemed, justly, quite proud of his son—"keep your plows agoing if you want to fetch corn. I never let the ground settle on the top; if it is beaten down by rain, or begins to look a kind of rusty on the surface, I pitch into it, and keep it as mealy as flour. The fact is our farmers raise more corn than they can tend, they can't go over the corn more than once or twice, and that'll never do, and I guess I'll show old Billy R—— that it's so."

Some ambitious farmers are pleased to "lay by" the corn very early; but it is not wise; for the grass is always more forward to grow about this season than any other; and the ground will become very foul where corn is too early laid by, and, what is more to the purpose, a great deal of the nourishment of a crop is derived from the air and dew *conveyed to the roots*. This can be done only when the surface is kept thoroughly open.

* * *

PLOW TILL IT IS DRY, AND PLOW TILL IT IS WET.

SPEAKING of corn, a very intelligent gentleman remarked: "Well, by a five minutes' talk, I made Mr. —— produce the best crop he ever had on a certain field." He was looking over the fence where his corn was, at a flat field, upon furrows full of water; as I came by he said: "Well, I shall never get a crop off this piece of land; it's going just as it always does when I plant here." I told him of an old man in Indiana, who was a good farmer, to whom I once said when at his house one morning:

"Deafenbaugh, how is it that you always have good corn when no one else gets a half crop?"

"*Why*," said he, "*when it is wet I plow it till it is dry, and when it is dry I plow it till it is wet.*"

The man to whom I told this anecdote, says our informant, tried the practice, and gained a fine crop.

Now the principle is *good*. Our Dutch friend would not, we suppose, plow a stiff *clay* in a wet condition, unless, possibly, to strike a channel through the middle between rows. But the gist of the story lies in this—*constant cultivation*. Stir, *stir*, STIR the ground.

------•◆•------

STIRRING THE SOIL.

NEXT to deep plowing we should urge the advantage of continually stirring the surface of the soil.

IT PRODUCES CLEANLINESS.—Weeds in a growing crop are witnesses which no good farmer can afford to have testifying against him. When seed is sown broad-cast, weeding cannot be performed. In Europe, where labor is cheap and children plenty, acres of wheat and such-like crops are weeded by hand. *Our* only chance is to clear out every field, to be sown broad-cast, by a thorough previous culture. In all crops which are drilled, or planted in rows, the hoe, or plow, or cultivator, should be kept in lively use through the season. This practice should begin early, that weeds and grass may not get a start, for often, if they do, it is nearly impossible to keep them down, especially if the season is a wet one.

But there are yet some important reasons for constantly stirring the soil among growing crops. No matter how thoroughly the earth was pulverized when the seed was put in, one or two rains will, except in very sandy loam, beat it down compactly. This crust is injurious in preventing the ingress of moisture. But that which is the most material of all is, that *it excludes the air*. It is well known that the air affords much nourishment to vegetation; but, perhaps, it is not as well known, that it supplies it *by the root* as well as by the leaf. If any one wishes to try the

5

experiment, and we have done it time and again, let two patches in a garden be treated in all respects alike, except in this—let one be hoed or raked *every two or three days* and the other not at all, or but once in the season.

The result will satisfy any man better than a paper argument. Indeed, we have found it impossible (in a garden) to perfect some vegetables without constantly stirring the soil.

While these advantages are gained, it is not to be forgotten that, in dry seasons, a thorough pulverization of the surface, will prevent the evaporation of the moisture *in the earth* and prevent deleterious effects of the drought.

——•••——

SUBSOIL PLOWING.

ONE of the great improvements of the age is the adoption in husbandry of the subsoil plow; or, as it is called in England, *Deanstonizing system*, from Mr. Smith, of *Deanstone*, who first brought the implement into general notice. They are designed to follow in the furrow of a common plow, and pulverize without bringing up the soil for eight or ten inches deeper. In ordinary soils two yoke of oxen will work it with ease, plowing from an acre to an acre and a quarter a day.

The use of this plow will renovate old bottom-lands, the surface of which has been exhausted by shallow plowing and continual cropping. It brings up from below fresh material, which the atmosphere speedily prepares for crops.

Old fields, a long time in grass, are very much benefited.

Constant plowing at about the same depth will often form a hard under-floor by the action of the plow, through which neither roots nor rain can well penetrate ; subsoiling will relieve a field thus conditioned.

Soils lying upon clay or hard compact gravel are opened

and remarkably improved by the process. The wet, level, beech-lands would be greatly benefited by deep plowing in the *fall of the year*, subjecting the earth, to a considerable depth, to the action of the frosts, rains, etc., and giving a downward drain for superfluous moisture.

Although we have incidentally alluded to the benefits of subsoiling, they deserve a separate and individual enumeration.

1. In very deep molds or loams it brings up a supply of soil which has not been exhausted by the roots.

2. In soils whose fertility is dependent upon the constant decomposition of mineral substances, subsoil plowing is advantageous by bringing up the disintegrated particles of rock, and exposing them to a more rapid change by contact with atmospheric agents.

3. Subsoiling guards both against too much and too little moisture in the soil. If there is more water than the soil can absorb, it sinks through the pulverized under-soil. If summer droughts exhaust the moisture of the surface they cannot reach the subsoil, which affords abundant pasture to the roots.

FIRE-BLIGHT AND WINTER KILLING.

THESE are two entirely different processes. The *Fire Blight* (of the middle and western States), is a disease of the circulatory system, induced by a freezing of the sap while *the tree is in a growing and excitable state*. It always *must* occur before the leaves are shed in the autumn. Winter-killing is of two kinds—resulting from severe cold, and from untimely heat. The loss of tender shrubs, roses, etc., at least, before they are fully established, and of half-hardy fruit-trees, is occasioned by the winter sun shining warmly upon them while frozen, and suddenly thawing them. The point of death is usually near the surface of the ground, where the under-ground bark and upper bark come together. Whole orchards are destroyed in this way; and, if examined, the bark may be found *sprung off* from the wood. This may occur at any time during the winter.

We are in doubt whether the winter-stored sap exists in a state to be affected by the expansion of the freezing fluids of the tree. If the expansion of congelation *did* produce the effect, it should have been more *general*, for there are fluids in every part of the trunk—all congeal or expand— and the bursting of the trunk in one place would not relieve the contiguous portions. We should expect, if this were the cause, that the tree would *explode*, rather than split. Capt. Bach, when wintering near Great Slave Lake, about 63° north latitude, experienced a cold of 70° below zero. Nor could any fire raise it *in the house* more than 12° above zero. Mathematical instrument cases, and boxes of seasoned fir, split in pieces by the cold. Could it have been the sap in *seasoned fir wood* which split them by its expansion in congealing?

We quote a paragraph from Loudon—"The history of frosts furnishes very extraordinary facts. The trees are often scorched and burnt up, as with the most excessive heat, in consequence of the separation of the water from the air, which is therefore very drying. In the great frost in 1683, the trunks of oak, ash, walnut, and other trees, were miserably split and cleft, so that they might be seen through, and the cracks often attended with dreadful noises like the explosion of fire-arms."

We don't exactly know whether to take the first part as Loudon's explanation of the facts in the second.

There can be no doubt that the nature of the summer's growth, very much determines the power of a tree to resist the severity of winter. When there is but an imperfect ripening in a cold and backward season, the tissues formed will be feeble, and the juices stored in them thin. Now the power to resist cold, among other things, is in proportion to the viscidity of the fluids in a plant.

It is highly desirable that the chemical researches which have revolutionized the art of cultivation, should be pushed into the *morbid anatomy* of vegetation. A close, exact analysis of all the substances in an injured condition, will save a vast deal of bootless ingenuity and fanciful speculation.

WINTER TALK.

Do not be tempted by fine weather to haul out manure —it will be half wasted by lying in small heaps over the field ; to spread it will be worse yet; manure should lie in a stack, as little exposed to the weather as possible.

Look to your fences; see that they are in complete order and leave nothing of this to consume your time in the spring when you will need all your force for other work. It is well to haul all the rails you will need for the year. The timber will last longer cut now. Do not leave rails or sticks of timber lying where you cleave them, on the damp ground, they will decay more in six months there, than in eighteen when properly cared for. Put two rails down and lay the rest across them so as to have a circulation of air beneath. If you have five or ten acres of *deadening* which you mean to clear up and put to corn, you may as well roll the logs now. Every good farmer should study through the winter to make his spring work as light as possible. Whatever can be done *now* do not fail to do it; you will have enough to do when spring opens ; and perhaps the season may be one which will crowd your work into a week or two. If you have young fruit-trees, or a lit-

tle home-nursery, look out for *rabbits*. They usually depre-
date just after a light fall of snow.

Overhaul all your plows, carts, shovels, hoes, etc., and
put everything in complete readiness.

While you are moving about and repairing holes in the
fence, putting on a rail here, a stake yonder, a rider in
another place, you may inquire of yourself whether your
character is not in some need of repairs? Perhaps you are
very careless and extravagant—the fence needs rails there;
perhaps you are lazy—in that case the fence corners may
be said to be full of brambles and weeds, and must be
cleared out; perhaps you are a violent, passionate man—
you need a stake and rider on that spot. And lastly, perhaps you are not *temperate*, if so, your fence is all going
down and will soon have gaps enough to let in all the hogs
of indolence, vice, and crime: and they make a large drove
and fatten fast. Now is a good time to plan how to get
out of debt. Don't be ashamed to *save* in *little things*,
nor to earn small gains: "*Many a mickle makes a muckle.*"
But set it down, to begin with, that no saving is made by
cheating yourself out of a good newspaper. No man reads
a good paper a year, without *saving* by it. Suppose you
put in your wheat a little better for something you see
written by a good farmer and get five bushels more to the
acre. One acre pays for a year's paper. One recipe, a
hint which betters any crop, pays for the paper fourfold.
Intelligent boys work better, plan better, earn and save
better; and reading a good paper makes them intelligent.
Besides, suppose you took a good paper a year, and found
nothing new during all that time (an incredible supposi-
tion!), yet every two weeks it comes to *jog your memory*
about things which you may forget, but ought not to forget.
It steps in and asks whether that little store bill is paid?
Whether that loan drawing a fatal *six*, *seven* or *ten per cent*
(poison! poison! deadly poison!) is being melted down?
whether the children are going to school? whether the

tools are all right? the fences snug? whether economy, and industry, and sound morals (the best crop one can put in), are flourishing? It will look at your orchard—peep over into your garden, pry into the dairy—nay, into the cupboard and bureau, and even into your pocket. Now, if you are a man willing to learn, it will give you hints enough in a year to pay ten times over for your paper.

"SHUT YOUR MOUTH."

WE heard a lad, in anger, use this expression to another. It was not very bad advice, though given somewhat roughly.

When we hear some of our mincing misses singing, now away up, and now away down, tossing their heads and rolling their eyes, we think, Well, miss, if you knew what folks thought of you, you'd *shut your mouth*.

We have seen many men ruined because they did not know how to *shut their mouth* when tempted to say " Yes," to a bad business.

When we see a man standing before the bar just ready to drink, we think, Ah! you fine fellow, if you will not keep your mouth shut before *that* bar, you will, by and by, find yourself before a Bar where it will be shut tight enough.

When we hear a fine lady scolding till every room rings; or tattling from house to house—or scandal-mongering, we think, Ah, you lady, with all your schooling, you never learned to *shut your mouth*.

SPRING WORK ON THE FARM.

THOROUGHLY overhaul your tools; let plows be sharpened; repair their stocks if anywhere started or weakened; look after the chains, the swingletrees, the yokes for your oxen, or the harness for your horses. Don't have any straps to replace, or harness to tie up with tow strings after you get into the fields, and when time is precious. Now IS THE TIME TO SAVE TIME, BY GETTING READY. Old rusty buckles will give way the moment the plow strikes a root; stitches which have been longing for some time to fall out and part, will be likely to do it when you have the least time to mend them. Then we shall hear talk; you'll be cursing the old horse or the old rickety harness, and declaring that your "luck is always on the wrong side;" and you may depend upon it, that it always will be, so long as you are not more careful. Good luck is a wary old fish which nibbles at everybody's hook, but the shrewd and skillful angler only catches it.

The opening of spring is usually debilitating both to man and beast. Your horses cannot stand hard usage at once; some of them will need physic—all of them should be put to work carefully; increase their task gradually; favor them, and you will get abundantly paid for it before their summer's work is done.

A good farmer may be known by the way he manages his spring work. Consider how much there is of it. Cows are calving; mares foaling; young heifers for the first time to be broken to milking; all the tools to be got ready; the ground to be broken up and seeded; the orchards to be set; or old ones to be attended to; a garden to be made; and a hundred other things to do. Now here is a chance for good management, and a yet better chance for bad management. There is as much skill in "laying out" a season's work for the farmer, as there is in "laying out" a frame for a house or barn.

Bethink you of all the *mistakes* you made last season; if you made any good hits, improve upon them this year. Every farmer should resolve to do *all things* as well as he did the last year, and *some* things a great deal better.

While everything is merry, birds singing, bees at work, cattle frisky, and the whole animated world is joyous, do but search and see if, among all beasts, birds, or bugs, you can find one that needs whisky to do its spring or summer work on?

Look again; seeds are sprouting; trees budding; flowers peeping out from warm nooks. Everything grows in spring-time. Youth is spring-time, habits are sprouting, dispositions are putting out their leaves, opinions are forming, prejudices are getting root. Now take at least as good care of your children as you do of your farm. If you don't want to use the land you let it alone, and *weeds* grow; but when you wish to *improve* a piece, you turn the natural weeds under, and sow the right seed, and tend the crop. I have heard good kind of folks object to much " *bringing up*" of their boys. They guessed the lads would come out about right. You break a colt, and break a steer, and break a heifer, and break a soil, and if you won't break your children, they will be very likely to break you—heart and pocket.

Fermenting manures should not be hauled or spread until you are ready to plow them under. [If you spread manure on meadows it should be fine, and well rotted, and let ashes be liberally mixed with it.] If you let manure lie a week or ten days exposed in the fields to the air, it will waste one half of " its sweetness on the desert air." Let the plow follow the cart as fast as possible, and the gases generated by your manure will then be taken up by the soil, and held in store for your grain.

DEEP PLOWING.—There may be some rare cases where, for special reasons, shallow plowing is advisable. But the standing rule upon the farm should be deep plowing. A

5*

good farmer remarked the other day to us, "One of my neighbors who is always talking of deep plowing was at it last summer, and I followed in the furrow, and his depth did not average more than four inches; he did not measure on the *land side* but on the mold-board side." The reasons are very strong for deep plowing.

1. When crop after crop is taken off the first four or five inches of top earth, it tends speedily to rob it of all materials required by grass or grain. Every blade taken from the soil, takes off some portion of that soil with it.

2. Deep plowing brings up from beneath a greater amount of earth, which, when subjected to the frosts, the atmosphere, and the action of the plow, becomes fit for vegetation.

3. Summer droughts seldom injure deeply-plowed soils; certainly not to that degree that they do shallow soils. The roots penetrate the mellow mould to a greater depth, and draw thence moisture when the top is as dry as ashes. Will not some one who is curious in such matters try two acres side by side plowed shallow and deep, respectively, and give us the history of their crop?

QUANTITY OF SEED.—It has been often said that American husbandry was unfavorably peculiar in stinginess of seed-sowing. It is certain that very much greater quantities are employed in Great Britain and on the Continent than with us, and that much greater crops are obtained per acre. In part the crop is owing to a superior cultivation; but those who have carefully studied the subject affirm that, in part, it is attributable to the use of much greater quantities of seed. We give a table showing the average quantity of seed per acre for different grains, in England, Germany, and the United States. The table was formed in that manufactory of so many valuable articles, the *Albany Cultivator*. It must be remembered that the average crop is not the average of the best farming States, but of the whole United States.

	GERMANY. Seed per acre—Product.		ENGLAND. Seed per acre—Product.		UNITED STATES. Seed per acre—Product.	
Wheat,	2½ bushels.	25 bushels.	2½ to 3½ bu.	28 bushels.	1 to 1½ bush	18 bushels.
Rye,	2 "	25 "	2 to 2½ "	25 "	1 to 1½ "	15 "
Barley,	2½ "	85 "	2½ to 4 "	86 "	1½ to 2 "	25 "
Oats,	2 to 4 "	40 "	4 to 7 "	32 "	2 to 3 "	35 "
Millet,	7 quarts.	85 "				
Peas,	2½ bushels.	26 "	8 to 8½ "	30 to 40 bu.	2 to 2½ "	25 "
Corn,	20 quarts.	86 "			20 to 30 qts.	80 "
Turnips,		80 to 85 tons	1 to 2 pints.	30 to 35 tons	1 to 2 lbs.	20 tons.
Buckwheat,	1 bushel.	27 bushels.	1 to 1½ bush	26 bushels.	16 to 20 qts	15 to 80 bu.
Clover,	14 pounds.		14 to 18 lbs.		5 to 10 lbs.	
Flax,	2 to 8 bush.	10 bu. seed.	2 to 8 bush.	10 bu. seed.	1 to 1½ bush	8 to 12 bush
Hemp,	2½ to 8 "	650 pounds.	8 "	550 pounds.	1½ to 2½ "	500 pounds.
Potatoes,	5 "	800 bushels.	8 to 12 "	250 bushels.	8 to 20 "	175 bushels.

———•◆•———

SPRING WORK IN THE GARDEN.

WHEN spring comes, everybody begins to think of the garden. A little of the experience of one who has learned some by making many mistakes will do you no harm.

TOO MUCH WORK LAID OUT.—When the winter lets us out, and we are exhilarated with fresh air, singing birds, bland weather, and newly-springing vegetation, our ambition is apt to lay out *too much work.* We began with an *acre,* in garden; we could not afford to hire help except for a few days; and we were ambitious to do things as they ought to be done. By reference to a Garden Journal (every man should keep one), we find that we planted in 1840, *sixteen* kinds of peas; *seventeen* kinds of beans; *seven* kinds of corn; *six* kinds of squash; *eight* kinds of cabbage; *seven* kinds of lettuce; *eight* sorts of cucumber, and *seven* of turnips—*seventy-six varieties of only eight vegetables!* Besides, we had fruit-trees to transplant in spring—flowers to nurture, and all the etceteras of a large garden. Although we worked faithfully, early and late, through the whole season, the weeds beat us fairly; and every day or two some lazy loon, who had not turned two spadefuls of earth during the season, would lounge along and look over, and seeing the condition of things, would very quietly say:

"Why, I heard so much about your garden—whew! what regiments of weeds you keep. I say, neighbor, do you boil that *parsley* for greens?" It nettled us, and we sweat at the hoe and spade all the harder, but in vain; for we *had* laid out more than *could* be well done. Nobody asked how much we *had* done—they looked only at what we had *not* done. To be sure so many sorts were planted only to test their qualities; but the laying out of so large a work in spring is not wise. *A* HALF *well done is better than a* WHOLE *half done.* Remember there is a *July* as well as an April; and *lay* out in April as you can *hold* out in July and August. We have profited by our own mistakes and have no objections that others should do it.

VEGETABLE GARDEN.—Before you meddle with the garden, do two things: first inspect your seeds, assort them, rejecting the shrunk, the mildewed, the sprouted, and, generally, the discolored. Buy early, such as you need to purchase. Do not wait till the minute of planting before you get your seeds. Second, make up your mind beforehand just what you mean to do in your garden for the season.

Preparation.—Haul your manure and stack it in a corner; do not spread it till the day that you are ready to turn it under; cut your pea-brush and put it under shelter; inspect your bean-poles and procure such as are necessary to replace the rotten or broken ones; inspect every panel of the garden fence; one rail lost, may ruin, in a night, two months' labor, and more temper and grace than you can afford to spare in a whole year. Clean up all the stubble, haulm, straw, leaves, refuse brush, sticks and rubbish of every sort, and cast it out, or burn it and distribute the ashes. If you intend to do your work in the best manner, see that you have the *sorts* of manure that you may need through the season: ashes, fine old barn-yard manure, green long manure, leaf-mold from the wood, top-soil from pastures, etc., etc. Every florist understands the use of these.

Coarse manure may be put upon your pie-plant bed, as a strong and succulent leaf-stalk is desirable. Let it be thoroughly forked, gently near the stools and deeply between the rows.

With an iron-toothed rake go over your old strawberry beds that are matted together, and rake them severely. Strawberries that have been kept in hills and cleanly tended should be manured between the rows and gently spaded or forked.

Early Sowings.—Tomatoes, egg-plant, early cucumbers, cabbage, cauliflowers, broccoli, lettuce, melons, celery for an early crop, should have been, before this, well advanced in a hot-bed. If not, no time is to be lost; and if a first sowing is well along, a second sowing should be made.

You cannot get too early into the ground after the frost is out and the wet a little dried, onions for seed or a crop, lettuce, radishes, peas, spinage, parsnip, early cabbage, and small salads.

ASPARAGUS.—The beds should be attended to; remove all weeds and old stalks; give a liberal quantity of salt to the bed—if you have old brine, or can get fish brine at the stores, that is better than dry salt. Asparagus is a *marine* plant, growing upon sandy beaches along the sea coast, and is therefore benefited by salt, to which, in its *habitat*, it was accustomed. Put about three or four inches of old, thoroughly rotted manure upon the bed; fork it in gently, so as not to wound the crowns of the plant. Directions for forming beds belong to a later period in the season.

ONIONS.—Should be sown or set early.

If you prefer seed, sow, across beds four feet wide, in drills eight inches apart; young gardeners are apt to begrudge *room*—give it freely to everything, and it will repay you; when they come up, thin out to one for every inch; as you wish young and tender onions for your table, draw these, leaving, at least, one every five inches in the row. If your soil is deep and very rich, onions can be grown in one season from the seed as well as from the set—we try it almost every year and *never fail*, although told a hundred times: "You could do that in the old States, but it won't do out here." It had to do, and did do, and always will do, where there is no lazy men about; but nothing ever does well in a slack and lazy man's garden; plants have an inveterate prejudice against such, and won't grow; but he is a darling favorite among weeds.

The white or silver skin, and the yellow Portugal have been favorite kinds with us to raise from seed. They are tender, mild flavored, but do not keep as well as the *Red. Strong onions always keep better than mild ones.*

If you prefer top-onion sets, or sets of any other kind, plant them out at the same distances, viz. eight inches between the row and five or six between the sets. Inexperienced gardeners are afraid that *little* sets no bigger than a pea, will not do well. It is a mistake—they will make large onions; put them *all* in, if they are sound. Plant the sets so that the top shall just appear above the surface.

If you plant out old onions for *seed*, let them be at least a foot apart and stake them when they begin to blossom. If you plant the *top-onion* for sets you need not stake them, for they cannot shed out their seed if they fall over. It is not generally known that the same onions may be kept for seed for many years.

TRANSPLANTING.—All fruit-trees, most kinds of shade trees, shrubs, *hardy* roses, honeysuckles, pinks, lilacs, peonies, etc., may be raised, divided, and transplanted in April unless your soil is *very wet.* All *hardy* plants may be safely transplanted just as soon as the ground is dry enough to crumble freely—and not till then. In planting out shrubs, remember that they will *grow;* if you put them near together, for the sake of present effect, in a year or two they will be crowded. We set at ample distances and fill up the spaces with lilies, peonies, phlox, gladiolus, and herbaceous plants which are easily removed.

FLOWER GARDEN.—Remove the covering from your bulb-beds; as soon as the earth is dry enough to crumble, with a small hoe carefully mellow the earth *between* the rows of bulbs, and work it loose with *your hands*, in the row itself. Leave the surface convex, that superfluous rain may flow off. Transplant roses that are to be moved. Divide the roots of such lilies, peonies, irises, etc., as are propagated by division, and replant.

As fast as the soil allows, spade up your borders, and flower compartments, giving first a good coating of very fine, old, pulverized manure.

If you have hot-beds you may bring forward most of your annuals, so as to turn them out into the open beds as soon as frosts cease.

But defer sowing in the open air until the first of April; and then, sparingly; sow again the middle of April, and on the first of May. Only thus, will you be *sure* of a supply. If you gain more than you need by three sowings, should all succeed, you have friends and neighbors enough, if you are a reasonably decent man, who will be glad to receive the surplus.

MANURE.—Corn and potatoes will bear green and unfermented manure. But all ordinary garden vegetables require *thoroughly* rotted manure. If the soil is sandy, leached ashes may be applied with great profit at the rate of seventy or eighty bushels the acre. The soil is made more retentive of moisture, and valuable ingredients are secured to it. Salt may be used with great advantage on all garden soils, but especially upon light and sandy ones. Thus treated, soils will resist summer droughts and be moist when otherwise they would suffer. Salt has also a good effect in destroying vermin, and it adds very valuable chemical ingredients to the soil. Soapsuds should be carefully saved and poured about currants, gooseberries and fruit-trees. Charcoal, pulverized, is excellent, as it absorbs ammonia from the atmosphere, or from any body containing it, and

yields it to the plants.   Let a barrel be set near the house
filled with powdered charcoal.   Empty into it all the *cham-
ber-ley*.   The ammonia will be taken up by the charcoal, and
the barrel will be without any offensive smell.   But as soon
as the charcoal is saturated, it will begin to give out the
peculiar odor of urine.   Let the charcoal then be mixed
with about five times its bulk of fresh earth and well worked
together, and it will afford a very powerful manure for vegetables and flowers.   In Europe, where manure is precious,
it is estimated that the excrementitious matter, slops, suds,
scraps, etc., of a family, will supply one acre, for each mem-
ber, with manure.*   There are few families whose offal
would not afford abundant material for enriching the garden, and with substances peculiarly fitted for flowers, fruits,
and esculent roots.

FALL WORK IN THE GARDEN.

PLANTING seeds may be performed for very early spring
use.   Lettuce, spinage, and radishes, may be sown in a sheltered spot, and they will come forward ten days or a fortnight
earlier than those which shall have been sown in spring.

Clearing up the garden should be thoroughly performed.
Let pea-brush be removed, bean poles and flower stakes be
collected and put under shelter.   Collect all refuse vines,
haulm, stems and stalks and wheel them to a corner to rot,
or to be ready for use in covering flower-beds.   Let the
alleys be hoed out for the last time, and it will be as good
as one hoeing in the spring, when they will probably be too
wet to hoe.   Gravel may now be laid in the walks ; if ashes
are to be spread, it may be done in autumn, and save time in
the spring.

* See note, p. 98, Colman's Tour, 2d part, where is given an estimate
by a distinguished agricultural chemist, Mr. Haywood.

All tender plants are to be removed or secured by covering.

The best covering to secure the earth from frost, that we know of, is a layer of leaves, say three inches thick when well packed down, and *upon them* two or three inches of chip dirt, with the coarsest part on top. We have had the soil unfrozen in severe winters when so covered. In this manner, tuberoses, gladiolus, dahlias, tiger flowers, etc., may be kept out through the winter. The gladiolus thus treated makes splendid tufts of blossoms. It may be prudent to try only a few at first, and adventure more as experience gives confidence.

CELERY which is to be left in the trenches should first be well covered with straw, and then boards should be placed upon the top in such a manner as to shed the rain. Great quantities of wet rot it when it is not growing; and freezing and thawing *in the light* destroys it.

If portions of the garden have been infested with cutworms, etc., let it be spaded and thrown up loosely just before freezing weather. A clay soil will be ameliorated by frosts, if treated in the same way. A light, loose soil, should not be worked in the fall.

GUARDING CHERRY-TREES FROM COLD.

THIS tree is peculiarly liable while young, but more especially when coming into bearing, to be roughly handled by our winters. The bark at the surface of the ground splits, and often the trunk, enfeebling the tree and sometimes destroying it. The evil does not result from the cold, but from the action of bright suns upon the frozen trunk. Let those having valuable young trees, prepare them for winter by giving a cheap covering to the trunks, so that the sun shall not strike them. This may be done by tying about them bass matting, long straw, corn-stalks, or any similar protection.

SHADE-TREES.

WE believe that no man ever walked under the magnificent elms upon the Boston Common, or beneath the Lindens in Philadelphia, or through Elm street in New Haven, without conviction of the beauty and utility of shade-trees. Trees not only are objects of beauty—the architecture of Nature—but they promote both health and comfort. Our ardent summers, from June to October, make open, unshaded streets, almost impassable, and reflect heat upon our dwellings from the side-walks and beaten road.

In this country the growth of trees is so rapid, and the supply from our own forests so abundant and convenient that every village and city, and every well-conducted farm should be lined with shade-trees. We will offer a few suggestions upon the kinds to be selected and the manner of setting.

THE LOCUST (*Robinia pseudacacia*).—This tree is very popular, and is almost the only one at the West set for shade-trees. It has a beautiful form, grows very rapidly, bears a profusion of beautiful and very fragrant blossoms (pendulous racemes of pea-shaped flowers), its foliage is singularly pleasing—the young leaves being of a light pea-green, and growing darker with age, so that in the same tree three or four distinct shades of green may be seen; it grows freely in all soils, and is not infested by any worms; its timber is almost as durable as cedar, and in the West, is not subject to the attacks of the *borer*, as it is in the East.

On the other hand, the tree becomes unsymmetrical with age, it is brittle, breaking easily at slight wounds, even when they have healed over. It is not a long-lived tree, and requires careful protection from cattle.

We would advise a more sparing use of it. Let *every other* tree be a Locust, and the alternate maple or elm, oak, tulip, etc. By this method the Locust will afford immediate shade, and when they become unsightly the intervening trees will have grown to a goodly size. The Locust should be transplanted just as the buds are ready to burst; they should be protected by frames as soon as set. Good cases may be made at a trifling expense, by taking strips of inch and a half stuff, three inches wide, and nine or ten feet long, sharpen the lower end, and drive it into the ground four or five inches, and in a box formed about the tree let cross-pieces be nailed at the top. Be careful that the tree does not *rub* upon the case, although the wound will heal over, yet in the first high wind, it will be apt to break off at that point. This tree is rather peculiar in that respect.

The Locust was introduced to Europe by a Frenchman named Robin. From him the genus (*Robinia*) took its name. There are but four species belonging to it, and they are all indigenous to North America, viz.:

Robinia pseudacacia (common Locust). *R. viscosa*, confined to the southwestern parts of the Alleghany Mountains, bearing *rose*-colored blossoms and being even more ornamental than the former; it is equally hardy, and if it could be introduced among us would form a valuable addition. Locusts nowhere appear to a better advantage than when planted in clumps of six or eight on a lawn, and if the *R. pseudacacia* and *R. viscosa* were contiguous, blending the pure white and the rose-colored blossoms, the world might be challenged for a finer effect.

The *R. hispida* (*rose-acacia* of our gardens) is a highly ornamental shrub, its branches are, like the moss-rose, covered with minute spines, which give it a fine appearance. A fourth species is said to exist in the basin of Red River. The favorable opinion here expressed of the Locust, will remove any impression of prejudice when we say, that *they are altogether too much cultivated.* Our forests are full of magnificent shade-trees whose claims can never, all things considered, be equalled by the Locust.

ELM (*Ulmus Americana*), commonly called White Elm. Of the four species of elms indigenous to the United

States, but two are particularly worth notice, the White Elm, and Slippery Elm (*U. pulva*). But the former of these is so incomparably the superior, that it should be selected wherever it can be had. It attains a height of one hundred feet, is very long-lived, grows more and more beautiful with age, its long branches droop over, forming graceful pendulous extremities; and no one who has seen the Boston Mall, or the New Haven elms, or those scattered along the villages of Connecticut, will think that Michaux exaggerated in pronouncing this tree to be *the most magnificent vegetable production of the Temperate Zone.* It is unquestionably the monarch among shade-trees, as superior to the oak for avenues and streets, as the oak is to it for parks and forests. The great main-street of every village should be lined with White Elms, set at distances of fifty feet, and Locusts between to supply an immediate shade, and to be removed so soon as the slower-growing elm has spread enough to dispense with them.

THE MAPLE.—The following varieties are in our forests, and are beautiful shade-trees for the borders of farms, door-yards, public squares, avenues, streets, etc. The Sugar Maple (*Acer saccharinum*), White Maple (*A. eriocarpum,*) Red Maple (*A. rubrum*). This last variety shows beautiful red flowers before its leaves put out in spring, and, like the sugar-maple, brilliant scarlet leaves in autumn. The maple is a beautiful tree of fine form, the leaves of the different varieties are variously shaped and all beautiful, it is free from disease and noxious insects.

Besides these, the ash, oak, tulip, beech and walnut, are all worthy of being transferred to our streets. Shade-trees for door-yards, and public squares, and pleasure-grounds, require a separate notice, as in some material respects they should be differently treated.

We warmly recommend in lining streets, that each alternate tree only be locust.

It is better for *effect* that each street, or at least continuous portions of each, have *one kind* of forest tree, so that an avenue of similar trees be formed. In planting grounds, it is well to group trees of different kinds, but in streets an avenue should be of elms, or of oaks, or of syca-mores, or of maples, and not all of them mingled together.

A PLEA FOR HEALTH AND FLORICULTURE.

EVERY one knows to what an extent women are afflicted with nervous disorders, *neuralgic* affections as they are more softly termed. Is it equally well known that formerly when women partook from childhood, of out-of-door labors, were confined less to heated rooms and exciting studies, they had, comparatively, few disorders of this nature. With the progress of society, *fevers* increase first, because luxurious eating vitiates the blood; *dyspepsia* follows next, because the stomach, instead of being a laboratory, is turned into a mere warehouse, into which everything is packed, from the foundation to the roof, by gustatory *stevedores*. Last of all come *neuralgic* complaints, springing from the muscular enfeeblement and the nervous excitability of the system.

Late hours at night, and later morning hours, early appli-cation to books, a steady training for *accomplishments*, viz. embroidery, lace-work, painting rice paper, casting wax-flow-ers so ingeniously that no mortal can tell what is meant lilies looking like huge goblets, dahlias resembling a battered cab-bage; these, together with practisings on the piano, or if something extra is meant, a little tum, tum, tuming, on the harp, and a little ting-tong on the guitar; reading "ladies' books," crying over novels, writing in albums, and original correspondence with my ever-adored Matilda Euphrosyne, are the materials, too often, of a fashionable education. While all this refinement is being put on, girls are taught from eight years old, that the chief end of women is to get a beau, and convert him into a husband. Therefore, every action must be *on purpose*, must have a discreet object in view. Girls must not walk fast, that is not lady-like; nor run, that would be shockingly vulgar; nor scamper over fields, merry and free as the bees or the birds, laughing till the cheeks are rosy, and romping till the blood marches merrily in every vein; for, says prudent mamma, "my dear, do you think Mr. Lack-a-daisy would marry a girl whom he saw acting so unfashionably?" Thus, in every part of education those things are pursued, whose tendency is to excite the brain and nervous system, and for the most part those things are not "*refined*," which would develop the muscular system, give a natural fullness to the form, and health and vigor to every organ of it.

The evil does not end upon the victim of fashionable education. Her feebleness, and morbid tastes, and preternatural excitability are transmitted to her children, and to their children. If it were not for the rural habits and health of the vast proportion of our population, trained to hearty labor on the soil, the degeneracy of the race in cities would soon make civilization a curse to the health of mankind.

Now we have not one word to say against "accomplishments" when they are *real*, and are not purchased at the expense of a girl's constitution. She may dance like Miriam, paint like Raphael, make wax fruit till the birds come and peck at the cunning imitation; she may play like Orpheus harping after Eurydice (or what will be more to the purpose, like a Eurydice after an Orpheus), she may sing and write poetry to the moon, and to every star in the the heavens, and every flower on earth, to zephyrs, to memory, to friendship, and to whatever is imaginable in the spheres, or on the world—if she will, in the midst of these ineffable things, remember the most important facts, that *health* is a blessing; that God made health to depend upon exercise, and temperate living in all respects; and that the great objects of our existence, in respect to ourselves, is a virtuous and pious character, and in respect to others, the raising and training of a family after such a sort that neither we, nor men, nor God, shall be ashamed of them.

Now we are not quite so enthusiastic as to suppose that floriculture has in it a balm for all these mentioned ills. We are very moderate in our expectations, believing, only, that it may become a very important auxiliary in main. taining health of body and purity of mind.

When once a mind has been touched with zeal in floriculture it seldom forgets its love. If our children were early made little enthusiasts for the garden, when they were old they would not depart from it. A woman's perception of the beauty of form, of colors, of arrangement, is naturally quicker and truer than man's. Why should they admire these only in painting, in dress, and in furniture? Can human art equal what God has made, in variety, hue, grace, symmetry, order and delicacy? A beautiful engraving is often admired by those who never look at a natural landscape; ladies become connoisseurs of "artificials," who live in proximity to real flowers without a spark of enthusiasm for them. We are persuaded that, if parents, instead of regarding a disposition to train flowers as a useless trouble, a waste of time, a pernicious romancing, would inspire the love of it, nurture and direct it, it would save their daughters from *false taste*, and all love of meretricious ornament. The most enthusiastic lovers of nature catch something of the simplicity and truthfulness of nature.

Now a constant temptation to female vanity—(if it may be supposed for the sake of argument, to exist) is a display of person, of dress, of equipage. In olden times, without entirely hating their beauty, our mothers used to be proud of their spinning, their weaving, their curiously-wrought apparel for bed and board. A pride in what we have *done* is not, if in due measure, wrong or unwise; and we really think that rivalry among the young in rearing the choicest plants, the most resplendent flowers, would be altogether a wise exchange for a rivalry of lace, and ribbons, and silks. And, even if poor human nature must be forced to allow the privilege of criticising each other something severely, it would be much more amiable to pull roses to pieces, than to pull caps; all the shafts which are now cast at the luckless beauty, might more harmlessly be cast upon the glowing shield of her dahlias or upon the cup of her tulips.

A love of flowers would beget early rising, industry, habits of close observation, and of reading. It would incline the mind to notice natural phenomena, and to reason upon them. It would occupy the mind with pure thoughts, and inspire a sweet and gentle enthusiasm; maintain simplicity of taste; and in connection with personal instruction, unfold in the heart an enlarged, unstraitened, ardent piety.

* * *

KEEPING YOUNG PIGS IN WINTER.

THERE is both negligence, and mistake, in the way of wintering pigs. I am not talking to those whose manner of keeping stock is, to let stock take care of themselves; but to farmers who *mean to be careful*. Hogs should be *sorted*. The little ones will, otherwise, be cheated at the trough, and overlaid and smothered in the sleeping-heap. There should not be too many in one inclosure; especially young pigs should not sleep in crowds; for, although they sleep warmer, they will suffer on that very account. Lying in piles, they get sweaty; the skin is much more sensitive to the cold, and coming out in the morning reaking and smoking, the keen air pierces them. In this way, young pigs die off through the winter by being too warm at night. If you have the land-shark and alligator breed, however, you should crowd these together, for the more they die off the better for the farmer.

SWEET POTATOES.

ALTHOUGH our practice has been more extensive, and is more skillful, in eating sweet potatoes than in raising them, we yet adventure some remarks: No root can live and grow without food from the leaf; if the tops be permitted to root, so much nutriment is subtracted from the tubers as is diverted to these new roots. Those who are best skilled in their cultivation, raise their vines up so as to detach the roots, but do not twist them round the hill; which, by crushing or covering the leaves, would render the vines unhealthy. As to vines of the *Cucurbitacæ*, their fruit not being under ground, it is not necessary that such an amount of prepared sap should go to the root as if tubers were formed. There is, in such vines, a great liability to disease and injury near the hill. The vines shrink and dry near the base; and however flourishing the running end may otherwise be, it is destroyed. If roots are secured at several points along the vine, we remove the chances of its prematurely dying, without withdrawing any sap necessary for the maturation of its fruit.

MANAGEMENT OF BOTTOM-LANDS.

ALMOST every kind of soil requires a management of its own. That proper for clays, and that proper for bottom-lands, cannot be interchanged. Bottom lands are usually composed largely of vegetable matter and sand; and are therefore light, and easy to work; yet, as they are now managed, they admit a less variety of crops than the tougher and more unmanageable clay lands.

BOTTOM-LANDS FOR CORN.—Our corn-lands, strictly so called, consist of rich intervales and river bottoms. On these corn is raised year after year, without manuring, fallowing, clover, or any change; but one constant, successive corn, corn, corn. It is supposed that corn may be had for an indefinite period, so far as mere exhaustion of the soil is concerned, if the right course is pursued. Some of the best farmers in this region *hog* their corn lands. *Hogging*, is turning the hogs in upon the ripe corn, and letting them harvest it in their own way. The saving of labor of gathering the corn and feeding it out is very great. Some single farmers fatten from one to five hundred head of hogs; but if this number were fed by hand and the grain gathered for them it would require a force which would eat up the profits. When the fatting hogs have eaten off the field (temporary fences divide large fields into inclosures of convenient size) they are turned into another, and the stock-hogs for another year, are let in to glean and root for the waste and trampled corn. In this way nothing is lost.

This method *takes very little off from the land;* for the droppings of the hogs returns a great amount of food for the soil; and the corn stalks being burned or turned under, the land continues in good heart. Land being hogged will be *free from cut-worms;* for the continual rooting of the stock-hogs, which continues until the ground freezes, throws up the eggs or insect to be destroyed by the winter. This method of cultivation is peculiarly suited to large farms, where extensive tracts of ground are kept under the plow.

But in the course of eight or ten years, this process renders the soil extremely light. The action of frost upon it, after the hogs have snout-plowed it, leaves it in the spring as light and dry as an ash-heap. The corn will still *grow* as well, but every high wind will throw it down; the soil has not tenacity enough to hold up its crop. *Clovering* has been resorted to by some good farmers as a remedy; but without pretending to know certainly, we suspect that clover will not fully answer the object. Clover on hard soils, separates the particles and renders the ground lighter, and adds vegetable matter to its composition. This is not what bottom land needs. It is *too* light, and rich enough in vegetable matter.

We believe a better course will be found in putting *bottom-lands to small grain.* To be sure, there are difficulties in the way of this; but good farming is nothing but a compromise of difficulties. If the month of May be cold and backward, wheat will do well and yield freely. But if the spring is forward, May warm and wet, the grain will run rank, break down when the head begins to fill, and, of course, the berry, however plump and well it might have looked in the milk, will, after it falls, for want of nourishment, light, and air, shrink and shrivel. But even in such springs, might not an over rankness be prevented by pasturing the grain; or even mowing it, when, as it sometimes happens, it gets ahead of what cattle are put upon it. But, at the worst, the grain is not lost; for if it lodges, and is spoiled for the sickle, hogs may be turned upon it and they will thrive well.

But now comes the advantage of small grain to the soil, which will be the same whether the crop is reaped or hogged. The straw or stubble, in either case, remains upon the ground. This should not be *plowed in*, but *burned, and the ashes plowed under.* To do this a strip of eight feet should be plowed about the whole field; and fire put to it, *on every side at once*, so that it may burn towards the centre; for fire, driven across a field, would leap many feet of open space at a fence. The more stubble the better, and the more weeds the better. The ashes will give to the soil just what it lacks, cohesion or firmness, and moisture. For, to make a dry soil moist, requires some substance to be added, which, having an affinity for moisture, shall attract and retain it. This is the nature of wood or straw ashes. A gentleman who will recognize in the above much of his own practical experience, mentioned to us a singular fact in corroboration of this reasoning. Having a very heavy wheat or oat stubble on a bottom-land field, which made it very hard for the plow, he burned it over; but a smart thunder-storm coming suddenly up, the fire was extinguished, leaving about five acres in the middle of the piece, unburned. The whole field was then plowed. It was found that the soil in the part burned over was more firm, and moist, all the ensuing summer; and the corn more even, and darker colored, than that upon the five acres which escaped the fire, and whose stubble had been plowed in.

At all events, there can be no doubt that wood-ashes would be very advantageous to bottom lands. And we are persuaded that such soils may be kept in wheat and corn for any length of time, if thus managed. In conclusion, corn your bottom-lands till they are too light, hogging instead of harvesting them; then put in wheat or oats; leave the stubble long, burn it over, and put it into wheat again, or to corn, as the case may be.

----•◦•----

CULTIVATION OF WHEAT.

THERE are two opinions which will prevent any attempt to improve the cultivation of wheat, or, indeed, of anything else. The first is the opinion that, what are called *wheat-lands*, yield enough at any rate: the second is the opinion of those who own a soil not naturally good for wheat, that there is no use in trying to raise much to the acre. We suppose that wheat will not *average* more than twelve bushels to the acre, as it is now cultivated in some parts. At that rate, and with too low prices, it is not worth cultivation for commercial purposes. The cost of seed, of labor in preparing the soil, putting in the crop, harvesting, thresh- ing, and carrying it to market, is greater than the value of the crop. At fifty cents a bushel, and twelve bushels to the acre, the farmer gets six dollars, which certainly does not cover the worth of his time and the interest on his land.

Is it possible, then, at an expense within the means of ordinary farmers, to bring a double or treble crop of wheat ? If nature has set limits to the produce of this grain to the acre, and if our farmers have come up to that limit, there is no use in their trying to do any better.   But if their crop is four fold behind what it ought to be, they will feel courage to reach out for a better mode of cultivation.   Vegetables collect food from the atmosphere, and from the soil ; and different plants select different articles of food from the soil, just as different birds, beasts, insects, etc., require different food.   One class of plants draws potash largely from the soil, as turnips, potatoes, the stalk of corn, etc. Another class requires lime, in great measure, as tobacco, pea straw, etc.   Liebig partially classifies plants according to the principal food which they require ; as silica plants, lime plants, potash plants, etc.

Every plant being composed of certain chemical elements, requires for its perfection a soil containing those elements. Thus chemistry has shown, by exact analysis, that good meadow hay contains the following elements :   Silica (sand), lime (as a phosphate, a sulphate, and a carbonate, i. e. lime combined with phosphoric, sulphuric, and carbonic acids), potash (as a chloride, and a sulphate), magnesia, iron, and soda.   Whatever soil is rich in these will be productive of grass.

The grain of wheat (in distinction from the straw) contains, and of course requires from the soil, sulphates of potash, soda, lime, magnesia, iron, etc.

Any vegetable, in its proper latitude, will flourish in a soil which will yield it an abundance of food; and decline in a soil which is barren of the proper nutritive ingredients.

A practical, scientific knowledge of these fundamental facts, will give an intelligent farmer, in grain-growing latitudes, almost unlimited power over his crops.   A good cook knows what things are required for bread; he selects these materials, compounds them to definite proportions— adding, if any one is deficient; subtracting, if any one is in excess. Raising a crop is a species of slow cooking. Here is a compound of such materials (called wheat) to be made. Nature agrees to knead them together, and produce the grain, if the farmer will supply the materials. To do this he *must* understand what these materials are. Suppose a cook perceiving that the bread was wretched, did not know exactly what was the matter; and should add, salt, or flour, or yeast, or water at hap-hazard? Yet that is exactly what multitudes of farmers do. They find that their fields yield a small crop of wheat. They do not know what the matter is. Is the soil deficient in lime, or sand, or clay? Is magnesia or potash lacking? Perhaps they do not even know that these things are requisite to this crop. "The land must be manured." Now, manure on an impracticable soil, is *medicine.* Of course if the farmer prescribes, he must tell *what* medicine, i. e. what manure. Is it vegetable matter or phosphates? alumina or silica? Suppose a doctor says: "You are sick and must take medicine," without knowing what the disease is, or what the appropriate remedy; and so should pull out a handful of whatever there was in his saddle-bags and dose the wretch? That's the way farming goes on. "The ten acre lot wants manure." To the barn yard he goes, takes the dung heap, plows it under, and gets an enormous crop of—straw. Nitrogenous manure was not what the soil wanted. He has added materials which existed in abundance already; but those elements, from the want of which his crop suffered, have not been given it. The land is sicker than it was before. It languishes for want of one element, it suffers from a surfeit of another. We are prepared to sustain these observations by a reference to authentic facts.

Massachusetts, a few years ago, was not a wheat-growing State. Cautious farmers had given up the crop, because neither soil nor climate was supposed to favor it. How then have both soil and climate been persuaded to relent, and permit from twenty to forty bushels to grow to the acre? It was no accident, and no series of blind but lucky blunders, that effected the change. It was *thinking* that did it. *It was a change wrought by science.* Elliot (in Connecticut), Deane (both clergymen), Dexter, Lowell, Fessenden, and many others, all men of science, were pioneers. Agricultural surveys, geological surveys, and skillful chemical analyses of the soil and its products have been made for, now, a series of years. A Hitchcock, a Dana, a Jackson have applied science to agriculture. Pamphlets, books, and widely circulated newspapers have diffused this knowledge. Agricultural societies, state and county; farmers' meetings for discussion, such as are held every winter in Boston, have awakened the *mind* of farmers, and by learning to treat their soils skillfully, good wheat is raised in large quantities on soils naturally very averse to wheat.

The average crop of wheat in great Britain is *twenty-six* bushels to the acre, but forty and fifty are common to good farmers; sixty, seventy, and even eighty have been raised by great care.

In the whole United States it will not average much more than fifteen. A comparison of the two countries will show a corresponding inferiority on our part in the application of *science* to agriculture. Scotland, formerly, hardly raised wheat. Since the formation of the Highland Agricultural Society in Scotland, wheat has *averaged* fifty-one bushels to the acre!—*Ellsworth's Report for* 1844, p. 16.

Lord Hardwicke stated, in a speech before the Royal Agricultural Society of England, that fine Suffolk wheat had produced *seventy-six* bushels per acre; and another and improved variety had yielded *eighty-two* bushels per acre! This was the result of "book farming" in a country where anti-book farmers raise *twenty-six* bushels to the acre. .

Those very operations which farmers call *practical*, and upon which they rely in decrying "book farming" were first made known by science, and through the writings of scientific men.

These views have an immediate and practical bearing on the cultivation of wheat in the Western States.

Hitherto the want of enough cleared land has led farmers to put in wheat among the corn, and *half* put it in at that. Others have plowed their fallows, or their grass lands, so early in the season, that rains and settling have made it hard again by seed-time. Then, without stirring it, the grain has been thrown (away) upon it, and half harrowed in and left to its fate. Equally bad has been the system of late single plowing. Others have given their grain no soil to bed their roots in; a scratched surface receives the grain; its roots, like the steward, cannot dig, and so get no hold; and are either winter killed, or subsist upon the scanty food of the three or four inches of top soil. With some single exceptions, wheat cannot be said to have been *cultivated* yet. The two great operations in rendering soil productive of wheat, are either the *development of the materials already in the soil; or, the addition to the soil of properties which are wanting.*

Much land yielding only twelve or fifteen bushels, by a better preparation would, just as easily, yield thirty. Let us suppose that a common plowing of four or five inches, precedes sowing. Out of this superficial soil the wheat is to draw its food. Constant cropping has, perhaps, already diminished its abundance. Then wheat is rank in stem, short in the head, and light in the kernel. But below there is a bed of materials untouched. The subsoil, if brought up, exposed to the ameliorating influence of the elements, will furnish in great abundance the elements required. The simple operation of deep and thorough plowing will, often, be enough to increase the crop one-half. Deep plowing gives a place for the roots, which will not be apt to heave out in winter; it saves the wheat from drought, it gives the nourishment of twice the quantity of soil to the crop.

Five acres may become ten by enlarging the soil *downward*. These remarks are desultory; and, while we intend to continue writing on the subject, we say to such as may be getting ready for the wheat-sowing, *plow deeply and thoroughly;* unlike corn, wheat can only be plowed once, and that at the beginning. It should be thoroughly done, then, once for all.

WHEAT LANDS ought to be so farmed as to grow better from year to year; certainly, they ought to hold their own. Lands may be kept in heart by the adoption of a rotation suited to each particular soil; or, if frequent wheat crops are raised, by fallows or manuring. It is a fact that in this neighborhood farms in the hands of careful men are yielding better crops of wheat every year; while multitudes of farmers think themselves fortunate in twelve or fifteen bushels to the acre, there is another class who expect twenty-five or thirty bushels, and in good seasons get it. This is encouraging. As our lands get older we may look for yet better things. Some farmers put in from 100 to 800, and even 1,000 acres of wheat. The native qualities of the soil are relied upon for the crop. To manure or clover such a body of land is impossible with any capital at the command of its owners. But with us, each owner of a quarter section puts in from ten to twenty acres, and it lies within his means to dress this quantity of land to a high degree.

SOILS FIT FOR WHEAT.—A vegetable mold cannot yield wheat, because it does not contain, and therefore cannot afford to the crop, silicate of potash, or phosphate of magnesia; the first of which gives strength to the stem, and the second of which is necessary to the grain. On such soil wheat may grow as a grass, but not as a grain.

A mere sand will not yield wheat; because wheat requires, and such soils do not contain, soda, magnesia, and especially silicate of potash.

All clays contain potash, which is indispensable to wheat, but they may be deficient in soda, in magnesia, and in other alkalies.

A calcareous clay-loam may be regarded as the best soil for wheat. And when it does not exist in a natural state, all the additions in the form of manure should be with reference to the formation of such a soil. If the land be light and sandy, clay, and marl, and wood ashes should be added, together with barnyard manure; if the soil is a tenacious clay, it should be warmed and mellowed by sand and manure; if it is deficient in lime, lime in substance, or in marl must be given; vegetable molds, if heavily dressed with wood-ashes and lime, may be brought to produce wheat.

To PREPARE THE GROUND.—This operation depends upon the condition of the soil. But, in all cases, the deepest plowing is the best. The roots of wheat, if unchecked, will extend more than *five feet*. Stiff, tough, soils, unbroken for years, and especially if much trampled by cattle, will require strong teams. Oxen are better than horses to break up with. It has been said, that a yoke of cattle draw a plow deeper, naturally, than a span of horses. They are certainly better fitted for dull, dead, heavy pulling. And if oxen have been well trained they will do as much plowing in a season as horses, and come out of the work in better condition.

Fallow lands should be broken up early in summer, as soon as corn planting is over; about midsummer plow again; and the last time early in September to prepare for seed.

A grass or clover lay * may be plowed under deeply at

---

* The word *lay*, or *ley*, is only a different way of spelling *lea*, the old English word for *field*, not used except in poetry or by farmers; and it is one, among many instances, of old Saxon English words being preserved among the agricultural population long after they have ceased to be generally used.

midsummer, and not disturbed till sowing-time ; and the fall plowing should not disturb the inverted sod.

When wheat is to be sown on wheat again, as large a part of the straw should be left in the harvest-field as possible. This is to be plowed under ; but, if it can be done without endangering the fences, it would be better to *burn it over ;* the ashes will contain all the valuable salts. On this point we extract the following note appended by the editor of *Liebig's Agricultural Chemistry.*

" In some parts of the grand-duchy of Hesse, where wood is scarce and dear, it is customary for the common people to club together and build baking-ovens, which are heated with straw instead of wood. The ashes of this straw are carefully collected and sold every year at very high prices. The farmers there have found by experience that the ashes of straw form the very best manure for wheat ; although it exerts no influence on the growth of fallow-crops (potatoes or the leguminosæ, for example). The stem of wheat grown in this way possesses an uncommon strength. The cause of the favorable action of these ashes will be apparent, when it is considered that all corn-plants require silicate of potash ; and that the ashes of straw consist almost entirely of this compound.

But this procedure does not depend upon theoretical reasonings ; it has been abundantly substantiated by the practice of English cultivators. We find on page 333 of the " British Husbandry, " an admirable work published under the superintendence of the Society for the Diffusion of Useful Knowledge, the following statement:

" The *ashes of burnt straw* have also been found beneficial by many intelligent practical farmers, from some of whose experiments we select the following instances. Advantage was taken of a fine day to fire the stubble of an oat-field soon after harvest, the precaution having been previously taken of sweeping round the boundary to prevent injury to the hedges. The operation was easily performed, by simply applying a light to windward, and it completely destroyed every weed that grew, leaving the surface completely covered with ashes; and the following crop, which was wheat, produced full five quarters per acre. This excited further experiment, the result of which was, that in the following season, the stubble having been partly plowed in according to the common practice, and partly burned, and the land sown with wheat, the crop produced eight bushels per acre more on that portion which had been burned, than on that which had been plowed in. The same experiment was repeated, on different occasions, with similar results; and a following crop of oats having been laid down with seeds, the clover was found perfectly healthy, while that portion on which the burning of the stubble had been omitted, was choked with weeds. It must, however, be recollected, that if intended to have a decided effect, the stubble must be left of a considerable length, which will occasion a material deficiency of farm-yard manure; though the advantages will be gained of saving the cost of moving the stubs, the seeds of weeds and insects will be considerably destroyed, and the land will be left unimpeded for the operation of the plow.

"On the wolds of Lincolnshire, the practice of not only burning the stubble, but even the straw of threshed grain, has been carried, in many cases, to the extent of four to six loads per acre; and, as it is described in the report of the county, has been attended, in all those instances, with very decidedly good effect. It is even said to have been found superior, in some comparative trials, to yard-dung, in the respective rate of five tons of straw to ten of manure!"

We frequently ride past immense piles of wheat straw, encumbering the yard or field where it was threshed; and never without thinking upon the unthriftiness of a farmer who ignorantly takes everything off his wheat land, returns nothing to it, and is content with annually diminishing crops.

SELECTION OF SEEDS.—The varieties of wheat, already very numerous, are constantly increasing. No farmer should be satisfied with anything short of the *best* kind of wheat. Suppose an expense of many dollars to have been incurred in procuring a new kind, if it yield only two bushels more to the acre than an old sort, it will more than pay for itself in the first harvest field. It should be observed that different soils require different varieties; and every farmer should select, after trial, the kind which agrees best with his land.

A standard wheat should be hardy, strong in the straw; not easy to shell and waste, prolific, thin in the bran, white in flour, and the flour rich in starch and gluten. The earliness or lateness of a variety affects its liability to disease.

Much may be done by every farmer to secure a variety suited to his soil from his own fields. Let a watchful eye observe every remarkable head of wheat—a very early one, a very long head, any which have an unusual sized grain, or is distinguished for any excellent property. By gathering, planting separately, and then culling again, each farmer may improve his own wheat ten fold. Indeed it has been in this way that several improved varieties have been procured.

Of spring wheat, the most valuable kinds are, *Italian Spring Wheat;* bearded, red berry, white chaff, head long, bran thick, flour of fair quality. *Tea* or *Siberian Bald;* bright straw, not long; berry white, bald; flour good; extensively cultivated in New England and northern part of New York. Valuable variety.

BLACK SEA WHEAT.—White chaff, bearded, berry red, long and heavy, bran thick, flour inferior. Ripens very early, and seldom rusts or mildews.

The following are also the spring varieties. *Egyptian Wild Goose or California.*—Large and branching head, bearded, berry small, bran thick, flour coarse and yellow, ripens late, and subject to rust.   Although branching, it is not productive.   There is a winter variety also.   *Rock Wheat*, from Spain.—Chaff white, bearded, berry red and long, bran thick, flour of fair quality, hardy, shows small, well adapted for new lands and late sowing.   *Black Bearded.*—Long cultivated in New York—stem large, heavy head, berry large and red, beard very long and stiff, produces flour well.   *Red Bearded*, English.—Chaff red, bearded, beards standing out, berry white, weighs from sixty to sixty-two pounds.   *Scotch Wheat.*—A large white wheat, berry and straw large.

Spring wheat does well on soils which heave and throw out winter wheat.   It is deemed a good policy to sow some spring wheat every year, that, if the winter wheat fails, a crop may still be on hand.

An account of the best varieties of winter wheat, we extract from the *Western Farmer and Gardener :*

" WHITE FLINT.—A winter wheat, very white chaff, withstood Hessian fly well, has yielded fifty-four bushels to the acre, weighing from sixty-three to sixty-seven pounds per bushel.   *Improved White Flint.*—This from early selection from the first.   *White Provence, from France.*—A white wheat—shows small heads, well filled and large.   *Old Red Chaff.*—White wheat, old—subject to fly.   *Kentucky, White Bearded.*—White wheat, sometimes called Canadian, Flint—early, good for clay soils.   *Indiana Wheat.*—White wheat—berry white and large, ripens early, not so flinty as the White Flint, good flour, valuable for clayey soils.   *Velvet Beard, or Crate Wheat.*—White wheat—English variety, chaff reddish, berry large and red, straw large and long, heads long and well filled, beard very stiff, flour yellowish.   *Soule's Wheat.*—A mixed variety, heads large, berry white, not very hardy.   *Beaver Dam.*—Old variety, berry red, flour yellowish, ripens late.   *Eclipse.*—English, not hardy. *Virginia White May*, from Virginia.—Winter, good flour, chaff white.   *Wheatland Wheat*, from

Virginia.—Chaff red, heads well filled, berry red, hardy. *Tuscan Bald,* from Italy in 1837.—Berry large and white, not hardy, flour good. *Tuscan Bearded.*—Head large, still less hardy. *Yorkshire,* from England, ten years ago. —Mixed variety of white and red chaff, bald, berry white, good flour, liable to injury from insects, subject to ergot. *Bellevere Tallavera.*—White variety from England, head large, tillers well, not hardy, insects like it much. *Pegglesham,* English.—Head large, berry white, and medium sized, tender for our winters—(all this is calculated for New York State.) *Golden Drop,* English.—Berry red, flour not first rate. *Skinner Wheat.*—Produced from crosses, berry red, chaff white, hardy, yield good, sixty-four pounds to the bushel. *Mediterranean.*—Chaff light, red bearded, berry red and long, very flinty, flour inferior. *Hume's White Wheat* from crosses.—A beautiful white wheat, berry large, bran thin, hardy and a valuable variety. *Blue Stem.* —Cultivated for thirty-three years, berry white, sixty-four pounds to the bushel, flour superior, bran thin, and very productive. *Valparaiso Wheat,* from South America.— Chaff white, bald, berry white, bran thin, a good variety.

PREPARING SEED FOR SOWING.—Seed wheat should be subjected to a process which shall separate all chess, cockle, etc., from it, together with the shrunken kernels of the wheat itself. This may be, in part, done by screening; but the light grain will float and may thus be detected in the process of brining. Two tubs, or half barrels, may be conveniently used. A strong brine of salt and water is preferred, and the wheat, in convenient parcels, is poured in, the light wheat skimmed from the top, the brine poured off into the second tub, and the heavy wheat at the bottom put into some suitable receptacle to drain for an hour. When in successive parcels the whole quantity to be used has been brined, let it be emptied upon a smooth floor, and limed at the rate of about a bushel of lime to ten of wheat.

By this process the chaffy grain is rejected, the smut, to which wheat is so liable, is entirely prevented; and the grain caused to germinate more rapidly and strongly. The lime should be what is termed *quicklime*, or that just slaked. The reason may be explained. No seed can germinate until it has rid itself of a large part of that carbon, which, being essential to its *preservation*, must be withdrawn in order that it may grow. The addition of oxygen from air and water converts the carbon to carbonic acid, which is emitted from the pores, and escapes. Newly slaked lime has a powerful affinity for carbonic acid; and by withdrawing it from the seed, puts it in a condition favorable to immediate germination. Lime that has been air-slaked or lain exposed to the air after being slaked by water, combines with the carbonic acid in the atmosphere, and when applied to wheat, being already a carbonate, it does not liberate the carbonic acid contained in the seed.

———•◆•———

PLEASURES OF HORTICULTURE.—There is no writing so detestable as so-called *fine writing*. It is painted emptiness. We especially detest fine writing about rural affairs —all the senseless gabble about dew, and zephyrs, and stars, and sunrises—about flowers, and green trees, golden grain and lowing herds, etc. We always suspect a design upon our admiration, and take care not to admire. In short, *geoponical cant, and pastoral cant, and rural cant* in their length and breadth, are like the whole long catalogue of cants, (not excepting the German Kant), intolerable. Now and then, however, somebody writes as though he knew something; and then a free and bold strain of commendation upon rural affairs is relishful.

PRACTICAL USE OF LEAVES.

THERE are two facts in the functions of the leaf, which are worth consideration on account of their practical bearings. The food of plants is, for the most part, taken in solution, through its roots. Various minerals—silex, lime, alumen, magnesia, potassa—are passed into the tree in a dissolved state. The sap passes to the leaf, the superfluous water is given off, *but not the substances which it held in solution.* These, in part, are distributed through the plant, and, in part, remain as a *deposit in the cells of the leaf.* Gradually the leaf chokes up, its functions are impeded, and finally entirely stopped. When the leaf drops, it contains a large *per cent.* of mineral matter. An autumnal or old leaf yields, upon analysis, a very much larger proportion of earthy matter than a vernal leaf, which, being yet young, has not received within its cells any considerable deposit. It will be found also, that the leaves contain a very much higher *per cent.* of mineral matter, than *the wood of the trunk.* The dried leaves of the elm contain more than eleven *per cent.* of ashes (earthy matter), while the wood contains less than two *per cent. ;* those of the willow, more than eight *per cent.,* while the wood has only 0.45 ; those of beech 6.69, the wood only 0.36 ; those of the (European) oak 4.05, the wood only 0.21 ; those of the pitch-pine 3.15, the wood only 0.25 *per cent.*[*]

It is very plain, from these facts, that, in forests, the mineral ingredients of the soil perform a sort of *circulation;* entering the root, they are deposited in the leaf; then, with it, fall to the earth, and by its decay, they are restored to the soil, again to travel their circuit. Forest soils, therefore, instead of being impoverished by the growth of trees, receive back annually the greatest proportion of those

---

[*] See Dr. Grey's Botanic Text Book, an admirable work, which every horticulturist should own and study.

mineral elements necessary to the tree, and besides, much organized matter received into the plant from the atmosphere; soils therefore are gaining instead of losing. If owners of parks or groves, for neatness' sake, or to obtain leaves for other purposes, gather the annual harvest of leaves, they will, in time, take away great quantities of mineral matter, by which the soil, ultimately, will be impoverished, unless it is restored by manures.

Leaf-manure has always been held in high esteem by gardeners. But many regard it as a purely *vegetable substance;* whereas, it is the best mineral manure that can be applied to the soil. What are called vegetable loams (not peat soils, made up principally of decomposed *roots*), contain large quantities of earthy matter, being mineral-vegetable, rather than vegetable soils.

Every gardener should know, that the best manure for any plant is the decomposed leaves and substance of its own species. This fact will suggest the proper course with reference to the leaves, tops, vines, haulm, and other vegetable refuse of the garden.

The other fact connected with the leaf, is its function of *Exhalation.* The greatest proportion of crude sap which ascends the trunk, upon reaching the leaf, is given forth again to the atmosphere, by means of a particularly beautiful economy. The *quantity* of moisture produced by a plant is hardly dreamed of by those who have not specially informed themselves. The experiments of Hales have been often quoted. A sun-flower, three and a half feet high, presenting a surface of 5.616 square inches exposed to the sun, was found to perspire at the rate of twenty to thirty ounces avoirdupois every twelve hours, or seventeen times more than a man. A vine with twelve square feet exhaled at the rate of five or six ounces a day. A seedling apple-tree, with twelve square feet of foliage, lost nine ounces a day.*

---

* Lindley's Horticulture, p. 42–44. Grey's Botany, p. 181.

These are experiments upon very small plants. The vast amount of surface presented by a large tree must give off immense quantities of moisture. The practical bearings of this fact of vegetable exhalation are not a few. Wet forest-lands, by being cleared of timber, become dry; and streams, fed from such sources, become almost extinct as civilization encroaches on wild woods. The excessive dampness of crowded gardens is not singular, and still less is it strange that dwellings covered with vines, whose windows are choked with shrubs, and whose roof is overhung with branches of trees, should be intolerably damp; and when the good housewife is scrubbing, scouring and brushing, and nevertheless, marvelling that her house is so infested with mold, she hardly suspects that her troubles would be more easily removed by the axe or saw, than by all her cloths and brushes. A house should never be closely surrounded with shrubs. A free circulation of air should be maintained all about it, and shade-trees so disposed as to leave large openings for the light and sun to enter. Unusual rains in any season produce so great a dampness in our residences that no one can fail to notice its effect, both on the health of the occupants, and upon the beauty and good condition of their household substance.

* * *

The following method to destroy weeds is pursued at the mint in Paris, with good effect: 10 gallons water, 20 lbs. quicklime and 2 lbs. flowers of sulphur are to be boiled in an iron vessel; after settling, the clear part is thrown off and used when needed. Care must be taken, for if it will destroy weeds it will just as certainly destroy edgings and border flowers if sprinkled on them. Weeds, thus treated, will disappear for several years.

SPRING-WORK FOR PUBLIC-SPIRITED MEN.

SHADE-TREES.—One of the first things that will require your action is, the planting of *shade-trees*. Get your neighbors to join with you. Agree to do four times as much as your share, and you will, perhaps, then obtain some help. Try to get some more to do the same in each street of your village or town.

Locusts, of course you will set for immediate shade. They will in three years afford you a delightful verdant umbrella as long as the street. But *maples* form a charming row, and the autumnal tints of their leaves and the spring flowers add to their beauty. They grow quite rapidly, and in six years, if the soil is good and the trees properly set, they will begin to cast a decided shadow. Elms are, by far, the noblest tree that can be set, but they will have their own time to grow. It is best then to set them in a row of other trees, at about fifty or a hundred feet apart, the intervening space to be occupied with quicker-growing varieties.

The beech, buckeye, horse-chesnut, sycamore, chestnut, and many others may be employed with advantage. Now, do not let your court-house square look any longer so barren.

Avenues may be lined with rows of trees, but squares and open spaces should have them grouped or scattered in small knots and parcels in a more natural manner.

MAY-WEED.—There was never a better time to exterminate this villainous, stinking weed than summer-time will be. Just as soon as the first blossoms show, "up and at it." Club together in your streets and agree to spend one day *a-mowing*. Keep it down thoroughly for one season and it will no longer bedrabble your wife's and daughter's dresses, nor fill the air with its pungent stench, or weary the eye with its everlasting white and yellow.

SIDE-WALKS.—What if your neighbors are lazy; what if

they do not care ? Some one ought to see that there are
good gravel walks in each village. You can have them in
this way : Take your horse and cart and make them before
your own grounds, and then go on no matter who owns,
and when your neighbors see that *you* have public spirit,
they will, by and by, be ready to help you. But the grand
way to do nothing, is, not to lift a finger yourself, and then
to rail at your fellow-citizens as selfish and devoid of all
public spirit.

PROTECT PUBLIC PROPERTY.—What if it does concern
everybody else as much as it does you ? Some one ought
to see that the fences about every square are kept in repair.
Some one ought to save the trees from cattle; some one
ought to have things in such trim as that the inhabitants
can be proud of their own town. Pride is not decent when
there is nothing to be proud of; but when things are worthy
of it, no man can be decent who is devoid of a proper
pride. The church, the schoolhouse, fences, trees, bridges,
roads, public squares, sidewalks, these are things which tell
tales about people. A stranger, seeking a location, can
hardly think well of a place, in which the distinction
between the house and stye are not obvious; in which every
one is lazy when greediness does not excite him, and where
general indolence leaves no time to think of the public
good.

When politicians are on the point of dissolving in the
very fervent heat of their love for the public, it would
recall the fainting soul quicker than hartshorn or vinegar to
ask them—Did you ever set out a shade-tree in the street ?
Did you ever take an hour's pains about your own village ?
Have you secured it a lyceum ? Have you watched over its
schools? Have you aided in any arrangements for the
relief of the poor ? Have you shown any *practical* zeal for
good roads, good bridges, good sidewalks, good school-
houses, good churches ? Have the young men in your place
a public library ?

If the question were put to many distinguished village patriots, What have you done for the public good?—the answer would be : "Why, I've talked till I'm hoarse, and an ungrateful public refuse me any office by which I may show my love of public affairs in a more practical manner."

——•◦•——

FARMERS AND FARMING SCENES IN THE WEST.

IF any one goes to Holland they are all Dutch farmers there; if he goes to England he finds British husbandry; iu New England it's all Yankee farming. A man must go to the West to see a little of every sort of farming that ever existed, and some sorts we will affirm, never had an existence before anywhere else—the purely indigenous farming of the great valley. Within an hour's ride of each other is the Swiss with his vineyard, the Dutchman with his spade, the "Pennsylvany Dutch" and his barn, the Yankee and his notions, the Kentuckian and his stock, the Irishman and his shillelah, the Welchman and his cheese, besides the supple French and smooth Italian, with here and there a Swede and a very good sprinkling of Indians.

Away yonder to the right is a little patch of thirty acres owned by a Yankee. He keeps good cows, *one* horse only (fat enough for half a dozen) ; every hour of the year, save only nights and Sabbath-days he is at work, and neat fences, clean door-yard, a nice barn, good crops, and a profitable dairy, and money at interest, show the results. What if he has but thirty acres, they are worth any two hundred around him, if what a man makes is a criterion of the value of his farm. But a little farther out is a jolly old Kentucky farmer, the owner of about five hundred acres of the best land in the county, which he tills when he has nothing else to do. He is a great hunter and must go out for three or four days every season after deer. He loves office quite well, and is always willing to "serve the public" for a consid-er-a-tion, as Trapbois would say. As to farming, he hires more than he works; but, now and then, as at planting or harvesting, he will lay hold for a week or a month with perfect farming fury, and that's the last of it. As to working every day and every hour, it would be intolerable! He is a great horse-raiser, is fond of stock, and if a free and easy fellow ready to laugh, not careful of his purse, nor particular about his time, will ride over his grounds, admire his cattle, his bluegrass pasture, his Pattons and his Durhams; and above all, that blooded filly, or that colt of Sir Archie's—our Kentucky farmer will declare him the finest fellow alive, and his house will be open to him from year's end to year's end again.

Right along side of him is a "Pennsylvany Dutch," good-natured, laborious, frugal and prosperous. He minds his own business. Seldom wrangles for office. Is not very public spirited, although he likes very well to see things prosper. He farms carefully on the old approved plan of his father, plants by the signs in the moon, seldom changes his habits, and on the whole constitutes a very substantial, clean, industrious, but unenterprising farmer.

Then there is a *New York* Yankee; he has got a grand piece of land, has paid for it, and got money to boot; he knows a little about everything; he "lays off" the timber for a fine large house—bossed the job himself. When it was up he stuck on a kitchen, then a pantry on to that, then a pump-room on that, then a wood-house on that, and then a smoke-house for the fag end; a fine garden, a snug little nursery well tended, good orchards; by and by a second farm, pretty soon a boy on it, all married and fixed off; by and by again another snug little farm, and then another boy on it, with a little wife to help him; and then a spruce young fellow is seen about the premises, and after a while a daughter disappears and may be found some miles off on a good farm, making butter and raising children, and has good luck at both. The old man is getting fat, has money lent out, loves to see his friends, house neat as a pin, glorious place to visit, etc., etc. But who can tell how many sorts more there are in the great heterogeneous West, and how amusing the mixture often is, and what strange customs grow out of the mingling of so many diverse materials. It is like a kaleidoscope, every turn gives a new sight. We will take our leisure, and give some sketches of men, and manners and scenery, as we have seen them in the West.

About eight years ago a raw Dutchman, whose only English was a good-natured *yes* to every possible question, got employment here as a stable-man. His wages were six dollars and board; that was $36 in six months, for not one cent did he spend. He washed his own shirt and stockings, mended and patched his own breeches, paid for his tobacco by some odd jobs, and laid by his wages. The next six months, being now able to talk " goot Inglish," he obtained eight dollars a month, and at the end of six months more had $48, making in all for the year $84. The second year, by varying his employment—sawing wood in winter, working for the corporation in summer, making garden in spring, he laid by $100, and the third year $125, making in three years $309.

With this he bought 80 acres of land. It was as wild as when the deer fled over it, and the Indian pursued him. How should he get a living while clearing it? Thus he did it. He hires a man to clear and fence ten acres. He himself remains in town to earn the money to pay for the clearing. Behold him! already risen a degree, he is an employer! In two years' time he has twenty acres well cleared, a log-house and stable, and money enough to buy stock and tools. He now rises another step in the world, for he gets married, and with his amply-built, broad-faced, good-natured wife, he gives up the town and is a regular farmer.

In Germany he owned nothing and never could; his wages were nominal, his diet chiefly vegetable, and his prospect was, that he would be obliged to labor as a menial for life, barely earning a subsistence and not leaving enough to bury him. In five years, he has become the owner in fee simple of a good farm, with comfortable fixtures, a prospect of rural wealth, an independent life, and, by the blessing of heaven and his wife, of an endless posterity. Two words tell the whole story—Industry and Economy. 'These two words will make any man rich at the West.

We know of another case. While Gesenius, the world-wide famous Hebrew scholar, was as school, he had a bench-fellow named Eitlegeorge. I know nothing of his former life. But ten years ago I knew him in Cincinnati as a baker, and a first-rate one too; and while Gesenius issued books and got fame, Eitlegeorge issued bread and got money. At length he disappeared from the city. Travelling from Cincinnati to Indianapolis, a year or two since, I came upon a farm of such fine land that it attracted my attention, and induced me to ask for the owner. It belonged to our friend of the oven! There was a whole township belonging to him, and a good use he appeared to make of it. Courage then, ye bakers! In a short time you may raise wheat instead of molding dough.

———•••———

A HOLE IN THE POCKET.—If it were not for these holes in the pocket, we should all be rich. A pocket is like a cistern, a small leak at the bottom is worse than a large pump at the top. God sends *rain* enough every year, but it is not every man that will take pains to catch it; and it is not every man that catches it who knows how to keep it.

7

ORNAMENTAL SHRUBS.

A DESCRIPTION of a few of the desirable flowering and ornamental shrubs for yards and lawns may enable our readers to select with judgment.

PRIVET.—This is quite beautiful as a single plant; but is universally employed for hedges, verdant screens, etc. There is an evergreen variety, originally from Italy, by far the best. The roots of this plant are fibrous, don't spread much; the limbs endure the shears very patiently; it grows very rapidly, two full seasons being sufficient to form a hedge; and it will flourish under the shade and drip of trees.

ROSE ACACIA (*Robinia hispida*).—This is a species of the locust, of a dwarf habit, seldom growing six feet in height, and covered with fine spines which give its branches a mossy appearance. Its blossoms resemble the locust, but are of a pink color. It is often grafted upon the locust to give it a higher head and better growth. It should be in every shrubbery.

VENETIAN SUMACH, or smoke tree (*Rhus cotinus*).—The peculiarity of this shrub is in the large bunches of russet-colored seed-vessels, looking, at a little distance, like a puff of smoke. The French and Germans call it *periwig-tree*, from the resemblance of these russet masses to a powdered wig. It grows freely, and is highly ornamental.

There are two other species of sumach worthy of cultivation; the *Rhus typhina*, or Stag's Horn sumach, of a fine flower, and whose leaves turn in autumn to a beautiful purplish red; and the *R. glabra*, or Scarlet sumach, having red flowers and fruit of a velvety scarlet appearance, changing as it ripens to crimson.

SYRINGA, or Mock Orange (*Philadelphus coronarius*), is a beautiful shrub, having, in the spring, flowers of a pure white, and of an odor only less exquisite than that of the orange; whence one of its popular names. The leaves have

the smell of the cucumber, and are sometimes used in spring
to flavor salads. It grows freely, even under the shade of
trees, which, in all low shrubs, is a valuable quality. There
is also a large flowered inodorous variety. The popular
name, Syringa, is the botanical name of the lilac; but
these plants are not in the remotest degree related to each
other.

LILAC.—This well-known and favorite little tree requires
only to be mentioned. There is a white variety, and deli-
cately-leaved variety called the Persian.

SNOWBALL (*Viburnum opulus*), everywhere known, and
everywhere a favorite ; and scarcely less so is the

WAXBERRY, or Snowberry, (*Symphora racemosa*), introduced by Lewis and Clark to the public attention, and first
raised from seed by McMahan, a gardener of some note.
When its fruit is grown, it has a beautiful appearance.

TAMARISK (*Tamarix gallica*), a sub-evergreen of very
beautiful feathery foliage, of rapid growth, and highly ornamental in a shrubbery. It will grow in very poor soil.

SHEPARDIA, or Buffalo Berry, from the Rocky Mountains,
a low tree, with small silvery leaves, a currant-like fruit,
which is edible. This is worthy of cultivation. It is diœ-
cious, and the male and female trees must therefore be
planted in proximity.

DWARF ALMOND (*Amygdalus nana*), but now called by
botanists Cerasus or Prunus japonica. This favorite shrub
is found in all gardens and yards. The profusion of its
blossoms and the delicacy of their color make it, during the
short time of its inflorescence, deservedly a favorite. As it
flowers before its leaves put forth, it requires a green background to produce its full effect. It should therefore be
planted against evergreens.

WOOD HONEYSUCKLE (*Azalea*).—This is a native of North
America, and is perfectly hardy. It flourishes best in a half
shade, and flowers freely. There have been a vast number
of varieties originated from crossing the species; and the

nurseries will supply almost every shade of color from white to brilliant flame color.

The *A. pontica*, is also hardy; but the Chinese species require a greenhouse. This is one of the most magnificent shrubs that can be cultivated, and deserves the special attention of those who wish to form even a moderately good shrubbery.

The BERBERRY (*Berberis vulgaris*) is quite beautiful when in fruit. It is easily propagated, grows in any soil, requires little pruning, and is very good for hedges.

GLOBE FLOWER (*Corchorus japonica*).—A very pretty shrub with double yellow flowers, which are in abundance early in the summer, and also, but sparingly, shown throughout the season.

" By some mistake *Kerria japonica* was at first supposed to belong to Corchorus, a genus of Tiliaceæ,.and of course nearly allied to the lime-tree; to which it bears no resemblance, though it is still called *Corchorus japonica* in the nurseries. It is also singular, that though the double-flowered variety was introduced into England in 1700, the species was not introduced till 1835. It is a delicate little shrub, too slender to support itself in the open air; but when trained against a wall, flowering in great profusion. It should be grown in a light, rich soil, and it is propagated by cuttings."—*Companion to the Flower Garden.*

LABURNUM (*Cytisus laburnum*).—This beautiful plant forms a small tree, which, in May, is covered with pendant yellow blossoms. Blooming at the same time with the lilac, the two planted together have an extremely beautiful effect. It is hardy, grows in any soil, and is propagated easily by seed.

The Scotch Laburnum (*C. alpinus*), is much more beautiful than the common kind, " the flowers and leaves being larger and the flower more frequently fragrant. They are also produced much later in the season, not coming into flower till the others are quite over."

ALTHEA, or Rose of Sharon (*Hibiscus Syriacus*).—One of the most desirable shrubs for yards and gardens. The form of the shrub is compact and sightly; flowers double, and may be had of every color; it is hardy, growing well in all soils, and blooms continually from the last of July till frost. It is beautiful in avenues, and, being patient of the shears, it will form a fine *floral* hedge, a good specimen of which may be seen on Mr. Hoffner's beautiful grounds near Cincinnati. The single altheas are not so desirable. We regard this shrub as worthy of much more extensive cultivation than it has received. Its flowers are coarse on a close inspection, but at a little distance, and among other plants its effect is excellent. It is very easily propagated by cuttings, or from the seed.

SWEET-SCENTED SHRUB (*Calycanthus Floridus*).—Chiefly desirable from the pine-apple fragrance of its brownish-purple flowers. They are used to scent drawers, to carry n the pocket, etc. It grows freely in any dry, ric soil, and is propagated by layers and suckers.

RED-BUD (*Cercis Canadensis.*)—This small tree is familiar to every one, being the first spring flowering tree of our woods. It flourishes in gardens and makes a finer appearance there than in its native localities.

———•◆•———

GOOSEBERRIES.—Let those who are accustomed to lose their fruit by mildew, drench their bushes with an alkaline wash. Lime-water, or diluted lye are the most convenient. With a watering-pot, copiously water the whole bush, on the upper and under side of the branches; which can be easily done, if one will lift the branches while another bestows the shower-bath. After they have done bearing, prune out the head, and the lower branches, so as to give a *free circulation of air* under and through the bush. Spade in about them a liberal dressing of leached ashes, and fine charcoal if procurable.

GARDEN-WORK FOR AUGUST.

Dahlias will require special attention to secure them from splitting down, and breaking; let every part be well supported by ties. The cool nights and warm days of approaching fall will give them their most vigorous growth.

SAVING SEED.—Beet, spinage, peas, celery, salsify, lettuce seeds will now be ripe and should be gathered. Even if not quite ripe, they may be plucked, as experiments seem to show that seeds are more injured by over-ripeness than under-ripening. Seal up your peas in bottles and put wax about the cork, according to Dr. Plummer's directions, and the larvæ of the pea-bug will die for want of air. Seeds are ripened best in their own pods or receptacles; and where they ripen nearly at the same time, and do not easily shake out, we hang the whole plant in an airy shed, barn, etc., until winter; and then, for convenience, thresh out and pack up.

As fast as your perennial plants have shed their flowers, let the seed plants be destroyed, unless you wish to save seed, as the ripening of seed exhausts the root.

Young peach-trees should have the side shoots cleared away and one strong centre stem secured for budding in the fall.

Onions may now be gathered. Let them lie a day or two on the bed or in the alley, and then be transferred to a cool and airy place. The sets for top onions may be tied in bundles and hung up till spring.

Where peas and bush beans have been cleared away, turnips may be sowed for a fall and winter crop.

Spinage seed should be got ready to be sown in September, if you wish a good supply of this choicest of all spring greens.

Celery plants will begin to grow strongly in the trenches;

water with liquid manure; if troubled with insects, dust with quick lime and water with salt water. Above all things be careful in drawing in the earth to keep it out from the heart of the plant, and let it be done in dry weather.

———•◦•———

PULLING OFF POTATO BLOSSOMS.

THE *Boston Cultivator*, speaking of this process, says: "As the qualities of the potato-ball or apple differ considerably from the root or tuber, it may be that the juices destined to nourish the balls will not, on removing the blossoms, go to increase the roots. This view is not unreasonable."

We do not suppose the theory to be, that the sap tending to the bloom and ball *returns* to the root. But, simply, that there will be so much less food to be prepared, and therefore so much less exhaustion to the vegetable economy. It is well known that the filling out and ripening of seeds is eminently exhausting to the plant. It has long been the custom of florists who wish show-flowers, to refuse their bulbous plants leave to bloom for one season, plucking off the bud, that they might be so much the stronger for the next year's blooming.

But we suppose the truth to be this. The sap is prepared in the leaf and enters the distributing vessels of the plant. It is conveyed to every organ; each part, receiving its portion, *modifies it by a farther chemical action peculiar to itself.* Thus in the case of an apple-tree. The elaborated sap which goes to the leaf, the alburnum, the liber, the blossom, the fruit is the same in all; but the fruit gives it a still further elaboration, by which it imparts the peculiar properties belonging to it, in distinction from the tissues; so of the bark, the blossom, etc. If, then, the seed-vessels are removed, so much less elaborated sap is consumed as they would have required; and this, or at least, portions of it, are given to the other parts of the vegetable economy.

BLADING AND TOPPING CORN.

No one performs these operations for the benefit of the ear, but to obtain fodder, and it is then justified on the ground that the corn is not harmed by it. The sap drawn from the root does not flow straight up into the ear and kernel, but into the *leaves* or blades. The carbonic acid of the crude sap is decomposed, oxygen is given off and carbon remains in the form of starch, sugar, gum, etc., etc., according to the nature of the plant. When sap has by exposure to light undergone this change it is said to be *elaborated*.

It is only now that the sap, passing from the upper side of the leaf to a set of vessels in the under side, is reconveyed to the stem, begins to descend, and is distributed to various parts of the plant, affording nourishment to all. But when the fruit of every plant is maturing, it draws to itself a large part of the prepared sap, which, when it has entered the kernel, is still farther elaborated, and made to produce the peculiar qualities of the fruit, whether corn or wheat, apple or pear. It is plain from this explanation that a plant stripped of its leaves is like a chemist robbed of his laboratory, or like a man without lungs.

If corn is needed for fodder, let it be cut close to the ground when the corn has glazed. The grain will go on ripening and be as heavy and as good as if left to stand, and the stalk will afford excellent food for cattle. Sheep are fond of corn thus cured, and will winter very well upon it. In husking out the corn, the husk should be left on the stalk for fodder.

MAPLE-SUGAR.

As most persons who have not informed themselves on the subject, imagine that we are indebted to cane-sugar for our main supply, and that maple-sugar is a petty neighborhood matter, not worth the figures employed to represent it, we propose to spend some space in stating the truth on this matter. We will exhibit, 1, the amount produced; 2, the proper way of manufacturing it; 3, the proper treatment of sugar-tree groves.

We shall confine our statistics to the most important Northern and Western States.

1. New York produces annually....	10,048,109	lbs.
2. Ohio.....................................	6,363,386	"
3. Vermont	4,647,934	"
4. Indiana	3,727,795	"
5. Pennsylvania...........................	2,265,755	"
6. New Hampshire.........................	1,162,368	"
7. Virginia.................................	1,541,833	"
8. Kentucky...............................	1,377,835	"
9. Michigan...............................	1,329,784	"
Total of nine States........................	22,464,799	"
Residue thus—add for Maine, Massachusetts, Connecticut, Maryland, Tennessee, Illinois, Iowa, Missouri and Wisconsin.............	2,030,853	"
	24,495,652	"

Something should be subtracted for beet-root and corn-stalk-sugar. But on the other hand, the statistics are so much below the truth on maple-sugar, that the deficiency may be set off against beet-root and cornstalk-sugar. That the figures do not more than represent the amount of *maple-sugar* produced in these States may be presumed from one case. Indiana is set down at 3,727,795; but in the four counties of Washington, Warrick, Posey and Harrison, no account seems to have been taken of this article.

7*

In Marion county, four of the first sugar-making townships, Warren, Lawrence, Centre and Franklin, are not reckoned. If we suppose these four townships to average as much as the others in Marion county, they produced 77,648 lbs., and instead of putting Marion county down at 97,064 it should be 174,712 lbs. It is apparent from this case, that in Indiana the estimate·is far below the truth; and if it is half as much so in the other eight States enumerated,* then 22,464,799 is not more than a fair expression of the *maple-sugar* alone.

Lousiana is the first sugar-growing State in the Union. Her produce, by the statistics of 1840, was 119,947,720, or nearly one hundred and twenty million pounds. The States of Mississippi, Alabama, Georgia, South Carolina and Florida, together, add only 645,281 pounds more.

> Cane-sugar in the United States 120,593,001 lbs.
> Maple " " " 24,495,652 "

Thus about one-sixth of the sugar made annually in the United States is made from the maple-tree.† It is to be

---

* Dr. J. C. Jackson puts Vermont at 6,000,000 lbs. per annum, while the census only gives about 4,000,000.

† The data of these calculations, it must be confessed, are *very* uncertain, and conclusions drawn from them as to the relative amounts of sugar produced in different States, are to be regarded, at the very best, as problematical. We extract the following remarks from an article in the *Western Literary Journal*, from the pen of Charles Cist, an able statistical writer:

"It is not my purpose to go into an extended notice of the errors in the statistics connected with the census of 1840. A few examples will serve to show their character and extent. In the article of hemp, Ohio is stated to produce 9,080 tons, and Indiana 8,605—either equal nearly to the product of Kentucky, which is reported at 9,992 tons, and almost equal, when united, to Missouri, to which 18,010 tons are given as the aggregate. Virginia is stated to raise 25,594 tons, almost equal to both Kentucky and Missouri, which are given as above at 28,002 tons. Now the indisputable fact is, that Kentucky and Missouri produce more than hemp all the rest of the United States, and ten times as much as either Ohio, Indiana remembered too that in Louisiana it is *the* staple, while at the North maple-sugar has never been manufactured with any considerable skill, or regarded as a regular crop, but only a temporary device of economy. Now it only needs to be understood that maple-sugar may be made so as to have the flavor of the best cane-sugar, and that it may, at a trifling expense, be refined to white sugar, and the manufacture of it will become more general, more skillful, and may, in a little time, entirely supersede the necessity of importing cane-sugar. Indiana stands fourth in the rank of maple-sugar making States. Her annual product is at least *four million pounds*, which, at six cents the pound amounts to $160,000 per annum. A little exertion would quickly run up the annual value of her home-made sugar to half a million dollars.

Maple-sugar now only brings about two-thirds the price

or Virginia, which three States are made to raise 50 per centum more than those two great hemp-producing States.

"The sugar of Louisiana is given at 119,947,720 lbs., equal to 120,000 hhds., 160 per cent. more than has been published in New Orleans, as the highest product of the five consecutive years, including and preceding 1840.

"But what is this to the wholesale figure-dealing which returns 3,160,949 tons of hay, as the product of New York for that article! a quantity sufficient to winter all the horses and mules in the United States.

"Other errors of great magnitude might be pointed out; such as making the tobacco product of Virginia 11,000 hhds., when her inspection records show 55,000 hhds., thrown into market as the crop of that year. Who believes that 12,233 lbs. pitch, rosin and turpentine, or the tenth part of that quantity, were manufactured in Louisiana in 1840, or that New York produced 10,093,991 lbs. maple-sugar in a single year, or twenty such statements equally absurd, which I might take from the returns?"

Mr. Cist will find in the appendix to Dr. Jackson's Final Report on the Geology of New Hampshire, a statement, that Vermont makes 6,000,000 pounds of sugar annually. If this be so, we may, without extravagance, suppose that New York reaches 10,000,000 lbs. So far as we have collateral means of judging, the amount of maple-sugar is *under*-stated in the census of 1840.

of New Orleans.   The fault is in the manufacturing of it.
The saccharine principle of the *cane and tree are exactly
the same*.   If the same care were employed in their man-
facture they would be indistinguishable; and maple-sugar
would be as salable as New Orleans, and if afforded at a
less price, might supplant it in the market.   The average
quantity of sugar consumed in England by each individual
is about thirty pounds per annum.

MAPLE-SUGAR MAKING.—Greater care must be taken
in collecting the sap.   Old, and half-decayed wooden-
troughs, with a liberal infusion of leaves, dirt, etc., impart
great impurity to the water.   Rain-water, decayed vegetable matter, etc., add *chemical* ingredients to the sap, troublesome to extract, and injuring the quality if not removed.
The expense of clean vessels may be a little more, but with
care, it could be more than made up in the quality of the
sugar.   Many are now using earthen-crocks.   These are
cheap, easily cleaned, and every way desirable, with the
single exception of breakage.   But if wood-troughs are
used, let them be kept scrupulously clean.

The kettles should be scoured thoroughly before use,
and kept constantly clean.   If rusty, or foul, or coated with
burnt sugar, neither the color nor flavor can be perfect.
Vinegar and sand have been used by experienced sugar-
makers to scour the kettles with.   It is best to have, at
least, three to a range.

All vegetable juices contain *acids*, and acids resist the
process of crystallization.

Dr. J. C. Jackson* directs the one-*measured ounce* (one-
fourth of a gill) of pure lime-water to be added to every
gallon of sap.   This neutralizes the acid, and not only faci-
litates the granulation, but gives sugar in a free state, now
too generally acid and deliquescent, besides being charged

* Appendix to final Report on the Geology and Mineralogy of New
Hampshire, page 361.   This admirable Report is an able exposition of
the benefit of public State surveys.

with salts of the oxide of iron, insomuch that it ordinarily strikes a black color with tea.

The process of making a pure white sugar is simple and unexpensive. The lime added to the sap, combining with the peculiar acid of the maple, forms a neutral salt; this salt is found to be easily soluble in alcohol. Dr. Jackson recommends the following process. Procure sheet-iron *cones*, with an aperture at the small end or apex—let them be coated with white-lead and boiled linseed-oil, and thoroughly dried, so that no part can come off. [We do not know why earthen cones, unglazed and painted, would not answer equally well, besides being much cheaper.] Let the sugar be put into these cones, stopping the hole in the lower end until it is entirely cool. Then remove the stopper, and pour upon the base a quantity of strong whisky or fourth-proof rum *—allow this to filtrate through until the sugar is white. When the loaf is dried it will be pure white sugar, with the exception of the alcohol. To get rid of this, dissolve the sugar in pure boiling hot-water, and let it evaporate until it is dense enough to crystallize. Then put it again into the cone-moulds and let it harden. The dribblets which come away from the cone while the whisky is draining, may be used for making vinegar. It is sometimes the case that whisky would, if freely used in a sugar camp, go off in a wrong direction, benefiting neither the sugar nor the sugar-maker. If, on this account, any prefer another mode, let them make a *saturated* solution of loaf-sugar, and pour it in place of the whisky upon the base of the cones. Although the sugar will not be quite as white, the *drainings* will form an excellent molasses, whereas the drainings by the former method are good only for vinegar.

---

* If those who drink whisky would pour it on to the sugar in the refining cones, instead of upon sugar in tumblers, it would refine *them* as much as it does the sugar; performing two valuable processes at once.

CARE OF SUGAR ORCHARDS.—It is grievous to witness the waste committed upon valuable groves of sugar-trees. If the special object was to destroy them, it could hardly be better reached than by the methods now employed. The holes are carelessly made, and often the abominable practice is seen of cutting channels in the tree with an axe. The man who will murder his trees in this tomahawk and scalping-knife manner, is just the man that Æsop meant when he made the fable of a fellow who killed his goose to get at once all the golden eggs. With good care, and allowing them occasionally a year of rest, a sugar-grove may last for centuries.

As soon as possible get your sugar-tree grove laid down to grass, clear out underbrush, thin out timber and useless trees. Trees in open land make about *six pounds* of sugar, and forest trees only about *four* pounds to the season. As the maple is peculiarly rich in potash (four-fifths of potash exported is made from sugar-maple), it is evident that it requires that substance in the soil. Upon this account we should advise a liberal use of wood-ashes upon the soil of sugar-groves.

TAPPING TREES.—Two taps are usually enough—never more than three. For though as many as twenty-four have been inserted at once without killing the tree, regard ought to be had to the use of the tree through a long series of years. At first bore about two inches ; after ten or twelve days remove the tap and go one or two inches deeper. By this method more sap will be obtained than by going down to the colored wood at first. We state upon the authority of William Tripure, a Shaker of Canterbury, N.H., that about seven pounds of sugar may be made from a barrel of twenty gallons, or four pounds the tree for forest trees; and two men and one boy will tend a thousand trees, making 4,000 pounds of sugar.

We would recommend the setting of pasture-lands, and road-sides of the farm with sugar-maple trees. Their growth is rapid, and no tree combines more valuable properties. It is a beautiful shade-tree, it is excellent for fuel, it is much used for manufacturing purposes, its ashes are valuable for potash, and its sap is rich in sugar. There are twenty-seven species of the maple known, twelve of them are indigenous to this continent. All of these have a sacharine sap, but only two, to a degree sufficient for practical purposes, viz., *Acer saccharinum* or the common sugar-maple, and *Acer nigrum* or the *black* sugar-maple. The sap of these contains about half as much sugar as the juice of the sugar-cane. One gallon of pasture maple sap contains, on an average, 3,451 grains of sugar; and one gallon of cane-juice (in Jamaica), averages 7,000 grains of sugar.

But the cane is subject to the necessity of annual and careful cultivation, and its manufacture is comparatively expensive and difficult. Whereas the maple is a permanent tree, requires no cultivation, may be raised on the borders of farms without taking up ground, and its sap is easily convertible into sugar, and, if carefully made, into sugar as good as cane-sugar can be. Add to the above considerations that the sugar-making period is a time of comparative leisure with the farmer, and the motives for attention to this subject of domestic sugar-making seem to be complete.

LETTUCE.—Those who wish fine *head* lettuce should prepare a rich, mellow bed of light soil; tough and compact soil will not give them any growth. In transplanting, let there be at least one foot between each plant. Stir the ground often. If it is very dry weather, water at evening *copiously*, if you water at all; but the *hoe* is the only watering-pot for a garden, if thereby the soil is kept loose and fine. We have raised heads nearly as large as a drumhead cabbage by this method, very brittle, sweet and tender withal.

GEOLOGICAL DEFINITIONS.

MANY terms, in general use among scientific men, and usually employed in agricultural works, are obscure to young readers. For their sakes we will explain some of them; and shall not be angry if *old* men profit by the explanation.

SOIL.—The surface-earth, of whatever ingredients it may be composed. It may be a clay-soil, a sand-soil, a calcareous soil, as the surface is composed of clay, or sand, or clay strongly mixed with lime, etc.

SUBSOIL.—The earth lying below the ordinary depth to which the plow or spade penetrate. Sometimes it has hardened by the running of the plow over it for a series of years; then it is called *pan*, as hard-pan, clay-pan, etc. It is sometimes of the same nature as the top-soil, as in clay-lands; in others it is a different earth; as when a coarse gravel underlies vegetable mold, or when clay lies beneath sandy soil.

SUBSOIL PLOWING.—In ordinary plowing, the share runs from five to seven inches deep. A plow has been constructed (called subsoil plow), to follow in the furrow, and break up from six to eight inches deeper—so that the whole plowing penetrates from ten to sixteen inches.

SUBSOIL PLOW.—A plow having a narrow " *double share,* or a small share on each side of the coulter, and no mold-board." It is designed to break up and soften the subsoil, but not to bring it up to the top.

MOLD.—A soil in which decayed vegetable matter largely predominates over *earths*. Thus, leaf-mold is soil *principally* composed of rotten leaves; dung-mold, of dung reduced to a fine powdery matter; heath-mold, a black vegetable soil found in heath-lands; peat-mold, forest-mold, garden-mold, etc.

LOAM.—Clay, or any of the primitive earths, reduced to a mellow, friable state by intermixture of *sand*, or vegetable matter, is called loam.   Clay lands well manured with sand, dung, or muck, are turned, gradually, to a loam.

ARGILLACEOUS.—From the Latin (*argillaceus,*) soil principally composed of clay.

ALUMINA OR ALUMINE.—Generally employed to signify *pure* clay. It is, chemically speaking, a metallic oxide ; *aluminium* is the metallic *base,* and is an elementary substance.

It is generally known that the *diamond* is pure carbon (charcoal is carbon in an impure state), but it is not as generally known that the *ruby* and the *sapphire,* "two of the most beautiful gems with which we are acquainted, are composed almost solely of alumina," or pure clay in a crys- tallized state.

SILICIOUS.—An earth composed largely of silex. *Silex* or *silica* is considered to be a primitive earth constituting flint, and containing most kinds of sands, and sandstones, etc. China or porcelain, ware is formed from silica and alumina united, *i. e.* from silicious sand and clay.

CALCAREOUS.—A soil into the composition of which lime enters largely.   Limestone lands are calcareous.   Pure clay manured freely with marl becomes calcareous, for marl is, mostly, clay and carbonate of lime.

ALLUVIAL.—Strictly speaking, alluvium or our alluvial soil, is a soil formed by causes yet in existence.   Thus a bottom-land is formed by the wash of a river.   It is usually a mixture of decayed vegetable matter and sand.

DILUVIAL.—A diluvial soil or deposit is one formed by causes no longer in existence.   Thus a deposit by a deluge is termed *diluvial.* The word is derived from the Latin (*diluvium*), signifying a deluge.

The terms argillaceous, calcareous, silicious, alluvial and diluvial are constantly employed in all works which treat of husbandry.

FRIABLE.—A friable soil is one which crumbles easily. Clay is *adhesive,* or in common language *clammy:* leaf-mold is friable, or crumbling. Clay becomes friable when, by exposure to air or frost, or by addition of sand, vegetable matter, etc., it is thoroughly mellowed.

— ◆●◆ —

DRAINING WET LANDS.

BEFORE many years there will be thousands of acres pierced with drains. But the inducements to it which make it wise in England and New England do not yet, generally, exist in the West. The expense of draining one acre would buy two. Many farmers have already more arable land than they can till to advantage. Land redeemed from slough would not pay for itself in many years.

But although a general introduction of draining would not be wise, there are many cases in which, to a limited extent, it should be practised. Lands lying near to cities are sufficiently valuable, and the market for farming products sure enough, to justify the reclaiming of wet pieces of land. On small farms of forty and eighty acres, surrounded by high-priced lands, not easily procured for enlarging his farm if the owner should wish it, draining might be employed with advantage. A man with a *small* farm can *afford* expenses for high cultivation which would break a *large* farmer.

Some times a large meadow or arable field is marred by a wet slash through the middle of it; a farmer would not begrudge the labor of draining for the sake of having his favorite field without a blemish. Sometimes farms are intersected by wet lands, which make the passage from one part of the farm to another difficult at all times, and almost impassable at some seasons of the year. Draining might be resorted to in such a case, not so much for the sake of the land reclaimed, as for the convenience of the whole farm.

We know pieces of wet, peaty meadow land lying close by the farm-house, the only drawback to the beauty of the place. A good farmer would wish to recover such a spot for the same reason that he would prefer a handsome house to a homely one—a fine horse over a coarse-looking animal —a sightly fence, rather than a clumsy one. There is much strong land—but high, flat, and cold—which is wet through all the spring, resisting seed till long after other portions of the farm are at work, and which would, but for this backwardness, be regarded as the best land. If without great expense, such land could be cured, few farmers would mind the trouble or labor.

There are three kinds of draining which may be employed according to circumstances—subsoil-plowing, furrow-draining and ditch-draining. When a soil is underbound by a compact, impervious *subsoil*, all the rain or melting snow is retained in the soil until it can *exhale* and evaporate. For the subsoil acts like a water-tight floor, or the bottom of a tub. Subsoil-plowing, by thoroughly working through this under crust, gives a downward passage to the moisture ; water sinks as it does in sandy loams. Nor will such treatment be less useful to prevent the injury of summer drought ; for the depth of soil affords a harbor for roots from whence they can draw moisture when the top-soil is dry as ashes.

But there is a limit put to this treatment by the amount of clay contained in the subsoil. It has been experimentally ascertained in England, that when the soil contains as high as forty-three per cent. of alumina (clay) subsoil-plowing is useless, because the clay soon *coalesces* and is as impervious as ever. In such cases, if the land has a slight inclination in any direction, furrow-draining may, in some measure, relieve it. The ground is marked out in lands as for sowing grain and plowed with back-furrows, throwing the earth toward the centre. The rain and snow will run to either side, and flow off by the channels left between each strip. This treatment does not relieve the land, to any great extent, of water contained in it, but acts as a preventive, by carrying off the rain and snow before they are absorbed.

———•◦•———

O DEAR! SHALL WE EVER BE DONE LYING?

An honest old gentleman, in telling us his troubles, gave great prominence to the necessity he was frequently under of disappointing his customers, whose work could not be finished as soon as he had promised. After explaining the difficulty, he looked up with great earnestness, and exclaimed, " *O dear! shall we ever be done with this lying?*"

We have often wondered ourselves whether such a consummation would ever take place. "Your boots shall be done on Saturday night without fail." Nevertheless, you have to go to church with gaping shoes for want of them. "Your coat shall be sent home by nine o'clock on Saturday night;" and you get it, in fact, the Wednesday after. "Will you lend me your wheel-barrow? I will return it to-night." You wait for it till next week, and then *send* for it. My carpenter solemnly agreed to finish my house by November; but it was July before I could get the key. My wood was to be split on Saturday afternoon—enough for the Sabbath; so it was—but I had to do it. My money was to be paid me the next week; and then, *next* week; and then, NEXT week—and *then*, as soon as he could get it; he did get it and spent it; and then it should be paid when he got it again—he got it again, and paid another debt because the man treated him more savagely than I would. The strength laid out in running for this money, if it had been economically applied to labor, would, nearly, have *earned* the whole debt. The fellow never paid me at last; but Death came along, and he paid him promptly. "O dear! shall we ever get done with this lying?" It is one of the few domestic manufactures which need no protection, and flourishes without benefit either to the producer or consumer.

———◆◆◆———

CARE OF STOCK IN WINTER.

PERHAPS no better sign of careful husbandry can be found than in the attention paid to brute animals. We always expect a thriftless fellow to neglect and abuse his stock. When we see them well cared for, we always judge the owner to be a good farmer. Cattle ranging out often have had good picking, and if partly fed at the rack, will come out in the spring well-conditioned. Where hay and grain are a drug, we suppose that all cautions about wasting them will be laughed at. *Care* and *economy* are not the peculiar features of western farming; profusion and easiness are the more characteristic. But there are some points of attention to which every farmer should give heed.

CLEANING THE STABLE.—When cattle lie out, this trouble is saved in their case. But it is almost universally the practice to let the manure accumulate in stables for horses from autumn to spring, and sometimes from year to year, until its quantity compels its removal. This is all well enough for the sake of the manure—it is sheltered, and its strength preserved. But it is at the expense of the horse. The concentrated effluvia is bad; and lying down upon manure, night after night, causes the skin to break out in blotches; and sometimes the whole ham is affected so much that the hair comes off, and the skin is inflamed and covered with running sores. The ammonia of urine (which abounds in

horse manure), is caustic, and acts upon the skin like a blis-
ter upon the human flesh. If Providence had ordained that
a sore should break out on the owner, for every one on his
stock occasioned by his negligence, animals would have
a much better time than they now do.

Cows with Calf.—Especial attention should be paid to
these. As they grow heavy, toward spring, they should
not be chased by horses or dogs, or beaten by unmannerly
boys and men. Their food should be abundant and nutricious. A cow brought to calving in spring in a very thin
and lean condition will not recover through the whole summer, no matter how carefully tended. The cow, the calf,
and your own profit in both, require that you should bring
your cows to the spring in first-rate condition. If you have
roots, feed them ; but if not, give a slop of shorts, meal, and
flax-seed cake. This last ingredient is eminently ser, service-
able in laying on flesh.

Milking Cows.—Let them be milked regularly without
regard to weather. A careless girl will, if not watched,
milk irregularly, and what is worse, leave the cow *unstript*.
The morning work presses, or the cold pinches, or she is in
haste, at night, to go a visiting, or some one of a hundred
other reasons tempt her to milk out the full flow, and leave
the strippings. A cow so abused will be injured, in a short
time, so much, that all the care in the world will not bring
her back again.

See that stock are treated with gentleness and patience.
It is a shame to abuse a kind and docile animal, and it is
useless to thrash those that are not so. In either case, kindness is the best policy. A man who is brutal to cattle is
more of a beast than they are. We have seen many a man
who, if he had two more legs, would not fetch the price of
a stock-hog.

DEEP PLANTING.

WE saw recently a potato which grew at the depth of *twenty-five feet* below the surface of the earth. This is an extraordinary depth. Few things planted at that depth would vegetate. The fact in this case is unquestionable. The top was terminated by a cluster of *blossoms*, and the potatoes were of the size of small hickory-nuts.

P. S. Another fact, which like to have been omitted in this account, is, that it grew at the bottom of an *open well.*

CORN AND MILLET FOR FODDER.

THE practice of sowing grains for fodder has been practised with great success. MILLET is sown in May, June, or July, at the rate of three pecks of seed to the acre. It is, usually, ready for the scythe in about ninety days. Thick sowing is best. Cut when the grain is fairly out of the milk, and cure it like hay. Four tons is a fair yield—two tons is a small crop.

INDIAN CORN should be sown broadcast at the rate of four to five bushels to the acre. Corn belongs to the tribe of *grasses.* Cultivating it for the grain, in rows, with every stimulant of air, light, and manure, develops the stalk almost to a tree form. When sown for fodder, the object should be to produce it, as nearly as possible, like a *grass.* Thick sowing will tend to do it, and each stalk being small and tender, the crop will be easily masticated by cattle. By good management six or eight tons may be cut to the acre —cutting twice in the season. The first mowing should be about the period of *silking.* The next, whenever the shoots have grown again to a proper size. If but one mowing is intended, it should be permitted to stand a week or two later than when two crops are to be taken. For, all plants prepare the most of nutritious juices at the period of their *fruiting*. Indian corn is the richest in saccharine matter at about the time its grain is turning from a milky to a mealy state. Cattle will eat either of the above grains, treated like a grass crop, with great avidity ; and every one knows that it is desirable to give them a *change* of food through the winter.

SEED SAVING.

THE seeds of cucumber, melon, etc., are better, at any rate, when four of five years old than when fresh ; and we have well authenticated instances of seeds retaining their vitality much longer than this. There is *no* fixed period during which seeds will keep. There is no reason to suppose that they would lose their vitality in any assignable number of years *if the proper conditions were observed.* De Candolle says that M. Gerardin raised kidney beans, obtained from Tournefort's herbarium, which were at least a hundred years old ; but beans left to the chances of the atmosphere are not good the second year, and hardly worth planting in the third. Professor Lindley raised raspberry plants from seed not less than sixteen or seventeen hundred years old. Multitudes of other instances might be given. In reply to the first question, it may, then, be said, that the length of time through which seeds will keep depends upon the method of preserving them.

We do not suppose it to be essential to inclose apple, pear, and quince seeds in earth for the purpose of preserving their vitality during a single winter. But if exposed to the air, the rind becomes so hard and rigid as to make germination very difficult from mere mechanical reasons. The moisture of the soil keeps the covering in a tender state, and it is easily ruptured by the expansion of the seed.

The shell of peach, plum, and other stone-fruit seeds would form, if left to dry and harden, a yet more hopeless prison. If kept for two years, the most stone-fruit pips, it is to be presumed, would not germinate. Some, however, would have vigor enough to grow even then. We have forgotten who it was, but believe it to have been a reliable person, recently mentioned the fact, that a peach or apricot stone was for several years kept as a child's plaything; but upon being planted, grew, and is now a healthy tree. Such cases are, however, rare.

The intercourse between Great Britain and her distant colonies, and the various expeditions fitted out from her shores for purposes of botanical research and for the acquisition of new plants from distant regions, have made the subject of seed-saving at sea a matter of much experiment.

In general, the conditions of preservation are three; a low temperature, dryness, and exclusion of air. But it often happens, that all these cannot be had, and then a choice must be made between them. Heat and moisture will either germinate the seeds or corrupt them. In long voyages, and in warm regions, *moisture contained in the seed*, if in a close bottle, is sufficient to destroy the seed. Glass bottles have therefore been rejected. Seeds for long voyages, or for long preservation, are thoroughly ripened and thoroughly dried; but dried without raising the *temperature* of the air, as this would impair their vitality. They are then wrapped in coarse paper, and put, loosely, in a coarse canvas bag, and hung up in a cool and airy place. In this way seeds will be as nearly secure from heat and moisture—their two worst enemies—as may be. It is probable that some seeds have but a short period of vitality under any circumstances of preservation. Seeds containing much oil, are peculiarly liable to spoil. Lindley suggests that the oil becomes rancid.

8

The preservation of seeds from one season to another, for home use, is not difficult, and may be described in three sentences: ripen them well, dry them thoroughly, and keep them aired and cool.

———•◦•———

RHUBARB.

RHUBARB or *pie-plant* is becoming as indispensable to the garden as corn, or potatoes, or tomatoes.   No family should be without it.   It comes in after winter apples are gone and before green apples come in again for tarts.   By a little attention it may be had from the last of March through the whole summer.   Indeed, it may be had through the whole year.   The root contains within itself all the nourishment required to develop the leaves and stalks at first, without any other aid than warmth and moisture. ` If then it be lifted late in the fall or during open weather in winter, and put in large pots, nail kegs, boxes, etc., put in a warm room, or cellar, it will soon send up a supply of leaves.   It is not even necessary that there should be much light, for the want of it only makes the stem whiter and of a milder acid.   The roots thus used may either be thrown away, or set out again and not· used until they have recovered, which will be in about one summer.

For early spring use, select a warm spot in the garden, and late in the fall dig in around your roots a good supply of rotten manure.   Cover them with coarse manure, straw, or litter.   As soon as the frost comes out of the ground, knock out the ends of a barrel and put one over each plant from which you propose to gain an early supply.   Put a quantity of coarse manure around the outside of the barrel to maintain the warmth, and, in cold nights and during cold rains, lay a board over the open top.   Thus treated, you may have tarts in March.   But the main supply of this wholesome plant is to arise from open cultivation. The roots may be gained from seed or from division of old roots. Eastern writers recommend sowing the seed in autumn; but in the West spring sowings have vegetated much better than an autumnal planting. In April sow the seed in deep mellow and rich beds. Keep the plants free from weeds and in a growing state during the summer. They may require a little shading during the hottest days of summer. The next spring we transplant them to a trial-bed; for, it is to be remembered, that the seed does not necessarily give a plant like its parent. Let them be set two feet apart every way, and during the season it can be seen which are the largest and best; these are to be raised in the fall, divided and transplanted, and the rest thrown away. Out of a hundred plants, not more than two or three may be worth keeping. In the spring of 1842 we planted seed obtained in New York, for the Victoria Rhubarb (a new kind), which had been imported but a few months. Of fifty plants only three proved worth keeping—one of these for its earliness and the others for size.

When you have secured roots from which you wish to form a bed for your main supply, divide them either in the fall or spring into as many pieces as there are buds on the crown, each piece having, of course, a bud. The smallest slice of root will live, although a large portion is preferable. Do not be too timid in dividing; the plant is exceedingly tenacious of life—it can hardly be killed. We have had roots lying in the open air for weeks, and when replanted growing with undiminished vigor. Every one who has, for a single season, tended a garden, knows what *dock* is, and how tenacious of life, so much so, as to make it quite a trouble. The rhubarb is a full-blooded vegetable brother, belonging to the same family of plants.

This plant thrives most luxuriantly in a rich, sandy loam; the earth should be spaded and mellowed to at least twenty inches depth. We prepare ground for it as follows: Mark

out the row with a line, throw out the top earth on one
side; throw out a full spade depth of subsoil upon the
other side. Throw back the top dirt, mixing it freely
with well rotted manure. Now put in the soil which was
taken from the bottom of the trench; as this is comparatively poor—mix it largely with manure. We make rows
four feet apart, and set the plants three feet apart in the
row. Very little care is needed in after cultivation. The
large leaves will shade the ground and check weeds. A
good supply of fresh manure, well dug in once a year, will
keep the plants in heart and health for a long time.

PEAS.

PEAS should be planted among the earliest of seeds.
They are a hardy vegetable, and will bear severe frosts in
the spring without injury. A light, sandy soil is the best.
If manured, let only the most thoroughly rotted be used.
Two sorts of peas are sufficient for all ordinary purposes—
one early kind, and one for the later and main supply. The
number of kinds advertised by seedsmen is very great, and
every year adds to the new varieties. Many of them are
of little value, and many, hitherto esteemed, are supplanted
by better ones. The Early Warwick and Cedo Nulli are
fine early peas, unsurpassed till the Prince Albert appeared.
This is now esteemed the earliest of peas, ripening at Boston
in fifty-three days from the time of sowing, and in England
in forty-two days. We hope to be able, soon, to have this
variety for distribution. Early peas are seldom of high
flavor; none that we ever raised are comparable to the
larger and later peas, and it is, therefore, except for market
purposes, not desirable to plant very largely of early sorts.

Of late peas we have, after trying many sorts, fallen back

upon the old-fashioned *Marrowfat*, and now raise it exclusively. It will be fit for the table in from seventy to eighty days after planting. *Knight's tall marrowfat* is recommended in Hovey's Magazine (a standard authority), as of " delicious quality and producing throughout the whole season." We have never had an opportunity of proving it.

We prefer *buying* our seed to *raising* it. In this region the pea-bug pierces every seed-pea, and, although the germ is not usually destroyed by this depredator, the seed is weakened, and the certainty of growth very much diminished. If one *must* plant buggy peas, let them have *scalding* water poured upon them and turned off again immediately. The bug will be destroyed and the pea not injured.

When peas are up they require but one or two hoeings, as they soon shade the ground so as to prevent weeds from growing. They should be well supplied with brush, strongly set in the ground. When peas are allowed to fall over, they become mildewed and rot. This also happens when the rows are planted so near together as to prevent free circulation of air.

When large quantities of peas are desired they should be sown broad-cast, at the rate of about three bushels to the acre—more rather than less. It leaves the land in fine tilth, smothering all weeds. Thirty bushels to the acre is a fair crop; but eighty-four, and eighty-eight, have been taken.

——•••——

AUTUMN-PLANTED ONIONS.—Onions for seed should be planted in October; and, like their more brilliant, but less perfumed, friends of the tulip and hyacinth connections, they will thoroughly root themselves during the autumn and mild winter weather, and be ready for early work, the moment the frost rises from the ground.

PLANT SHADE-TREES.

WE would suggest to the editors of newspapers the propriety of establishing in their columns a permanent agricultural department. We are much pleased to see that many excellent papers are doing it, and that others insert occasional articles. Great advantage cannot fail to accrue to our town and rural population by putting into their hands every week, able articles from practical farmers and gardeners upon the various topics of agriculture and horticulture. Let every paper urge the setting out of shade-trees in our villages. It is greatly to be desired, that all our towns should be filled with elms, maples, ashes, locusts, etc. The cultivation of fruit may be much encouraged and promoted by a frequent republication of articles on that subject. The gardens and conservatories of a few very wealthy gentlemen do not constitute a horticultural community. They are of great use in the procuration and cultivation of new varieties of plants, and in testing important matters by expensive experiments. But affluent men and their pleasure grounds are to horticulture, what universities are to common schools; that State is best educated whose *whole* population are the most thoroughly trained; and that is *the* horticultural State, *all* of whose villages, towns, farms, and gardens, are in the highest state of cultivation.

Our desire is to diffuse a love for rural affairs, husbandry, and horticulture among the whole mass of the community.

———•••———

WEEDS IN ALLEYS.—It is said that weeds may be entirely destroyed for years by copious watering with a solution of lime and sulphur in boiling-hot water. This, if effectual, will be highly important to such as have garden gravel walks, pavements, etc., through which grass and weeds grow up.

H O T · B E D S.

AFTER a little practice any one can make and manage a simple hot-bed. For a common family one twelve by four feet will be large enough, and nine by four will answer for a small family. *Frame.*—The frame should be made of two-inch stuff (pine or poplar). The back must be as high again as the front, in order to give the right inclination to the sash. The ends should be nailed fast to corner posts, say four inches square. The back and front are to be attached to those parts by iron bolts, which may be screwed or unscrewed at pleasure. The frame may be taken to pieces, if so made, and put away during the season it is not in use. A frame twelve by four, will take four sash of three feet wide, the other sized frame will take three sash. Where the sash meet, a piece of wood three inches broad and two thick, should be let in from back to front, for the sash to run upon, and it may be allowed to extend back for two feet beyond the body of the frame. Three coats of paint should be put on the outside and inside of the frame, and then, with good care, it will last twenty years. Mark out the ground six inches larger every way than your frame. Dig it out a foot deep. Take fresh, strong horse-dung. Shake it up and mix it thoroughly. Lay it into the bed evenly, beating it down with the back of the fork, *but never treading it.* Raise the bed three feet above the surface, making the thickness in all four feet. In a week's time this will have settled six or eight inches. We have for the sake of a gentler and longer continued heat, laid alternate layers of manure and *tan-bark,* and thus far it has done well with us. Put on the frame and sash and let it stand till the heat begins to raise, which will be two or three days. Then raise the sash to let the steam pass off. In about four days take off the frame, put on about six inches of light, good soil, evenly, all over the bed; replace the frame, and in a day thereafter it will be ready for seed.

Cabbage, cauliflower, tomatoes, egg plants, peppers, celery, cucumbers, lettuce, together with savory herbs, as sweet marjoram, sweet basil, thyme, sage, lavender, etc., etc. may be sown in drills in the soil prepared as above.

It is difficult to give, on paper, the directions for the care of the bed. The greatest dangers of all, are that of *burning* the plants by excessive heat, or of damping them off, by too little air. These evils must be guarded against by the admission of as much air as possible. In mild days let the sash be partly open all day, and in very cold days, endeavor to procure a half hour even, at mid-day, for raising the sash and airing the plants. As they grow up, if crowded, they should be thinned out, so as not to run up spindling.

ORIGINAL RECIPES.

WHEN we say *original*, we don't mean that no one ever employed the same recipes, but only this, that we have obtained them, not from books, but from good and skillful housewives.

EPICURE'S CORN BREAD.—Upon two quarts of sifted corn-meal, pour just enough boiling water to scald it thoroughly; if too much water is used it will be heavy. Stir it thoroughly, let it get cold; then rub in a piece of butter as large as a hen's egg, together with two teaspoonfuls of fine salt; beat four eggs thoroughly, and they will be all the better if the whites and yolks are beaten separately, add them to the meal and mix thoroughly. Next, add a pint of sour cream, or butter-milk, or sour milk (which stand in the order of their value). Dissolve two teapoonfuls of saleratus in hot water, and stir it in. Put it in buttered pans and bake it.

In winter, it may be mixed over night and in that case, the eggs and saleratus should not be put in until morning. When ready for the oven, the mixture ought to be about as thin as good *mush*, and if not, more cream should be added.

If you are not an epicure already, you will be in danger of becoming one, if you eat much of this corn cake— *provided it is well made.*

SUGAR GINGER-BREAD.—To three-quarters of a pound of butter and not quite a pint of finely rolled brown sugar, add a great spoonful of ginger, and a little cinnamon and nutmeg ; beat these up to a foam ; beat four eggs thoroughly and add and mix well, with the butter and sugar. Add a teacup of rich cream, a great spoonful of saleratus dissolved in hot water. Stir in sifted flour as long as it can be worked. Pound and knead the dough very thoroughly. Roll out quite thin, cut into small cakes, bake in a quick oven. They will be hard, but tender and crisp.

HOOSIER BISCUIT.—Add a teaspoonful of salt to a pint of new milk, warm from the cow. Stir in flour until it becomes a stiff batter; add two great spoonfuls of lively brewer's yeast; put it in a warm place and let it rise just as much as it will. When well raised, stir in a teaspoonful of saleratus dissolved in hot water. Beat up three eggs (two will answer), stir with the batter, and add flour until it becomes tolerable stiff dough ; knead it thoroughly, set it by the fire until it begins to rise, then roll out, cut to biscuit form, put in pans, cover it over with a thick cloth, set by the fire until it rises again, then bake in a quick oven. If well made, no directions will be needed for eating.

As all families are not provided with scales and weights, referring to the ingredients generally used in cakes and pastry, we subjoin a list of weights and measures.

WEIGHT AND MEASURE.

Wheat flour	one pound	is one quart.
Indian meal	one pound two ounces,	is one quart.
Butter, when soft	one pound one ounce,	is one quart.
Loaf-sugar, broken,	one pound	is one quart.
White sugar, powdered,	one pound one ounce,	is one quart.
Best brown sugar	one pound two ounces,	is one quart.
Eggs	ten eggs	are one pound.

LIQUID MEASURE.

Sixteen large tablespoonfuls	are	half a pint
Eight large tablespoonfuls	are	one gill.
Four large tablespoonfuls	are	half a gill.
A common sized tumber holds		half a pint.
A common sized wine glass holds		half a gill.

Allowing for accidental differences in the quality, freshness, dryness, and moisture of the articles, we believe this comparison between weight and measure to be as nearly correct as possible.

COOKING VEGETABLES.

WHILE we believe meat to be necessary to laboring men, we are equally sure that it is used to excess; for persons of a sedentary habit, vegetable diet is supposed to be much more wholesome, because much less stimulating than meat. Whatever shall make vegetables more relishful will extend their popular use, and therefore any *simple* recipe for cooking them is a public good. The following are taken fresh from the kitchen, and we will vouch for their being good, although there may be other ways still better.

1. GREENS.—The articles employed for greens are numerous; we merely mention the following:—sprouts of turnip

and cabbage, dandelions, lamb's quarters, red-rooted plantain, cowslip, wild pepper-grass, purslain, young beet-tops, lettuce, and spinage—the best of all greens.

In gathering plantain, care must be taken to select *only* the red-rooted, the white being thought poisonous. With the exception of spinage, all these should be boiled in salted water, or in water with a piece of salt pork, for half an hour, then taken out, drained, and served up with butter gravy.

Spinage is boiled, as above, for half an hour, then taken out, thoroughly drained, put into a skillet with cream, butter and pepper, and if need be, a little more salt. Place it over the fire and stir it up with a knife all the time it simmers, until it becomes a paste. About five minutes are enough for this last process—then dish and serve it.

2. Asparagus.—Asparagus should never be cut *below the surface of the ground*, although books and papers, almost universally, direct to the contrary. The white part of the stem is always tough and inedible. Let it spring up about six or eight inches and then cut it *at* the surface of the ground. Lay it in the pan or kettle in which it is to be cooked, and sprinkle salt over it. Pour boiling water over it, until it is just covered; boil from fifteen to twenty-five minutes, according to the age of the asparagus. Have two or three nicely toasted slices of bread in the dish which is to go to the table; lay the asparagus upon the toast, putting first sweet butter and pepper upon it according to your taste; lastly pour over it the liquor in which it was boiled. Many throw away the water in which it was cooked and substitute cream and butter, but thereby the finest flavor of the vegetable is thrown away and lost.

3. Beets.—While young, beets may be boiled tops and all; as the tops get tough the root alone is boiled in salted water until tender, viz. from three-quarters of an hour to an hour and a half, according to the size of the beet. Quarter or slice them if large, and add fresh sweet butter and pepper.

4. PEAS.—No vegetable depends more for its excellence upon good cooking than peas. Have them freshly gathered and shelled, *but never wash them.* If they are not perfectly clean, roll them in a dry cloth; but even this is seldom required, and then only through carelessness. Pour them dry into the cooking dish, and put as much salt over them as is required, then pour on boiling water enough to cover them; boil them fifteen minutes if they are young; no pea is fit to cook which requires more than half an hour's boiling. When done, put to a quart of peas three great tablespoonfuls of butter, and pepper to your taste. Put all the water to them in which they were boiled. The great mistakes in cooking peas are in cooking too long, and in deluging them with water.

STRING or SNAP beans are cooked like peas, only they require longer boiling.

5. CORN should be boiled in salted water from twenty to thirty minutes, according to its age; if boiled longer it becomes hard and loses its flavor. We have given in the *Western Farmer and Gardener,* p. 231, a recipe for corn and beans, but as all may not see that periodical, we extract the substance of it.

We give directions for a mess sufficient for a family of six or seven.

To about half a pound of salt pork put three quarts of cold water; let it boil. Now cut off three quarts of green corn from the cobs, set the corn aside and put *the cobs* to boil with the pork, as they will add much to the richness of the mixture. When the pork has boiled, say half an hour, remove the cobs and put in one quart of freshly-gathered, green, shelled beans; boil again for fifteen minutes; then add the three quarts of corn and let it boil another fifteen minutes. Now turn the whole out into a dish, add five or six large spoonfuls of butter, season it with pepper to your taste, and with salt also, if the salt of the pork has not proved sufficient. If the liquor has boiled away, it will be necessary to add a little more to it before taking it away from the fire, as this is an essential part of the affair.

6. SALSIFY OR OYSTER-PLANT.—This vegetable is raised exactly as are carrots and parsnips. Like the latter—they require a little frosting before their flavor is fully developed.

They should be scraped and washed (but *not* soaked in vinegar, as English cooks direct, to extract a bitter taste, which they do *not* contain), and sliced; sprinkle enough salt upon them to season them, pour on just enough boiling water to cover them; boil till perfectly tender, which will be, say fifteen minutes. Put butter and pepper to them; stir up a little flour in cream to make a thin paste and pour in enough to thicken a little the water in which they were boiled. Dish with or without toasted bread, as may suit the taste.

7. TOMATOES.—The recipe which we gave in the *Farmer and Gardener* has been universally copied, and, we believe, has beguiled thousands to the love of tomatoes. It has been introduced to cook-books under the name of " Indiana Recipe for Cooking Tomatoes."

8. ONIONS should be boiled for half an hour in salted water, then drained, put into sweet milk, boiled again for five or ten minutes, seasoned with butter, pepper and salt, and served up.

9. PIE-PLANT.—This important vegetable—among the earliest, the most wholesome, and of the easiest culture—should be found in every garden, and served up on every table during the spring and early summer. To prepare it for use, strip off the skin, slice it thin, put into a dish with a few spoonfuls of boiling water, just enough to keep from sticking, for its own juice will afford liquid enough after it is cooked. Boil until it is perfectly tender, stirring it constantly. If the plant is good and the fire quick, it ought to be boiled in five minutes. Stir in all the sugar needed while it is in a scalding state. A little nutmeg or lemon

peel, put in while it is hot, improves the flavor. When cool, it may be used for tarts, or pies, with or without upper crust; it also makes a better *apple*-sauce than apples do themselves.

10. EGG-PLANT.—Boil in salted water a few minutes; cut slices, put a little salt between each slice, and let them lie for half an hour. Then fry them in butter or lard until they are brown.

11. CAULIFLOWER AND BROCCOLI.—The only difference between these, so far as the cook is concerned, is in color. Take off the outside leaves and soak them for an hour in salted water. Pour boiling water to them and boil for about twenty minutes. Serve them up with butter and pepper. The Savoy cabbages are next in delicacy of flavor to the cauliflower, and may be cooked in the same way.

———◆◆◆———

FARMERS, TAKE A HINT.

IT is very surprising to see how slow men are to take a hint. The frost destroys about half the bloom on the fruit-trees; everybody prognosticates the loss of fruit; instead of that, the *half* that remains is larger, fairer, and higher flavored than usual; and the trees instead of being exhausted, are ready for another crop the next year. Why don't the owner *take the hint* and thin out his fruit every bearing year? But no; the next season sees his orchard overloaded, fruit small, and not well formed; yet he always *boasts* of that first-mentioned crop without profiting by the lesson it teaches.

We heard a man saying, " the best crop of celery I ever saw, was raised by old John ——, on a spot of ground where the wash from the barn-yard ran into it after every hard shower." Did he take the hint, and convey such liquid manure in trenches to his garden? Not at all; he bragged about that wonderful crop of celery, but would not take the hint.

We knew a case where a farmer subsoiled a field and raised crops in consequence which were the admiration of the neighborhood; and for years the field showed the advantage of deep handling. But we could not learn that a single farmer in the neighborhood took the hint. The man who acted thus wisely, sold his farm and his successor pursued the old way of surface-scratching.

A stanch farmer complained to us of his soil as too loose and light; we mentioned ashes as worth trying; "well, now you mention it, I believe it will do good. I bought a part of my farm from a man who was a wonderful fellow to save up ashes, and around his cabin it lay in heaps. I took away the house and ordered the ashes to be scattered, and to this day I notice that when the plow runs along through that spot, the ground turns up moist and close-grained." It is strange that he never took the hint! There are thousands of bushels of ashes lying not far from his farm about an old soap and candle factory with which he might have dressed his whole farm.

A farmer gets a splendid crop of corn or grain from off a grass or clover lay. Does he take the hint? Does he adopt the system which shall allow him every year just such a sward to put his grain on? No, he hates book-farming, and scientific farming, and "this notion of rotation;" and jogs on the old way.

A few years ago our farmers got roundly into debt; and they have worried and sweat under it, till some of them have grown greyer, and added not a few wrinkles to their face. Do they take the hint? Are they not pitching into debt again?

A few years ago *mules* commanded a high price; everybody raised mules forthwith; the market of course was glutted; the price fell; everybody quit the business; markets became empty and the price rose; a few men who had stuck to the business pushed in their droves and made money; and now everybody is raising mules again. The same game is played every four or five years with pork; men make when pork is scarce, but few farmers have stock on hand. They instantly rush into the business, flood the country with hogs and get almost nothing for them. Why don't men take the hint? *A moderate stock all the time,* makes more money than that system which has none when the price is high and too many when the price is low.

Because one year, the wheat crop has been very large and fine, and the price low, not half so much will be put in another year. Those who are wise, foreseeing this fact and sowing largely, will, if the season favors wheat, reap a handsome profit.

Auctioneers tell us that a "wink is as good as a word." We give both, and hope our readers will *take the hint.*

—•••—

MIXING PAINT, AND LAYING IT ON.

It is convenient, and oftentimes, on the score of economy, necessary for persons (who have not been apprenticed to the trade), to do their own painting. To enable such to practise with success, we propose giving a few hints.

RESPECTING THE ARTICLES USED.

WHITE LEAD.—This is extensively manufactured in all of our principal cities. Low priced leads are always adulterated by *chalk,* or, as it is called in its prepared state, *whiting.* It is sometimes so largely mixed with this, as to be worthless, and every one has observed houses, painted for a year or so, from which the paint rubs off like whitewash, in consequence of the use of adulterated lead. The poorest lead is sold *without any brand.* The common article is branded as No. 1, with the maker's name. The best article is branded with the maker's name, as PURE, or SUPERIOR. It is the best economy always to use the pure lead.

OIL.—Linseed oil is that usually employed in painting. It contains a large amount of fatty substance and of other impurity, which should be separated from it before it is used. *This is to be done by boiling.* For outside work, the oil should *always be boiled,* no matter what the painter says about it. Great care should be taken in doing this. Let the kettle be set out of doors, the heat be increased gradually, but never enough to produce violent boiling, as the oil will expand, run over, and take fire, when nothing can save it, or the house either, oftentimes, if you have been foolish enough to do it within doors. As fast as impurities rise to the surface, skim them off—when the oil has a clear look, slack off the fire and let the oil cool; carefully turn off the clear portion, leaving the *sediment* undisturbed.

DRYERS.—Substances used to make paint dry quickly are called *Dryers.* For light work sugar of lead is the best; for colored paint, litharge and red lead are employed. Spirits of turpentine is used for the same purpose. Litharge and red lead are usually boiled in with the oil at the rate of about a quarter of a pound of litharge to a gallon of oil.

MIXING AND LAYING ON.—Paint is purchased in kegs, containing twenty-five pounds of lead ground in oil, and ready for mixing. The kegs themselves make excellent paint-pots. The lead is to be mixed according to the work to be done. If paint is laid on in heavy coats it will crack and peel off. If several thin coats are successively laid on, it forms a solid body. The first coat is called *priming.* The lead is made quite thin with oil for priming. Before laying it on, let the work be cleaned, all dust and dirt be removed. The surface is then covered evenly with paint, and allowed to dry thoroughly.

SECOND COAT.—Let nail-holes, cracks, etc., be filled with putty; for colored painting, red-lead putty is the best. The paint should be mixed to the thickness of thin cream, and laid on *evenly*, but not in too great quantities. In nice work, after this coat has thoroughly dried, it should be rubbed down with pumice-stone or fine sand-paper. The third coat is to be laid on as was the second. Three coats, at least, are required for good painting. Four or five will be still better.

Paint mixed with boiled oil usually has a glossy appearance. If it is desired to increase this, small portions of varnish are added. This is usually confined to outside work.

In cities the glossy surface of paint, is dis-esteemed for inside work; and instead, a *flatted* white is laid on. This is produced by mixing the lead for the last coat with turpentine instead of oil, by which a dull white is made. Flatted colors are not susceptible of being cleaned by washing more that once or twice, whereas common paint will endure washing, if carefully performed, for years. If painting is *well done*, and the paint is of the best materials, it ought to last twenty years. But the trash too often daubed upon buildings, does not last five years.

White will keep its color best for outside work. Some tint is thought to be more agreeable for inside work. Much judgment is required in preparing colored or tinted paints; and verbal directions cannot well be given for it in any moderate space. The usual pigments employed in making up the tints most in fashion, are for *grey*—white lead, Prussian blue, ivory black, and låke, or Venetian red; for *pea* and *sea greens*—white, Prussian blue, and yellow; for *olive green*—white, Prussian blue, umber, and yellow ochre; for *fawn color*—burned terra sienna, umber, and white.

We add two recipes taken from an English work, for a cheap paint for inside walls.

"MILK PAINT.—A paint has been used on the Continent with success, made from *milk* and *lime*, that dries quicker than oil paint, and has no smell. It is made in the following manner: Take fresh curds and bruise the lumps on a grinding-stone, or in an earthen pan, or mortar, with a spatula or strong spoon. Then put them into a pot with an equal quantity of lime, well slacked with water, to make it just thick enough to be kneaded. Stir this mixture without adding more water, and a white-colored fluid will soon be obtained, which will serve as a paint. It may be laid on with a brush with as much ease us varnish, and it dries very speedily. It must, however, be used the same day it is made, for if kept till next day it will be too thick: consequently no more must be mixed up at one time than can be laid on in a day. If any color be required, any of the ochres, as yellow ochre, or red ochre, or umber, may be mixed with it in any proportion. Prussian blue would be changed by the lime. Two coats of this paint will be sufficient, and when quite dry it may be polished with a piece of woollen cloth, or similar substance, and it will become as bright as varnish. It will only do for inside work; but it will last longer if varnished over with white of egg after it has been polished."

" *The following recipe for milk paint* is given in 'Smith's Art of House Painting:' Take of skimmed milk nearly two quarts; of fresh-slaked lime about six ounces and a half; of linseed oil four ounces, and of whiting three pounds; put the lime into a stone vessel, and pour upon it a sufficient quantity of milk to form a mixture resembling thin cream; then add the oil, a little at a time, stirring it with a small spatula; the remaining milk is then to be added, and lastly the whiting. The milk must on no account be sour. Slake the lime by dipping the pieces in water, out of which it is to be immediately taken, and left to slake in the air. For fine white paint the oil of caraway is best, because colorless; but with ochres the commonest oils may be used. The oil when mixed with the milk and lime entirely disappears, and is totally dissolved by the lime, forming a calcareous soap. The whiting or ochre is to be gently crumbled on the surface of the fluid, which it gradually imbibes, and at last sinks: at this period it must be well stirred in. This paint may be colored like distemper or size-color, with levigated charcoal, yellow ochre, etc., and used in the same manner. The quantity here prescribed is sufficient to cover twenty-seven square yards with the first coat, and it will cost about three halfpence a yard. The same paint will do for outdoor work by the addition of two ounces of slaked lime, two ounces of linseed oil, and two ounces of white Burgundy pitch: the pitch to be melted in a gentle heat with the oil, and then added to the smooth mixture of the milk and lime. In cold weather it must be mixed warm, to facilitate its incorporation with the milk."

We add several recipes of various convenient kinds of paint to be employed in particular situations, and for special purposes.

"*A coating to preserve wood in damp situations* may be made by beating twelve pounds of resin in a mortar, and adding to it three pounds of sulphur and twelve pints of whale oil. This mixture must then be melted over a fire, and stirred well while it is melting. Ochre of any required color, ground in oil, may be put to it. This composition must be laid on hot, and when the first coat is dry, which will be in two or three days, a second coat may be given; and a third, if necessary."

"*Gas tar*, with yellow ochre, makes a very cheap and durable green paint for iron rails and coarse woodwork."

" *Composition to lay on a boarded building, to resist the weather and likewise fire.*—Take one measure of fine sand, two measures of wood-ashes well sifted, three of slaked lime ground up with oil, and mix them together; lay this on with a brush, the first coat thin, the second thick.   This adheres so strongly to the boards covered with it, that it resists an iron tool, and the action of fire, and is impenetrable by water."

" *A flexible paint for canvas* is made by stirring into fifty-six pounds of common oil paint a solution of soap lye, made of half a pound of soap and three pounds of water: it must be used while warm."

" *A black coloring for garden walls* may be made by mixing quicklime, lampblack, a little copperas, and hot water."

GARDEN WEEDS.

AFTER hot weather sets in many are naturally inclined to relax their garden labors; they have eaten their salads, their radishes and peas; their beans and corn require but little attention, and as for the rest, it is left to the company of weeds.

WEEDS.—If the garden be thoroughly hoed twice or three times, the labor of keeping down weeds the rest of the summer will be small.   It is best to go over a compartment first with the hoe, to cut off weeds and loosen the soil, then with a rake go over it again, levelling and smoothing the surface, and collecting the weeds into heaps, which should be wheeled to the manure-corner and left to decay.   In raking, tread backward so that your tracks will be covered by the rake, and the bed left even.

Among the most vexatious weeds may be mentioned the purslain (*Portulacca oleracea*), commonly called pussly. It comes in May and lasts through the summer.   One plant

bears seed enough for a whole acre. It is very tenacious
of life. The least bit of root sprouts again, and when
rooted up, if a single fibre touches the soil, it starts off in
full vigor. When boiled it furnishes a very palatable article
of "greens." We go over the ground with a hoe, then
rake it into heaps and wheel it to the barn-yard. Hogs
are fond of it, and it is said to fatten them well. It is
somewhat amusing to those who are vexed at its insuper-
able intrusiveness and its inevitable vigor, to hear English
garden-books speaking of it as "somewhat tender," of raising it on hot-beds, of drilling it in the open garden, of
watering it in dry weather thrice a week, and cutting it
carefully so that it may sprout again! Cut it as you please,
gentlemen! rake it into alleys, let an August sun scorch it,
and if there is so much as a handful of dirt thrown *at it*, no
fear but that it will sprout again. It is a vegetable type of
immortality. The Jamestown weed (called jimpsum), the
Spanish needle, lamb's-quarters, etc., are easily eradicated
for the season by one or two hoeings. The grasses which
infest gardens, spreading into a cultivated ground from the
grass-plat, or brought in with manure, are easily weeded
out if plucked while small; but if left, the long spreading-
roots tear up tender plants along with them.

It is said that if no seeds were brought into the land by
wind or manure, or growth, the stock of weeds might be
eradicated in eight years. But so long as corners and
fence edges are reserved as weed-nurseries, to furnish an
annual supply of seed, no one need fear that gardening will
become too easy from want of work.

We know of but two reasons for letting weeds grow to
any size. In a large garden, when all the ground is not to
be planted at once, the reserved portions may be suffered
to sprout all the weeds, and when six or eight inches high,
if turned under, they will furnish good manure. Again,
when cut-worms are very numerous, when tomatoes and
cabbages have been set out on a clean compartment, we

have lost from a half to two-thirds of the plants. If the weeds are kept down just about the hill, and permitted to grow for a few weeks, between the rows, although it has a very slovenly look, it will save the cabbages, etc., by giving ample foot to the cut-worm. When the plants grow tough in the stem the weeds may be lightly spaded in, and the surface levelled with a rake.

LUCERNE.

THIS admirable plant is not so well known as it should be. It resembles a clover, and is used for green food for cattle, for which it is peculiarly adapted both by its nutriciousness and its endurance of repeated cuttings. Care must be taken to put it upon the right soil and it will bear mowing four or five times a year, and will last for ten years—with care five years more! The soil for it is a *deep*, a very deep vegetable loam, which drains itself perfectly and yet without becoming dry. It has a fusiform root, which, as the plant grows older, extends downward from four to six feet. The subsoil is regarded by Flemish farmers as *of* more importance than the surface soil. A stiff, cold, clay, a wet and springy soil; a hard, cold, wet subsoil of any sort, is unfavorable to it. It should therefore be tried on warm, dry, and rich soils, than which none are better than our sandy alluvions or bottom lands. During its first year it requires some care, to keep down weeds, as it is easily smothered; but when once established it rules the soil in defiance of anything. If the ground is *very* clean, it may be sown broadcast; but it is always safer and often *necessary* to drill it. Authors vary as to the quantity of seed required per acre, Von Thaër says six to eight pounds, while his French editor says from sixteen to eighteen. We suppose that from ten to twelve pounds will be a fair amount.

When the plants are well established they will be improved by severe harrowing every spring, a sharp harrow being used until the field looks as if it were plowed.

Lucerne has been tried by a few cultivators in the West, but by more in the East, with great success, and it has this peculiar excellence, that, thanks to its very long roots, it withstands our severest droughts; indeed our hottest and dryest summers are those which it seems to delight in.

—•♦•—

FAMILY GOVERNMENT.

"WILLIAM! stop that noise, I say—*won't* you stop! Stop, I tell you, or I'll slap your mouth."

William bawls a little louder.

"William, I tell you! ain't you going to stop? *Stop* I say! If you don't stop I'll whip you, sure."

William goes up a fifth, and beats time with his heels.

"I never saw such a child!—he's got temper enough for a whole town; I'm sure he didn't get it from me. Why don't you be still! Whist. Wh-i-st. Come, come, be still, won't you? Stop, *stop*, STOP, I say! Don't you see this— don't you see this stick? See here now," (cuts the air with the stick).

William, more furious, kicks very manfully at his mother —grows redder in the face, lets out the last note, and begins to reel, and shake, and twist, in a most spiteful manner.

"Come, William! come dear—that's a darling—naughty William! come, that's a good boy; donty cry, p-o-o-r, little fellow; sant ab-o-o-s-e you, sall eh! Ma's ittle man, want a piece of sooger? Ma's little boy got cramp, p-o-o-r little sick boy," etc., etc.

William wipes up, and minds, and eats his sugar, and stops.

AFTER SCENE.—The minister is present, and very nice talk is going on upon the necessity of governing children. "Too true," says mamma, "some people *will* give up to their children, and it ruins them—every child should be governed. But then it won't do to carry it *too* far; if one whips all the time it will break a child's spirit. One ought to mix kindness and firmness together in managing children."

"I think so," said the preacher; "firmness first and then kindness."

"Yes, sir, that's my practice exactly."

———•♦•———

CATALOGUE OF FLOWERS, SEEDS, AND FRUITS.

WE have received from different directions catalogues of seeds, flowers, and fruits. Instead of a mere mention of them, we shall employ them as *texts* for some remarks on the departments to which they belong.

The kinds, and varieties of the same kind of vegetables advertised are satisfactory. There is evidence that the easily besetting sin of seed establishments has been resisted and very much overcome, viz.: *a prodigal multiplication of varieties.* Now we do not wish to tie down a seedsman to only one variety of cucumber—one pea—one bean; for there is great advantage in having many varieties of the same vegetable. Some love mild radishes, and some love the full peppery taste; as both qualities cannot exist in the same variety it is desirable to have two. But some radishes which do admirably in the spring and early summer, lose their good qualities if planted in summer. We therefore seek and find a summer variety. This again fails for late

9

autumnal use, and we procure a (so called) winter sort.
We need one pea for its *earliness:* but early fruit seldom
has size or a high flavor ; we desire other varieties, therefore, for flavor, even though, in giving them a longer
period to perfect their juices, we have a late pea. But some
men raise peas for *market,* and cannot afford to raise a pea
merely because fine-flavored, unless also it is *prolific.* Then,
once more, market peas must be raised, usually as a *field-
pea,* and sown broadcast. Some peas stand up stronger
than others, and these are of course preferred. Now, as we
cannot find any vegetable that combines all the qualities of
earliness, size, flavor, and adaptation to variety of soil and
diversity of cultivation, we come as near to it as possible,
by gaining *varieties,* in which some one or more of these
qualities are better developed than in any others. The reasons for multiplying varieties afford a rule by which they
may be limited.

The fact that a seed is a variety different from all others
is no good reason for retaining or cultivating it; it must, in
SOME *respects, surpass others* now in use, or it only encum-
bers the garden. What is the use of ten varieties of peas
ripening at the same time of one size, and differing from
each other in not one assignable particular ? When a catalogue enumerates *fifty varieties* of cabbage, or pea, or bean,
are we to believe that each of the *fifty* has a virtue peculiar
to itself? If not, if two-thirds of them have no merit
which is not found, and found in a higher degree, in the
one-third they have no business to be retained. Let the
one-third, stand and the rest be erased. We regard a *very*
fat catalogue as we do a very fat man—all the worse for its
obesity. In comparing catalogues, we are not left as much
without an authoritative standard of judgment, in respect
to a proper extension of the number of varieties, as might
at first appear. English gardening has been carried to such
a degree of excellence, both as an art and as a science, that
we may regard the deliberate judgment of the best gar-

deners as law on this subject.   When Loudon published his
invaluable "Encyclopedia of Gardening," he was permitted
by the London Horticultural Society to avail himself of the
services of the distinguished Monro in the department of
culinary vegetables.

Let us compare the catalogues of three first rate seedsmen
as it respects a multiplication of varieties, with Mr. Monro's
selections :

	Cucumber.	Melon.	Celery.	Beet.	Turnip.	Cabbage.	Peas.	Beans.	Lettuce.
Landreth...................	2	15	2	5	9	10	7	15	8
Breck....	9	10	6	8	22	18	20	24	12
Prince....................	17	25	8	9	30	49	47	61	56

Mr. Monro names *nineteen* kinds of peas only, instead
of *forty-seven : twenty-two* kinds of beans instead of *sixty-
one ;* seven varieties of turnip instead of *twenty-two,* or,
worse yet, *thirty; fourteen* sorts of lettuce, instead of *fifty-
two.*

To the uninitiated a catalogue may look meagre with only
eight kinds of lettuce instead of *fifty ; fifteen* beans instead
of *sixty-one,* etc., but these corpulent catalogues make
meagre pockets, except in the case of the *seedsman.* A
much greater latitude of varieties is allowable in a nursery
catalogue than in a seedsman's list. But in even these
there is a disposition to extravagance which needs to be cor-
rected. Where the disproportion of knowledge between
the buyers and seller is so great as it is, and for some time,
must be, in horticultural matters, it becomes nurserymen
and seedsmen who *are* honest (and we have many such, and
they are increasing)—those who regard their business as an
honorable branch of *science,* as well as a proper means of
livelihood, and who hope to gain a high *reputation,* even

more than they do wealth, it becomes such to render the lists SELECT; and while the monstrously bloated catalogues of boasting and avaricious men continue to perplex and deceive the unwary, let all intelligent cultivators *sustain* those who rely on the *quality* rather than *quantity* of their articles.

GARDEN SEEDS.

GOOD seeds are the very first requisite for a good garden; soil and culture cannot make good crops out of bad seed.

1. As a general rule, *buy your seeds*. The reasons for it are so many and so good, that you will certainly do it, unless *economy* prevent; but it is better to economize elsewhere.

In the first place, seed-raising is a delicate business; and, for many reasons, will be better done by those who make it their business, than by those who do not. A reputable seedsman never dreams of raising, himself, all the seeds which he sells. For example, one sort of seed is let out to a farmer who contracts to raise it in a given soil and manner, and at a distance from all other seeds. One man raises the beet seed—another man, very often hundreds of miles distant, another sort. Peas are sent to Vermont and to Canada, where the pea-bug does not infest them. Some seeds, for which this climate is not favorable, are imported from Italy, from Guernsey—just as flowering bulbs are from Holland. We suppose this to be true of Landreth, Thornburn, Prince, Breck, Risley, etc. In cases where seeds are raised upon the premises of the seedsman, they are put on different parts of the farm, as far apart as possible.

These precautions are indispensable to the procuration of the *best* seeds of esculent vegetables. Species of the same genus, with open flowers, are so easily *crossed*, that, if grown contiguously, they cannot be kept pure. All *cucurbi-taceous* plants, such as squashes,. pumpkins, melons, cucumbers, gourds, etc., will mix and degenerate if planted even in the same garden. Let any one who wishes to see how it is done, watch the bee covering itself with golden pollen as it searches for honey in the cells of the flower, and darting off to another, mingling the fertilizing powder of the two. In a single morning, cucumbers will be mixed with each other, and with canteloupes; squashes will be crossed, and in the next generation will show it. Where the organs of flowers are protected, as in the pea, bean, etc., by a floral envelope, insects do not mix their pollen. I I have never known pure beet seed raised in a private garden which had more than the single kind in it—or when another garden was near which had other sorts.

We prefer, *generally*, northern seeds to those raised elsewhere. A mere change of soil and climate is often advantageous to seeds. But besides this, greater care and skill are usually employed at the north in producing sound and safe seeds.

We can recommend, from repeated trials, the seeds of Risley, Chatauque county, N. Y., and of Mr. Breck of Boston. Landreth of Philadelphia has a high reputation, but we have been unfortunate in using his seeds—very probably from lack of skill. We shall try them again next summer. Our early York cabbages proved to be trifling flower seeds—Lima beans were the white Dutch runners. Not one of five of their peas vegetated. The beets were not good seed, and the variety (blood beet) not pure. The experience of others, at this point, is like ours. Unless more care is taken in that establishment their seeds will lose all credit. Their lettuce seed has always proved good, and such others as are easy to raise.

2. We insert a table, exhibiting the years which different seeds will retain their vitality.

TIME THAT SEEDS WILL KEEP.

	YEARS.		YEARS.
Asparagus	4 or 18	Marjoram	4
Balm	2	Melon	8 or 10
Basil	1 or 3	Mustard	8 or 4
Beans	1 or 2	Nasturtium	2 or 3
Beets	8 or 10	Onion	8
Borage	2	Parsley	5 or 6
Cabbage	6 or 8	Parsnip	1
Carrot	1 or 7	Pea	2 or 8
Celery	6 or 8	Pumpkin	8 or 10
Corn	2 or 3	Pepper	5 or 6
Cress	2	Radish	6 or 8
Cucumber	8 or 10	Rue	3
Caraway	4	Ruta Baga	4
Fennel	5	Salsify	2
Garlic	8	Savory	8 or 4
Leek	3 or 4	Spinage	8 or 4
Lettuce	8 or 4	Squash	8 or 10
Mangel Wurtzel	8 or 10	Turnip	8 or 4

Some seeds retain their power of germination to an astonishing length of time, as will appear from facts stated by Prof. Lindley:

"Not to speak of the doubtful instances of seeds taken from the Pyramids having germinated, melons have been known to grow at the age of 40 years, kidney beans at 100, sensitive-plant at 60, rye at 40; and there are now growing, in the garden of the Horticultural Society, raspberry plants raised from seeds 1600 or 1700 years old." (See "Introduction to Botany," ed. 3, p. 358.)

But in selecting seeds, *fresh* ones should be had if possible. Where, however, the vegetable is cultivated for the sake of its flower, or its fruit, it is sometimes better to select old seed. Thus balsamines (the touch-me-not) and the cucumber, squash and melon tribe do better on seeds three or four years old; for fresh seeds produce plants whose growth will be too luxuriant for producing fruit; whereas from old seed, the plants have less vigor of growth but a greater tendency to fruit well.

FARMER'S GARDENS.

FARMERS are apt to have very inferior gardens. The plea is, that in the spring they have no time; the farm crops are of more importance. In consequence of such a decision, no garden will be had unless the housewife is willing to be gardenwife too. At her importunity at length one horse is put to the plow and the garden is broken up—say four inches deep. Possibly the boy is allowed to throw up the beds, but very often even this is left to woman's hand. She has to hunt up seed; peppers are pulled off from the ceiling and eviscerated; drawers are ransacked for the bag of radish seed or the paper of lettuce seed; the old broken pitcher is taken from its long seclusion on the top of the cupboard and emptied of its beans and peas; withal a few flower seeds are added to grace the stock—four o'clocks, poppies, marigolds, and touch-me-nots. Our gardenwife is not so admirable for lily hands or fair face, or fairy form. She cannot walk over dewy flowers without crushing them, as can a true heroine; for her specific gravity gives evidence of a good constitution, health and habits.

Her praise is, that in a new country where woman unquestionably suffers the most of hardships, she is cheerful, contented, industrious, enterprising, and, like women the world over, seeks to draw around herself objects of taste and beauty to decorate and cheer her husband's and her children's home; and, if necessary, to do it by the field-labor of her own hands. We could not forbear saying so much of the meritorious gardener of more than half the rural gardens in the West.

The seeds all mustered, she may be seen, after the breakfast things are all done up, busy with spade and hoe, hiding her treasures. And thus she does it. First a liberal suit of onion beds—savory vegetables to the tongue and most unsavory to the nose—making it almost impossible for these respectable neighbors to live together in peace, one or other of them being in bad odor with the other. Next, a seed-bed full of cabbages—significant to the imagination of cold-slaw, sourcrout, etc. A good row of peas, and a few hills of running beans are added. The alleys are ruffled with bush beans; a few early potatoes, some corn for roasting-ears, with a slender bed for beets, complete the stock of esculents. But sage, and summer savory, and thyme, and rue, and sweet marjoram, tansy, boneset and wormwood are attended to; a part for stuffing ducks and chickens— and the others for curing those who have been too much stuffed *with* them. The garden yields in due time its first fruits; the potatoes come and go, the corn is early plucked, lettuce shoots up its seed-stalk, peas render their tribute and grow sere, beans rattle in the pod, and before August her work is done and her garden forsaken except a small retinue of flowers, which are nursed to the last. Weeds now make up for lost time, and in a few weeks a weedy forest hides every trace of cultivation. This is not a fancy sketch; we have been far from drawing a picture from the worst specimens; it is a fair average case.

Our business is, not to quarrel with the farmer, but to suggest a better plan for his garden. We saw the plan stated some years ago; where, we have forgotten, but think well of it. It is simply this: let the garden be an oblong— say three times as long as it is broad—and cultivate it with the *plow*. Instead of having beds, let all seeds be planted in rows running the whole length of the garden. For example, begin with one row of beets—or more if wanted; next a row or rows of carrots, parsnips, cabbages, potatoes, corn, and all about three feet apart. The same system should be followed for small fruits—currants, gooseberries, strawberries, raspberries, etc.—and it will have this advantage over common gardens, that the bushes will have sun and air on all sides, and be more fruitful and more healthy for it. The whole garden, thus arranged, can be kept in order with very little labor. A single-horse plow will dress between the rows of the whole garden in a very little time and save all hand-hoeing. The hand-weeding in the row may be performed by women or children.

In large towns ground is scarce and labor abundant. Gardens, therefore, are properly laid out for economy of space. In the country the reverse is true; land is abundant but labor scarce and dear; of course gardens should be laid out not to save room, but to economize labor. The plan suggested will save labor, improve the garden, and take from the wife the drudgery of the spade and hoe.

EARLY DAYS OF SPRING.

If the soil be thrown up during the open weather into ridges, an immense number of insects will be unburrowed and destroyed; stiff clayey soils will be rendered more crumbling and mellow by exposure to frost. If advantage is taken of the weather to haul manure, let it be stacked up, and a little earth thrown over it, else the volatile and most valuable portions will escape. Ashes may be spread over the garden; a small portion of refuse salt will benefit the ground, and may be sown now. Clear the ground of all vines, stalks, haulm. If you have flowering bulbs, cover slightly with coarse manure—they will not be so much tried by the changes of temperature and moisture, and will flower stronger for it. Bright, dry days afford a fine time for going to the woods and cutting poles for your beans, stakes for your trees and dahlias, brush for peas, etc. While you are about it, collect moss from old logs, and put away in the barn or shed to cover the ground in summer where roses and shrubs have been newly set out, and require to be kept moist. If not done before, put two or three forks full of coarse green manure about tender shrubs

—Noisette and China roses. Freezing and thawing at the crown of the roots, destroys them oftener than anything else.

On mild days when the earth is open, sow lettuce seed in a warm corner, beat it gently with the back of the shovel, and cover it slightly with fine earth or old crumbling manure. You will have lettuce ten days earlier for your trouble. Pepper-grass and radishes may be sowed in like manner.

☞ Let alone the knife and saw. Your vines and trees will not be benefited by any pruning at this season.

PARLOR FLOWERS.

WATER freely such as are in pots, while in blossom. The flower stalks will be apt to shoot up taller and weaker than in the garden, and will require rods to support them. Let the rod be thrust down about *two inches* from the centre of the flower, and attach the flower stem to it by one or two ligaments. Flowers in small stove rooms can be kept in health with extreme difficulty. The heat forces their growth, or injures the leaves. They should be washed off once a week (either on a mild day out of doors, or in a warm room within, if the weather be severe), as the dust settles upon the leaf, and stops up the stomata (mouths) by which the leaf perspires and breathes. If green *aphides* infest them, put a pan of coals beneath the stand, and throw on a half-handful of coarse tobacco. In half an hour every insect will tumble off. Let such as lie on the surface of the earth be removed or crushed, as they will else revive. Plants should have *fresh air* every day.

A SALT RECIPE.

THERE is a great fashion, now-a-days, in all papers, to set forth useful recipes for every imaginable purpose. Every newspaper has its weekly budget of recipes. Our magazines have a page of original recipes; and, before long, why should not the *North American Review*, or the *Edinburgh Review* come out with their quarterly bill of fare reciped in full? So practical is our nineteenth century, that our literary men and women feel it to be a solemn duty to indite novel recipes for cooking, seasoning, removing stains, curing diseases, etc.; and why not? If one can invent a sonnet, an elegy, or worse yet, a poem, and thus draw people's brains a wool-gathering in the regions of imagination, ought they not to atone for their license by an invention equally substantial for the body? Miss Leslie writes a beautiful story, and a recipe for manipulating lobsters. Miss Martineau writes travels, political economies and suggestions on plum pudding. Mrs. Sigourney tunes her lyre with a hand most redolent of pies, cakes and gingerbread. Such is the aspect of culinary affairs, and the rights of women, that the day seems at hand when no learning will sustain a man, and no accomplishments a woman, who does not understand the art and mystery of cooking. It will be the duty of some future Heyne to give accurate recipes for all the feasts of Homer's heroes, the ingredients of all the Horacian drinking-bouts—the dishes of Virgil's fine fellows, as well as the minor matters of armor, language, manners, and customs; and a good lexicon, Hebrew, Greek, or Latin, must contain clearly written recipes for all the dishes used by the people whose language it sets forth. We have been led into this grand prairie of reflections by a recipe found in a country paper, which unquestionably is *salty*.

"INDIAN BAKED PUDDING.—Indian pudding is good and wholesome, baked. Scald a quart of milk, and stir in seven table spoonfuls of salt, a tea-cupful of molasses, and a great spoonful of ginger, or sifted cinnamon. Bake three or four hours. If you want whey you must be sure and pour in a little cold milk, after it is all mixed. Try it."

If Misses Leslie, Childs, etc., refuse to mother such a recipe, with *no* Indian meal in it, but *seven* mortal spoonfuls of salt, then we will consider it as emanating from Lot's wife. We are sure if one should eat many such puddings, he would speedily come to her estate.

———•◦•———

CULTURE OF CELERY.

WE know of no vegetable which requires more care and skill in its cultivation, from beginning to end, than celery. An inexperiened hand will be apt to fail in planting his seed, fail in preparing the trenches, and fail in earthing up the plants and bleaching them. And yet, celery is so generally a favorite that every family desires it, and every gardener is willing to cultivate it.

SEED SOWING.—The seed is exceedingly slow in germination, and, if not assisted artificially, will lie three and sometimes four weeks without sprouting. We soak the seed in water, (a solution of oxalic acid would be much better), for twenty-four hours: turn off the water, and then add and stir up a few handfuls of sand, well moistened, and let the seed stand in a stove room or other warm place, for two or three days. The sand will now be nearly dry; if it be not, add dry sand to it until it is perfectly powdery, and can be sown without falling in lumps. Besides hastening its germination, mixing the seed with sand enables the operator to sow it with greater facility and evenness. Select a *shaded* spot, let the earth be rich, rather inclined to moisture, and perfectly mellow. Sow the seed broadcast, and cover *very thinly* by sifting over it finely pulverized mold. Beat the bed gently with the back of the spade to settle the earth firmly about the seed. Don't fear that the seed will be troubled by beating; every seed should have the earth pressed to it by a smart stroke of the hoe, hand, spade, or by the pressure of a roller. If the weather is exceedingly warm and dry, cover your seed-bed with matting or old carpet, to retain the moisture. When up let them be well weeded, until they are six inches high, when they are to be removed to the trench for blanching.

FIRST TRANSPLANTING.—The process here detailed may be wholly omitted by those who are *obliged* to economize time and labor. But those who wish to do the very best that can be done—who wish to avoid spindling, weak plants, and secure strong and vigorous ones—transplant their celery to a level bed of very·rich soil, placing the plants four inches apart every way. They are cultivated here for about five weeks, when they will have attained a robust habit, or, technically, they will have became· *stocky*—for which purpose they were thus transplanted.

CELERY TRENCHES.—Dig your trenches about eighteen inches wide, and one foot deep, laying a shovelful of dirt alternately on each side of the trench, that it may be conveniently drawn in on both sides when you *earth up.* If you are favored with a very deep and rich loamy soil, such as often abounds in Western gardens, you will need little or no manure. But usually about four inches of *vegetable mold* and very *thoroughly rotted* manure, should be placed in the bottom of the trench and gently spaded in. No part of the culture is more critical than manuring. If the soil is slow, poor, and stingy, the celery will be dwarfish, tough and strong. On the other hand, if you employ new, rank, fiery manure, although you will have a vigorous growth, the stalks will be hollow, watery, coarse and flavorless. Let the manure be very thoroughly decayed and mixed half and half with leaf or vegetable mold.

Set the plants five inches apart, water them freely with a fine rosed watering pot, and, if the sun is fierce, cover the trenches daily from ten A.M. till evening with boards. In about a week they will begin to grow and will need no more shading.

Let them alone, except to weed, until the plants are from twelve to fifteen inches high—at which time they are to be earthed up.

EARTHING UP.—In dry weather, with a short, hand-hoe, draw in the earth gently from each side and bring it up carefully to the stalk. The soil must be kept *out of the* plant, and it is best for the first and perhaps the second time of earthing, to gather up the leaves in the left hand, and holding them together, to draw the earth about them. Fill in about once in two weeks, and *always when the plants are dry*. When the trench is full, the process is still to go on, and at the close of the season your plants will be exactly reversed—instead of standing in a trench they will top out from a high ridge.

SAVING CELERY IN WINTER.—Three ways may be mentioned. Letting it stand in the trench—in which case it should be covered with long straw and boards so laid over it that it will be protected from the *wet*, which is supposed to be more prejudicial to it than mere cold.

The Boston market gardeners dig it late in autumn, trim off the fibrous roots, cut off the top, lay it for two days in an airy shed, turning it, say twice a day, and then pack it in layers of perfectly *dry* sand, in a barrel. After laying two days to air it goes into the barrel much wilted, but regains its plumpness, and comes out as fresh as from the trench.

Lastly, it may be put in rows on the cellar bottom, without trimming, and earth heaped up about it. Set a plank at an angle of forty-five degrees and bank up the earth against it, set a row of roots and cover them with dirt, then another row and so on.

Solid celery is not a particular variety—any celery is solid when properly grown—and if grown too rankly the most *solid* celery in the world will be hollow.

We have seen it recommended to water the trenches once or twice during the season with a weak brine of salt and water. Besides the fertilizing effect of salt, it will have the effect of retaining moisture in the soil, and what is of yet more moment, it destroys the parasitical fungus (*Puccinca Heraclei*) which attacks and rusts the plant, and probably would, also, guard it against a maggot which is apt to infest and very much injure it. There is an insect, which, in very dry weather, is apt to sting the leaf and cause it to wilt. While the dew is on in the morning, sift lime over the plants once or twice, and it will check the fly.

If any think these directions too minute and the process vexatious, they are at liberty to try a cheaper method—and may, once in a while, succeed. But a certain crop, year by year, cannot be expected without exact and very careful cultivation. We have learned this by sorrowful experience.

The main crop of celery need not be placed in the trenches until the middle of July or the first of August. It's greatest growth will be in the fall months.

———•◆•———

SEEDLING TREES.—Many trees which are entirely hardy when grown, are very tender during the first and second winters. Cover them with straw, refuse garden gatherings, leaves, etc. Sometimes it is best to raise them and *lay them in by the heels*, by which those gardeners designate the operation of laying trees in trenches or excavations, and covering the roots and a considerable portion of the stems. This will not be extra labor in all cases when the young trees are to be reset, at any rate, the second year in nursery rows.

CULTURE OF PIE-PLANT.

BEGINNERS should in all cases, if possible, obtain a supply of plants, from a proved sort, by dividing the root. Raising from seed is an after, and an amateur practice. The first object with every man is to supply his family with this esculent, and not to experiment with new sorts. Let him buy or beg from garden or nursery, enough buds to establish a bed, of some kind already known to be good.

The *best* season of the year for dividing the root is in the spring; the next best is in late autumn; and the worst in midsummer—as we have abundantly ascertained by experiment. The reason is plain. Like bulbs, and tubers, the root of the pie-plant stores up in itself during one season, a supply of organizable matter enough to enable it to start off the next season, without any dependence upon the soil. Dahlias, potatoes, onions, turnips, cabbages, etc., it is well known, are able to grow for a considerable time, in the spring, without any connection with the soil; being sustained by that supply which they had treasured up within themselves the previous autumn. When this is exhausted, they will die, if they have not been put in connection with food from without. When pie-plant is divided in the spring, it is full of the material of life, and a bud cut off from the main root with a portion of the root attached, has a supply of food until new roots are emitted, which in good soil and weather will be in about a week. There is the same vitality in autumn, and the only reason why it is not so good for transplanting as spring, is the risk that the buds and roots will rot off during the winter. A uniform winter will scarcely injure one in a hundred, but constant changes, freezing and thawing, will weaken, if not destroy many of them. When, however, it is necessary to divide and transplant in the fall, cover the bed full four inches deep with coarse, strong manure. Although great care will enable one to transplant a section of the root in midsummer, yet we have found that when no more attention is paid than in spring, nine plants are lost out of ten. The reason is obvious. There is no reserved treasure of sap in the root in summer, such as gives it vitality in spring or autumn. If for any reason we *must* take up a root in summer, let every possible fibre be saved, the plant well watered and sheltered until it begins to grow again.

RAISING FROM SEED.—The origination of new varieties of fruits, flowers and esculent vegetables is one of the greatest rewards of gardening. Almost every seed of the pie-plant will produce a variety. We have thought ourselves repaid for trouble if one in fifty seedling plants were worth saving. It requires a full two years' trial to improve a sort. Of fifty plants, say twenty-five may be rejected peremptorily the first season, the petioles being mere wires. Of the other twenty-five, one or two will give great promise, and the others will be doubtful. Let them be transplanted in the spring of the second season, into very mellow, rich, deep loam, full three feet apart every way, and here they may stand until the owner is fully satisfied, by the trial of one or more seasons, which are good and which inferior. In marking seedling plants, the cultivator should bear in mind that there are *two* kinds required, viz. a very early sort, and one for the later and main supply. If a plant has small stalks, and is *late* too, reject it of course. If it be very *early*, it may be valuable even if quite small. Some sorts are fit for plucking five or six weeks before others; we have a variety which comes forward almost the moment the frost leaves the ground in the spring, or in warm spells in winter.

In selecting a late sort from your seedlings, several qualities must be consulted. The plant should manifest an indisposition to go to seed; should be apt to throw out an abundance of leaves, to supply those taken off; the petioles should be large; the meat rich and substantial. There is great difference between one sort and another in the amount of sugar required, in the delicacy of flavor, and in the property of stewing to a pulp, without wasting away.

A good variety of pie-plant, then, should be a vigorous grower, prolific, large in the stalk, not apt to flower, of a sprightly acid without any earthy or woody taste, not stewing away more than one-third when cooked, and not requiring too much sugar.

We have observed in our trials that seedlings having smooth leaves, with the upper surface varnished and glossy, are seldom good; while every plant which we have thought worth keeping, had the upper surface of its leaves of a deep, dull, lack-lustre green.

FORMATION OF A BED.—Select a strong and rich loam Let it be spaded full two feet deep. If the subsoil has never been worked, and is clay, or gravel, a large supply of old manure should be mixed with it. Our working-method is this: Mark off the square, begin on one side, lay out a full spadeful of the top-soil clear across the bed; lay four or five inches of manure in the trench, and then spade it down a full twelve inches deep; beginning again by the side of the first trench, put the top-soil of the second into the first; add manure and spade as before; and so across the bed. The surface-soil thrown out of the first trench may be wheeled down and put into the *last* one. This process will leave the bed much higher than it was; let it stand one or two weeks to settle. If the bed is prepared in autumn it will be better, and in the spring it may be half-spaded again before planting.

Mark out, by line, rows three feet apart, and set your plants in the rows three feet from plant to plant, if of the large kind, and two feet, if of the small. Very large varieties require four feet every way. The buds should be left just below the surface of the soil.

AFTER CULTURE.—Through the summer keep the surface mellow and free from weeds. In the fall of the year, when the leaves show signs of falling, form a compost heap of

fine charcoal, if you can get it from blacksmith's or elsewhere, vegetable mold, ashes, and very old manure. Spread
and spade in a good coat of this, spading lightly near to the
plants and deeply between them. When frost destroys the
tops wholly, cover the bed with coarse, strong manure
about four inches deep, smooth it down, and let it remain
thus. The next spring stir the surface smartly with a rake,
and no further care will be required except to pluck out any
weeds that grow through the summer.

GATHERING.—Leaves are constantly springing from the
centre. Of course the full-grown ones will be on the outside. These should be harvested, leaving the inside ones
to mature. By going regularly over your bed, and taking
in turn the outside leaves, a bed may be used till July without the slightest injury. Other fruit, after that time,
usually displaces pie-plant and leaves it to rest the
remainder of the year. The leaf-stalks should not be *cut*
off. Slide the hand down as near as possible to the root,
and give the stalk a backward and sidewise wrench and it
will be detached at a joint or articulation, and no stump
will be left to rot and injure the root—we usually cut off
the leaves on the spot, leaving them about the root, both
for shade to the ground and for manure.

———•••———

PRESERVE YOUR POT-PLANTS.—We warn ladies having
pot-plants designed for winter-wear, to be prudent *before
hand*, or some frosty night will cut every tender plant left
out, and *then* prudence will be good for nothing. Every
one who pretends to keep parlor plants should own a
thermometer. If at sundown or at nine o'clock it stands
anywhere near forty degrees, your plants are in danger.
Sometimes it will fall, in one night, from fifty degrees to
below thirty-two degrees, which last is the freezing point.

SUN-FLOWER SEED.

To some extent this is likely to become a profitable crop. Medium lands will yield, on an average, fifty bushels; while first-rate lands will yield from seventy to a hundred bushels.

MODE OF CULTIVATION.—The ground is prepared in all respects as for a corn crop, and the seed sown in drills four feet apart—one plant to every eighteen inches in the drill. It is to be plowed and tended in all respects like a crop of corn.

HARVESTING.—As the heads ripen, they are gathered, laid on a barn floor and threshed with a flail. The seed shells very easily.

USE.—The seed may be employed in fattening hogs, feeding poultry, etc., and for this last purpose it is better than grain. But the seed is more valuable at the *oil-mill* than elsewhere. It will yield a gallon to the bushel without trouble; and by careful working, more than this. Hemp yields one and a fourth gallons to the bushel, and flax-seed one and a half by ordinary pressure; but two gallons under the hydraulic press.

The oil has, as yet, no established market price. It will range from seventy cents to a dollar, according as its value shall be established as an article for lamps and for painters' use. But at seventy cents a gallon for oil, the seed would command fifty-five cents a bushel, which is a much higher price than can be had for corn.

It is stated, but upon how sufficient proof we know not, that sun-flower oil is excellent for burning in lamps. It has also been tried by our painters to some extent; and for *inside* work, it is said to be as good as linseed oil. Mr. Hannaman, who has kindly put us in possession of these facts, says, that the oil resembles an *animal*, rather than a vegetable oil; that it has not the *varnish* properties of the linseed oil. We suppose by varnish is meant, the albumen and mucilage which are found in vegetable oils. The following analysis of *hemp-seed*, and *flax-seed*, or as it is called in England lint or linseed, will show the proportions of various ingredients in one hundred parts.

	Hemp-seed. (Bucholz.)	Linseed. (Leo Meier.)
Oil,	19.1	11.3
Husk, etc.	38.3	44.4
Woody fibre and starch,	5.0	1.5
Sugar, etc.	1.6	10.8
Gum,	9.0	7.1
Soluble albumen (Casein?)	24.7	15.1
Insoluble do.	—	3.7
Wax and resin,	1.6	3.1
Loss,	0.7	3.0
	100	100

The existence of impurities in oil, such as mucilage, albumen, gum, etc., which increase its value to the painter, diminishes its value for the *lamp*, since these substances crust or cloy the wick, and prevent a clear flame. All oils may, therefore, the less excellent they are for painting, be regarded as the more valuable for burning. *Rape-seed* is extensively raised in Europe, chiefly in Flanders, for its oil, and is much used for burning. Ten quarts may be extracted from a bushel of seed. We append a table representing the richness of various seeds, etc., in oil.

	Oil per cent.
Linseed (flax)	11 to 22
Hemp-seed,	14 to 25
Rape-seed,	40 to 70
Poppy-seed,	36 to 33
White mustard-seed,	36 to 48
Black mustard-seed,	15
Swedish turnip-seed,	34
Sun-flower seed,	15
Walnut kernels..	40 to 70

Hazel-nut kernels,...............................	60
Beech-nut kernels,.. ....,.....	15 to 17
Plum-stone do.	33
Sweet almond kernels,...........................	40 to 54
Bitter do. do...............................	28 to 46

————•••————

APRIL GARDEN-WORK.

EVERY one will now be at work in the garden. A few suggestions may make your garden better.

PLOWING GARDENS.—We do not like the practice except when the garden is large, and the owner unable to meet the expense of *spading*. But if you must plow, let that be well done. Those contemptible little one-horse plows, with which most gardens are plowed, should be discarded. The best plowing will be too shallow, but these spindling little plows, drawn by a little meagre horse, will skim over your ground, averaging from three to four inches deep, and preparing your soil to receive the utmost possible detriment from summer droughts. What chance have young roots, or the finer fibres of plants, to penetrate more than a few inches of surface-soil? Persons come to our garden and wonder why some vegetables flourish so well, while they never have luck with them, "It must be a difference of soil." No, it is the difference of working it. Give your vegetables a chance to descend eighteen or twenty inches if they incline to it, and you will have no more trouble. A large plow should be used, and you should stand by and *see* that it is *put in to the beam*. A garden soil is usually mellow, and a plow can go to its full depth without hurting the horses.

SPADING.—This mode of working the ground will always be employed by those ambitious of having a *first-rate* garden. Indeed, where there is much shrubbery and permanent beds. as of asparagus, pie-plant, strawberry, and plantations of currants, raspberries, etc., spading is the only method which *can* be employed.

SPADING SHRUBBERY.—Let very fine manure be spread about roses, honeysuckles, and ornamental shrubs (where they are not standing in a grass-lawn). Beginning at the plant, with great care turn over the soil one or two inches deep, yet so as not to injure the fibres; gradually deepen the stroke of your spade as you go out from the plant; at two feet from the shrub you may put in the spade half its depth, and at three feet to its full depth. You will of course cut many roots, but they will very soon re-form and send out fibres, and by the manure spaded in, be supplied with abundant nourishment for the season.

SPADING FLOWER BEDS.—This requires a practised hand. There is danger of wounding and displacing clumps of flower-roots, or of filling the crowns with dirt, or of leaving the surface uneven, and the edges ragged. If there is a skillful gardener to be had, hire it done, and watch while he performs, for any man who has seen a thing done in a garden once, ought to be ashamed if he cannot himself do it afterwards.

SPADING VEGETABLE BEDS.—Asparagus, pie-plant, straw-berries, etc., require enriching every year, and to have the manure forked or spaded in. It is easy to perform this upon strawberries, and a spade is preferable. A three or four-pronged fork is better for asparagus and pie-plant. Be careful not to tear or cut the crowns of the plants. No material injury ensues from clipping the side fibres, *in the spring;* in summer, when a plant requires all its mouths to supply sap for its extended surface of leaf, it is not wise to cut the roots or fibres at all, but only to keep the surface mellow and friable.

DEEP SPADING.—Ames' garden-spades measure twelve inches in length of blade. In a good soil the foot may gain one or two additional inches by a good thrust. Thus the soil is mellowed to the depth of fourteen inches. This will do very well; but if you aspire to do the very best, another course must be first pursued. The first spadeful must be thrown out, and a second depth gained, and then the top soil returned. This is comparatively slow and laborious, but it need not be done more than once in five years, and by dividing the garden into sections, and performing this *thorough-spading* on one of the sections each year, the process will be found, practically, less burdensome than it seems to be.

GETTING POOR ON RICH LAND AND RICH ON POOR LAND.

A CLOSE observer of men and things told us the following little history, which we hope will plow very deeply into the attention of all who plow very shallow in their soils.

Two brothers settled together in —— county. One of them on a cold, ugly, clay soil, covered with black-jack oak, not one of which was large enough to make a half dozen rails. This man would never drive any but large, powerful, Conastoga horses, some seventeen hands high. He always put *three* horses to a large plow, and plunged it in some ten inches deep. This deep plowing he invariably practised and cultivated thoroughly afterward. He raised his seventy bushels of corn to the acre.

This man had a brother about six miles off, settled on a rich White River bottom-land farm—and while a black-jack clay soil yielded seventy bushels to the acre, this fine bottom-land would not average fifty. One brother was steadily growing rich on poor land, and the other steadily growing poor on rich land.

One day the bottom-land brother came down to see the black-jack oak farmer, and they began to talk about their crops and farms, as farmers are very apt to do.

"How is it," said the first, "that you manage on this poor soil to beat me in crops?"

They reply was "*I* WORK *my land.*"

That was it, exactly. Some men have such rich land that they won't *work* it; and they never get a step beyond where they began. They rely on the *soil*, not on labor, or skill, or care. *Some men expect their* LANDS *to work, and some men expect to* WORK THEIR LAND;—and that is just the difference between a good and a bad farm er.

When we had written thus far, and read it to our informant, he said, "three years ago I travelled again through that section, and the only good farm I saw was this very one of which you have just written. All the others were desolate—fences down—cabins abandoned, the settlers discouraged and moved off. I thought I saw the same old stable door, hanging by one hinge, that used to disgust me ten years before; and I saw no change except for the worse in the whole county, with the single exception of this one farm."

GETTING READY FOR WINTER.

HAUL tanbark and bank up around the house to insure a warm cellar. Cellar windows should be kept open through the day, and closed after the nights begin to freeze, as late in the season as possible. See that dry walks are prepared from the house to all the out-houses. Do not be stingy of your materials; make the paths high and rounding, so as to insure dryness, especially about the barn. See that stones, gravel, or timber are laid so as to be out of the way of cattle's feet, and just in the way of your own. We have seen swamp-barn-yards, before going into which a prudent man would choose to make his will. Mud on the shoes from roads and fields is all well enough; but mud from one's own

10

yards, shows that the owner has not fixed up as he ought to have done.

If your stables are old, examine the floor; or some night may let a horse through, to come out lame for life. If you have a dirt floor, see that it is carefully laid, and remember that if it be inclined either way, it should be *from* the rack and not *toward* it. Let your wagons, carts, plows, etc., be repaired during the fall and winter, and not be left till spring. See that your shingles are all sound on the house, barn, and shed. The leak which you have allowed to drop, drop, drop all summer has at last taken off a yard or two of plaster, and it is time now to put on a shingle or two. There is another leak or two that *must* be stopped. That pocket of yours which has let out dime after dime for liquor, the hole getting bigger and bigger every year, now is the time to sow *it* up, or it will rip *you* up. A pocket is a small place, to be sure, but we have seen barns, cattle, and acre after acre slip through a hole in it which, at first, was only large enough to let sixpence through.

See that all your tools have a safe and dry standing-place; hoes rakes, scythes, sickles, yokes, spades, shovels, chains, pins, harrows, plows, carts, and sleds, axes, mattocks, hammers, and everything, but your geese and ducks, should be kept from wet and snow.

If you have no stables for your cattle, you should have good sheds provided, opening to the south. Even when cattle are allowed to run through the stock-fields, there ought to be in some warm place an ample shed to which they can resort during wet and cold weather; and one sufficiently snug can be made without calling in the carpenter or buying lumber.

ESCULENT VEGETABLES.

WE mention some of the more common kinds of garden esculent vegetables, to point out the best kinds, and give some hints for their cultivation. If more vegetables were raised and eaten in the place of meat, there would be fewer diseases, and less expense for medicine than is now the case among those who eat so heartily and liberally of the *fat* of the land.

BEET.—The turnip-rooted blood beet should be sown for the earliest crop; the long blood beet for the late crop, and for winter use. The *blood beet* is the proper garden beet. The *scarcity*, the sugar beets (so called), white, yellow, and red, are inferior for table use. Every year we see accounts of new varieties, which are seldom mentioned a second time, while these old standard sorts hold their own from year to year. We see people running around among their neighbors for *beet*-seed, careless whether it is early or late, coarse fleshed or fine grained, sweet or insipid. It is just as easy and cheap to have the best seed of the best kinds, as to have refuse seed of worthless kinds. Lately, a variety introduced from France, called *Bassano*, has attracted attention and commendation.* It is early, tender, and sweet. If you attempt to raise your own seed, let only *one* sort stand in the garden; otherwise bees and other insects will mix them, and the purity of the variety will be

---

* A new variety called the *Bassano* has been recently introduced into France, and extensively cultivated; and it is said to be found in all the markets from Venice to Genoa, in the month of June. It is remarkable for the form of the root, which is flattened like a turnip. The skin is red, the flesh white, veined with rose. It is very tender, very delicate, preserving its rose colored rings after cooking, and from two to two and a half inches in diameter. This description is from the *Bon Jardinier* for 1841. The edition for 1842 states that this variety is highly esteemed in the north of Italy, and that it is, in fact, one of the best kinds for the table.—*Hovey's Magazine.*

lost. We very seldom see an unmixed variety in common gardens, unless seed have been bought from good seedsmen.

The best seed is a small black seed about the size of a pin head, enveloped in a ragged, rough, two or three lobed husk. Every *seeming* seed planted, then, is a mere envelope of two or more seeds, and two or three plants come up, very much to the surprise of the inexperienced, for each husk. When a little advanced, they are to be thinned out to one in a place.

We prefer planting very early, and in rows eight inches apart and at about *one inch* distant in the row. As the plants begin to gain size they make very delicate greens; and for this purpose are to be boiled, leaf, root, and all. Continue to thin out until one is left for every six inches for full growth.

Every year a great ado is made about monstrous beets— twenty and thirty pounders. There is no objection to these giants, unless they beget an idea that *size* is the test of merit. For table-use, *medium sized* fruits and vegetables are every way preferable; a beet should never be larger than a goose-egg.

It is equally foolish to suppose that large, coarse-grained vegetables, whether potatoes, beets, parsnips, ruta bagas, or anything else, are as good for stock, though not so palatable to men. To be sure they fill up. But that which is nutriment to man is nutriment to beast; a vegetable which is rank and watery is no better for my cow than for us. It is not the *bulk* but the *quality* that measures the fitness of articles for food.

PARSNIP.—This vegetable is, to those who are fond of it, very desirable, as coming in at a time when other things are failing. For, although the parsnip attains its size by autumn, yet its flavor seems to depend upon its receiving a pretty good frosting. It may be dug at open spells through the winter and early in the spring. It gives one of the first indications of returning warmth, and its green leaves are among the first which cheer the garden. On this account it must be dug early in the spring and housed, or it will spoil by growth.

We know of no difference in varieties. The *Guernsey*, is not a different sort from the common, but only the common sort, very highly cultivated in that island, where it sometimes grows to a length of four feet. The *hollow-crowned* and *Siam* are mentioned in English catalogues, as fine fleshed and flavored, but we have never been able to obtain seed of them.

The parsnip (*Pastinacea sativa*) is a native of Great Britain and is found wild by the road-sides, delighting particularly in calcareous soils. It has hitherto been supposed that the seed would not retain its germinating power more than one year, but Mr. Mendenhall states that he has raised freely from four year old seed. The parsnip is much sown as a field crop at the east, yielding 1,000 bushels, on good land, to the acre. They are invaluable both to cows and horses. The quantity and quality of milk in cows is improved; and no farmer with whom butter-making is a considerable object of interest, should be without a root crop—beet, carrot, or ruta baga.

CARROT. (*Daucus carota*).—This is a native of Great Britain. The early horn and Altringham are the best varieties sold by our seedsmen. Beside their use upon the table, they are largely and deservedly cultivated in the field for stock. A horse becomes more fond of them than of oats, and they do not, like the potato, require boiling before feed ing out. A thousand bushels may be raised to the acre. The premium of the New York Agricultural Society for the year 1844, was to a crop of 1,059 bushels the acre. The seed should be new each year, as it will not come well even the second year, and not at all if kept yet longer.

RADISH.—Every garden has its bed of radishes, and they

are among the first spring gifts. They will grow in any soil, but not in all equally well. A mellow sandy loam is best; or rather that soil is best which will grow them the quickest. If they are a long time in growing, they are tough and stringy. It is said that a compost of the following materials will produce them very early and finely. Take equal parts of buckwheat bran and fresh horse-dung, dig them in plentifully into the soil where you intend to sow. Within two days a plentiful crop of toadstools will start up. Spade them under, and sow your seed, and the radishes will come forward rapidly, and be tender and free from worms.

The *short-top scarlet*, is the best for spring planting. It is so named, because, from its rapid growth the top is yet small when the root is fit for the table. There is a white and red turnip-rooted variety, also good for spring use. The turnip-rooted kinds have not only the shape, but something of the sweetness and flavor of the turnip, and are by some preferred to all others. For summer planting, there is a yellow turnip-rooted sort and the summer white. For fall and early winter, the white and black Spanish are planted. When radishes are sown broadcast, it must be very thinly, for if at all crowded they run to top, and refuse to form edible roots. For our own use, we sow on the edges of beds, devoted to onions, beets, etc., and thrust each seed down with the finger.

The radish (*Raphanus sativus*) is a native of China, and was introduced to England before 1584.

SALSIFY, OR VEGETABLE OYSTER.—We esteem this to be a much better root for table use than either the parsnip or carrot. It is cultivated in all respects as these crops are. Some have been skeptical as to their possessing an oyster flavor. They seldom attain the true taste until, like the parsnip, they have been well frosted. But if dug up during spells in winter and early in the spring, and cooked by an orthodox formula, they are strikingly like the oyster.

We have just consulted the oracle of our kitchen, and give forth the following method of cooking it: First, oblige your husband to raise a good supply of them. When you have obtained them, scrape off the outside skin—cut the root lengthwise into thin slices—put them into a spider and iust cover with hot water. Let them boil until a fork will pass through them easily. Without turning off the water, season them with butter, pepper, and salt, and sprinkle in a little flour—enough to thicken the liquor slightly. Then eat them.

The success of this gustatory deception depends, more than anything else, upon the skill in seasoning. If well done they are not merely an apology, but they are a very excellent substitute for the shell-fish himself; a thousand times better than pickled can-oysters—those arrant libels upon all that is dear in the remembrance of a live oyster.

Every one may save seed for himself, as it will not, if well cultivated, degenerate. It is a biennial, and roots may either be set out, or left standing where they were planted. When the seed begins to feather out it must be immediately gathered, or like the dandelion or thistle, it will be blown away by the wind. This vegetable should be much more extensively cultivated than it is.

BEANS.—There are three kinds—English dwarf, kidney dwarf or string, and the pole beans. The first kind, so far as our experience has gone, are coarser than the others, and, in our hot and dry summers, are very difficult to raise.

Of kidney or bush beans, there is a long catalogue of sorts. The *Mohawk* is good for its hardiness, enduring spring frosts with comparative impunity. The *red-speckled valentine* is highly commended. But after a trial of some twenty kinds, we are entirely contented with one—the *China red-eye*. It is early, hardy, very prolific, and well flavored.

Of the pole beans, one sort, the *Lima*, might supersede all others were it a little earlier. It is immensely prolific;

its flavor unrivalled, and nearly the same in the dry bean as when cooked in its green state, a quality which has never, we believe, been found in any other variety. To supply the deficiency of this variety in earliness, we know of none equal to the *Horticultural*. With these two kinds one has no need of any other. Pole beans will not bear frost, and are among the last seeds to be planted, seldom before the last of April. The bush-bean may precede them a fortnight.

The English dwarf (*Vicia faba*) is a native of Egypt; but has been cultivated in England from time immemorial, and, it is supposed, was introduced by the Romans.

The kidney dwarf (*Phaseolus vulgaris*) is a native of India, and was introduced into England about the year 1597.

The pole bean (*Phaseolus 'multifloris*) is a native of South America, and was introduced to England in 1633.

Pole beans are not strictly annuals. In a climate where the winter does not destroy them they bear again the second year, and we believe yet longer. Gov. Pinney, of Liberia, on the African coast, stated in a lecture, speaking of the vegetable productions of that region, that the bean was a permanent vine like the grape, bearing its crops from year to year without replanting. The bush bean is strictly an annual. If the pole bean were protected in the ground, or raised and put away like sweet potatoes, dahlias, etc., in the cellar and replanted in the spring it would bear again the second season. Perhaps an earlier crop of beans might thus be secured.

The bean crop, by field culture, is not to be overlooked. Great quantities of dried beans are consumed by families, by the army and in the navy, and they always bear a good price, when they are well grown and well cured. They are excellent for sheep, not from their fattening properties, but for improving their fleece. Analysis has shown them to be rich in those properties which are " wool-gathering."

FIELD ROOT CROPS.

FROM mid-winter, and especially *just before* spring opens, beets, carrots, parsnips, potatoes, ruta baga, and mangel wurtzel are of the highest utility. After months of dry fodder, and of slops thickened with corn-meal, cattle need—their stomach, their blood need—a change of diet; and none can be better than roots. At the East it is no longer a debatable question—root crops are as regularly laid in as grain or grass crops. The chief difficulty at the East, in introducing "new-fangled notions," arises from the regular routine habits of farmers and their settled aversion to change from old ways. Very little of this spirit exists at the West. There the very essence of life is *change*. The population have broken up from old homesteads, moved off from old States, abandoned the comforts and settled life of long tilled agricultural districts—to come into a new country, where they *have* to practise new ways, live differently, and labor by new methods; and, by consequence, the farming community of the West are remarkably free to meet and adopt agricultural improvements. But the difficulty lies in a different direction. The farmers have large farms—are ambitious of large crops, large herds of cattle, large droves of hogs, and of a style of husbandry which brings in a large pile, and all at once; so that the idea of *good* farming is *large* farming. Many a sturdy Kentuckian will very patiently plow, two or three times, his fifty or hundred acres of corn, and think nothing of it; but to put in half an acre of carrots, or beets, to weed and work, to harvest and store the vexatious little crop, this seems a piddling business. Our big prairie farmers, our heavy bottom-land farmers, our stock farmers who "hog" one or two hundred acres of corn, of their own planting or of their neighbor's, they do not love *little* work. We know a man who lives on thirty acres of land of about a middling quality. He winters seven cows, two horses, and two pigs. He raises corn and grass

10*

enough for his own use, and sells none. Every year he puts in about a quarter of an acre of parsnips, or ruta baga, for winter and spring fodder. His garden in summer, and his dairy all the year round, are represented in market. He probably does not receive five dollars at *once*, on any one sale, through the year. We never looked into that old chest under his bed; but we will venture much, that if the shrewd housewife would keep her eagle eyes off long enough to give us a chance, it would be found that this man has made, and laid up, more money in the last five years from his thirty acres, than any farmer about here from six times the amount. Our farmers *have not grown rich on large and careless farming; but many are growing rich on small farms and careful husbandry.*

When the dairy shall be more thought of—when wintering stock, and fattening it, shall be more carefully studied— we predict that our farmers will annually raise thousands of bushels of roots, and have capacious cellars under their barns to store them in.

— • • • —

CULTIVATION OF FRUIT-TREES.

WE must give up thinking of *remedies* for blights and diseases of fruit-trees and seek after *preventives*. Amputation may limit its ravages; but surgery is not a remedy, but a resource after remedies fail. We must, it seems to us, look for a preventive in a wiser system of fruit cultivation. To this subject we shall now speak.

The effect of cultivation in changing the habits of plants is familiar to all. Incident to this artificial condition of the plant, there will be new diseases, vegetable vices, which, as they result from cultivation, must be regarded in every perfect system of cultivation.

Where trees are grown for timber, or shade, or orna-

ment, everything can be sacrificed to the production of
wood and foliage.   But in fruit-trees wood is nothing and
fruit is everything.   We push for *quantity* and *quality* of
fruit; and would not regard the wood or foliage at all, if it
were not indispensable as a means of procuring fruit.   That
is the most skillful treatment of fruit-trees which involves a
just compromise between the wants of the *tree*, and the
abundance and excellence of *fruit*.   There is a way of gaining fruit by a rapid consumption of the tree; and there is a
method of gaining fruit by invigorating and prolonging the
tree.   Two systems of cultivation grow out of these different methods—a natural system and an artificial system.
All *cultivation* is artificial, even the rudest.   By natural
system, then, is only meant a treatment which interferes
but *little* with nature; and by artificial, a system in which
skill is applied to every part of the vegetable economy.
For conservatories, gardens, and experimental grounds,
there is no reason why an artificial system should not exist.
Moral considerations restrain us from stimulating a man or a
beast to procure a quick or a large return at the expense of
life and limb; but in vegetable matters our *preference* or
interest is the only restraint.   If any reason exists for forcing a tree to bear young, and enormously, and after ten
years' service for throwing it away, it is proper to do it.
For larger show-fruit we *ring* a limb expecting to sacrifice
the branch; we diminish the life of the pear by putting it
to a dwarf habit by violent means.   If we have any sufficiently desirable object to accomplish, there is no reason
why we should not do it.   There may be as good reasons
for limiting a tree to ten years as a strawberry bed to
three.

   There is another form of the artificial system in which
there *is* much to censure.   When fruit-trees are set in gardens, yards, etc., to be permanent, and *long-lived*, it is folly
to apply to them that high-toned treatment which belongs
to an artificial system as I have spoken of it above.

Impatient of delay, the cultivator presses his trees forward by stimulating applications, or retards them by violent interference—by prunings at the root or branch, by bending or binding; everything is sacrificed for early and abundant bearing. Fine fruit yards, designed to last a hundred years, are served with a treatment proper only to a conservatory or experimental garden. This high-toned system is still more vicious when applied to orchards and especially to pear orchards; and it seems to us that much is to be learned and much unlearned before we shall have attained a true science of pear culture. Let us consider some facts. It is well known that seedling apple-trees are generally longer lived than grafted varieties, and obnoxious to fewer diseases. The same is true of the pear-tree. It has frequently been said that *seedling* and *wilding* pears were not subject to the blight. This is not true if such trees are undergoing the same cultivation as grafted sorts; it is not always true when they exist in an untutored state; but when they are left to themselves, they certainly are *less* obnoxious to the blight and to disease of any kind, than are grafted and cultivated varieties. A comparison between wild and tame, between cultivated and natural, between seedling and and grafted fruit, is certainly to the advantage of seedling uncultivated fruit, *in respect to the* HEALTH *of the tree*—of course it is not in respect to quality of fruit. In connection with these facts, consider another, that seedling and wilding fruit is nearly twice as long in coming into bearing as are cultivated varieties. The seedling apple bears at from ten to fourteen years. The pear bears at from fifteen to eighteen years. But upon cultivation the grafted pear and apple bear in from five to eight years. It is noticeable that, although the pear as a wilding is four or five years longer in coming to a bearing state than the apple, yet, upon cultivation, they both bear at about the same age from the bud or graft. In a private letter from Robert Manning (we prize it as among the last he ever wrote; another, received not long after, was *dictated;* but signed by his tremulous hand in letters which speak of death), he says, " *Pears bear as soon as apples of the same age;* on the quince much sooner," etc.

It appears, then, that while cultivation accelerates the period of fruit-bearing and perfects the fruit, it is also accompanied with premature age and liability to diseases. we do not wish to be understood as opposing the habit of *cultivating* fruit, or as prejudiced against grafted varieties —we are neither opposed to the one nor to the other. But we would deduce from facts, some conclusions which will enable us to perfect our fruits by a more discriminating treatment.

The question will arise, Is it only by accident that liability to disease increases, with increase of cultivation? Is there an *inherent* objection in *all* artificial treatment? or is there objection only to particular methods of artificial cultivation?

Although there may be too many exceptions, to allow of our saying, that quickly-growing timber is not durable, it may be said in respect to trees of the same species, that the durability of the timber depends (among other things) on the slowness of its growth. Mountain timber is usually tougher and more lasting than champaign wood; timber growing in the great alluvial valleys of the West, is notoriously more perishable than that grown in the parsimonious soils of the North and East.

The reason does not seem obscure. In a rich soil, and under an ardent sun, not only is the growth of trees greater in any given season, than in a poor soil, but the growth is coarser and the grain coarser. But what is a *coarse* growth, and what is fine-grained, or coarse-grained timber?—timber in which the vascular system has been greatly distended, in which sap-vessels and air-cells are large and coarse. Where wood is formed with great rapidity and with a superabundance of sap, not only will there be large ducts and vessels, but the sap itself will be but imperfectly elaborated by the leaves. We may suppose that overfeeding in vegetables is, in its effects, analogous to overfeeding in animals. The sap is but imperfectly decomposed in the leaf—it passes into the channels for elaborated sap in a partially undigested state—it deposits imperfect secretions, and the whole tissue resulting from it will partake of the defects of the *proper juice.**

Thus a too rapid growth not only enlarges the sap passages, but forms their sides and the whole vegetable tissue of imperfect matter. This accounts, not only for the perishableness of quickly-grown timber, but, doubtless, for the short-lived tendency of cultivated fruit in comparison with *wildings*. For where the tissue is imperfectly formed, general weakness must ensue.

These reasonings do not include plants which, in their original nature, have a system of large sap-vessels, etc., and which naturally are rapid growers, but respects only plants which have been forced to this condition by circumstances.

Has this condition of the vegetable substance nothing to do with the health of a tree? Does it not very much determine its liability to disease?—its excitability? Where are trees liable to diseases of the circulation? In England, in New England, where, by climate and soil, growth is slow?—or in the Western and Middle States, where, by climate, by soil, and by vicious treatment, the growth is excessive? This leads me to review the methods employed in rearing fruit-trees.

The nursery business is a commercial business, and aims at *profit*. It is the interest of nurserymen to sell largely, and to bring their trees into market in the shortest possible time from the planting of the seed and the setting of the

---

* For the young reader it may be necessary to say, that when sap is first taken up by the roots it is called *true sap ;* but after it has undergone a change in the leaves it is called *proper juice.*

bud, to the sale of the tree. But independently of this, few nurserymen know, accurately, the nature of the plants which they cultivate, and still less the habits of each variety. Why should they, when learned pomologists are content to know as little as they? The trees are highly cultivated and closely side-pruned. The *vigor* of a tree, *i. e.* the rapidity with which it will grow, determines its favor. Sorts which take time, and require a longer treatment, are regarded with disfavor. Everything is sacrificed to rapid growth and early maturity.

Next, and proceeding in the same evil direction, comes the orchard cultivation. From what quarter have we, mostly, derived our opinions and practices in fruit cultivation? From French, English, and New England writers. But is the system which they pursue fit for us? There is an opposite extreme to high cultivation; there are evils besetting low-cultivation. In cold, wet, stiff, barren soils, and in a cool, or humid, or cloudy atmosphere, trees require stimulants. The soil needs drying, warming, manuring; and the tree requires pruning. But such a system is ruinous, where the soil is full of fiery activity, bursting out with an irrepressible fertility and a superabundant vegetation; where the long summer days are intensely brilliant, and the *air* warm enough to ripen fruit even in the densest shade of an unpruned tree.

A traveller in Lapland would require the most bracing and stimulating food; but in New Orleans it would produce fever and death. A region, subject to all the diseases and evils of vegetable plethora, has adopted the practice of regions subject to the opposite evils. While receiving with gratitude, at the hands of eminent foreign physiologists and cultivators, the *principles*, we must establish the ART of horticulture, by a practice conformable to our own circumstances. A treatment which in England would only produce healthful growth, in this country would pamper a tree to a luxurious fullness. Let us not be deluded by the fallacious appearance of our orchards. The evils which we have to fear are not shown forth in the early history of a tree or an orchard. On the contrary, the appearance will be flattering. The apple is a more hardy tree than the pear, and will endure greater mismanagement; but in the long run we shall have to pay for our greedy cultivation, even in the apple family. Our pear-trees are already evincing the evils of a too luxuriant habit; and if the West is ever to become the pear-region of America, the culture of this tree must be adapted to the peculiarities of western soil and climate.

It will be borne in mind that our remarks upon the cultivation of fruit-trees are not applicable to the processes of art employed in experimental gardens, or in climates requiring a highly artificial culture, but to gardens and open orchards of the pear and apple in the middle and Western States.

Our climate and soil predispose fruit-trees to excessive growth. There is, in the States of Ohio, Indiana, Illinois, and in the thickly settled portions of Missouri and Kentucky, very little poor soil. Limestone lands, clay lands, sandy loams and alluvions, afford not only variety of soil, but the strongest and most fertile. The forest trees of the West compared with the same species east of the Alleghany ridge, exhibit the difference of soils. Artificial processes may produce better soils, it may be, but there is not probably on earth so large a body of land which is, as uniformly, deep, strong, quick, and rich in all mineral and vegetable substances. It is cultivated under a climate most congenial to vegetation, both in respect to length and temperature. Our spring is early. In 1835 we gathered flowers from the woods, near Cincinnati, on the 22d of February. In 1839 we gathered them at Lawrenceburgh, in the last week of February. We find in our garden journal at Indianapolis, latitude 39°55′ north, March 11, 1840, " rose-bushes, honey-suckles, and willow trees had been in leaf for some days," and seed-sowing had begun. In 1841, seed was sown in open ground, April 8th. In 1842, pie-plant broke ground March 8th, and all early seed were in the ground by the 21st. In 1843, seeds were in by April 20. In 1844 ground was in a working state Feb. 23d, and seeds put in by March 1. Trees, varying according to the nature of the season, complete the *first* growth, on an average, about the 1st of September. Their second growth continues, usually, into November. In 1844 we had noisette roses pushing out terminal leaves after *Christmas ;* but this is not a frequent occurrence. Upon an average, the middle of March and the 1st of November, may be taken as the limits of the vegetable year—a period of more than seven months. During this season rains are copious, and frequent. Our midsummer droughts are seldom so severe upon vegetation as they seem to be in New England. During the months of June, July and August, the temperature of mid-day seldom falls below 70° Fahren. and ranges between 70° and 100°.

One other cause of rapid growth is to be mentioned —the nature of our winters. Except when the roots are frozen, they are supposed never to be inactive. During the winter they slowly absorb materials from the soil, and fill the whole system with sap. When the winters are severe, they are usually very long; and the slowness of its winter action is compensated by the length of time afforded to the plant. In the western States, though the winters are short, yet there is scarcely a week in which trees may not accumulate their stores. The spring growth will be vigorous in proportion to the amount of true sap collected in the vegetable system. As the whole winter is mild enough for this process to go on, the growth of trees is rampant in spring. Thus, the quality of the soils, and the nature of the seasons—the mildness of winter—the earliness of spring and length of summer—its heat and great atmospheric brilliancy, all conspire to produce very rapid and strong

growth in herb, shrub, and tree; and I repeat, as a fundamental consideration, that our SOIL AND SEASON PREDIS-
POSE FRUIT-TREES TO EXCESSIVE GROWTH.   From this fact
we should take our start in every process of orchard, nursery, and garden cultivation of fruit-trees; and if philoso-
phically employed it will, we will not say revolutionize, but
materially modify the processes of cultivation peculiar to
colder climates and poorer soils.   In respect to esculent
vegetables—cabbages, radishes, celery, rhubarb, lettuce,
etc., this rank and rapid growth is beneficial, since it is not
the *fruit* but the *plant* which we eat.   The reverse is true
in fruit-trees.   Observant cultivators have conformed to
this indication of nature, in some things; for instance, in
the treatment of the grape.   The German emigrants who
settled in these parts, having been conversant with vine-
dressing in Europe, were usually employed to cut and lay
in the vines of such as were desirous of the best gardens.
But, gradually, their practice has been rejected, and now,
instead of reducing our vines to niggardly stumps, the
wood is spared and laid in long.   If pruning be close, the
vine may be said to overflow with excess of new wood,
which does not ripen well.   Our remarks more especially
apply to regions below 40° of north latitude.

Below this line, our efforts need not be directed to the
forcing of growth, for that, naturally, will be all-sufficient.
Our object must be *compact and thoroughly ripened wood.*
These reasonings may be applied to many practices now
generally in vogue.

1. It is the practice of nurserymen to force their trees by
cultivation, and by pruning.   It is very well known, to
those conversant with the nursery business, that great growers and early growers are the favorites (and, so far as an
expeditious preparation of stock for sale is concerned, justly), that slow and tedious growers are put upon rampant
growing stocks to quicken them.   In some cases manures are
freely applied to the soil, as directed by all writers who teach

how to prepare ground for a nursery. But such writers had their eye upon the soil of England or New England. The still more vicious practice of side trimming and free pruning is followed, which forces the tree to produce a great deal of wood, rather than to ripen well a little. A well-informed nurseryman ought not to look so much at the *length* of his trees, as to the *quality of their wood*. The very beau ideal of a fruit-tree for our climate is one that, while it is hardy enough to grow steadily in cool seasons, is not excitable enough to grow rampantly in warm ones, and which completes its work early in the season, ripens its wood thoroughly, and goes to rest before there is danger of severe frost. Such trees may be had, by skillful breeding, as easily, as, by breeding, any desirable quality may be developed in cattle or horses. But of this hereafter.

The subject of pruning will be separately treated; but it is appropriate here to say, that every consideration should incline the nurseryman to grow his trees *with side brush from top to bottom*, and by shortening these, to multiply leaves to the greatest possible extent all over the tree. In every climate we should idolize the *leaf*—in which are the sources of health and abiding vigor.

2. The mistakes of the nursery are carried out and developed by the purchaser, in the following respects—by bad selection, pernicious cultivation, and by improper pruning.

First, trees are selected upon a bad principle. Men are very naturally in a hurry to see their orchards in bearing; precocious trees, therefore, and all means of prematurity are sought. In respect to the pear, it is the popular, but incorrect, opinion that it takes a man's lifetime to bring them into fruit. Hope deferred, very naturally in such cases, makes the heart sick. But certain talismanic words found in catalogues and fruit manuals restore the courage, and you shall find the pencil mark made upon all pears, described as " of a vigorous growth," " a rampant grower," " comes early into bearing," " bears young," " a great and early bearer." But such as these—"not of a very vigorous growth," " does not bear young," " the growth is slow but healthy," " grows to a large size before producing fruit,"— are passed by. Many farmers judge of a tree as they would timothy grass. A short-jointed, compact branch, is " *stunted;*" but a long, plump limb, like a water shoot, or a Lombardy poplar branch, is admired as a first-rate growth. Some pears have but this single virtue : they make wood in capital quantities, but very poor pears. Now our selection must proceed on different principles if our orchards are to be *durable* and *healthy.* We should mark for selection pears described as—" of a compact habit," " growth slow and healthy," " ripens its wood early and thoroughly." A tree which runs far into the fall, and makes quantities of wood more than it can thoroughly ripen, must be regarded as unsafe and undesirable.

There is another marked fault in selecting trees—a disposition to get long and handsome trees with smooth stems. This principle of selection would be excellent when one goes after a bean-pole, or a cane. A fruit-tree is not usually cultivated for such uses. In the first place, it is not wise to expose the trunk of a fruit-tree to the full sun of our summers. We have seen peach trees killed by opening the head so much as to expose the main branches to the sun. A low head, a short trunk should be sought. When land is scarce, and orchards cultivated, high trimming is employed for the sake of convenience, not of the tree, but of its *owner.* And in cool and humid climates, such evils do not attend the practice, as with us. Beside picking long shanked trees, one would suppose that a leaf below the crotch would poison the tree from the assiduity with which they are trimmed off. It ought to be laid down as a fundamental rule with us, that a tree is benefited *not by the amount of its wood, but by the extent of its leaf surface.* Every effort should be used to make the length of the wood moderate, and the amount of its leaves abundant. The leaf does not depend for its quality on the wood, *but the wood takes its nature from the leaf*. Young trees ought to be grown with side brush from the roots to the fork. Water shoots from the root are to be removed, but leaves upon the trunk are to be nursed. By cutting in the brush when it tends to a long growth, it will emit side shoots, and still increase the number of leaves.

Secondly. There is great evil in pruning too much. France and England have given us our notions upon pruning. There, their own system is wise, because it conforms to the climate and soil. But their system of pruning is totally uncongenial with our seasons and the habits of our trees. In England, for instance, the peach will not ripen in open grounds, except, perhaps, in the extreme southern counties. In consequence, it is trained upon walls, and its wood thinned, to let light and heat upon every part of it. It is very right to husband light and heat when it is scarce, and by opening the head of a tree to carry them to all parts of the sluggish wood. But we often have more than we want. A peach will ripen, on the lowest limb and inside of the tree, by the mere heat of the atmosphere. Even in New England, the English system of pruning proves too free. Manning says, "From the strong growth of fruit-trees in our country and the dryness of its atmosphere, severe pruning is less necessary here than in England." We are not giving rules *for* pruning; but cautions *against* pruning too freely. There is not a single point in fruit cultivation where more mistakes are committed than in *pruning*.

Thirdly. Great mistakes are committed in stimulating the growth of trees by enriching the soil. Books direct (and men naturally and innocently obey), the putting of manure to young trees. We have no doubt that the time will come, when manures will be so thoroughly analyzed and classified, that we can employ them just as a carpenter does his tools, or the farmer his implements; if we wish *wood*, we shall apply certain ingredients to the soil and have it;

if we wish fruit, we shall have at hand manures which promote the fruiting properties of the tree; if we want seed, we shall have manures for it. But manures as now employed, are, usually, not beneficial to orchards of *young* trees. A clay soil, very stiff and adhesive, may require sand and vegetable mold to render it permeable to the root; some very barren soils may require some manure; but the average of our farms are rich enough already, and too rich for the good of the young tree. It would be better for the orchard if it made less wood and made it better.

If these directions make the prospect of fruit so distant as to discourage the planting of orchards, we will add, plant your orchard; and if you cannot wait for its healthful growth, plant also trees for immediate use, and serve them just as you please; manure them, cut them, get fruit at all hazards; only make up your minds that they will be short-lived and liable to blight and disease.

A LIST OF CHOICE FRUITS.

OUR readers may desire a list of fruits, which are universally admitted to be of first-rate excellence. We cannot include, of course, *all* that are first rate; but we put none in that are not so.

I. APPLES.

I. SUMMER.

Red or Carolina June.
Summer Queen.
Yellow Hoss.
Sweet Bough.

Prince's Harvest.
Kirkbridge White.
Sweet June.
Daniel.

II. AUTUMN.

Maiden's Blush.	Fall Harvey.
Wine.	Gravenstein.
Holland Pippin.	Ashmore.
Rambo.	Porter.

III. WINTER.

Black.	White Belle Fleur.
Golden Russet.	Michael Henry Pippin.
Newtown Spitzenberg.	Pryor's Red.
Rhode Island Greening.	Green Newtown Pippin.
Hubbardston Nonsuch.	Jenetan or Rawle's Janet.
Vandeveer Pippin.	Putnam Russet.
Yellow Belle Fleur.	

II. PEARS.

I. SUMMER PEARS, *or such as ripen from the first of July to the last of August.*

1. Madeleine, or Citron des Carmes.
2. Bloodgood.
3. Summer Francreal.
4. Dearborn's Seedling.
5. Julienne.
6. Williams' Bon Chretien.

II. AUTUMN PEARS, *or such as ripen from September to the last of November.*

7. Stevens' Genesse.
8. Belle Lucrative.
9. Henry the Fourth.
10. Washington.
11. Dunmore.
12. St. Ghislain.
13. Seckel.
14. Beurre Bosc.
15. Andrews.
16. Marie Louise.
17. Doyenne or fall butter.
18. Dix.
19. Petre.
20. Duchesse D'Angouleme.

III. WINTER PEARS, *or those which ripen during the winter and spring months.*

21. Beurre Diel.
22. Hacon's Incomparable.
23. Passe Colmar.
24. Beurre Ranz.
25. Columbia.
26. Beurre D'Aremberg.
27. Van Mons Leon le Clerc.
28. Beurre Easter.
29. Chaumontelle.
30. Glout Morceau.
31. Prince's St. Germain.
32. Winter Nelis.

Those who wish only *four* trees, may select Nos. 2, 6, 20, 26. Those who have room for *eight*, to the above may add 13, 23, 25, 32. Those who wish sixteen trees, to the above may add, 1, 3, 11, 14, 18, 21, 24, 28.

III. PEACHES.

I. EARLY.

1. Red Magdalen.
2. Early Royal George.
3. Early York.

4. Morris' Red Rareripe.
5. Crawford's Early Melocoton.

II. MEDIUM.

6. Apricot Peach.
7. Baltimore Rose.
8. Swalsh.
9. Noblesse.
10. Coolidge's Favorite.

11. Malta.
12. Brevoort.
13. Douglass.
14. Grosse Mignonne.

III. LATE.

15. Heath.
16. Crawford's late Melocoton.

17. Lemon Cling.
18. La Grange.

IV. APRICOTS.

1. Large Early.
2. Breda.

3. Peach Apricot.
4. Moorpark.

V. CHERRIES.

1. Bauman's May or Bigarreau de Mai.
2. Black Eagle.
3. Knight's Early Black.
4. May Duke.
5. Elton.

6. Bigarreau, or Spanish Yellow.
7. Belle de Choisy.
8. Black Tartarian.
9. Downer's Late.
10. Napoleon.

For a collection of two trees, 4, 9; for four trees, add 6 and 10.

VI. PLUMS.

1. Green Gage.
2. Jefferson.
3. Huling's Superb.
4. Coe's Golden Drop.
5. Purple Gage.

6. Cruger's Scarlet.
7. Washington.
8. Red Gage.
9. Smith's Orleans.
10. Royal de Tours.

For two trees, 1 and 4; for four add 2 and 7. The following are said to be suitable for light sandy soils, on which plums usually drop their fruit: Cruger's Scarlet, Imperial Gage, Red Gage, Coe's Golden Drop, Bleeker's Gage, Blue Gage.

VII. STRAWBERRIES.

Early Virginia.	Hudson.
Hovey's Seedling.	Ross Phœnix.

No one man can make out a list that will suit all; and those who are acquainted with fruits will reject some from the above list and insert others. But it may be safely said, that he who has in his collection the above varieties, will have a collection comprising the best that are known, and without one inferior sort, although there may be many others *as* good; which may be added by such as have room for them.

—◆◆◆—

THE NURSERY BUSINESS.

THE great interest in the cultivation of fruit which has been excited within a few years, has given rise to many nurseries to supply the demand, and every year we see the number increasing. Or rather, we see new adventurers in this line, for the failure of many and the abandonment of the business, prevents the number from becoming so great as one would suppose.

We are very glad to see the art of fruit culture increasing, and we are very glad to see competent men embarking in the nursery business. But we are sorry to see the impression gaining ground that it is a business which anybody can conduct, and that every man can make money by it who knows how to graft or to bud. Let no man embark in it under such misapprehension.

11

In the first place, the time, and labor, and patience required for a successful nursery business is much greater than any one suspects beforehand. If a man has a large capital he may begin sales at once upon a purchased stock. But if one is to prepare his own stock for market, and this must be the case with by far the greater number of western nurserymen, it will require several years of expensive labor before he can realize anything. Nor even then will he be apt to receive profits which will at all meet his expectations. During these years of preparation on what is he to live? If he has means, very well; but let no man suppose that he can get along, especially with a family on his hands, during the early years of his nursery, if he has nothing else to depend upon. The mere physical labor of keeping a nursery in proper order is such as to make it no sinecure.

But all this is a less consideration than the special skill and vigilant care required to conduct a nursery in an honorable manner. Nowhere do mistakes occur more easily, and nowhere are they more provoking, both to the buyer and seller. It is rare that assistants can be had upon whom reliance can be placed. There are men enough to plow, and grub, and clean; but to select buds and grafts, to work the various kinds, and plant them safely by themselves, this, usually, must be done by the proprietor. Where a nursery is carried on by assistants, it makes almost no difference how much care is used, mistakes will abound.

The extent to which an error goes is not unworthy of a moment's attention. We purchased of a very highly respectable nurseryman, the *Royal George* peach. The first season many buds were distributed from it. An expert nurseryman in the vicinity, among others, got of it. The credit of the original proprietor of the tree was such that it was thought safe to propagate at once, and thousands of trees were worked with these buds; from him, nurserymen from neighboring counties procured scions, and now the Royal George, which has proved to be no Royal George at all, is scattered all over the country. When a nursery contains from fifty to a hundred kinds of apples, thirty or forty kinds of pears, ten to twenty sorts of cherries, thirty or forty kinds of peaches, besides plums, nectarines, apricots, etc., there will be some two or three hundred *separate varieties* of fruit to be propagated each year, and of each sort from a hundred to a thousand or more trees, according to the business of the nursery. Two things are apparent from this view; first, that such unremitting and sagacious vigilance is required that not every one is fit to be a nurseryman; and, secondly, that not every nurseryman is a scamp who puts upon you trees untrue to their names. No doubt there are roguish nurserymen; no doubt, too, there are culpably careless men in this, as in all other forms of business. But no one will be so charitable to nurserymen as those who understand the difficulties of their business; and a mistake, and many of them, may occur in well-appointed grounds, which no care could well have prevented.

We think this to be a business to which no man should turn, except under two conditions; first, that he will, if he has not already, serve a faithful apprenticeship to it—we do not mean by regular indenture, but by practising for several years in a good nursery until the prominent essential parts of the business have become practically familiar.

The other condition is, that he make up his mind to *see to it himself*.

—•◦•—

REMEDY FOR YELLOW BUGS.—A gentleman informs us that he has always saved his vines by planting *poppies* among them. Those on one side of an alley, without poppies, would be entirely eaten, while those on the other side, with poppies, would not be touched.

THE BREEDING OF FRUITS.

BECAUSE, as yet, no certain rules can be laid down for the production of a given result by crossing flower on flower, it does not follow that there are not certain invariable principles which govern the process. It is but a little while since breeding animals had any pretension to scientific rules. But, by careful practice and observation, the most important improvement has been attained in all the animals belonging to the farm. And if careful research and experiment do not result in absolute certainty, they will yet render the production of fine varieties of fruit, by the crossing of the old ones, a matter of much less chance than it now is.

The art of cross-fertilization is being much more practised by florists than by pomologists, and for obvious reasons. What the breeder of annuals can do in a few months requires more than as many years from him that essays to raise new fruits. Many florists' flowers, however, require as long and even a longer time than apples or pears; and it is a marvel that the phlegmatic patience of the tulip-loving Dutch Jobs should not have found imitators in the orchard. If a man can wait ten years to ascertain that all his seedling bulbs are good for nothing, or at the best, that out of ten thousand, but one or two are worth keeping, surely the patience of an enthusiast in fruit ought not to snap by being drawn through such a space.

Two methods for originating new varieties of fruit have been practised; the *natural* method of Van Mons, and the *artificial* method of Knight. Van Mons, born at Brussels in 1765, was a man of fine genius and thorough education. Although he is chiefly known as a pomologist, his labors in the nursery were only incidental to the regular occupation of a public scientific life. M. Poiteau quaintly says of him that he writes " on the gravest subjects, in the midst of noise, in a company of persons who talk loudly on frivolous subjects, and takes part in the conversation without stopping his pen."

Van Mons' theory is founded upon two physical facts:

1. *That all seeds in a state of nature can be made by cultivation to vary from their condition, which variations may be fixed, and become permanent.*

2. *That all cultivated seeds have a tendency to return toward that natural state from which they originally varied.* We say *toward*, for he supposed that an improved fruit would never return absolutely to the original and natural type.

It was upon this last principle that Van Mons accounted for the fact, that as a general thing, the seeds of fine old varieties of fruit produced only inferior kinds. Recourse could not be had therefore to seeds of improved fruit.

On the other hand, the seed of fruits absolutely wild would produce fruits exactly like their original. If the seed of the wild pear be gotten from the wood and planted in a garden, every seed will yield only the wild pear again. But if a wild pear be transplanted, and put under new influences of soil, climate and cultivation, its fruit will begin to augment and improve. The change is not merely upon the size and appearance of the fruit, it affects also the qualities of the *seed*. For if the seed be now planted, the difference between a wild pear, *in a state of nature* and the same wild pear-tree *in a state of cultivation* will at once appear in this, that whereas the seed of the first is *constant*, the seed of the second shows an inclination to *vary*. Here then is a starting. When once the habit of *variation* is gained, the foundation of improvement is laid. In a short time the enthusiasm of Van Mons had collected into his garden 80,000 trees upon which he was experimenting, nor can the result of his labors be better stated than in the words of M. Poiteau:

"That so long as plants remain in their natural situation, they do not sensibly vary, and their seeds always produce the same; but on changing their climate and territory several among them vary, some more and others less, and when they have once departed from their natural state, they never again return to it, but are removed more and more therefrom, by successive generations. and produce, sufficiently often, distinct races, more or less durable, and that finally if these variations are even carried back to the territory of their ancestors, they will neither represent the character of their parents, or ever return to the species from whence they sprung."

Accordingly, Van Mons began to sow the seeds of natural and wild fruit which were in a *variable* state. By all means within his power he hastened his seedlings to show fruit. The first generation showed only poor fruit but decidedly better than the wild. Selecting the seed of the best of these, he sowed again. From the fruit of these he sowed the third generation. From the third, a fourth; and from the fourth, a fifth; as far as the eighth generation.

His experience showed that there was great difference among different species of fruit in the number of generations through which they must pass before they were perfect. The apple yielded good fruit in the fourth generation. Stone fruits produced perfect kinds in the third generation. Some varieties afforded perfect fruit in the fifth generation, while others go on improving to the eighth.

The time required for this renovation diminished at each remove from the normal or wild state. Thus, the trees from the second sowing of the pear-seed fruited in from ten to twelve years; those from their seed, or of the third generation in from eight to ten years; those of the fourth generation in from six to eight years; those of the fifth generation, in six years, and those in the eight, in four years. These are the *mean* terms of all his experiments.

To obtain perfect stone fruits, through four successive generations, from parent to son, required from twelve to fifteen years; the apple required twenty years, and the pear, when carried only to the fifth generation, required from thirty to thirty-six years.

HYBRIDIZATION, OR KNIGHT'S METHOD.—Andrew Knight, one of the most original and philosophic horticulturists that ever lived, pursued an entirely different method—that of *cross-fertilization.* He carefully removed the anthers from the blossoms upon which he wished to operate, so that the stigma should not receive a particle of the pollen belonging to its own flower. He then procured from the variety which he wished to cross, a portion of the pollen, and artificially impregnated the prepared blossom with it. When the fruit thus produced had ripened its seeds, they were sown, and by regular process brought into bearing. The progeny were found to combine, in various degrees of excellence, the qualities of both parents.

REMARKS ON THE TWO METHODS.

1. Both Van Mons and Knight believed in a degeneracy of plants; but the degeneracy of the one system is not to be confounded with that of the other.

Knight believed that varieties had a regular period of existence; although, as in animal life, care and skill might make essential difference in the longevity, yet they could in nowise avert the final catastrophe; a time would come, sooner or later, at which the vegetable vitality would be expended, and the variety must perish by exhaustion—by *running out.*

Van Mons believed that an improved variety tended to return to its normal state—to its wild type; and although he did not believe that it could ever be entirely restored to its wild state, it might go so far as to make it worthless for useful purposes.

Knight believed in absolute decay; Van Mons, in retrocession. According to Knight's theory, varieties of fruit cease by the natural statute of limitation; according to Van Mons, they only fall from grace.

There can be no reasonable doubt that Van Mons held the truth, and as little, that Knight's speculations were fallacious. Bad cultivation will cause anything to run out; no plant will perfect its tissues or fruit without the soil affords it elementary materials. The so-called exhausted varieties renew their youth when transplanted into soils suitable for them.

2. Against Van Mons' method it is urged, that it enfeebles the constitution of plants; that, *enfeebling* is the very key of the process. This Mr. Downing urges with emphasis, saying that, "the Belgian method (Van Mons') gives us varieties often impaired in their *health* in their very origin." It is one thing to restrain the energy of a plant, and another to enfeeble it. It may be enfeebled until it becomes unhealthy, but rampant vigor is as really an unhealthy state as the other extreme. A tree refuses fruit and is liable to death from a coarse, open, rank growth, as much as from a languor which suppresses all growth.

No; that which we imagine Van Mons to have effected was a smaller, but more *compact* and *fine* growth. Nor are we aware that, *as a matter of experience*, the Belgian pears prove to be any more tender than the English. Doubtless, there are trees of a delicate and tender habit in the number, but as few, in proportion to the great number originated, as by any other method.

The two main objections to the plan are the *time required*, and the utter *uncertainty of the results*. To imitate the process would require a Van Mons' patience, in which, probably, he was never surpassed, and his enthusiasm, which was extraordinary even for a horticulturist, a race of beings supposed to be anything but phlegmatic.

The *uncertainty* is such as to prevent any determinate improvement. We get, not what we may wish, but whatever may happen to come. Nothing that art can do would affect the size, color, hardness, or in any respect, the general character of the fruit.

It is in these aspects that Knight's method must always be preferred as a practical system. We can obtain a return for our labor in *one-fifth* the time ; and, what is even more important, we can regulate, before-hand, the results within certain limits. The new fruit is to be made up of the qualities of its parents in various proportions. We cannot determine what the proportions shall be, but we can determine what parents shall be selected. Nor is it at all improbable that, when knowledge has become more exact by a longer and larger' experience, the breeder of fruit may cross the varieties with nearly the same certainty of result as does the breeder of stock. It is upon this feature, the power which science has over the results to be obtained, that we look with the greatest interest ; and we urge upon scientific cultivators the duty of perfecting our fruits by judicious breeding.

PRUNING ORCHARDS.

THE habit of early spring pruning has been handed down to us from English customs, and farmers do it because it always has been done. Besides, about this time, men have leisure, and would like to begin the· season's work; and pruning seems quite a natural employment with which to introduce the labors of the year.

It is not possible for America, but more emphatically for western cultivators to do worse than to pattern upon the example of British and Continental authorities in the matter of orchards and vineyards. The summers of England are moist, cool, and deficient in light. Our summers are exactly the reverse—dry, fervid, and brilliant. The stimuli of the

11*

elements with them are much below, and with us much above par. In consequence, their trees have but a moderate growth; ours are inclined to excessive growth.

Their whole system of open-culture, and wall-training is founded upon the necessity of *husbanding all their resources*. To avail themselves of every particle of light, they keep open the heads of their trees, so that the parsimonious sunshine shall penetrate every part of the tree. Let this be done with us, and there are many of our trees that would be killed by the force of the sun's rays upon the naked branches in a single season, or very much enfeebled. For the same general reasons, the English reduce the quantity of bearing-wood, shortening a part or wholly cutting it out, that the residue, having the whole energy of the tree concentrated upon it, may perfect its fruit. Our difficulty being an excess of vitality, this system of shortening and cutting out, would cause the tree to send out suckers from the root and trunk, and would fill the head of the tree with rank water-shoots or *gourmands*. What would be thought of the people of the torrid zone should they borrow their customs of clothing from the practice of Greenland? It would be as rational as it is for orchardists, in a land whose summers are long and of high temperature, to copy the customs of a land whose summers are prodigal of fog and rain, but penurious of heat and light.

Except to remove dead, diseased or interfering branches, do not cut at all.

But if pruning is to be done, wait till after corn-planting. *The best time to prune is the time when healing will the quickest follow cutting.* This is not in early spring, but in early summer. The elements from which new wood is produced are not drawn from the rising sap, but from that which descends between the bark and wood. This sap, called *true sap*, is the upward sap after it has gone through that chemical laboratory, the leaf. Each leaf is a chemical contractor, doing up its part of the work of preparing sap for use, as fast as it is sent up to it from the root through the interior sap-passages. In the leaf, the sap gives off and receives, certain properties; and when thus elaborated, it is changed with all those elements required for the formation and sustentation of every part of vegetable fabric. Descending, it gives out its various qualities, till it reaches the root; and whatever is left then passes out into the soil.

Every man will perceive that if a tree is pruned in spring before it has a leaf out, there is no sap provided to repair the wound. A slight granulation *may* take place, in certain circumstances, and in some kinds of plants, from the elements with which the tree was stored during the former season; but, in point of fact, a cut usually remains without change until the progress of spring puts the whole vegetable economy into action.

In young and vigorous trees, this process may not seem to occasion any injury. But trees growing feeble by age will soon manifest the result of this injudicious practice, by blackened stumps, by cankered sores, and by decay.

If one must begin to do something that looks like spring-work, let him go at a more efficient train of operations. With a good spade invert the sod for several feet from the body of the tree. With a good scraper remove all dead bark. Dilute (old) soft soap with urine; take a stiff shoe-brush, and go to scouring the trunk and main branches. This will be labor to some purpose; and before you have gone through a large orchard faithfully, your zeal for spring-work will have become so far tempered with knowledge, that you will be willing to *let pruning alone till after corn-planting.*

Two exceptions or precautions should be mentioned.

1. In the use of the wash; new soap is more *caustic* than old; and the sediments of a soap barrel much more so than the mass of soap. Sometimes trees have been injured by applying a caustic alkali in too great strength. There is little danger of this when a tree is rough and covered with

dead bark or dirt; but when it is smooth and has no scurf it is more liable to suffer. *Trees should not be washed in dry and warm weather.* The best time is just before spring rains, or before any rain.

2. Where fruit-trees are found to have suffered from the winter, pruning cannot be too early, and hardly too severe. If left to grow, the heat of spring days ferments the sap and spreads blight throughout the tree; whereas, by severe cutting, there is a chance, at least, of removing much of the injured wood. We have gone over the pear-trees in our own garden, and wherever the least affection has been discovered, we have cut out every particle of the last summer's wood; and cut back until we reached sound and healthy wood, pith and bark.

SLITTING THE BARK OF TREES.

THIS is a practice very much followed by fruit-raisers. Downing gives his sanction to it. Mr. Pell (N. Y.), famous for his orchards, includes it as a part of his system of orchard cultivation. Men talk of trees being *bark-bound*, etc., and let out the bark on the same principle, we suppose, as mothers do the pantaloons of growing boys. We confess a prejudice against this letting out of the tucks in a tree's clothes. We do not say that there may not be cases of diseased trees in which, as a remedial process, this may be wise; but we should as soon think of slitting the skin on a boy's legs, or on a calf's or colt's, as a regular part of a plan of rearing them, as to slash the bark of sound and healthy trees. *Bark-bound!* what is that? Does the inside of a tree grow faster than the outside? When bark is slit, is it looser around the whole trunk than before? When granulations have filled up this artificial channel, is not the bark just as tight as it was before? Mark, we do not say that it is *not* a good practice; but only that we do not yet understand *what* the benefit is.

" Why, the bark bursts sometimes."

Yes, disease may thus affect it; and when it does, *cut if necessary.*

" Does it do any harm?" Perhaps not; neither would it to put a weathercock on the top of every tree; or to bury a black cat under the roots, or to mark each tree with talismanic signs. Is it worth while to do a thing just because it does no harm?

" But when a tree is growing too fast, does it not need it ?" Yes, if it can be shown that the bark, alburnum, etc., do not increase alike. That excitement which increases the growth of one part of a tree will, as a general fact, increase the growth of every other. In respect to the *fruit and seed*, doubtless, particular manures will develop special properties. But is there evidence that such a thing takes place in respect to the various tissues of the wood, bark, etc?

" But if a tree be sluggish, and bound, will it not help it?" Whatever excites a more vigorous circulation will be of advantage. Whether any supposed advantage from the knife arises in this way, we do not know. But a good *scraping*, or a scouring off of the whole body with sand, and then a pungent alkaline wash—(soft soap diluted with urine) would, we think, be better for bark-bound trees than the whole tribe of slits, vertical, horizontal, zig-zag, or waved.

----◦◦◦----

Hovey's Magazine of Horticulture.—We recommend all who can afford three dollars a year for a sterling monthly, beautifully got up, in the best style of Boston typography, to send to Boston for Hovey's Magazine. We give it an unqualified recommendation, and those who take it one year will be loth to part with it.

DOWNING'S FRUIT AND FRUIT-TREES OF AMERICA.

WHEN a book is hopelessly weak or incorrect, it should be the object of criticism to exterminate it. But when a work is admitted to be, upon the whole, well done, criticism ought to be an assistance to it, and not a hindrance. Praise by the wholesale is better for the publisher than for the reputation of the author; since, in a work like Downing's, every pomologist knows that perfection is not attainable, and indiscriminate eulogy inclines the better-read critic to rebut the praise by a full development of the faults. Thus on one side there is general praise and faint blame; and on the other, faint praise and general blame.

We shall, at present, confine our attention to the catalogue of apples and pears, for all other fruits of our zone together are not of importance equal to these; and if an author excels in respect to these, his success will cover a multitude of sins in the treatment of small fruits, and fruits of short duration. Mr. Downing has shown good judgment in making out his list of varieties; his descriptions, for the most part, seem to be from his own senses; he has added many interesting particulars in respect to fruits not recorded before, or else scattered in isolated sentences in magazines and journals.

But are his descriptions thorough and uniform? While he has added. *materials* to pomology, has he advanced the *science* by reducing such materials to a consistent form? If we compare Mr. Downing's descriptions with those of Kenrick, or even of Manning, he excels them in fullness. If he be compared with classic European pomologists, he is decidedly inferior, both in the conception of what was to be done, and in a neat, systematic method of execution. Indeed, Mr. Downing does not seem to have settled, before hand, in his mind, a *formula* of a description; sometimes only three or four characteristics are given. Downing sins in excellent company. There is not an American pomological writer who appears to have *conceived*, even, of a systematic, scientific description of fruits. European authors, decidedly more explicit and minute than we are, have never reduced the descriptive part of the science to anything like regularity. We do not suppose that there can be such exact and constant dissimilarities detected between variety and variety of a species, as exists between species and species of a genus. We do not think a description of fruits to be imperfect, therefore, merely because it is less distinctive than a description of plants. But the more variable and obscure the points of difference between two varieties, the more scrupulously careful must we be to seize them. Where differences are broad and uniform, science can afford to be careless, but not where they are vague and illusory. We can approximate a systematic accuracy. But it must be by making up in the *number* of determining circumstances, that which is wanting in the invariable distinctiveness of a few that are *specific*.

1. Downing's descriptions are quite *irregular* and *unequal*. Both his pears and apples are imperfect, but not alike imperfect. The descriptions of pears are decidedly in advance of those of the apple. It would seem as if the improvement which he gained by practice was very easily traced in its course on his pages.

Hardly two apples are described in reference to the same particulars. With respect to color of skin, size and form, eye and stem, he approaches the nearest to uniformity. But with respect to every other feature there is an utter want of regularity, which indicates not so much *carelessness* as the want of any settled plan or conception of a perfect scientific description.

We will, out of a multitude of similar cases, select a few as specimens of what we mean. Of the *Pumpkin Russet*, he says, "flesh exceedingly rich and sweet;" but he does not speak of its *texture*, whether coarse or fine; whether brittle or leathery. *Pomme de Neige*—"flesh remarkably white, very tender, juicy and good, with a slight perfume;" but is it sweet or sour, or subacid, or astringent? No one can tell by reading the joint descriptions of the *Red* and the *Yellow Ingestries* what their flavor is, since it is only said that they are "juicy and high flavored"—but whether the high flavored juice is sweet or sour, does not appear. These are not picked instances. They occur on almost every page of his list of apples. The *Summer Sweet Paradise* is, of course, sweet, since we are three times told of it, once in the title and twice in the text. The SWEET *Pearmain* also, is a "sweet apple" "of a very *saccharine* flavor." Of course it is *sweet*. Nos. 67, 68, 69, 74, 75, and very many more, are described without information as to their flavor except that, whatever it is, it is "brisk," or "high," or "rich" —forlorn adjectives unaffianced to any substantive which they may qualify. Sometimes the health of the tree and its hardiness are given, and as often omitted. Some times its habit of bearing is mentioned, but oftener neglected. The color of the flesh is given in No. 82, but not in 83; in 84, but not in 85; from 86–92 inclusive, but not to the *second* 92, for the Bedfordshire Foundling and the Dutch Mignonne are both numbered 92. The color of the flesh is not given in 93, 97, 100, 101, 103, 110, although the intermediate numbers have it given. Why should one be minutely described, and another not all? We should regard it an ungrateful requital for all the pleasure and profit which this volume has afforded us to hunt up and display what, to some, may seem to be mere "jots and tittles," were it not that these, in themselves, unimportant things mark decisively the absence in the author's *plan*, of a style of description which pomology always needed, but now begins imperiously to demand. And we are confident that a pomological manual *on the right design*, is yet to be written. Our hearty wish is, that Mr. Downing's revised edition may be that manual.

2. We are led, from these remarks, to consider, by itself, the *imperfect scale* of descriptions adopted by all our

American pomological writers, upon which Mr. D. has not materially improved.

The description of the *tree* is very meagre or totally neglected. *Nothing at all* is said of it in cases out of the 174 apples numbered and described. The general shape of the tree is given in but *thirty-eight* instances in the same number.

The *color of the wood* is, usually, noticed in the account of pears; but in the account of apples in not one case, we should think, in ten.

The peculiar *growth of the young wood,* in a great majority of cases, is not noticed; but more frequently in the pear than in the apple list. The least practised observer knows how striking is this feature of the face of a tree. We do not remember an instance where the *buds* have been employed as a characteristic. Are distinctive marks so numerous that such a one as this can be spared? The shape, color, size, prominence, and shoulder of buds, together with their interstitial spaces, form too remarkable a portion of trees ·to be absolutely overlooked in a book describing the "fruits and *fruit-trees* of America."

Equally noticeable is the almost entire neglect of the *core and seed,* as identifying marks. Once in a while, as in the case of the Belle Fleur, the Roman Stem, the Spitzenberg, and the Pomme Royale, we are told, that the cores are hollow. But neither among pears nor apples, is the core or seed made to be of any importance. This is the more remarkable as being a decided *retrocession* in the art of description. Prince, wisely following continental authors, is careful in his description of pears, to give, and with some minuteness, the peculiarities of the seed. But Downing, injudiciously misled by, in this respect, the decidedly bad example of British authors, has, almost without exception, neglected this noble criterion. There is not another single feature, either of fruit or fruit-trees, which we could not spare better than the *core and seed.* Not only may varie-

ties be marked by their seeds, but they form, in connection
with the core, important elements of diagnosis of *qualities*.
A long-keeper, usually has a very small, compact core, with
few seeds. A highly improved and luscious pear, not unfrequently is wholly seedless; while fruits not far removed
from the wild state abound in seeds. Whenever a *system
of description* shall have been formed, we venture to predict
that the *core and seed* will be ranked at a higher value in it
than any one other element of discrimination and description.

The same neglect or casual notice is bestowed upon the
leaf. If anything about it is remarkable it is mentioned,
not otherwise: but is there a page of any book that was
ever printed, that has more reading on it than is on a leaf,
if one is only taught to read it? *It,* too, is not only a sign
of difference but very often of *quality*. Mr. D. has availed
himself of this criterion in describing peaches. Is it a legible
sign only in the peach orchard? He that is ignorant of
these marks, and only can tell one *fruit* from another, is yet
in the a b c of pomology. Who but a tyro, on importing
Coe's Golden Drop, would not at once perceive the imposition, if there was one, the moment his eye saw a bud, or its
shoulder? Van Mons learned to select stocks for his experiments, as well by the wood and bud in winter, as by the
leaf and growth of summer. In a large bed of seedlings
every experimenter ought to know by wood and leaf what
to select as prognosticating good fruit, and what to reject,
without waiting to see the fruit. Nurserymen of our
acquaintance, without book, label, or stake, can tell every
well-known variety on their grounds. One of our acquaintance never had a mark, label, stake, or register, of any
kind upon his ground; a culpable reliance on his ability to
read tree-faces; for, on his throwing up the business suddenly, his successor fell into innumerable mistakes. It is
just as easy for a pomologist to know the face of every
variety, as for a shepherd to know the face of every sheep
in his flock, or a grazier every animal of his herd.

3. Although the "Fruit and Fruit-trees of America" professes to give the process of management only for the *garden and the orchard*, it ought to include, and we presume was designed to embrace the essential features of nursery culture. Every cultivator of fruit must be a private nurseryman; he needs the same information, the same directions as if he were a commercial gardener. He that designs planting an orchard ought to know the *disposition* of each variety of fruit-tree, that he may suit the circumstances of his soil, or provide for the peculiarities of a tree, as a farmer needs to know the peculiarities of the different breeds of hogs and cattle. With a large number of persons it would be enough to say of fruits, "superb," "extra-superb," "superlatively grand," "extra magnificent;" for such, a *princely* catalogue would answer every purpose. But such as have some knowledge, and every year, we are happy to believe, the number of such increases, ask, not the author's bare eulogy, but a definite statement of all those special qualities on which such eulogy is founded. The exact *taste* of each variety of fruit should be studied in respect to soil; some, and but few, love strong clays; yet fewer thrive upon wet soils; but some will, as the Sweet or Carolina June, which does well on quite wet soils; some refuse their gifts except upon a warm and rich sand; some, and by far the greatest number, love a deep loam, with a subsoil moist without being wet. The buds of some varieties escape the vernal frosts by their hardiness; some by putting forth later than their orchard brethren. Some varieties thrive admirably by ground or root grafting, while very many, so worked, are killed off during the first winter; some varieties, if budded, grow off with alacrity, others are dull and unwilling; some form their tops with facility and beauty; others, like many men, are rambling, awkward, and averse to any head at all. Some sorts, put upon what stock you will, have singularly massive roots; others have fine and slender ones. Every variety of tree has traits of

disposition peculiar to itself; and in respect to traits possessed in common, even these may be classified. In every description there should be, at least, an attempt at giving these various nursery peculiarities. It cannot be done, as yet, with any considerable accuracy. *Fruit-trees have not yet been minutely studied.* A florist can give you a thousand times more minute and special information in respect to the peculiar habits and wants of his flowers, than an orchardist can of his trees. Doubtless, it is easier to do it in plants which have a short period; whose whole life passes along before the eye every season, than in plants whose very youth outlasts ten generations of Dahlias, Pansies, Balsams, etc. But that only makes it the more important that we should be up and doing. Let no work be regarded as classic which does not take into its *design* the most thorough enunciation of all the peculiarities of fruits, and pomology will receive more advantage in ten years, than it could by a hundred years of rambling, unregulated, discursive descriptions.

The ability which Mr. D. has shown as a horticultural writer, his industry in collecting materials for this, his last work; the skill which he has shown himself to possess in describing fruits, give the public a right to expect that he will " go on unto perfection;" and if Mr. D. will adopt a higher standard and set out with a design of a more systematic description of fruits, every liberal cultivator in the land will be glad to put at his disposal whatever of minute observation he may possess.

———•••———

BUCKWHEAT is a corruption rather than a translation of the Saxon word *Buckwaizen*, the first syllable signifying beech, the tree of that name, whose nut the kernel of the grain so much resembles in shape. The grain, therefore, might be properly called beech-wheat.

LETTER FROM A. J. DOWNING.

WE give below a letter from Mr. Downing, long known as an eminent pomologist and more recently yet more distinguished for his writings upon Horticultural matters. Although a private letter, it is of general interest, and he will, we hope, indulge the liberty taken.*

"HIGHLAND GARDENS, NEWBURGH, NEW YORK,
Feb. 29*th*, 1845.

"MY DEAR SIR: I thank you for the interesting article on horticulture in the West, which appears in the last No. of *Hovey's Magazine.*

"My particular object in writing you at this moment is to call your attention to the remarks you make on the 'Golden Russet,' which you call 'the prince of small apples.' From your description of this fruit it is the 'Sheep-nose,' or 'Bullock's Pippin' of Coxe, well known here, and one of the most melting and delicious of apples. I understand from Professor Kirtland, of Cleveland, that this is the apple known by the name of Golden Russet in his region.

"Will you do me the favor, for the sake of settling the synonyms, to send me two or three cuttings of the young wood, by mail? I can then determine in a moment. The Sheep-nose has long shoots of a peculiar *drab* color. If your apple proves the same, I think I shall cancel the title 'Sheep-nose'—(a vile name), known only in New Jersey, and substitute 'American Golden Russet'†—this being its common title in New England and the West. I speak now in relation to my work on fruits, now in press.

"What do you mean by the 'White Bell-flower of Coxe?' The Detroit I have carefully examined, and it is quite

* Mr. Downing's untimely end by drowning, is well known.
† There is an English Golden Russet, distinct and quite acid.

different from the Yellow Bellflower. The Monstrous Bell-flower—the only other one Còxe describes—is a large autumn fruit, while the Detroit keeps till April?

"My work on Fruits has cost me a great deal of labor, but will still contain many imperfections. When it is out of press—in about six weeks—I promise myself the plea-sure of sending it with the copy of each of my previous works for the acceptance of your Horticultural Society. And I then hope to be favored with your criticism. Hoping an early answer to my queries herein,

"I am sincerely yours,
"A. J. Downing.

"H. W. Beecher."

We should have said "Monstrous Bellflower" instead of White.

The Bellflower here mentioned is the White or Green Bellflower of Indiana, the *Ohio Favorite* of western Ohio about Dayton, etc., the *Hollow-cored Pippin of some;* and it has been inquired for, at Mr. Alldredge's nursery, as the *Cumberland Spice*. Mr. A—— considered, from the description given, that the white Bellflower only could have been meant. But from the following description of Cumberland Spice in Kenrick, from Coxe, I am inclined to think that the true Cumberland Spice may have been inquired for.

"The tree is very productive; a fine dessert fruit, large, rather oblong, contracted toward the summit; the stalk thick and short; of a pale yellow color, clouded near the base; the flesh white, tender, and fine. It ripens in autumn, and keeps till winter, and shrivels in its last stages."

The fruit was brought to Wayne County, Indiana, by Mr. Brunson. He came from New York to Huron county, Ohio, and thence to Wayne County, Indiana. It is univer

sally diffused through the eastern and central parts of
Indiana, and is esteemed a first-rate apple. The *tree* strikingly resembles the Green Newtown Pippin, but its brush is
not so small, and there is less of it, the top being rather
more open. The wood is brittle, and, as the tree is a free
and constant bearer, it tends to break, and is troublesome
to keep in good order. Mr. Ernst and other gentlemen of
Cincinnati suppose the variety to be the *Detroit.* We
cannot say one thing or another, except that it is of the
Bellflower family. The Detroit of New York is a widely
different fruit, of a bright scarlet color, and we never heard
of any other *Detroit,* until the name was applied to this
apple.

There is not the least doubt that the *Golden Russet* of the
West is the *Bullock Pippin* and *Sheep-nose* of New Jersey,
and we hope that the proposed name "*American Golden
Russet*" will deliver us, for ever after, from eating any
more *sheep-noses.* Names are of importance in classifying
fruits, and there is a pleasure also in having a decorous name
to a good fruit. It is amusing to look through a catalogue
of singular names.

The *Hoss* apple is popularly the *Horse* apple, and when,
on a certain contingency a gentleman promised to eat a *hoss*
it was not so hazardous a threat as some have imagined.
The French, in naming their fruits, exercise a freedom with
things human and divine, to which we occidentals are not
accustomed (as, *Ah Mon Dieu! Grosse Cuisse Madame,*
etc.), and an innocent person, recapitulating his pears, might,
if .overheard by neighbors understanding French, be
thought very profane, or worse. There are other names
which have a tendency to make the mouth water, as *Onion
Pear.* One must have pleasing associations while eating
the *Toad Pear.* (See Prince's Pom. Man. p. 24 and 34.)
The French *Bon Chrétien* (or Good Christian) is called in
these parts the *Bon Cheat-em.* Then, there is the Demoi-
selle, the Lady's Flesh, and Love's Pear (Prince, 58, 34,

and 117)—very proper for young lovers. Then, there is the *Burnt Cat* (*Chat Bruslé* of the French, Prince 89), which undoubtedly has a musk flavor. We have less objection to the *Priest's Pear* (*Poire de Prêtre*, Prince, 108). Piscatory gentlemen would always angle in our nurseries for the *Trout* pear (Prince 130), and if they did not get a bite, the pear *would*, as it is a fine variety. How did those who named pears, *Louise Bonne de Jersey*, or *Van Mons leon le clerc*, expect common folks to hold fast to the true name? But he must have a short memory indeed, who forgets the emphatic name of *Yat* or *Yut*.

But to return from our digression. We give the description of the Golden Russet from three sources, and indorse their general accuracy:

GOLDEN RUSSET.—(DR. PLUMMER.)

" SIZE.—2 2-10 inches long; 2 7-10 inches wide.

" FORM.—Rather smaller at the summit; moderately flattened at the ends.

" PULP.—Very tender, juicy, yellowish white.

" COLOR.—Deep yellow, with brown and russet clouds; or wholly brown and russet.

" SURFACE.—Nearly dull; ruffled by the confluent lineoles; dots hardly discoverable.

" FLAVOR.—Sweet and delicious.

" STEM.—Slender; half to one inch long, reaching to a considerable distance beyond the verge.

" EYE.—In rather contracted cavity; closed.

" Ripens in the tenth month.

" It is one of our best apples, and keeps well through the winter."

" Whether the Leathercoat and the Glass apple are the same as are now known under those names, it is impossible to determine. Near Poughkeepsie, in the State of New York, the Leathercoat used to be a favorite fruit; and whether it is the same as the Golden Russet, described above, I am not now able to say; but my recollection of that apple after a lapse of twenty-three years, induces me to think it is no other than the Golden Russet; and, indeed, Trevelyan calls it also the '*russet* appell.' The Glass apple was described in a former number of 'The Orchard.' If the 'lethercott' has descended to us under the name of Golden Russet, the fine flavor of this apple would lead us to believe that it had not deteriorated, after a period of more than two centuries and a half."— *West. Farm. and Gard.*, 1843.

BULLOCK'S PIPPIN, OR SHEEP-NOSE.—(COXE.)

Golden Russet of Cincinnati. Golden Russet of the Eastern nurseries.—(Dr. Kirtland.)

"Neither the size nor appearance of this fruit would attract attention; yet it sells more readily in markets where it is known than any other apple. Its flavor is rich and pleasant, and many people consider it the best fruit of the season. In northern Ohio it matures at New-Year's, while in Cincinnati it is in perfection in November."— *West. Farm. and Gard.*, 1841.

GOLDEN RUSSET—BULLOCK PIPPIN, OR SHEEP-NOSE.— (A. HAMPTON.)

"This apple is below medium size; the skin is yellow, inclined to a russet; the flesh yellow, rich, juicy, tender and sprightly. I know of no apple more generally admired for its richness and excellent flavor than this; commanding a high price, and ready sale, in market; it makes very rich cider; a great and constant bearer; and keeps well till spring."— *West. Farm. and Gard.*, 1841.

We do not know another apple whose *flavor* and *flesh*

12

are so admirable.   A gentleman in Ohio, on being asked for a list of a hundred trees for an orchard, replied, " set out ninety-nine Golden Russets, the other one you can choose for yourself."

ATTENTION TO ORCHARDS.

CLEAN OUT your orchards.   Let no branches lie scattered around.   If in crops, let the tillage be thorough and clean. In plowing near the tree be careful not to strike deep enough to lacerate the small roots and fibres.   An orchard should be tended with a *cultivator* rather than a plow, and the space immediately about the tree should be worked with a hoe.   Look to the fence corners, and grub out all bushes, briers and weeds.   A fine orchard with such a ruffle around it, is like a handsome woman with dirty ears and neck.

Pruning may still be performed.   Those who are raising young orchards ought not to prune at *any* particular time between May and August, but *all along* the season, as the tree needs it.   If a bad branch is forming, take it out while it is small ; if too many are starting, rub them out while so tender as to be managed without a knife and by the fingers. If an orchard is rightly educated from the first, there will seldom be a limb to be cut off larger than a little finger, and a pen-knife will be large enough for pruning.   In the West there is more danger of pruning too much, than too little.   The sun should never be allowed to strike the inside branches of a fruit-tree.   Many trees are thus very much weakened and even killed if the sun is violently warm. Over-pruning induces the growth of shoots at the root, along the trunk, and all along the branches.

Grub up suckers, and clear off from large and well established trees all side-shoots.   After a tree is three inches in diameter through the stem, it may be kept entirely free of side-shoots. But young trees are much assisted in every respect, except appearance, by letting brush grow the whole length of their stem, only pinching off the ends of the whips, if they grow too rampantly. In this way the leaves afford great strength to the trunk, and prevent its being spindling or weak-fibred.

Scour off the dead bark, which, besides being unsightly, is. a harbor for a great variety of insects, and affords numerous crevices for water to stand in. We have previously recommended soft soap, thinned with urine to the consistence of paint, as a wash for trees; we have seen nothing better.

Examine grafts if any have been put in. See if the wax excludes the air entirely; rub out all shoots which threaten to overgrow and exhaust the graft; if it is growing too strongly, it must be supported, or it will blow out in some high wind.

LOOK OUT FOR BLIGHT.—All trees that have shown no indications of blight, will be safe for the season. But those which have shown the affection may be expected to continue to break out through the season. It is all important to use the knife freely; for although there is no contagion from tree to tree, yet the diseased sap will, in the same tree, be conveyed from part to part over the whole fabric. But prompt pruning will remove the seat and source of the evil. Where a branch is affected, cut chips out of the bark along down for yards; indeed, examine the limb entirely home to the trunk, and you may easily detect any spots which are depositories of this diseased sap, which, by its color, and whole appearance, will be identified by the most unpractised eye. Cut everything, below and aloft, that has this feculent sap in it, even if you take off the whole head by the trunk, and leave only a stump; for, the stump may send new shoots; but if the tree is spared from false tenderness you will lose it, bough, trunk, and root.

WINE AND HORTICULTURE.

" Look not thou upon the wine when it is red, when it giveth his color in the cup, when it moveth itself aright."

Now, the Cincinnati Horticultural Society appointed a committee to do just what Solomon says must not be done. Their report is a very artful document, so drawn up that the unwary would suppose that this was a mere business affair—passing off quite respectably. But we were not to be deceived; we instantly saw through it; and pencil in hand, we noted all places in the report proper to shock a true Washingtonian heart.

Although the array of forty kinds of wine save one, did not intimidate these hitherto respectable gentlemen, it inspired them with prudence; and a German Committee called in, to ferret out any foreign wines which might have been smuggled in to the confusion of the judges.

The committee only darkly intimate their *modus operandi;* if they had given us a journal of their doings, made out on the spot, by some trusty clerk, what a bacchanal mystery would have been disclosed! but they had discretion enough left to defer this until they were sober again.

But Washingtonianism is abroad, and can detect all the mysteries of ebriety, however graced with authority from a Horticultural Society. We can imagine the impatience with which the bottles were preliminarily eyed—the entire moderation with which each sipped a few first specimens; we can see them gradually warming with their subject—tasting with alacrity—nodding at each other, squinting through the ruddy glass, smacking their too often dewy lips, or wagging their heads with more than ordinary satisfaction as a beaker of great merit made the *facilis descensus averni.* Laughter interrupts sober attention to business; in vain the chairman thumps the table for order;

he gets more jokes than attention. Many a sly story is told; some of them have visited wine countries and now begin long yarns thereof; the clamor of laughing, and anecdote, and criticism—the necessity, in consequence, of re-tasting, and tasting again to arrive at a conclusion, brought them, we doubt not, to a most lamentable conclusion, although the report only obscurely hints of it, as we shall see. Had any of them married into the Caudle connection we might have had a graphic account of their several arrivals at their homes—at what time, by whose help, in what condition, etc.

The tabular report given in has evidently been studiously framed. We suspect that if the opinions had been set down just in the order of their occurrence, they would have afforded an index of the condition of the committee as well as of the wine. But though they have mixed them up, they cannot elude our vigilance—we can pick out the chronological order. At first such opinions as these were given: "Tolerably good," "Inferior," "Poor, fermented on skins." They were critical yet; but warming a little they express more generous sentiments; "Good," "Very good Cape," "Very good, resembling old Madeira." The next step shows the genial advance—some were getting disputatious. "Good, considered by some better than No. 8, by others not so good,"—they evidently had a row about it. They next advanced into the patriotic mood as is seen in the judgment of our foreign wines, "Good dry wine, but supposed to be foreign," "Inferior, a foreign wine," "Not American wine." Here the gradations of contempt are very plain. We have next, melancholy evidence of their progress in the necessity of a stronger body to their wines,—"Not liked, supposed to have been injured in the bottle." Why not say it right out, that it was a weak, thin wine? Here we have it, "*Good strong* wine." The last record made is "Good new, not in a state for judgment." Does this refer to the wine or to the committee?

To the latter we suppose; and at this point, probably perceiving their condition, they laid aside their official character and made it a private, personal, and somewhat miscel-
laneous affair. We see now the meaning of a sentence
which follows the tabular exhibit: "The judgments pronounced and recorded in the foregoing table, were as
nearly unanimous as can ever be expected among so many
judges."

The committee state in respect to western wines: "That
the pure juice of the grape when judiciously managed will
furnish the finest kind of wine, without any addition or
mixture whatever; that no saccharine addition is necessary
to give it sufficient body to keep for any length of time in
this climate."

We submit that the *keeping* properties of wine are not
altogether intrinsic; but depend much upon the persons
having access to them, or, as we were taught in school,
"on time, place, and person." In *our* cellar American
wines would doubtless have great longevity. We wish to
call the attention of Mr. Gough to the closing sentence of
the report: "A taste for the wines of this region appears
to be well established, since all that can be produced finds
a ready market at good prices; and the committee are of
opinion, that the period is not distant when the wines of
the Ohio will enjoy a celebrity equal to those of the
Rhine."

Here's work on hand for him. In conclusion, we
respectfully suggest that the same committee be continued
from year to year, as there is no use in spoiling a fresh set
every year. If the specimens multiply, perhaps more help
will be required—at any rate a by-law should be passed,
so that there shall be one committee-man to at least every
ten bottles.

DO VARIETIES OF FRUIT RUN OUT.

Is there such similarity between animals and vegetables, in their organic structure, development and functions, as to make it safe to reason upon the properties of the one from the known properties of the other?

It is admitted that the lowest forms of vegetable existence are extremely difficult to be distinguished from a corresponding form of animal existence. As we approach the lower confines of the vegetable kingdom, flowers, and of course, seeds, disappear. The distinction between leaves and stem ceases; and, at last, the stem and root are no longer to be separated, and we find a mere vegetable sheet or lamina whose upper surface is leaf and whose lower surface is root. In a corresponding sphere, animal existence is reduced to its simplest elements. Whatever resemblances there are in the lowest and rudimentary forms of vegetable and animal life, it cannot be doubted that when we rise to a more perfect organization, the two kingdom become distinct and the structure and functions of each are in such a sense peculiar to itself, that he will grossly misconceive the truth who supposes a structure or a function to exist in a vegetable, because such structure or function exists in an animal, and *vice versâ*. To be sure, they resemble in *generals* but they differ in *specials*. Both begin in a seminal point but the seed is not analogous; both develop —but not by an analogous growth; both require food, but the selection, the digestion and the assimilation are different. The mineral kingdom is the lowest. Out of it, by help of the sun and air, the vegetable procures its materials of growth; in turn the vegetable kingdom is the magazine from which the animal kingdom is sustained; to each, thus the soil contains the original elements; the vegetable is the chemical manipulator, and the animal, the final recipient of its products. The habit of reasoning from one to the other, of giving an idea of the one by illustrations drawn from the other, especially in popular writings, will always be fruitful of misconceptions and mistakes.

The next idea set forth in the paragraph which we review, is, the *essential dissimilarity of buds and seeds.* The writer thinks that a plant from a seed is a *new* organization, but a plant from a bud or graft (which is but a developed bud) is but a continuation of a previous plant. With the exception of their integuments, a bud and a seed are the *same thing.* A seed is a bud prepared for one set of circumstances, and a bud is a seed prepared for another set of circumstances— it is the same embryo in different garments. The seed has been called, therefore, a " primary bud," the difference beng one of *condition* and not of *nature.*

It is manifest, then, that the plant which springs from a bud is as really a new plant as that which springs from a seed ; and it is equally true, that a seed may convey the weakness and diseases of its parent with as much facility as a bud or a graft does. If the feebleness of a tree is general, its functions languid, its secretions thin, then a bud or graft will be feeble,—and so would be its seed ; or if a tree be thoroughly tainted with disease, the buds would not escape, nor the tree springing from them—neither would its seed, or a tree springing from it. A tree from a *bud* of the Doyenne pear is just as much a new tree as one from its *seed.*

The idea which we controvert has received encouragement from the fact, that a bud produces a fruit like the parent tree, while, oftentimes, a seed yields only a *variety* of such fruit. But, it is probable that this is never the case with seeds except when they have been brought into a state of what Van Mons calls variation. In their natural and uncultivated state, seeds will reproduce their parent with as much fidelity as a bud or a graft.

The liability of a variety to run out, when propagated by bud or graft, is not a whit greater than when propagated by seed, *in so far as the nature of the vegetable is concerned.*

But it is true that the conditions in which a bud grows render it liable to extrinsic ills not incidental to a plant springing from seed. A seed, emitting its roots directly into the earth, is liable only to its own ills; a bud or graft emitting roots, through the alburnum of the stock on which it is established, into the earth, is subject to the infirmities of the stock as well as to its own. Thus a healthy seed produces a healthy plant. A healthy bud may produce a feeble plant, because inoculated upon a diseased branch or stem.

Instead of a limitation in their nature, there is reason to suppose that trees might flourish to an indefinite age were it not for extrinsic difficulties. A tree, unlike an animal, is not a single, simple organization, it is rather a *community* of plants. Every bud separately is an elementary plant, capable, if disjoined from the branch, of becoming a tree by itself. In fact, each bud emits roots, which, uniting together, go down upon a common support (the trunk) and enter the earth, and are there put in connection with appropriate food. Every fibre of root may be traced upward to its bud from which it issued.

In process of time, the elongation of the trunk exposes it to accidents; the branches are subject to the force of storms; in proportion as the distance from the roots increases, and the longer the passages through which the upper sap, or downward elaborated sap travels, the more liabilities are there to stoppage and injury. The reason of decline in a tree is not to be looked for in any exhaustion of vital force in the organization itself, but it is to be found in the immense surface and substance exposed to the wear and tear of the elements.

It would seem, if this view be true, that no bounds can be placed to the duration of perennial plants, if, by any means, we could diminish their exposure, by reducing their expansion, by keeping them within a certain sphere of growth. *Now this is exactly what is accomplished by bud-*

12*

ding. A bud, far removed on the parent stock from the root and connected with it through a long trunk, is inoculated upon a new stock. It now grows with a comparatively limited exposure to interruption or accident. The connection with the soil is short and direct.

In this manner a variety of fruit may be perpetuated to all generations, *if the laws of vegetable health be regarded in the process.* Healthy buds, worked upon healthy stocks and planted in wholesome soil, will make healthy trees; and from these another generation may proceed, and from these another. By a due regard to vegetable physiology, the Newtown Pippin, and the Seckle Pear, may be eaten two thousand years hence, *provided, always,* that expounders of prophesy will allow us the use of the earth so long for orchard purposes. A disregard of the laws of vegetable physiology in the propagation of varieties, will, on the other hand, rapidly deteriorate the most healthy sort. There is no clock-work in the branches of the tree, which finally runs down past all winding up; there is no fixed quantity of vitality, which a variety at length uses up, as a garrison does its bread. Plants renew themselves and every year have a fresh life, and, in this respect, they differ essentially from all forms of animal existence. Any *one* tree may wear out; but a *variety*, never.

We need not say, therefore, that we dissent from Knight's theory of natural exhaustion and from every supplement to it put forth since his day. Van Mons' theory of *variation* and the tendency of plants to return toward their original type, is to be regarded as nearer the truth.

THE STRAWBERRY CONTROVERSY.

No man will deny that in their cultivated state, strawberries are found, in respect to their blossoms, in three conditions: first, blossoms with stamens alone, the pistillate organs being mere rudiments; second, blossoms with pistillate organs developed fully, but the stamens very imperfect, and inefficient; third, blossoms in which staminate and pistillate organs are both about equally developed.

There are two questions arising on this state of facts; one, a question of mere vegetable physiology, viz., Is such a state of organization peculiar to this plant originally, or is it induced by cultivation? The other question is one of eminent practical importance, viz., What effect has this state of organization upon the success of cultivation?

Passing by the first question, for the present, we would say of the second that, a *substantial* agreement has at length, been obtained. It is on all hands conceded that staminate plants, or those possessing only stamens, and not pistillate organs, are unfruitful. Any other opinion would now be regarded as an absurdity. It is equally well understood that pistillate plants, or those in which the female organs are fully, and the male organs scarcely at all developed, are unfruitful. No one would attempt to breed a herd of cattle from males *exclusively*, or from *females;* and, for precisely the same reason, strawberries cannot be had from plants substantially male, or substantially female, where each are kept to themselves.

But a difference yet exists among cultivators as to the facts respecting those blossoms which contain *both* male and female organs, or, as they are called, *perfect* flowering plants.

Mr. Longworth states, if we understand him, substantially, that perfect-flowering varieties will bear but moderate crops, and, usually, of small fruit.

On the other hand, Dr. Brinkle, whose seedling strawberries we noticed in a former article, Mr. Downing, and several other eminent cultivators adopt the contrary opinion, that, *with care*, large crops of large fruit may be obtained from perfect-flowering plants. This question is yet, then, to be settled.

It is ardently to be hoped that, hereafter, we shall have less premature and positive assertion, upon unripe observations, than has characterized the early stages of this controversy. We will take the liberty of following Mr. Hovey in his magazine, between the years 1842 and 1846, not for any pleasure that we have in the singular vicissitudes of opinion chronicled there, but because an eminent cultivator, writer, and editor of, hitherto, the only horticultural magazine in our country, has such influence and authority in forming the morals and customs of the kingdom of Horticulture, that every free subject of this beautiful realm is interested to have its chiefs men of such accuracy that it will not be dangerous to take their statements.

In 1842, Mr. Longworth communicated an article on the fertile and sterile characters of several varieties of strawberries for Mr. Hovey's magazine, which Mr. H. for subject-matter, indorsed. In the November number, Mr. Coit substantially advocated the sentiments of Mr. L.; and the editor, remarking upon Mr. Coit's article, recognized distinctly the existence of male and female plants.

He (Mr. H.) says that, of four kinds mentioned by Mr. C. as unfruitful, two were so "*from the want of staminate or male plants;*" and "the cause of the barrenness *is thus easily explained.*" And he goes on to explain divers cases upon this hypothesis; and still more resolutely he says, that all wild strawberries have not perfect flowers; "in a dozen or two plants which we examined last spring *some were perfect* (the italics are ours) having both stamens and pistils; *others, only pistils,* and *others, only stamens;* thus showing that the *defect, mentioned by Mr. Longworth, exists in the original species.*" He closes by urging cultivators to set rows of early Virginia among the beds for the sake of impregnating the rest.

Mr. Hovey's next formal notice was exactly one year from the foregoing, November, 1843, and it appears thus: "We believe it is now the generally received opinion *of all intelligent cultivators* (italics are ours again) that there is *no necessity of making any distinction in regard to the sexual character of the plants when forming new beds. The idea of male and female flowers*, first originated, we believe, by Mr. Longworth, of Ohio, is now considered *as exploded*." Such a sudden change as this was brought about, he says, by additional information received during that year by means of his correspondents, and by more experience on his own part. He says nothing of male blossoms and female blossoms, *which he had himself seen in wild strawberries*. Mr. Hovey then assumed the theory that *cultivation*, good or bad, is the cause of fertile or unfertile beds of strawberries, and he says: "in conclusion, we think we may safely aver, that there is not the least necessity of cultivating *any one strawberry near another* (our italics) to insure the fertility of the plants, *provided* they are under a proper state of cultivation."

Mr. Hovey now instituted experiments, which he promised to publish, by which to bring the matter to the only true test; and he, from time to time, re-promised to give the result to the public, which, thus far, we believe, he has forgotten to do.

His magazine for 1844 opens, as that of 1843 closed; and in the first number he says, "the oftener our attention is called to this subject, the more we feel confirmed in the opinon that the theory of Mr. Longworth is entirely unfounded; that there is *no such thing as male and female plants*, though certain causes may produce, as we know they have, fertile and sterile ones."

Nevertheless, in the next issue but one this peremptory language is again softened down, and a doubt even appears, when he says, " IF *Mr. Longworth's theory should prove true,*" etc. We, among others, waited anxiously for the promised experiments; but if published we never saw them. The subject rather died out of his magazine until August, 1845, when, in speaking of the Boston Pine, a second fine seedling of his own raising, he is seen bearing away on the other tack, if not with *all* sails set, yet with enough to give the ship headway in the right direction: " Let the causes be what they may, it is sufficient for all practical purposes, to know, that *the most abundant crops* (italics ours) can be produced by planting some sort abounding in *staminate* flowers, in the near vicinity of those which do not possess them." P. 293. And on p. 444 he reiterates the advice to plant near the staminate varieties. In the August number for 1846, p. 309, Mr. Hovey shows himself a thorough convert to Mr. Longworth's views, by indorsing, in the main, the report of the committee of the Cincinnati Horticultural Society. We hope after so various a voyage, touching at so many points, that he will now abide steadfast in the truth.

We look upon this as a very grave matter, not because the strawberry question is of such paramount, although it is of no inconsiderable importance; but it is of importance whether accredited scientific magazines should be trustworthy; whether writers or popular editors should be responsible for mistakes entirely unnecessary. We blame no man for vacillation, while yet in the process of investigation, nor for coming at the truth gradually, since this is the necessity of our condition to learn only by degrees, and by painful siftings. The very first requisite for a writer is, that he be worthy of trust in his statements. No man can be trusted who ventures opinions upon uninvestigated matters; who states facts with assurance which he has not really ascertained; who evinces rashness, haste, carelessness, credulity, or fickleness in his judgments. The question of perfect or imperfect blossoms depends upon the simplest exercise of eyesight. It requires no measurements, no process of the laboratory, no minute dissections or nice calculations; it requires only that a man should *see* what he *looks* at.

When a boy, playing "how many fingers do I hold up," by dint of peeping from under the bandage, we managed to make very clever guesses of how many lily-fingers some roguish lassie was holding in tempting show before our bandaged eyes; but some folks are not half so lucky with both eyes wide open, and the stamens and pistils standing before them.

If such a latitude is permitted to those who conduct the investigations peculiar to horticulture, who can confide in the publication of facts, observations or experiments? Of what use will be journals and magazines? They become like chronometers that will not keep time; like a compass that has lost its magnetic sensibility; like a guide who has lost his own way, and leads his followers through brake, and morass, and thicket, into interminable wanderings. Sometimes, the consciousness of faults in ourselves, which should make us lenient toward others, only serves to produce irritable fault-finding. After a comparison of opinions and facts, through a space of five years, with the most distinguished cultivators, East and West, Mr. Longworth is now universally admitted to have sustained himself in all the essential points which he first promulgated—not *discovered*, for he made no claims of that sort. The gardeners and the magazines of the East have, at length, adopted his practical views, after having stoutly, many of them, contested them.

It was, therefore, with unfeigned surprise, that we read Mr. Hovey's latest remarks in the September number of his magazine, in which, with some asperity, he roundly charges Mr. Longworth with manifold errors, and treats him with a contempt which would lead one, ignorant of the controversy, to suppose that Mr. Hovey had never made a mistake, and that Mr. Longworth had been particularly fertile of them. Thus : " Mr. Longworth's remarks abound in so many errors and inconsistencies, that we shall expect scarcely to notice all." " Another *gross assertion*," etc. Referring to another topic, he says, " This question we, therefore, consider as satisfactorily settled, without discussing Mr. Longworth's conflicting views about male and female, Keen's," etc.

This somewhat tragical comedy is now nearly played out, and we have spoken a word just before the fall of the curtain, because, as chroniclers of events, and critics of horticultural literature and learning, it seemed no less than our duty. We have highly appreciated Mr. Hovey's various exertions for the promotion of the art and science of horticulture, nor will his manifest errors and short-comings in this particular instance, disincline us to receive from his pen whatsoever is good.

We hope that our remarks will not be construed as a defence of western men or western·theories, but as the defence of the truth, and of one who has truly expounded it, though, in this case, theory and its defender happen to be of western origin. Whatever errors have crept into Mr. Longworth's remarks should be faithfully expurgated ; and perhaps it may be Mr. Hovey's duty to perform the lustration. If so, courtesy would seem to require that it should be done with some consciousness, that through this whole controversy Mr. Longworth is now admitted to have been right in all essential matters ; and if, in error at all, only in minor particulars, while Mr. Hovey, in all the controversy, in respect to the plainest facts, has been changing from wrong to right, from right to wrong, and from wrong back to right again. We do not think that the admirable benefits which Mr. Longworth has conferred upon the whole community by urging the improved method of cultivating the strawberry, has been adequately appreciated. We still less like to see gratitude expressed in the shape of snarling gibes and petty cavils.

We will close these remarks by the correction of a matter
which Mr. Downing states.   While he assents to all the
practical aspects of Mr. Longworth's views, he dissents as
to some matters of fact and philosophy, and among others,
to the fact that Hovey's seedling is *always* and *only* a pistillate plant.   He thinks that originally it had *perfect* flowers, but that after bearing twice or thrice on the same roots
the plants degenerate and become either pistillate or staminate.   He says, " Hovey's seedling strawberry, at first,
was a perfect sort in its flower, but at this moment more
than half the plants in this country have become pistillate."

Mr. Hovey himself states the contrary on p. 112 of his
magazine for 1844.   He denies that there are two kinds
of blossoms to his seedling, and says, "the flowers are all
of one kind, with both pistils and stamens, *but the latter
quite short and hidden under the receptacle.*"   This is the
common form of all *pistillate* blossoms, and shows, in so far
as Mr. Hovey's observations are to be trusted, that, at its
starting-point and home, Hovey's seedling was, as with us it
now invariably is, so far as we have ever seen it, a pistillate
plant.

———•••———

STRAWBERRIES.

DIRECTIONS for the culture of the strawberry will vary
with circumstances; as, whether it is raised for private use,
or for market.   But, for whatever purpose cultivated,
respect must be invariably had to the fact of staminate and
pistillate flowers, or male and female.   Each flower contains
the rudiments of both the male and female organs.   But the
male organs are more or less defective in one set of plants
and the female in another "and, in the Hudson and some
others, it amounts to a complete separation of the sexes.
In some of the male (staminate) varieties more or less of

the blossoms are also partially perfect in the female organs and will produce some fruit.

" Every flower contains both the male and female organs ; and, in the white and monthly, both organs are always perfect in the same blossom, as far as my experience goes. In other kinds, the male organs are more or less defective in one set of plants, and the female in the other ; and, in the Hudson and some other varieties, it amounts to a complete separation of the sexes. The male organs are so defective in one set of plants, and the female in the other, that an acre of either would not produce a single fruit. In some of the male (staminate) varieties, more or less of the blossoms are also more or less perfect in the female organs, and will produce more or less fruit ; but I have never seen a female plant with the male organs sufficiently developed to produce a single perfect fruit. Hovey's seedling, and some others, may produce deformed berries."—*Longworth.*

Mr. Longworth, in consequence of this fact, always has a compartment allotted to male and one to female plants, and out of these he forms his beds, being able thus to insure a proper proportion of males to females. Mr. S. S. Jackson, a very skillful nurseryman of Cincinnati, usually, in selling plants, puts up ninety females to ten males in the hundred.

We shall now give the time and manner of planting of some of the best cultivators in the West, at the East, and in England.

Mr. Jackson says : " I plant any time from the first of April, till they are in bloom. I, one year, planted twenty-five square roods of ground ; the plants were all in bloom when set out ; and the next year I picked thirty-eight bushels, and there were fully ten bushels left on the vines.

" I plant them in this way : first plow or spade the ground ; harrow it smooth ; then strain a line on one side nine inches from the edge, and a row from twelve to fifteen inches apart; then move the line eighteen inches, and plant another row; then move it three feet, and again eighteen inches—and so on till the ground is planted. I then go over and put one male plant every six feet, between the two rows. Keep them clear of weeds through the summer, and let them spread as much as they will.

"In the fall dress the out-walks eighteen inches wide, which will leave the beds three feet wide; and when it sets in cold, give them a light covering of straw; rake it off in the spring. You may then expect a full crop. It is best to make a new bed once in two or three years."

But plantations may be made through the summer, and as late as September; of course, the earlier in the season the better established the plants will become before winter, and the larger the next summer's crop. Thus, a bed formed in September would bear very scantily; while Mr. Jackson's beds, formed in the spring, produced a large crop the next season.

Mr. Kenrick gives the following methods as practised by market gardeners near Boston; the first one strikes us as being the most economical way of working strawberries, on a large scale, that we have seen:

"In the vicinity of Boston, the following mode is often adopted. The vines are usually transplanted in August. The rows are formed from eighteen inches to two feet asunder. The runners, during the first year, are destroyed. In the second year, they are suffered to grow and fill the interval, and in the autumn of that year, the whole old rows are turned under with the spade, and the rows are thus shifted to the middle of the space. The same process is repeated every second year.

"Another mode, which may be recommended generally, is to plant the strawberries in rows thirty inches asunder, and nine inches distant in the row, and suffer the vines to extend to the width of eighteen inches, leaving twelve inches' space for an alley; or allow eighteen inches' width

to the alleys, and three feet asunder to the rows; and to
form new beds every three years, or never to suffer the bed
to exist over four years; and to plant out in August in
preference to spring."

Dr. Bayne of Alexandria, D. C., gives his method
of producing very large fruit. The peculiarity of his
treatment is the use of undecomposed or green manure.
Almost every other cultivator recommends *well rotted*
manure; and, we are inclined to think, with the better
reason. We have found some English cultivators who
agree with him; but the most dissuade from the practice,
as making plants productive of leaves rather than fruit.

"To produce strawberries of extraordinary size for exhibition, I would recommend the following preparation:
select the best soil and trench it at least two feet deep;
incorporate well with the first twelve inches an abundance
of strong undecomposed manure; pulverize and rake the
ground well, then mark off the rows twelve or fifteen inches
asunder, and set the plants in the rows from twelve to
fifteen inches, according to the luxuriance and vigor of the
variety. During the first year, the runners must be carefully and frequently destroyed before they become rooted.
By this means the stools become very vigorous and bear the
most abundant crops. In the spring after the fruit is set,
place around each plant a small quantity of straw, or what
is much better, cover the whole surface of the ground one
inch thick with wheat chaff. This prevents evaporation,
protects the fruit from the earth, improves the flavor, and
will greatly increase the size."

Loudon gives Garnier's method of treating the strawberry as an *annual*. It is peculiarly applicable to small
gardens. The observations on the depth of soil required,
are worthy of especial attention:

"Early in August, or as soon as the gathering is over, I
destroy all my beds, and proceed immediately to trench,
form, and manure them in the manner before directed, to

receive the plants for the crop of the ensuing year, taking care to select for that purpose the strongest and best-rooted runners from the old rejected plants. If at this season the weather should be particularly hot, and the surface of the ground much parched, I defer the operation of preparing my beds and planting them till the ground is moistened by rain. Such is the simple mode of treatment which I have adopted for three successive years, and I have invariably obtained upon the same spot, a great produce of beautiful fruit, superior to that of every other garden in the neighborhood. Depth of soil I have found absolutely necessary for the growth and production of fine strawberries, and when this is not to be obtained, it is useless, in my opinion, to plant many of the best varieties. It is not generally known, but I have ascertained the fact, that most strawberries generate roots, and strike them into the ground, nearly two feet deep in the course of one season. The practice of renewing strawberry plantations every year, and even of using runners of the current year for forcing, is now become very general among gardeners. Mr. Knight generally adopts this mode, and, notwithstanding the increased labor attending it, it is even adopted by some market-gardeners about London for their earliest crops. It is invariably found that by this mode the fruit not only comes larger, but somewhat earlier. It must always be recollected, however, by those who intend practising it, that almost the whole of the success depends on bringing forward the earliest runners, by encouraging them to root. This is done by stirring the soil beneath them, hooking them down, or retaining them in their proper places by small stones; or, when the object is to procure plants for forcing rooting them into small pots."

RASPBERRIES, STRAWBERRIES, GOOSEBERRIES AND CURRANTS.

CURRANTS, Gooseberries, Raspberries, Strawberries, etc., are termed "Small Fruit." We will give some directions for spring-work which these require.

RASPBERRIES.—The sorts usually found in our gardens are rejected from all good collections as worthless. The Antwerp, red and white, have, until lately, been regarded as the best. Two new kinds are very highly thought of— the *Franconia* and the *Fastolf.* This last is an English variety; was found growing on a gentleman's ground among some lime and brick rubbish—evidently a seedling —and removed to his garden. It was a number of years before it attracted attention; but, lately, it has been much in demand and bids fair to claim a rank among the first, if it is not *the* first.

A deep, rich, loamy soil which is moist, proves best for this fruit. It prefers a half shady position.

When first planted, put them four feet apart in the row, and the rows three feet from each-other.

In old beds cut out the *last year's bearing wood,* now worthless, and also all the new shoots but four or five to a root; grub up all that have come up between the rows. Cut those which are reserved for bearing to about five feet in length, and tie them gently to a stake. Thus treated from year to year, and well manured, raspberries will return a rich reward.

STRAWBERRIES.—The number of kinds is immense. Knight, late president of the London Horticultural Society, had *four hundred* kinds in his garden, and most of them seedlings of his own raising. The early *Virginia* is regarded as the best early kind. Hovey's, Warren's and Keen's seedlings are admirable sorts. Wiley's and Motter's seedlings originated in Cincinnati and are esteemed. There are many other fine sorts which an amateur cultivator would wish, not necessary to common gardens, where two or three choice sorts will suffice.

Almost every cultivator has a way of his own in raising strawberries.

In private gardens, in a soil well enriched and deeply spaded, let beds be formed about four feet wide; upon these set three rows of hills and the plants about fifteen inches apart in the row. *Pinch off all runners through the season*, unless they are wanted for new plants.

Old beds, grown over and matted, had better be destroyed; but if, for any reason, it is desirable to save them, mark out lines every eighteen inches and dig alleys through the bed, by turning the plants under. In this way the patch will be thrown into beds of eighteen inches width. Before this is done take an iron-toothed rake and rake the bed severely. Do not be afraid of tearing the plants; go over the whole bed thoroughly. It will seem as if scarcely a dozen plants were left, but in a few weeks your bed will be entirely covered with a strong growth.

GOOSEBERRIES.—This fruit is very much neglected because its merits are only little known. There are two sorts found in our gardens, the common gooseberry and *English*, by which name is meant a large, coarse, thick-skinned green variety. It is not generally known that there are any other cultivated sorts; and as these are inferior they are little cared for. The Lancashire (England) Nurserymen publish 300 varieties! The select list of Mr. Thompson of the London Horticultural Society's garden comprises *fifty-six* varieties; the still more condensed select list of *Robert Manning* (Mass.) includes *twenty-eight* sorts. Some of these bear fruit as large as a medium-sized plum. There are four colors, red, yellow, green and white; to each color are two sizes, large and small fruits. Those who have not seen and tasted the Scotch and Lancashire varieties of the gooseberry do not know what the fruit is. In sending for them, select a *trustworthy* nurseryman, and request him to send, of each color, such kinds as have proved, with him, the best; and in such numbers as you may wish. The gooseberry delights in three things, a very rich soil, a shady position, and a free circulation of air. If accommodated in these respects, it will be free from mildew and give a sure and ample crop of delicious fruit.

Hill-tops are the best sites. In gardens the open and airy parts should be selected; in low and confined situations they mildew. Hog manure is esteemed the best for this fruit. When the fruit begins to set, if threatened with blight, take a moderately strong lime-water (sulphur added will be all the better) or, if lime is not convenient, lye from wood ashes, and drench the bushes freely with it. A large watering-pot should be employed. Gooseberries may be increased from cuttings like the currant, and with the same ease.

CURRANTS.—There are very few varieties of this fruit. Our common red and white, if well cultivated, are very good. The Large Dutch Red, and White, are much larger varieties and generally preferred in the best Eastern gardens. Every farmer, if he has nothing else, has a long row of currant bushes, and gets, usually, five times as many currants as he can consume. Very few fruits have so few diseases incident to them as the currant. It is not infested with worms, its fruit is subject to no blight, it bears every year, is rarely affected either by severe winters or late frosts, and we do not remember a season in our lives when there was not, at least, a partial currant crop.

We advise those who are careful in such matters to train their currants to a *tree form;* let a cutting be set, rub out all the buds but two or three at the top; at about twelve or fifteen inches from the earth let the branches put out, and never permit suckers to grow, or branches to stand lower than this. The difficulty which some have found in tree currants, that they are top-heavy and require staking to prevent their being bent by winds and their own weight, arises from having the stem too long. We have seen two feet and even more allowed. If twelve or fifteen inches be allowed, the stem, in a few years, will become strong enough to withstand winds and sustain its own top. Thus formed they are beautiful to the eye, convenient for borders, allow a free circulation of air under and through them, are easy to work in spring or for manuring, and easy to prune, when, as should be done every year, you take out the old wood.

Gooseberries will do better to be trained in this way, than in the bush form. The top once formed, there is no difficulty in keeping it so. If you are faithful to grub up every sucker for one season you will have few to plague you after that.

Gooseberries, Raspberries, Strawberries and Currants ought to be found in every farmer's garden. The trouble of cultivation is slight and the return of wholesome fruit very great. One woman can, for the most part, bestow all the attention which they need.

SPRING-WORK IN THE ORCHARD.

1. THERE is a great deal more pruning done than is needful or healthful. Our hot summers and strong growth of wood make every leaf on the tree precious. Dead limbs should be taken out. Where the tree is really *tangled* with wood, thin out. Where branches are rubbing across each other *severely*, take off one of them. Grub up *every* water-sprout from the roots. If you can avoid it, do not use them for trees, for the tree thus obtained will inherit the same propensity of sending up water-shoots. Sometimes, in scarcity of stock, they are used rather than to have none, but it is then only a lesser of two evils.

2. TIME OF PRUNING.—There is a bad practice abroad of pruning before the leaves are out. English books direct to

13

prune in February, and we suspect that the custom sprang up at the East from the old country example. It is not safe for us to follow the *specific* processes of Great Britain or the Continent. OUR OWN *well settled experience is to be our rule of practice.*

There is no better month in the year to prune, *than that month in which the tree is making the most wood.* It is plain that the sooner a wound heals the better; and equally plain, that a tree which is *growing* will heal a wound quicker than an inactive tree. All the matter which goes to form wood, or to form the granulations by which a cut heals, comes from the *downward* current of sap, or sap which has been elaborated in the leaf. Of course when the tree has the most leaves, and the leaves are preparing the greatest quantity of *proper juice* or elaborated sap, that is the time for pruning, because the time for healing. In this climate we have preferred the last of May for spring pruning, and the last of August for summer pruning—the exact week varying as the season is forward or backward.

3. INSTEAD OF PRUNING AT THIS EARLY PERIOD, LET TREES BE THOROUGHLY SCRAPED AND SCOURED.—A three-sided scraper, such as butchers use to clean their blocks with, or any convenient implement, may be applied to the trunk and large branches with force sufficient to take off the *dry*, *dead* bark. Only this is to be removed. Take soft soap and reduce it by *urine* to the consistence of paint. With a stiff shoe-brush rub the whole trunk and the limbs as far up as is practicable. The bark will grow smooth and glossy; insect eggs will be entirely destroyed; all moss and fungous vegetation removed, and the bark stimulated and made healthier. THIS IS BETTER THAN ANY WHITEWASH, and just as convenient.

4. Lime is better used as follows : remove the earth from the trunk, and put about half a peck to each tree. Every spring, spread and dig in the old lime, and put new in its place. Unleached ashes are good to be dug in around a

tree. If your soil is calcareous, full of lime, these applications are not needful. Thoroughly rotted manure, or better yet, black vegetable mold may be dug in liberally, and will supply the soil with nutriment, and the roots will find their way in with great facility.

5. When a tree is manured, remember that the *ends* only of the roots take up nourishment, and that the ends of the roots are not found close by the *trunk*. We often see heaps of manure piled about the *trunk*, and the ends of the roots are three yards or more distant from it. You might as well put your fodder down at your cattle's hind legs, and wonder that they did not get fat on it. Treat your trees as you do your stock—put their food where their mouths are. YOUNG ORCHARDS are better without stimulating manure. Let the soil be mellowed, and then give the trees their own time, and if they do not bear quite as soon, they will live longer and be less subject to disease.

MIRACLES IN FRUITS.

WHEN a traveller was relating, in Cowper's presence, some prodigious marvels, the poet smiled somewhat incredulously. "Well, sir, don't you believe me? I saw it with my own eyes." "Oh, certainly, I believe it if *you* saw it, but I would not if I had seen it *myself*." Even so we feel about the thousand and one physiological fooleries which run the monthly rounds of the papers.

How on earth do men suppose a fruit to receive its characteristic quality? Is it from the root, trunk, pith, bark, branch, or leaf? One would think that it made no difference which. We have long supposed that the leaf digested the sap, returned it to the passages of distribution to be employed in the formation of fruit, wood, tissue, etc. Is this the function of the leaf? or have recent investigations exploded this doctrine? If not, it will be apparent that all grafting of scions together, cannot change the quality of fruit, unless the leaves are also amalgamated. Is a red, green, yellow, and white fruit, sweet, sour, or bitter, be put upon the same tree, each will maintain its characteristics; because, each bud or scion has its own peculiar leaves, from whose laboratory the fruit is sweetened or acidulated and colored with all its hues. To be sure, fruits are affected by the stock on which they are put; but their characteristic elements are not altered, but only pushed along in the same line and made more perfect.

There is no doubt that trees indulge, occasionally, in rare antics. A sober apple-tree will sometimes let down its dignity, in what gardeners call a "sport," *e. g.* a sweet apple may grow on a sour tree, and *vice versâ*. An apple may on one side be sweet and on the other sour. But, in such cases, the same general law is seen governing yet. We all know that great changes of temperament occur in men. A nervous temperament often becomes abdominal, and a little, wiry, fussy, peevish, minikin, becomes a round, plump, rosy, corpulent spot óf good nature. Similar changes may occur, through disease, or the peculiarity of the season, or from unknown causes, in the structure of the leaves of a branch, and then the fruit will follow the change of the leaf.

But the fruit itself digests still further the elaborated sap sent to it from the leaf. If, then, from any hidden causes, the fruit should in part change its structure, the juices elaborated would be altered. If stamens and pistils may change to petals, if petals may change to leaves, if leaves may extend to branches, we know of no reason why the whole or the half of a fruit may not, also, alter its structure; and with its peculiarity of function, also, of course, the character of the fruit. While then we are not skeptical of "monsters," "marvels," "sports," "singularities," we think we can trace the original law through all the transmutations.

PROTECTING THE ROOTS OF FRUIT-TREES.

CULTIVATORS are frequently urged in Horticultural papers to *cover the roots* of the peach-trees with heaps of snow, etc., that they may be retarded in the spring, and escape injury from late frosts upon their blossoms. This direction takes it for granted that the warmth of the ground starts the root, and the root starts the sap, and the sap wakes up the dormant branch. By covering the soil and keeping it back, the whole tree is supposed to be secured. But, unfortunately for this process, the motion of the sap is *first* in the BRANCHES, and last in the roots. Light and heat, exerted upon the branches for any considerable length of time, produce a high state of excitability; the sap begins to move toward the bud, its place is supplied by a portion lower down, and so on until the whole column of sap through the trunk is in motion, and last of all in the ROOT. But suppose warm, spring days, with a temperature of from sixty degrees to sixty-five degrees, have produced a vigorous motion of the sap in the branches and trunk, while the root, (thanks to snow and ice piled over it to keep it frozen), is dormant, what will result? The sap already within the tree will be exhausted, the root will supply none, the light and heat still push on the development of bud and leaf and the tree will exhaust itself and die. We not long since observed a remarkable confirmation of these reasonings. A gentleman of our acquaintance, in reading these unskilfull directions to cover the peach-tree root, opened trenches about his trees, and filled them with snow, heaping bountifully also all about the trees. The next spring, long after his trees should have been at work, the snow held the root fast; the buds swelled and burst, lingered, shrivelled and died—and the *trees too*. This might have been prognosticated. There are partial methods of protecting the peach from too early development, but they all have respect to the protection of the *limbs.* If the branches can be covered during the random and prematurely hot days of spring, the tree will not suffer. High, and cool-aired aspects, north hill-sides, northern sides of houses, barns, etc., will answer this purpose. When it can be afforded, long boards may be set up upon the east and south sides of choice trees, upon a frame slightly made and easily removed.

The reason why more damage has not been done by covering peach-tree roots, than has occurred, is, that the ground has been superficially frozen, and many of the roots extending deeper and laterally beyond the congealed portions, have afforded a supply of sap after a motion had been imparted to it in the branches.

PRUNING GRAPE VINES.

ALL know that after the sap begins to flow in the spring, a vine, if cut, will bleed. It seems that at this early period of its development the sap vessels have no power of contraction. Many suppose that the same state of things continues throughout the growing season, and are afraid to cut their vines. But after the vine has begun to grow freely (when the leaves, for example, are as large as the palm of one's hand), a wound very soon contracts, bleeds little or none, and heals over as in a tree. Any pruning which is necessary upon the old wound may, therefore, be fearlessly performed.

Some inexpert cultivators, in order to let the sun fall upon the grapes, pluck off the leaves; hoping thus to procure sweeter grapes. This is the very way to have acid fruit. Where is the sugar prepared for the cluster but in these very leaves which are taken off? Without leaves, the sap which flows into the cluster has undergone but imperfectly those chemical changes on which the fruit depends. Every leaf in the neighborhood of the fruit is precious.

-----•◦•-----

MILDEW ON GRAPES.

MANY permit the fruit of the vines to perish before their eyes from the ravages of mildew, ignorant that an effectual remedy is within their reach. It is simply to dust the branches with flowers of sulphur. It is best done while the dew is on.

When vines are trained upon the sides of a house or fence, it is well to whitewash the surfaces on which they are fastened with a wash in which flowers of sulphur has been largely mixed.

It is recommended by some cultivators to employ such a whitewash for the *wood* of the vine, covering all the main stems with it; but all these methods result in the one thing —the application of sulphur as a remedy for mildew.

-----•◦•-----

HOW TO OBTAIN GRAPE VINES.

GRAFTING is only practised on the vine for special reasons, and we have never had occasion to try it. We shall speak of a better mode of obtaining vines.

The best method of " getting a start " of grape vines is, by the employment of cuttings. These may be planted immediately after the spring pruning of established vines. But cuttings of native grapes are as well planted *in the fall*. The granulation, from which the roots spring, will form during the winter, and the cuttings, starting early in the spring, will make good growth the first year. Cuttings are the best, because they can be procured easily, abundantly, and cheaply; they will bear carriage to any distance, are exceedingly tenacious of life, and they make thriftier plants. Cuttings may be set, either where they are to remain, in which case several should be set, to allow for failures, and only the strongest finally retained; or, they may be set in nursery rows, eight inches apart. Cuttings should be inserted about eight inches deep, and have two eyes or buds above the surface. The *two* buds are merely precautionary; that if one fails the other may sprout; one only, and that the strongest, should finally be permitted to grow.

An old and skillful cultivator of the vine says that *cuttings are the best of all modes of* securing a supply of vines. "For my part I am for scions without roots, after many experiments. All the advantage the one with roots has over the other, is that they are more sure to live; but they will not in general, *make as thrifty plants*." —*J. J. Dufour.*

This only objection to cuttings—that a part of them fail to root—is of little practical importance, as they are easily obtained in any quantity.

—•••—

AUTUMNAL MANAGEMENT OF FRUIT-TREES.

ORCHARDISTS and cultivators of garden-fruit will have need of all their skill to prepare tender fruit-trees for winter. It is the misfortune, alike of the English summers, and of ours in the West, that trees do not properly ripen their wood. But in Great Britain it is from the want of enough, and in America, from too much summer. Our long and hot summers give two or three *separate growths* to fruit-trees, and the last one is usually in progress at a period so late

that severe frosts and freezings overtake the tree while yet
in an excitable state, pushing new wood, and with a top
quite unripened for severe frosty handling.

The year 1845 furnished a fine type of western summers.
The spring came in very properly, and at so late a period
that the usual frosts, after the expansion of leaves, were
avoided. The summer opened warmly and continued with
almost unvarying heat throughout. At the same time there
were frequent and copious rains.

By this statement the average temperature of June was
71°, and the rain 6¹ inches; of July, average noon heat
80°, rain 3¼ inches; of August, average noon heat 80°, rain
5½ inches. Nights were exceedingly warm. The day
repeatedly opened and closed at 80°. Our thermometer on
the north of our house, in a shady yard, stood for eight and
ten days together between 94° and 100°, twice attaining
the latter height.

Under such stimulus our pear, apple and plum-trees, made
their first growth by the first of July. They soon started
into a second growth, which wound up during the last of
August and the first of September, plum-trees entirely
shedding their leaves and standing as bare as in January.

Let orchards be examined when frosts begin to occur,
and every *side-shoot, sucker* or *water-sprout,* cut cleanly
out. These succulent, raw sprouts are the breeding-spots
of disease. Cold-blight invariably manifests itself in them
in the most positive form.

Garden trees, choice pears, and stone-fruits, should, in
addition to this operation, if still in growth at the last of
September, receive a fall pruning. From the first to the middle of October, according to the season, cut off two-thirds
of the new growth, or back to strong, ripe wood. It is well
known that the newest buds, near the extremity of young
wood, are the most sensitive and apt to break and grow,
whereas the buds near the base of a branch are dormant.

13*

It is the repose of the older buds which makes fall pruning, if performed with judgment, so valuable. Because it forces the tree to expend its energies in ripening its wood instead of making more, and it also tends to induce fruitfulness by changing leaf-buds to fruit-buds. The great art of fall pruning is to relieve the tree of its crude wood *without causing its dormant buds to break*. If performed too early, or if but the tips of the fine wood are removed, the new buds may break and side-shoots issue, leaving the tree worse off than before.

Young trees *just coming into bearing* should have their trunks protected. That there is a change in the economy of a tree when it begins to bear is plain; and experience seems to teach that trees are peculiarly tender at the time of this change, since they are far more apt to die when coming to fruit, than either before or afterward. Cherry-trees and pear-trees should have brush, or corn-stalks, or straw, or matting, as is most convenient, so placed from the ground to the branches, as to exclude the sun without excluding air. An hour's attention may save much regret.

PEARS GRAFTED UPON THE APPLE STOCK.

WE do not think the pear does so well in any other way as on its own root. But it has been found extremely difficult to obtain the requisite stock. Pear-seeds are scarce. When obtained, the seedlings have proved intractable, and left the nurseryman oftentimes in the lurch. The first and best substitute for pear-stock, is the *root of the pear*—great quantities may be obtained when removing pear-trees in the autumn from the nursery, and also without any injury to the trees, roots may be taken from old bearing-trees.

These are to be grafted in the manner already described in our pages. Next to this, the quince stock is to be chosen. The pear is dwarfed upon it. In other words, the two are but imperfectly suited to each other, and the scion does not develop according to its original nature. But this very dwarfing adds something to the good qualities of the fruit, affords trees so small that, at eight feet apart, they make beautiful linings to a walk or border, and, morever, brings the pear to its fruit several years earlier than if it were on its own bottom. But on the other hand, the pear on quince is comparatively short-lived. The white-thorn has been tried as a stock and not without success, but it is hardly to be used except in extremities.

Last, and worst of all, comes the apple. The scion grows as vigorously upon the apple as upon a stock of its own species, and we do not know that the fruit deteriorates. But the trees seem to *have no constitution.* After a few bearings they seem struck with irremediable weakness, and soon run down and die. Nurserymen ought not, therefore, to graft the pear upon the apple. To do so, if advised of the foregoing facts, cannot be honest. Our attention has been called to the subject by some painful experience of our own.

———•••———

NESHANOC POTATO.—This potato (pronounced *Mesha-noc*), was raised from the seed about the year 1800, by John Gilkey, Mercer county, Pennsylvania. He called it *Neshanoc*, from a creek near to which he lived. It was called by some, *Mercer*, from the county in which it was raised. It is extensively cultivated, and deserves to be. Mr. Gilkey was an Irishman—of course a judge of good potatoes.

SEEDLINGS FROM BUDDED PEACHES.

MR. NICHOLAS LONGWORTH inquires: "Will the pit of the budded peach produce the same fruit as the bud, or as the stock, or a mixture of the two?" And he also says, "I have never fairly tested the question, but my experience led me to believe that the budded pit produced the same fruit as the original stock."

So far as this question can be determined (independently of experiment) upon the known laws of the vegetable kingdom, we say that it will *not* produce fruit like that of the original stock; nor will it, on the other hand, with any certainty, reproduce the budded kind.

If the pit of a budded variety takes after the *stock*, we must very much change our theory of the office of leaves, and perhaps of the bark. At present, the received and orthodox teaching is, that the sap from the root is crude and undigested until it has received in the leaf a chemical change. Until then, the sap does not materially influence the vegetable tissue, nor form new substance, or affect the fruit. But *after* its elaboration in the leaf, a returning current of prepared sap (similar in its functions to arterial blood), sets downward, distributing to every part of the vegetable economy the properties required by each. The sap arising from the root, does not touch the channel of fruit until it has been chemically changed; and the difference exhibited in the fruit of one tree compared with another, arises, primarily from the nature of the sap which it receives; the sap receives its qualities by a digestion in the leaf.* In all cases, then, we suppose the *leaf* to determine the nature of the fruit (and the root in no case, and the trunk in no case), since the stem is, so far as sap is concerned, but a bundle of canals for its passage—a mere high-

---

* The fruit itself still further elaborates the sap, else a peach would be as acrid as the juice of the peach leaf.

way for transmission—and not like the leaf, a laboratory for its preparation ! *

We may be reminded that a *stock*, in point of fact, *does* influence the fruit. It is indisputable that pears are changed on quince roots. The *Wilkinson*, grafted upon the quince, is smaller, more prolific, higher flavored, and of a brighter red cheek than if grafted on the pear. The Duchesse d'Angoulême is larger and better on the quince than on its own roots. But what is *the* influence in this case? When a free-grower is put upon a slow-grower, the point of junction becomes a point of comparative *obstruction* to the return-sap. It is only a wholesome process of *ringing, or decortication.* Lindley says:

" When pears are worked upon the wild species, apples upon crabs, and peaches upon peaches, the scion is, in regard to fertility, exactly in the same state as if it had not been grafted at all: while, on the other hand, a great increase of fertility, is the result of grafting pears upon quinces, peaches upon plums, apples upon the thorn, and the like. In these cases, the food absorbed from the earth by the root of the stock is communicated slowly." And

---

* Loudon (Encyclopædia of Gardening, p. 448), has the following remarks:

" The bark is the medium in which the proper juices of the plant, in their descent from the leaves, are finally elaborated and brought to the state which is peculiar to the species. From the bark these juices are communicated to the medullary rays, to be by them deposited in the tissue of the wood. The character of timber, therefore, depends chiefly upon the influence of the bark: and hence it is that the wood formed above a graft never partakes, in the slightest degree, of the nature of the wood below it. The bark, when young and green, like the leaves, is supposed, like them, to elaborate the sap, and hence may be considered as the universal leaf of a plant.

These views corroborate the reasoning above, although Loudon extends the functions of the leaf to the *bark*. We have not been able, in our limited range of books, to find any other authority for this statement, respecting the " young and green bark."

Manning adds: "No other influence have we ever noticed exercised by the scion upon the stock."

But if, after all, it can be shown by actual trial, that the pits of budded peaches DO *go back to the fruit of the stock*, why we must receive it, in spite of all theory; for, (and some would do well to heed the maxim), facts must rule our theories, and not theories our fact. But we may properly put any facts seeming to contravene the received theory of the functions of plants in producing fruit, *upon their oath*, and refuse them, unless they are unquestionable and relevant.

Suppose a budded peach not to yield a fruit at all like the bud, suppose it to resemble the fruit of the stock, it does not follow that the *stock* influenced the fruit to such a change. Mr. Longworth knows how freely some peaches "sport," and that all peaches may be made to do it. If a Melacatune be budded upon a Red Rareripe, and the Melacatune pit shows a fruit resembling the Red Rareripe, it must be shown that the blossom had not been crossed by the busy offices of flies, bees, etc., with the pollen of contiguous Red Rareripe-trees.

When a tree is even *solitary*, it does not follow that a change in fruit which shall make it resemble the stock more than the graft, results from the force *of the stock* on the grafted fruit, for seedlings of grafted fruit are, notoriously often, base and degenerate; and the resemblance might be accidental, for seedlings of different origin are often strikingly alike.

While we are aware of no facts which justify Mr. Longworth's suspicion, that the pits of budded varieties produce kinds like the stock on which the bud was put, we have facts enough showing that "budded pits" produce their own kind.

It may be added that *thoroughly* ripe peaches are less inclined to "sport" than those which are partially green.

CARE OF PEACH-TREES.

TAKE a light hoe and remove the earth from the trunk of your trees. If there are worms there you may detect them from the gum which has exuded, or by the channels which they have made in the bark, or if by neither of these, by the discoloration of the bark in spots. Scrape the bark gently with the back of a knife, and you can easily detect the traces of worms if any are there. Cut freely and boldly both ways along their track so as to lay bare the channel in its whole length—remove the worm, and the bark will very soon heal. Sometimes four, six, and even more will be found in one tree. The ashes of stone coal, blacksmiths' cinders, wood ashes, lime, the refuse stems of tobacco, planting tansy around the trunk, these, and dozens of other remedies are proposed. For our own part we rely solely on our jack-knife. In March or April, and then again in August or September, according to the season, we search the trunk thoroughly. We can attend to twenty trees in an hour or two; and when eating freely of delicious peaches we never had a qualm of regret for having so spent the time.

We have practised sowing salt under fruit-trees with decided advantage. If one pound of saltpetre be added to every six pounds of salt, it will be yet better. We sow enough to make the ground look moderately white, and prefer to do it in wet weather.

* * *

THE most salable butter, quality being equal, is that which is neatest done up. There is a great deal in the *looks* of a thing. You'll always find it so.

RENOVATING PEACH-TREES.

THE peach-tree inclines to thicken at the top, the small inside branches die, and are removed by every neat cultivator. As the branches shoot up, this tree is disposed to abandon its lower branches, and, like the vine, to bear on the wood the farthest from the root, *i. e.* the young and new wood. In a few years the tree has a long-necked trunk, sometimes several of them; while the weight of foliage and fruit is situated so as to act like a power applied to a lever; and as the fruit grows heavy, or a storm occurs, the tree is broken down. We have practised the following method with success. In the month of July we saw off the top of one half of the tree, leaving about ten or twelve feet of stem, measuring from the ground. New shoots will now put out along the whole trunk; a part of these should be rubbed off, according to the judgment of the cultivator, leaving such as will give symmetry to the tree, *and form a head low down.* The second year, these branches will bear fruit, and the other side may then be treated in the same way.

This new head will require little meddling with for about four years. At this time, or whenever the tree is outrunning itself, the same process is to be renewed. But this time the tree will be composed of a multitude of smaller branches, instead of two or three main ones as at first. Some of these should be wholly cut out, and the wound smeared with a residuum of paint, or a thick white paint, or grafting wax, or anything that will exclude the air while the cut is granulating. The others are to be cut within, say, five inches of the old, original wood—leaving, thus, a stem of mere stumps. If the branches are taken entirely off, leaving only the oldest wood, the buds which would break from it would not be as healthy or vigorous as those which will spring from the stumps of the later branches.

Probably twenty or thirty whips will come to each stump;

these should from day to day be reduced in number, until, at last, all are removed but one, and that one should, if possible, spring from the nearest point where the stump joins the old stem. When this new branch is obtained and fairly established, remove the stump with a fine saw, so as to leave the new branch, as nearly as possible, in the place of the old one. We remove the whips from a stump gradually in order to give the tree the advantage of their leaves as long as it can be done without interfering with the branch or branches which we are training out.

This method is to the peach what pruning is to the grape. The tree is kept in hand instead of sprawling abroad, a prey to its own weight and to storms; there is always a plenty of young wood for the fruit, which can be easily reached when one thins out, or gathers for use.

One of our trees taught us this method of its own accord in the summer of 1843. The weight of fruit was so great that we applied a prop to the middle of the branch; in a few days the branch broke short off at the point of the prop. It so happened that the three main limbs on one side of the tree acted in this manner. That same fall a strong growth of new wood shot out, and the next season I had on *that side* as fine a top as ever I had on any peach-tree.

----•••----

EVERY farmer who expects his wife to make good butter, after furnishing her with some good, well-fed milk cows, should provide her with good milk-pans—large and shallow, so as to present a large surface for the cream to rise on, and enough of them to hold all her milk, and allow it to remain undisturbed long enough for all the cream to rise. These pans should be nicely washed every time the milk is emptied out of them, and always be clear and bright when filled.

AN APOLOGUE OR APPLE-LOGUE.

Two men planted out each one hundred apple-trees. In six or seven years they began to bear. One had spared no pains to bring his orchard into the highest condition. He had constantly cultivated the soil about them, scraped off the rough bark, washed them with urinated soap, picked off every worm and nursed them as if they had been children. The other, pursuing a cheaper plan, simply let his trees alone; but the moss, and canker-worms took his place and attended to them every year. When the orchards began to bear, the careful man had the best fruit, and the careless man covered his folly by cursing the nursery-man for selling him poor trees. In a year or two the careful man had two bushels to the other's one from each tree. Not to be outdone, the latter determined to have as many apples as the former, and set out another hundred trees. By and by, when they bore, the other orchard had so improved that it produced twice as many yet; another hundred trees were therefore planted. In process of time the first orchard of one hundred trees still sent more fruit to market than the three hundred trees of the careless man, who now gave up and declared that he never did have luck, and it was of no use to try *on his soil* to raise good fruit.

1. When a man is too shiftless to take good care of two horses, he buys two more, and gets from the four what he might get from two.

2. A farmer who picks up a cow simply because it is not an ox, and *is*, nominally, lactiferous, and then lets the creature work for a living, very soon buys a second, and a third, and a fourth, and gets from them all, what he should have had from one good one.

3. A farmer had one hundred acres. Instead of getting seventy-five bushels of corn to the acre, he gets forty and makes it up by cultivating twice as many acres; instead of thirty bushes of wheat he gets twelve, and puts in acres

enough to make up; instead of making one hundred acres do the work of three hundred, he buys more land, and allows thrèe hundred to do only the work of one hundred.

4. A young woman, with a little pains, can have three times as many clothes as she needs, and then not look so well as a humble neighbor who has not half her wardrobe; wherefore, we close with some. proverbs made for the occasion:

Active little is better than lazy much.

Carefulness is richer than abundance.

Large farming is not always good farming, and small farming is often the largest.

SELECT LIST OF APPLES.

It is impossible to frame a list of apples which will suit ῾very cultivator. Men's taste in fruits is widely different. The delicacy and mildness of flavor which some admire, is to others mere insipidity. The sharp acid, and coarse grain and strong flavor which disgust many palates, are with others the very marks of a first-ratè apple. The object of the cultivator in planting an orchard, whether for his own use, for a home market, for exportation, for cider-making, or for stock-feeding, will very materially vary his selection.

The soil on which an orchard is to be planted should also determine the use of many varieties, which are admirable only when well suited in their locality.

Regard is to be had to climate, since some of the finest fruits in one latitude entirely betray our expectations in another. The hardiness and health of different varieties ought to be more an object of attention than hitherto. As in building, so in planting an orchard, a mistake lasts for a century, and a bad tree in a good orchard is like bad timber in a good mansion.

However select, then, a list may be, every cultivator must exercise his own judgment in adapting it to his own circumstances.

SUMMER APPLES.

1. CAROLINA JUNE.—This is identical with the Red June of the principal nurseries; but many inferior varieties scattered through the country, called Red June, are to be discriminated from it.

The tree is upright with slender wood, which, when loaded with fruit, droops like a willow. It is a healthy tree, ripens its wood early in the fall, and is not subject to frost-blight. It comes early into bearing, is productive and bears every year. The fruit is of medium size though specimens grow large; the flavor is sprightly, subacid, the flesh tender. It has flourished well on sand-loams, common clays, and on strong limestone clay. Ripens from the first to the twentieth of July. A valuable market fruit. Four trees, in one county, sent *eighty dollars'* worth to market in one season. Not mentioned by eastern writers, nor found in eastern catalogues, but described at the West by Hampton and Plummer, and found in Ohio and Indiana nurseries.

2. SWEET JUNE.—Tree upright, wood moderately strong; ripens its wood early in fall; not subject to frost-blight; flourishes on all soils, even if quite wet; bears very young, often while in nursery rows; bears every year and abundantly. The fruit is of medium size; color a pale yellow; form globular; flavor sweet and pleasant. Ripens at same time as the Carolina June.

3. KIRKBRIDGE WHITE.—Not found in any catalogues but those of Western nurseries. Tree upright, wood strong and stubbed; grows slow while young, but vigorously when fully established; ripens its wood early in autumn; not subject to frost-blight; bears moderately

young, and is very productive. *Its fruit ripens in succession for six weeks from first of July to middle of August*, and is peculiarly valuable on that account; color nearly white; it is largest at base and tapers regularly to the eye, and is ribbed; flavor, mild, pleasant acid; flesh melting, and, if fully ripe breaks to pieces in falling to the ground.

4. PRINCE'S HARVEST.—Manning pronounces this "the earliest apple worthy of cultivation." It may be in Massachusetts, but it is preceded by many at the West. Manning's description is good.

"The form is flat, of medium size; the skin, when perfectly ripe, is of a beautifully bright straw color; the flesh tender and sprightly; if gathered before they are fully ripe, it has too much acidity. The finest fruits are those which drop ripe from the tree; the branches make very acute angles, by which it is readily distinguished from most other trees in the orchard; it bears young. Ripe early in July."

Our nurserymen regard it as a shy bearer.

5. SUMMER QUEEN.—Extensively cultivated in the West under the name of *Orange Apple*. The tree is spreading; a rapid grower; not subject to frost-blight; wood moderately strong; comes late into bearing; productive when the tree is fully grown, according to the books, but in this region with some exceptions has proved to be a poor bearer. Fruit large, yellow, striped with red; flesh, breaking; flavor strong, and not delicate.

6. SWEET BOUGH.—Two varieties of this name are cultivated in the West—Coxe's and Mount's. Coxe's sweet bough, is that of the books and catalogues. Ripens at the same time; not quite so high in flavor. Coxe's trees are large limbed and spreading; bearing on the point of the limbs, and are shy bearers; Mount's variety is of upright growth; bears on spurs along the branches; is a good bearer and ripens from middle of July to August.

"A variety under the name of Philadelphia Jennetting is known in Trumbull County, Ohio. It ripens two weeks later than the common kind, otherwise it is not essentially different."—*Dr. J. P. Kirtland.*

7. SUMMER PEARMAIN.—There seem to be two varieties of this name cultivated in Ohio and Indiana.

(1.) That of Coxe, which is the one generally cultivated, and deservedly popular.

"The fruit-buds seem to be unusually hardy, and often resist the impression of late spring frosts, while others are killed. In 1834, when our fruits were universally cut off by that destructive agent, a tree of the summer pearmain and another of the Vandeveer, matured a dozen or two apples, while not another tree in an orchard containing over five hundred, bore a solitary fruit. It is worthy of more extensive cultivation."—*Dr. Kirtland.*

(2.) A variety evidently allied to Coxe's, but all things considered a more desirable variety. The fruit resembles Coxe's, but is larger; the flavor is the same, but not quite as high; Coxe's is oblong; this variety is Vandeveer pippin shape; color the same, and the period of ripening, viz., July and August. The trees are very distinct; Coxe's is upright, this is spreading; Coxe's of a slender growth, and stinted habit, and is hard to bring forward in the nursery; this has a vigorous growth, and strong wood, and strikingly resembles the Vandeveer pippin-tree. It bears early and abundantly in all soils.

This second variety was brought, by a man named Harlan, Fayette County, Indiana, from South Carolina, where it is extensively cultivated.

8. DANIEL.—The tree is upright, nearly pear-tree shape; wood strong and healthy; leaves, above all varieties, dark green and glossy; bears young and abundantly. Fruit medium size; it has a yellow ground covered with blotches of dull red; flavor rich, sweetish, and high. Ripens in

succession from first to middle of August. A desirable variety.

9. Hoss, improperly pronounced *Horse*, and so written in Prince's catalogue. Originated in North Carolina; largely cultivated in both Carolinas and southern Virginia; named from the originator. It has been propagated by suckers, grafts, and *even by seeds ;* in this latter case, the product very nearly resembles the parent. Three varieties, however, may be discriminated. Tree upright, wood strong and healthy; bears yearly and abundantly; flesh melting : flavor rather too acid until thoroughly ripe, and then fine. Ripens in August and September. Desirable in the most select orchards.

The *time of ripening* I have set down for the latitude of Indianapolis. Upon the Ohio River, near Cincinnati, it will be ten days earlier.

AUTUMN APPLES.

10. MAIDEN'S BLUSH.—Tree moderately spreading, open top, limbs slender; grows late in fall, and somewhat liable to winter-killing; grows well on all good soils; bears young and very abundantly every year. The fruit large when the tree is not allowed to ripen too large a crop; white, and blush toward the sun; tender, melting, very juicy, decidedly acid. The fruit is, even in unfavorable seasons, very free from cracks, knots, and is always fair; one of the best for drying and excellent for marketing; should be plucked before it is dead ripe; ripens from August to October. It is the same as the English Horthornden. It does not do well grafted on the root; being apt to burst the first or second winter; buds well, and should be thus propagated in the nursery. It is a native of New Jersey.

11. WINE APPLE.—Tree spreading but not sprawling; medium grower, healthy; limbs rather slender; does well

on all soils; bears very young, largely, and every year. Fruit large on young, and medium-sized on old trees; deep yellow ground covered with red, and russet about the stem; tender, melting, very juicy, high-flavored, sweet, with a spicy dash of subacid. One of the richest cooking apples; one of the most desirable for drying, resembling dried pears. Where known, it is worth, dried, a dollar and a half a bushel, when other apples command but seventy-five cents. Ripens first of September and has passed its prime by November. Eastern writers call it a winter apple, and Kenrick gives October to March as its season; but, in the West, it seldom sees the first winter month. Takes by graft and bud pretty well; does well grafted upon the root; favorable for nursery purposes.

12. HOLLAND PIPPIN.—Tree large and spreading; strong growth; wood short and stubbed, healthy; bears moderately young; they are averse to heavy clay and wet soils; on light, dry, rich, sandy soils bears largely, and of high color and flavor; bears every other year. Fruit large, very bright yellow, tender, juicy, subacid. The pulp in the mouth becomes rather viscid, as if the fruit were mucilaginous, which is agreeable or otherwise according to the taste of the eater. It is sometimes, but rarely, water-cored. Ripens in October and November; will keep later, but apt to lose in flavor. Good for drying, but usually sold green, being a very marketable fruit. Not a good tree for nurserymen; not willing to come if grafted on the root; does well by crown-grafting; moderately well by budding, the eye being apt to put out simply a spur, which can seldom be forced into a branch if permitted to harden.

13. RAMBO.—This apple is known in New Jersey by the names of Romanite, Seek-no-further, and Bread and Cheese. The first two names belong to entirely different apples. The rambo is not to be confounded with the *Rambours*, of which there are several varieties. Tree upright,

and the most vigorous growth of all trees cultivated in the West; the easiest of all to bud with, a bud seldom misses, and makes extraordinary growth the first season; it may well be called the nurseryman's favorite; bears very young, abundantly every year, good on all soils. Fruit medium size, yellow ground with red stripes and the whole overlaid with a bloom, like a plum; tender, juicy, melting, subacid, rich; it has a peculiarity of ripening; it begins at the skin and ripens toward the core; often soft and seemingly ripe on the outside while the inside is yet hard. Ripens from October to December. One of the best of all fruits.

14. GOLDEN RUSSET.—This admirable apple is put in the list of fall fruits, because, though it will keep through the winter, it ripens in November, and sometimes even in October. Tree, strong grower, upright, compact top-healthy, grows late in fall and therefore subject to winter-killing; will grow on all soils, but delights in rich sandy loams, on which it bears larger and finer fruit. Fruit small, rather oblong; color yellow, slight red next to the sun; although called *russet*, there is but a *trace* of it on the fruit of healthy trees; tender, melting, spicy, very juicy; in flavor it resembles the St. Michael's *pear* (Doyenné) more nearly than any other apple.

This fruit is the most popular of all late, fall, or early winter apples, and deservedly, and should be put at the head of the list. A gentleman near Belfre, Ohio, being applied to for a list of apples to furnish an orchard of a thousand trees for marketing purposes, replied, "Take nine hundred and ninety-nine golden russets, and the *rest* you can choose to suit yourself." For nursery purposes it is rather a backward apple; the buds apt to fail, which occasions much resetting. It will not do well grafted on the root, being tender and always largely winter-killed when so wrought. They graft kindly on well established stocks.

14

If a larger list of fall apples is desired, we recommend the Fall Harvey, Gravenstein, Lyscom, Porter, Red Ingestrie, Yellow do. The Ashmore is a desirable fruit—difficult to raise in the nursery, and therefore avoided, but the fruit is fine. The Ross Nonpareil is a very admirable fall fruit of Irish origin.

The list of autumn apples is very large and continually augmenting. But fall apples are, ordinarily, less desirable than any others; not from inferior quality, but because they ripen at the season of the year when peaches and pears are in their glory.

WINTER APPLES.

15. GLORIA MUNDI or *Monstrous Pippin*. Tree, one of the most upright, top close, and resembling the pear. Wood medium sized, healthy, vigorous growth, wood ripens early, not subject to frost-blight; bears on moderately young trees. It works well from the bud, and also extremely well grafted on roots, and grows straight and finely for nursery purposes. Fruit very large, green, changes when dead-ripe to a yellowish white. Flavor mild, subacid; flesh melting and spicy. Ripens in November, at the same time with the Golden Russet, but will not keep as long. A native.

16. BLACK APPLE.—Tree low, spreading, and round topped; wood of medium vigor, healthy, ripens early, and not subject to frost-blight. Grafts on the root kindly; not so favorable for budding as the No. 15; bears remarkably young, and abundantly to a fault. Fruit medium sized; color very dark red, almost black, with grey rusty spots about the stem; flesh tender, breaking; moderately juicy, flavor rather sweet, though not a real sweet apple. No apple would stand fairer as an early winter fruit, were it not for a peculiar, dry, raw taste, somewhat resembling the

taste of uncooked corn meal. Ripens from November to January. It is a native.

17. NEWTON SPITZENBURG.—Tree, not large, upright but not compact, top open; wood of medium size and vigor of growth; healthy, ripens early, and yet, now and then, it takes the frost-blight; bears moderately young, every other year, very abundantly; grafts well on the root, buds only moderately well, good for nursery handling. Fruit, varying much in size, but often large, flesh melting, juicy; flavor rich, spicy, subacid; ripens from November to January.

18. RHODE ISLAND GREENING.—Tree large, very spreading and drooping, grows vigorously, healthy, ripens early, not subject to frost-blight; bud takes well; but, whether grafted on the root, or budded, it will plague the nurseryman by its disposition to spread and twist about like a quince bush. It should be budded on strong stocks at the height at which the top is to be formed; but it always overgrows the stock. Fruit very large, color green' with cloudy spots dotted with pin-point black specks; flesh breaking, tender and juicy: flavor mild, rich, subacid; a very popular fruit. Ripens from November to January.

19. HUBBARDSTON NONESUCH.—Admirable in nursery; works well on root or by bud. We give Downing's description, as it has not fruited in this region.

"A fine, large, early winter fruit, which originated in the town of Hubbardston, Mass., and is of first rate quality. The tree is a vigorous grower, forming a handsome branching head, and bears very large crops. It is worthy of extensive orchard culture.

"Fruit large, roundish-oblong, much narrower near the eye. Skin smooth, striped with splashes, and irregular broken stripes of pale and bright red, which nearly cover a yellowish ground. The calyx open, and the stalk short, in a russeted hollow. Flesh yellow, juicy, and tender, with an agreeable mingling of sweetness and acidity in its flavor. October to January."

20. MINISTER.—We give Manning's description:

"This fine apple originated in Rowley, Mass. The size is large, the form oblong like the Bellflow‹r, tapering to the eye, with broad ridges the whole length of the fruit; the skin a light greenish yellow, striped with bright red, but the red seldom extends to the eye; flesh yellow, light, high flavored and excellent. This is one of the very finest apples which New England has produced. It ripens from November to February, and deserves a place in every collection of fruits, however small. This apple received its present name from the circumstance of the late Rev. Dr. Spring, of Newburyport, having purchased the first fruit brought to market."

21. VANDERVEER PIPPIN.—Tree large, one of the most vigorous, spreading, but not drooping; ripens its wood late, occasionally touched with frost-blight and liable to burst at the surface of the ground during the winter. Bears young, every year, and very abundantly. Buds well, grafts well on the root, grows off strongly, forms a top readily, and will please nurserymen. Fruit large, more uniformly of one size all over the tree than any in the orchard; shape of fruit flat; color, red stripes on a yellow, russety ground. Flesh coarse, gritty; flavor strong, penetrating, without aroma; December to March. This fruit is remarkable for having almost every good quality of tree and fruit and being notwithstanding a third-rate apple. The tree is hardy, its bloom, from peculiar hardiness, escapes injury from frost, and even a second set of blossoms put out, though feeble ones, if the first are destroyed. The fruit is comely, cooks admirably, keeps well; but a certain sharpness and coarseness will always make it but a second or third-rate fruit. No tree is sought by farmers in this region, with more avidity. Its origin is doubtful. Brunson, of Wayne County, brought it to Indiana, and all our nurseries trace their stock to his. It was carried for the first time to New Jersey, by Quakers visiting that region,

from his orchard. It should have been mentioned, that it holds its age remarkably well, very old trees producing as largely, and as fair, sound fruit as when young.

22. YELLOW BELLE FLEUR, OR BELLFLOWER.—Tree spreads and droops more than any tree of the orchard, the Newark pippin, perhaps, excepted; wood very slender and whip-like, healthy, ripens early, not subject to frost-blight, grafts well on the root, but is rather tender during the first winter when so worked; buds well, but from its drooping, sprawling habits, is hard to form into a top. Bears moderately young (not so young as the white); abundantly. Flesh melting and tender and juicy; flavor fine and delicate rather than high; color deep yellow when ripe; ripens from December to March. One of the most deservedly popular of winter apples and always salable in all markets.

23. WHITE BELLE FLEUR.—This apple is cultivated in Ohio under the names of *Hollow-cored Pippin*, *Ohio favorite*, and, by the Cincinnati pomologists, of *Detroit*. It is also the *Cumberland Spice* and *Monstrous Bellflower* of Coxe. It was taken to the West by Brunson of Wayne County, Indiana, and thence disseminated in every direction; and it may be called *the* Bellflower of Indiana, since it and not the yellow, predominates in all orchards, The yellow, however, within five years, has been largely distributed. Tree, medium sized, spreading; wood stronger than the yellow belle fleur, healthy, ripens its wood early, but liable to after-growth in warm falls, and therefore subject to frost-blight. The tree, from its habit of growth, more liable to split and break under a full crop than any tree of the orchard. One of the youngest bearers in the nursery; fruitful to a fault. Grafted on the root it kills off in winter; buds well and forms a top without difficulty. Fruit above medium and sometimes very large; color, greenish white, and, in some seasons with a blush on the sunny side; flesh breaking at first, but when fully ripe,

melting and juicy; flavor mild and delicate. It is not apt
to cloy, and more can be eaten than of almost any variety.
Ripe from December to March.

24. BALDWIN.—Works well in nursery by root or bud,
and is fine for nurserymen. Top forms easily. Not upright, as Downing says, but a round, spreading top. We
give Downing's description:

"The Baldwin stands at the head of New England
apples, and is unquestionably a first-rate fruit in all respects.
It is a native of Massachusetts, and is more largely cultivated for the Boston market than any other sort. It
bears most abundantly, and we have had the satisfaction
of raising larger, more beautiful, and highly favored specimens here, than we ever saw in its native region. The
Baldwin, in flavor and general characteristics, evidently
belongs to the same family as Esopus Spitzenburg, and
deserves its extensive popularity.

"Fruit large, roundish, and narrowing a little to the eye.
Skin yellow in the shade, but nearly covered and striped
with crimson, red, and orange, in the sun; dotted with a
few large russet dots, and with radiating streaks of russet
about the stalk. Calyx closed, set in a rather narrow
plaited basin. Stalk half to three fourths of an inch long,
rather slender for so large a fruit, planted in an even,
moderately deep cavity. Flesh yellowish white, crisp, with
that agreeable mingling of the saccharine and acid which
constitutes a rich, high flavor. The tree is a vigorous,
upright grower, and bears most abundantly. Ripe from
November to March, but attains its greatest perfection in
January."

25. MICHAEL HENRY PIPPIN.—Tree upright, with a
round-shaped top; wood strong, rather slow grower, ripens
its main growth of wood early, but liable to fresh growth
in warm, wet falls; bears very young, every other year
abundantly and not a single apple in the next year. Should
not be grafted on the root; and it is rather troublesome

when budded, from a disposition to make dwarf spur-like branches, rather than upright limbs. Fruit medium-sized, long, large about the base, sharpening toward the eye; color green, clouded and black speckled; flesh tender, melting; flavor rich, inclined to sweet, and very fine. Ripens from December to March.

26. RED SWEET PIPPIN.—Tree handsome, round-topped, but rather spreading; wood strong, and vigorous growth, ripens early; tree very healthy, apt to grow with very smooth bark affording little shelter for insects; bears young, every year and abundantly. Works well in the nursery either by grafting on the root, or by budding. Fruit medium size inclining to large; color red with grey stripes on the shaded side; flesh breaking and firm; flavor sweet and rich. It bakes well, is good for pies, eats well, and its kitchen and table qualities combined make it a desirable fruit. Ripe from December to April.

27. PRYOR'S RED.—Tree upright; wood slow growing, slender, and the branches full of small wood, healthy, not subject to frost-blight; comes very late into bearing, requiring ten or twelve years for full bearing; bears only moderate crops; every year. Difficult to work in the nursery, but does better by grafting on the root than by budding. Fruit above medium size; color, red dotted with white specks; the whole surface covered with slight bloom; flesh melting; flavor very rich and high, and by some thought to be even richer than the golden russet. If this apple only grew on the Vanderveer pippin tree, it would require nothing more to render it perfect. Ripens from December to March. Its keeping properties are more in danger from the *teeth* than from ordinary decay. A very salable and popular apple, which, when once had, none would consent to lose. It is unknown in New England and New York except by description; and is not even described by Downing, and but little more than mentioned by Kenrick.

28. GREEN NEWTOWN PIPPIN.—Tree spreading, wood slender and slow growing; ripens early, making it often troublesome for nurserymen to procure buds fit for late work; not subject to frost-blight. The tree requires vigorous cultivation to redeem it from a feeble growth; the bark is inclined to crack on the branches and scale up, and when once roughened it is difficult ever again to make them smooth. Late coming into bearing, bears abundantly every other year. They should never be grafted on the root; they should be budded on strong healthy stocks and high up in order to do well. Fruit large, green, changing to yellow when dead-ripe; flesh firm, breaking; flavor very rich. Ripe from February to May. This apple is cultivated in extraordinary abundance at the East both for home and foreign markets. They sell in London, at sixpence a piece. The farm of R. L. Pell contains 2,000 bearing trees of this variety; a note descriptive of which we give from Downing:

" One of the finest orchards in America is that of Pellham farm, at Esopus, on the Hudson. It is no less remarkable for the beauty and high flavor of its fruit, than the constant productiveness of trees. The proprietor, R. L. Pell, Esq., has kindly furnished us with some notes of his experiments on fruit-trees, and we subjoin the following highly interesting one on the apple.

" ' For several years past, I have been experimenting on the apple, having an orchard of 2,000 bearing Newtown Pippin-trees. I found it very unprofitable to wait for what is termed the ' bearing year,' and it has been my aim to assist nature, so as to enable the trees to bear every year. I have noticed that from the excessive productiveness of this tree, it requires the intermediate year to recover itself—to extract from the earth and the atmosphere the materials to enable it to produce again. This it is not able to do, unassisted by art, while it is loaded with fruit, and the intervening year is lost; if, however, the tree is supplied with proper food it will bear every year; at least such has been the result of my experiments. Three years ago, in April, I scraped all the rough bark from the stems of several thousand trees in my orchards, and washed all the trunks and limbs within reach with soft soap; trimmed out all the branches that crossed each other early in June, and painted the wounded part with white lead, to exclude moisture and prevent decay. I then, in the latter part of the same month, slit the bark by running a sharp-pointed knife from the ground to the first set of limbs, which prevents the tree from becoming barkbound, and gives the young wood an opportunity of expanding. In July I placed one peck of oyster-shell lime under each tree, and left it piled about the trunk until November, during which time the drought was excessive. In November the lime was dug in thoroughly. The following year I collected from these trees 1,700 barrels of fruit, part of which was sold in New York for four, and others in London for nine dollars per barrel. The cider made from the refuse, delivered at the mill two days after its manufacture, I sold for three dollars and three-quarters per barrel of thirty-two gallons, exclusive of the barrel. In October I manured these trees with stable manure in which the ammonia had been fixed, and covered this immediately with earth. The succeeding autumn they were literally bending to the ground with the finest fruit I ever saw, while the other trees in my orchard not so treated were quite barren, the last season having been their bearing year. I am now placing round each tree one peck of charcoal dust, and propose in the spring to cover it from the compost heap.

" ' My soil is a strong, deep, sandy loam on a gravelly subsoil. I cultivate my orchard grounds as if there were no trees on them, and raise grain of every kind except rye, which grain is so very injurious that I believe three successive crops of it would destroy any orchard younger than twenty years. I raised last year in an orchard containing

14*

twenty acres, trees eighteen years old, a crop of Indian corn which averaged 140 bushels of ears to the acre.'"

29. RAWLE'S JANET, OR JENNETTING. — Tree round topped, a little spreading and handsome. Wood strong, slow growth, short jointed, and the healthiest, perhaps, of all orchard trees. Does not bear young; but when established, a great bearer every year, unless overloaded, when it rests a year. It is the finest of all apples to graft on the root, and should be always so propagated in the nursery; if budded, it being a late starter in spring, the stock will put out its branches before the bud, and make great trouble. Fruit medium sized; color green striped with red; roundish but inclined to sharpen toward the eye; flesh white, melting, very juicy; flavor mild and delicate. Ripens from February to May. This is, and deserves to be, an exceedingly popular apple in all the West. The tree is remarkably healthy; it blooms ten days later than other varieties, and therefore seldom loses a crop by spring frost; but the bloom is very sensitive to frost if overtaken; the fruit is very relishful; keeps as well as the Newtown Pippin, and by many, and by this writer among the number, is much preferred to that noted variety. It has the peculiar excellence of enduring frost without material injury; a property which has enabled cultivators to save thousands of bushels of fruit which by sudden and early cold had been severely frosted.

———•◆•———

THE reason that the Cockle-bur, that great pest on farms, cannot be destroyed by being cut off once a year, is that nature has provided for its propagation by bestowing on it seed vessels which ripen at two different times of the year. This will be found to be the case on careful examination.— *Western Farmer and Gardener.*

ORIGIN OF SOME VARIETIES OF FRUIT.

THE history of our fine fruits has many curious points of interest to the zealous pomologist. It is made up of skill, felicitous blunders, discoveries, and profitable accidents.

The Flemish pears, with which so large a portion of the calendar of new pears is filled, were the products of scientific efforts. In like manner, many of the finest fruits originated by Knight, were by a scientific, although a different, process. On the other hand it would be difficult to find fruits superior to those in the making of which only Nature had a hand.

The *Duchesse d'Angoulême*, a pear without a rival, in its season, was found in 1815, growing wild in a hedge, near Angers, in the department of Maine et Loire, France.

The *Washington*, one of our finest native pears, was likewise discovered in a thorn hedge, at Naaman's creek, Delaware, by Gen. Robertson. He was removing a fence on his farm about forty-five years ago; he found the young tree nearly grown.

The *Lewis* is a native of Massachusetts. Mr. Downer, of Dorchester, a critical judge of fruits, was acquainted with the original tree ten years before he thought it worth a place in his garden. He visited it three times, and was each time disinclined to cultivate it; it was not until he had seen a tree taken from it, growing in cultivated ground, that he adopted it. It now ranks among the finest native pears.

Dearborn's Seedling was discovered by General Dearborn in a cluster of syringas and rose bushes, forming a part of a border to an avenue. Pears seem to have great fondness for hedges, borders, etc. The discoverer attempted to remove the tree, then, apparently, about five years old, to his nursery for a stock; but digging two feet deep, and finding no root but the tap root, he feared that deplanting might kill it. It was left to grow, and has proved to be one of the first-class pears.

Downer's late cherry, was a stock in the nursery row, and several times budded with other kinds; the buds always failing, the tree was allowed to fruit, and proved one of the best, if not *the* best, of late cherries.

Knight's Black Eagle was raised from the seed of the Bigarreau fertilized by the May Duke. When it bore, the fruit was so inferior that the London Horticultural Society peremptorily rejected it. Mr. Knight determined to head the tree down and graft into it other sorts. But he had given the tree to a daughter, with whom it was a favorite, and she refused to have it sacrificed. Each year, subsequently, showed an improvement in the fruit; and now it stands in the first class of cherries. This is one among many instances, which show that young seedlings do not exhibit the true qualities of the fruit for several years after they come to bearing.

The *Red-cheek Melocoton* peach was accidentally obtained by the late Wm. Prince, Flushing, Long Island. He had budded the Kennedy's Caroline upon a stock, and below the point of inoculation a branch of the original stock had shot up into bearing. Sending a servant to gather the budded fruit, he was surprised by his bringing, and, as he declared, from this tree, a free-stone peach. On examining, he found the cause as stated above, and was so much pleased with the new kind that he cultivated it.

———•••———

THE best stock a man can invest in, is the stock of a farm; the best shares are plow-shares; and the best banks are the fertile banks of the rural stream: the more these are broken the better dividends they pay.

THE QUINCE.

WE have nothing to say that has not been well said by Downing, in his most interesting chapter on the Quince. His *Fruit and Fruit Trees of America*, by the way, is beyond all question the best pomological manual, all things considered, which has appeared at home or abroad.

To return to the quince; we marvel that so few trees have found a place in our collections of fruit. Quinces bear transportation, and will, upon an average, bring two dollars a bushel. They sell extravagantly high every year, and yet no one seems to take the hint.

Our favorite mode of increasing the quince, is by layers. The tree being low and inclined to be bushy, there is always an abundance of suitable wood to lay down. Twenty or thirty or even more rooted plants may be obtained in a single season; and the layers throw out such a profusion of roots that the only difficulty will be to separate each plant with its roots from the tough and matted abundance which will be found to have filled the soil. If laid down in the spring, they may be removed by midsummer, a cool and moist day being chosen, and the plants shaded until they start again to growing. If this is done, a second set of layers may be put down to remain over fall and winter and be removed the next spring.

Trees intended for the fruit-compartment of the garden should be trained to a *single* stem, when they will make a low and not altogether unsymmetrical tree; at any rate, a tree much more convenient than the quince *bush* which we usually find in our garden corners.

Where the seed is to be planted, they should be *prepared ;* they are covered with a thick mucilaginous matter which restrains their quick germination. Let them be put into water for twelve hours, and the water will become nearly as thick as paste. Pour it off and repeat the operation until they are nearly clean; mix them with sand and sow them immediately.

CUTTING AND KEEPING GRAFTS.

MANY experienced orchardists suppose the best time for cutting grafts to be immediately on the fall of the leaf in autumn.

Grafts should be cut in mild weather, when the wood is entirely free from frost. Select the *outside* limbs and the last year's growth of wood.

Too much care cannot be observed in *keeping the varieties separate*. Tie up in bundles and mark the names of each kind as soon as cut. A moment's carefulness may save years of vexation.

When the grafts are to be used at home, it is well to lay them in the cellar where frost will not reach them, and slightly cover them, *so that they shall not evaporate the moisture which they contain*. Too much wet injures them. Half-dry sand is as good as anything, and if packed in an old nail-keg and put in a cool place, they will require no further attention until it is time to use them.

When grafts are to be sent to a considerable distance, they should be carefully wrapped in moist cloth, with folds enough to exclude the air entirely. For convenience of carrying they may be packed, in this condition, in a box, and the space filled in with cotton-wool, chaff, bran, or any similar substance.

It is stated by some, that grafts taken from the lower limbs of trees will produce fruit the soonest; while those from the middle and top and from the upright shoots will make trees of the finest form. We confess a slight prejudice against the lower limbs of trees, as it was thence that "switches" were cut in the mischievous days of our youth, wherewith to apply Solomon's doctrine of discipline. Whether they will make upright trees, we cannot say; but they are supposed to have a tendency to make upright men.

FROST-BLIGHT.

It is a matter of great importance that all cultivators of fruit unite in making observations on this subject, and that it may be done with some unity of purpose.

1. Let the examiner select trees upon which are seen small *water-shoots*, that have evidently grown late in the fall. Usually, a tuft of withered leaves will indicate them. Examine also all the new wood which retains terminal leaves or is winter-killed at the tips.

2. The pith will be, in apples, an iron-rust color, and in pears greenish black or pepper color; the inner skin will be discolored, and the wood of a greenish, waxy appearance. On cutting down to the point where these shoots unite with the branch or trunk, the diseased sap will be found to have discolored the whole neighborhood. In many cases which we have examined, half the trunk is affected. We examined a bearing pear-tree, which to the eye has not one sign of unhealthiness, but which, on cutting, is found to be affected throughout, and will, undoubtedly, die in spring.

3. Let a comparison be instituted between trees in different circumstances.

Is there any difference between slow-growing varieties and those which grow rapidly?

Is there any difference between trees in cold, northern aspects, whose sap, in autumn, would not be likely to be excited, and those with southern aspects?

Is there a difference between trees upon a fat clay or rank loam of any kind, and those upon a warm, dry, sandy loam. It is supposed that any causes which produce a coarse, watery, flabby tissue in a tree, predispose it to injury by frost, and thus to the blight; and that the fineness and firmness of texture of trees growing in a sand-loam on a gravelly subsoil give them great power of endurance.

4. Let trees which are found to be in an injured condition be marked and examined again as follows:

(1.) At the breaking up of winter, to see if any change of condition has taken place.

(2.) At the breaking of the bud into leaf.

(3.) At the full development of leaf and when the downward current of sap is begun.

5. It is a matter of great importance to ascertain whether the character of the season which follows such frost-injuries as have befallen fruit-trees in this region, modifies the disease. Some think that blight will follow without regard to the ensuing season; others suppose that a *dry*, and warm season will very much prevent the mischief; but that a *moist* and warm spring and summer, will give it a fatal development.

It is ardently to be hoped that accurate observations will be made, and upon a large scale. We presume that it need not be added that the *exact truth of facts* is the first step toward any sound explanation; and that our object should be to *find out facts*, and then, afterward, to deduce principles.

———•❖•———

Boiling Potatoes.—Not one housekeeper out of ten knows how to boil potatoes properly. Here is an Irish method, one of the best we know. Clean wash the potatoes and leave the skin on; then bring the water to a boil and throw them in. As soon as boiled soft enough for a fork to be easily thrust through them, dash some cold water into the pot, let the potatoes remain two minutes, and then pour off the water. This done, half remove the pot-lid, and let the potatoes remain over a slow fire till the steam is evaporated; then peel and set them on the table in an *open* dish. Potatoes of a good kind thus cooked, will always be sweet, dry and mealy. A covered dish is bad for potatoes, as it keeps the steam in, and makes them soft and watery.

SEEDLING FRUITS.

ALREADY the varieties of hardy fruits have become so numerous, that not only can they not all be cultivated, but the mere list of names is too bulky to be printed. Downing's book gives a list of 181 apples. The London Horticultural Society's Catalogue, expurgated at that, gives 900 kinds of apples, and 1,500 have been tested in the Society's gardens. Manning's experimental grounds and nursery at the time of his death, contained 1,000 named varieties of the pear! Swollen as is the list, there are scores annually added; many under the advice of scientific bodies; many have popular approbation; many from the partialities of some parental nurseryman; and many come in, as evil came into this world, no one can tell how.

It has become necessary, therefore, to exclude many from the catalogue, and especially necessary that none should enter without the very best passport. In the main, one set of tests will serve, both for receiving and expurgating; for no matter how long a fruit has been on the list, it should be ejected if, being out, its qualities would not gain it a fresh admission. There are no hereditary rights, or rights of occupancy, in pomological lists.

Titles, rank, antiquity, pedigree and other merciful means of compensating a want of personal merit, may do for *men* but not for *apples*. A very glorious pomological reformation broke out in the London Horticultural Society's gardens at Chiswick, and that Luther of the orchard, Mr. Thompson, has abolished an astonishing number of sinecures, and reformed, if not worthless rotten boroughs, very worthless apples and pears. The Society's first catalogue issued in 1826. Its third catalogue was published in December of 1842. The experience of the intervening sixteen years led to the total rejection from their list, on the ground of inferiority, or as synonyms, of 600 varieties of apples; 139 of cherries; 200 of gooseberries; 82 of grapes,

80 of strawberries; 150 of peaches; 200 of pears; and 150 of plums. Only *twenty-eight* peaches are allowed to stand; and only *twenty-six* strawberries out of the hundreds that were proved. We have no similar society in the United States whose authority would be generally acknowledged. Our only resource is the diffusion of the very best fruits that every neighborhood may have a standard of comparison by the reduction of experience to the form of rules. Although it is difficult to lay down general rules on this subject, there are three which may be mentioned.

1. *No fruit should be admitted to the list and none retained upon it, which is decidedly poor.*—One would suppose this truism to be superfluous as a rule. But it is only necessary to go out into seedling orchards in any neighborhood to find small, tough, and flavorless apples, which hold their place alongside of orchards filled with choice grafted fruit.

2. *No seedling fruit · should be added to the list, which is in no respect better than those of the same period of ripening already cultivated.*—It is not enough that an apple is nearly or quite as good as another favorite apple. It must be *as* good in flavor, and better in some of its habits.

3. *In testing the merits of fruit, an estimate should be the result of a consideration of all the habits, jointly, of the tree and of the fruit.*—It is in the application of this rule that great experience and judgment are required. This will be plain, if one considers how many essential particulars enter into a first-rate fruit beside mere flavor.

Of two fruits equal in flavor, one may surpass the other in tenderness of flesh, in juiciness, in delicacy of skin, and in size. It is rare that any single fruit combines all these excellences, and therefore it is that we retain several varieties, among which such properties are distributed.

There are many fruits which, having good substance and flavor, derive their value from some single peculiarity.

Thus a fruit may be no better than many others, but the tree, blooming very late in spring, is seldom overtaken by prowling and irregular frosts. Some of our best fruits have stingy bearing-trees, or trees of very tender and delicate habit; and we are obliged to tolerate more hardy and prolific trees with fruit somewhat inferior.

A few fruits are retained on the list because they have the singular property of being uninjured by frosts, and others because, though not remarkable for flavor, they are endless keepers, of both which properties the Rawle's Jennetting is an example.

In fruits designed for market, beauty and abundance must be allowed to supersede mere excellence of flavor. Some very rich fruits are borne in such a parsimonious way that none but amateurs can afford tree-room.

Nor are we to overlook nursery qualifications; for, of two fruits equally good, preference should be given to that which will work the kindliest in the nursery. Some will bear grafting on the root, some will not; some take well by budding, and grow off promptly and with force; others are dull and slugglish, and often reluctant to form the new partnership. While then it will always be to the nurseryman's interest to work such kinds as he can sell the most of —he has a right, in so far as he directs the public judgment of his neighborhood, to give a preference, among equal fruits, to such as work the surest and strongest. It is as much the interest of the purchaser and the public to have the freest growing sorts, as it is the nurseryman's interest. Thus, if another Seckle pear could be found growing on the tree of Williams' *Bon Chrétien*, it ought to supplant the old Seckle tree, which, in spite of its incomparable fruit, is a vexatious thing to manage; and, as often in the case of other and fairer fruit, makes one wonder how such amiable and beautiful daughters ever had such a surly and crusty old father.

A pomological censor must also have regard to varieties

of taste among men, and to commercial qualities of fruit, and to its adaptation to soil and climate.

No one man has a right to make his tongue the monarch over other people's tongues. Therefore, for instance, it is none of our business, if a rugged mouth chooses to roll a slice of the austere Vanderveer pippin, like sin, as a sweet morsel under his tongue. The mild delicacy of an apple, which fills our mouths with admiration, would be mere insipidity to all who are favored with leather mouths. So that there must be toleration even among apple-mongers.

Nor are the humbler tests of cooking to be overlooked. Some fruits are good eaters and poor cookers; some cook well but are villainous to the taste when raw; some will stew to a fine flavor and sweetness *without sugar*, and some have remarkable jelly properties. But after the largest allowance is made for taste, hardiness, keeping, prolific bearing, color, size, texture, season, adaptation to soils, etc., etc., there will be found, we think, a large number of tenants in our nurserymen's catalogues, upon whom should be instantly served a writ of ejectment.

* * *

TIME FOR PRUNING.

WE do not believe in severe pruning at *any* time. If a man has the education of his orchard from the start, it is an utter abomination to leave his trees in such a condition as to require it. If, however, one comes into possession of a much abused orchard, or of a seedling orchard; or, if a single tree is to be changed, or an old tree is to be headed back for health's sake, then it may be necessary to prune with a free hand. But in such cases, the change should not be attempted in one season, but divided between two.

There is, we suppose, a critical time in which pruning will injure the tree. It is after the sap is in full motion, the vegetable system impleted, *but before the pores and sap passages have acquired a contractile power.* Thus, if a grape is pruned when the buds begin to swell, the wood does not contract, and the vine bleeds to excess. But if pruned after the leaves are as large as the palm of the hand, no injury ensues from cutting, for now the sap passages contract and close speedily.

Thus if a tree be handled before or after this period, it does not suffer; but if pruned *at this critical state of the wood*, it will bleed, the stump part will become diseased, probably from the relaxed state of the woody tissue, and canker will ensue—a word indicating, we presume, simply a state of decay, covered by or accompanied with, some sort of fungus growth.

Pruning before this critical time, is sometimes the most convenient. But if it be a question, at which of the two periods is the tree in a state to suffer the least, and to recover the soonest, we say, *after it is in full leaf and well a-growing*, viz. the last of May and the first of June. The wood has then a contractile force, does not bleed; the tree is making new wood with great energy, and has therefore a full supply of organizable matter with which promptly to heal the wound.

Mr. O. V. Hill thus speaks in the *Boston Cultivator:*

"Fruit growers at the present day, are generally of the opinion, that the proper time for pruning is the last of May or early in June, when the tree is in full leaf and in a vigorous, growing state. This, on many accounts, appears to be the most suitable season, as the wounds heal much more rapidly, the tree throws out less suckers, canker is avoided and the sap circulates freely to every part of the tree; but there are some objections to pruning in the early part of summer, which I do not recollect to have seen noticed. Any one who is familiar with vegetable physiology is aware that there is a new layer of wood and a new layer of bark deposited every year, and that in June this process is in active operation; the newly-forming wood and bark are then consequently in a tender and imperfect state, and very susceptible to injury. Standing in the forks of the branches as it is sometimes necessary to do in pruning, will frequently separate the bark and wood, especially in young trees at this season. In grafting late in the season, this is frequently the case; sometimes where the ladder is placed against a branch it will remove the bark; and in sawing, unless the saw runs very clear, and the teeth are fine, the same results will follow; if pruning is done in June, it should be performed with the greatest caution."

The New York *Farmer and Mechanic*, commenting on the above, says:

"The best time for pruning apple-trees is, as yet, we believe, undetermined by the most experienced orchardists, but we are of opinion that the early part of June is, for reasons above given by Mr. Hill, to be preferred. The objection arising from the fear of injuring the bark of the tree can easily be obviated by having the operator use *moccasins* instead of shoes, and surrounding the upper round of the latter with straw or flannel."

Downing says:

"We should especially avoid pruning at that period in spring when the buds are swelling, and the sap is in full flow, as the loss of sap by bleeding is very injurious to most trees, and, in some, brings on a serious and incurable canker in the limbs.

"There are advantages and disadvantages attending all seasons of pruning, but our own experience has led us to believe that, practically, *a fortnight before midsummer is by far the best season, on the whole, for pruning in the northern and middle States.* Wounds made at this season heal over freely and rapidly; it is the most favorable time to judge of the shape and balance of the head, and to see at a glance which branches require removal; and all the stock of organizable matter in the tree is directed to the branches that remain."

Some of the western States are so much earlier than that of New York, that early June will be equivalent to the time specified by Downing. We have now fortified the opinion which we heretofore expressed, by good authority, and by what seems to us good reasons. As it is, however, with some, yet a debated question, we shall carefully insert the experience of any man for or against our position.

PLUMS AND THEIR ENEMIES.

MULTITUDES of men have had plum-trees, and every year, for ten years, have seen the fruit promise fair at first and then prematurely drop, without knowing the reason. Even well-informed men have said to us that it arose from some defect in the *tree*, from too much *gum*, from a worm at the *root*, etc.

The plum-tree is very hardy; is less subject to disease than most fruit-trees; its fruit is highly prized; and the varieties of it are numerous and many of them delicious. By a proper selection of trees a succession of fruit may be had from July to November. The trees are usually sure and enormous bearers, every year. With so many good qualities the cultivation of the plum is well-nigh prohibited, as a garden or orchard fruit, by the valor of one little bug!

The *Curculio* (a very hardy fellow, with a constitution yet unimpaired by such a name as *Rhynchœnus Nenuphar!*) is a small beetle, about a quarter of an inch long, which attacks the plums almost as soon as the fruit has set. They seek this, and almost all smooth-skinned fruits, as a place of deposit for their eggs. Many of the facts which we shall narrate, were mentioned to us by Mr. Payne of Madison, who has closely and curiously observed this depredator.

An incision is first made, of semicircular form, by a little rostra or lancet which he carries in his head for this very purpose. After the opening is made, the curculio deposits an egg therein; then changing positions again, it carefully, with its fore legs, secures the egg in its *nidus*, and pats the skin under the edge of which its treasure is hidden, with repeated and careful efforts of its feet. Where fruit abounds it deposits, usually, but one to a plum. But we have had trees, just beginning to bear, whose few plums were scarified all over.

The egg hatches to a worm, and this feeds on the plum, causing it prematurely to fall; the insect issuing from it, enters the ground, to undergo its transformations, and soon to reappear, a beetle, ready for fresh mischief-making propagation.

The climate of the West is entirely glorious for all manner of insects. They can put the East to shame in the matter of aphides, cockroaches, cutworms, army and wireworms, curculios, peach-worms, grubs, etc., etc. There are many questions relating to the history of insects, about which eastern writers are in doubt, not at all doubtful with us.

1. Do the larvæ remain in the ground all the residue of the summer, and come forth only in the ensuing spring? In cold latitudes it may be so. Harris says, that they undergo their transformation in twenty days. Downing admits this of a few stragglers. But the main supply of bugs, he thinks, remains all summer and until spring, in the ground. But with us the curculio is not exclusively an early summer insect. It is found, in its appropriate haunts, through the whole warm season. Mr. Payne put plums containing the worms into a glass, and in eleven days obtained full-grown curculios. In cool regions they probably have but an annual generation; but in warm and

long summers, in the West, they reproduce often in each season.

2. The mode of ascent has been a matter of doubt. J. J. Thomas, in the *Fruit Culturist* says: "It has the power of using its wings in flying; but whether it crawls up the tree or ascends by flight, appears not to be certainly ascertained."

Downing admits that it flies, but says, "How far this insect flies is yet a disputed point, some cultivators affirming that it scarcely goes further than a single tree, and others believing that it flies over a whole neighborhood."

Kenrick says: "They crawl up trees," and he quotes an author as saying: "That of two trees standing so near each other as to touch, the fruit of one has been destroyed and the other has escaped; so little and so reluctantly do these insects incline to use their wings." Dr. James Tilton says, in the "Domestic Encyclopedia," that "they appear very reluctant to use their wings, and perhaps never employ them but when necessity compels them to migrate."

It is true that the curculio, in cold and chilly weather, is disinclined to fly; but give it a right murderously hot day, and "McGregor's on his native heath again." Just before a thunder storm, in summer, in a still, sultry, sweltering day, they may be seen flying among the trees as blithely as any house-fly; alighting on your arm, or hand, and springing off again as nimbly as a flea.

All remedies founded on the idea of their crawling preferences will be signal failures. Troughs about trees, bats of wool, bandages of all kinds about the trunk to impede the ascent will be found as useful as would high fences to keep crows from a cornfield, or birds from the garden.

All remedies for this pest succeed to a charm where the curculio does not abound; and almost every one of them fails in places really infested them.

In cities, and in country places which are far removed

15

from all orchards or gardens, the crops may be saved. It
is not difficult to defend a tree against all the curculios that
are *bred upon it.*   Pavements; hard-rolled gravel; gathering up, daily, the fallen ⋅plums and destroying them; the
application of salt, and many other remedies may succeed
where the curculio from other gardens or orchards cannot
easily migrate to supply the trees with a fresh brood.
Trees in cities, and in retired places, on this account, often
bear plenteously.

But of what use is it to destroy five hundred larvæ, if
twice that number of emigrants, from some other quarter,
are anxious, the next spring, to *squat* upon your trees, or
to *enter* them, in land-office style, most nefariously? All
remedies founded on the destruction of the larvæ will be
totally useless if your trees can be reached from some
infected point abroad, as we have found to our sorrow.   In
our own experience, and in that of other amateur-cultivators
of fruit, the pavement, salt, and all have been " love's labor
lost."   But in the experience of others, in climates where
the curculio does not abound, or in secluded situations, they
have proved effectual.

The remedies to be employed, in ordinary cases, must be
such as will constantly molest the insect at his work.
Inclosures, in which swine root, and rub against the trees;
lanes, where cattle resort, to rub off their hair in spring, to
shade themselves in summer—these are the best situations.
In yards and gardens plum-trees should be placed upon the
most frequented paths; close to the well, by the kitchen
door, near the wood-house, so that, as often as possible,
they may be jarred in passing and repassing.

Where a few trees stand apart in the garden, it is said
that, daily, morning and evening, by spreading a sheet
under them, and giving the tree a sudden and violent blow
with a mallet, the insects will drop and may then be
gathered and destroyed. This should be performed while
it is cool, as then, only, the curculio is somewhat torpid. If

this course is pursued, a block should be put upon the tree, to receive the stroke, with a bit of carpet or some soft pad to it, that the bark may not be injured. A white sheet should be spread under the tree to catch the falling robber.

A few trees will suffice for a private family, and the fruit must be earned by careful watchfulness. Those who are too indolent, or careless, or indifferent to the luxury to bestow the requisite attention through the months of May and June, may spare themselves the trouble of planting plum-trees. Plum *orchards* are not to be thought of.

Although the curculio chiefly delights in the plum, it scruples at no fruit. It may be found upon peaches, cherries, nectarines, apricots, gooseberries and currants.

------●●●------

ROOT GRAFTING.

WHILE nothing can be done out of doors in the nursery, the process of root grafting may be carried on, and the stock be ready for setting as soon as the grounds are open in spring.

When this method of grafting is employed with discretion, it greatly aids the nurseryman. It is a resource in case he cannot procure stocks to bud or graft upon; it makes finer and handsomer trees; and it can be carried on at a season of leisure; and the scions, being early in the ground, have a longer season of growth by two months than buds, or ordinary grafts.

Although any healthy root with some fibres will answer to graft upon, yet experienced nurserymen prefer the *tap* roots of young seedling stocks. Those who have apple and pear stocks which are to be removed, should employ the open weather of winter to raise them. The tap roots may be taken for grafting purposes and the stocks put away in cellars, or buried in the ground.

We do not know that there is any difference in favor of the root of one variety over another; but it will not do to propagate every variety of fruit by this method. Experience has shown that some sorts do better by root grafting than in any other way; but other kinds are very apt to be winter-killed; and some varieties have such a straggling habit of growth, that it would be extremely difficult to train them to a good head; and such sorts, therefore, require to be budded or grafted high up on good stocks.

The roots being washed, are cut into four or five inch pieces; and the scions prepared as for ordinary grafting. Splice, or tongue grafting is the most convenient method. Woollen yarn, cut to ten or twelve inches' length, is wound around it closely at the point of junction. Let the grafting wax be kept in a melted state, by being put in a pan, over a few coals. Holding the work over the pan, with a spoon pour a portion of the liquid all over the yarn; it hardens immediately, and the whole may be set in rows in a box and covered above the point of union with moist sand, and kept in a cellar till it is time to turn them out in the spring.

———•◆•———

THE cherry, plum, pear and apple trees, in a diseased condition, will often throw up numerous and thrifty sprouts that will offer to an inexperienced cultivator inviting temptations to multiply his stock at a rapid rate with little labor. If he be deceived by these appearances, and propagate his valuable kinds upon these diseased growths, his efforts will ultimately result in his disappointment.

BLIGHT AND INSECTS.

IN an article on employing suckers of fruit-trees for stocks, which we shall copy, Dr. Kirtland says:

" The practice of grafting and budding pears upon this quality of stocks has extended a diseased action, a kind of canker among our pear orchards, that has, in some instances, been mistaken for *blight*, a disease that has its origin in the depredations of a minute coleopterous insect, which has been satisfactorily described in all its stages of transformation by Dr. Harris, and other Massachusetts entomologists."

That the fire-blight is, to any considerable extent anywhere, but especially at the West, occasioned by an insect, is an idea, we believe, totally unsupported by facts. That some injury has been done by the *scolytus pyri*, the investigations of Mr. Lowell and Professor Peck leave no room to doubt. But we are not satisfied that, even in these cases, they were the cause of the *blight*, but only an accidental concomitant. Did Mr. Lowell or Professor Peck *always* find this beetle upon blighted trees? Was it found in *every* blighted limb? Did not blight occur without these insects? Has any one of New England *since* found the blight to proceed from the gnawings of this beetle?

Has any one found this beetle *before* the blight occurred at its mischievous work, or is it only *after* the blight is seen that the beetle is found? If the *scolytus pyri* has been *found* only after the tree is thoroughly affected, there is reason to suppose that it did not *come* until after the disease had prepared the way for it.

We are seriously skeptical of this alleged cause. Whatever may be true of the blight at the East, the blight in the West is unquestionably not an effect of the *scolytus pyri*. We have examined with the utmost pains, multitudes of trees in all soils—several of our shrewdest nurserymen have searched year by year, and we have, unfortunately, had too much opportunity and too many subjects, and yet no insect or insect-track has been detected, except those which have attacked the tree in *consequence* of the blight.

To be sure, we can find bugs, black, brown, green and grey, but the mere presence of an insect is nothing, though with many, it seems enough, when a tree is blighted, if a bug is found on it, to determine the parentage of the mischief. Nor do the published accounts of insects, found on blighted trees, increase our respect for this theory. The observations seem to have been not thorough enough, and not carefully made, and the reasonings even less philosophical. Men have searched for a theory rather than for the mere facts in the case. But by far the greatest number of those who write, give no evidence of relying upon any observations which they have themselves made, but go back perpetually to the old precedents, Mr. Lowell and Professor Peck, without being at any pains to verify them. Has Dr. Kirtland ever found the *scolytus pyri?* Has he ever, in time of extensive blight, found it under such circumstances as to satisfy his mind that it was the real cause of fire-blight? or does he rest satisfied that blight is occasioned by an insect simply because so it is set down in good books? The canker may be mistaken for blight by those who have not been acquainted with either; but surely, no one who has ever attentively examined one real case of fire-blight would ever mistake it for anything else, or anything else for it.

The insect theory we regard as wholly untenable except for special, local, peculiar ravages which are not properly *blights.* The blight is a disease of the *circulation.* It affects every tissue of the plant. It is not a disease from exhaustion of sap by the suction of aphides, as Dr. Mosher, of Cincinnati, supposed, for the trees have a plethora rather than scarcity of sap; it lacerates the sap-vessels, bursts the bark, flows down the branches, and dries in globules upon the trunk. On cutting the tree, if the blight is yet new, the texture of the alburnum will be found to resemble what is called a *water-core* in the apple, its color is of a dirty greenish hue, soon changing by exposure to brown and black. But if the blight is old, the wood is of a dingy white, the alburnum colored like iron rust, and the bark of a brownish black. These appearances are incompatible with any idea of exhaustion by the gnawing of the *scolytus pyri*, or the suction of aphides, which would result in mere shrinking of parts, dryness and death. If insects have a hand in the mischief, it is by the secretion of poison, of which fact, we have never seen the trace of proof, although it has often been suggested, and is by some empyrically asserted. To our minds the insect-poison-theory is imaginary. It is entirely convenient to refer every excrescence, or shrinking of parts, every watery suffusion, wart, discoloration, crumpling leaf, wilting, etc., to poison, and still more convenient to find the insect so atomic that it cannot *be* found, and thus to heap the multiform sins of the orchard on the scape-goat of a hypothetical insect.

As to electricity, as no one knows anything about this elemental sprite, his out-goings or in-comings, we are like to have acted over again all the caprices of witch-times, when elves and gnomes cut up every prank imaginable, and when any prank, which was cut up, of course was performed by them. Everybody is agog about electricity. But we respectfully suggest that it is one thing to ascertain facts by cautious, guarded experiments or careful observation, and quite another to set down everything, which one does not know what else to do with, to electricity, simply because *it may be so for aught that we know to the contrary.* People reason somewhat in this wise ; electricity performs a vast number of very mysterious operations, therefore, every operation which is mysterious is performed by electricity. We believe electricity to have something to do with it, only because it seems to have concern with every living, growing thing.

We believe that the blight is, in all cases, the effect of

frost upon the sap. We have, until recently, supposed it to arise from autumnal freezing, while the tree is in full growth. We are now inclined to suppose that severe freezing and sudden thawing at any time, autumn, winter or spring, *when the sap is in motion*, will result in blight. The blight of 1844 was from the freezing of growing trees in the autumn of 1843, and the premonitory stages were clearly discernible in the tree during the whole winter months before it broke out in its last malignant form.

When a warm winter allows continuous motion of sap, and sudden, severe freezing with rapid thawing occurs, we *suppose* it to cause a variety of blight. We are making investigations on this head, but are not yet prepared to speak with certainty.

When a sudden violent freezing overtakes growing trees in spring, with rapid thaws, it, we suppose, results in a blight resembling the autumn-caused blight.

We are diligently searching into this whole matter, and hope to throw some light upon it.

But now comes *the* question. What is it that makes some trees so obnoxious to this evil while others escape? Why are some orchards generally affected, and contiguous orchards entirely saved?

It is very plain that the blight occurs, as a general disease, in some seasons more than in others, because it depends upon the peculiar condition of the season, the time and degree of frosts. But it does not seem so clear why, when these conditions are favorable to blight, one tree should suffer, and the next in the row should not; why one orchard should be depopulated, and another in the same town not touched.

We think that light will be afforded on this point by a consideration of the *texture* of trees.

When trees are rapidly grown by stimulating manures, or upon strong clay loams, or from any other cause, the wood is coarse, the passages enlarged, the tissue loose and spongy. The tree passes a great volume of sap—it is but imperfectly elaborated (as is seen by the late period to which such trees defer the bearing of fruit), and the tissues formed by it are correspondingly imperfect in wholesomeness, compactness, and solidity of parts. The tree is bloated —is dropsical.

On gravelly soils, or loams with a gravelly subsoil, or on any kind of soil, which gives a slow and thorough growth, the wood is fine, close and perfect; the vessels are not expanded, their sides are firmer, less sensitive to sudden changes of temperature, and when exposed to them better able to resist them.

Whatever soil produces rank or coarse wood, a flabby tissue will be subject to blights. Whatever soil induces a fine-grained, compact fibre, and vigorous tissue, will be free from blight. The same is true of the various methods of cultivation; those who drive their trees, who aim chiefly at a rapid and strong growth, will give their trees a condition requisite for blight. Those who pursue a more cautious, a slower method, and look to the *quality* rather than the *quantity* of their wood, will be comparatively free from blight.

To be sure, there may be seasons so extreme that blight will occur in the most healthy tree; so disease will occur in the most temperate men; yet temperance, conformity to the laws of nature, is the rule of health, and nonconformity the preparation for disease.

Meanwhile, will those who are unfortunate enough to have a good opportunity for observing, examine—

1. The soil and subsoil of blighted trees?

2. The habit of the tree, as to rankness of growth?

3. The character of the cultivation which has been employed?

4. In short, the relative condition of orchards and trees which have escaped or been blighted, as to fineness and closeness, and health of texture. It is high time that this matter should be minutely investigated. It is the *opprobrium cultorum*.

15*

APPLES FOR HOGS.

FARMERS are afraid of sour apples; if stock have *only* sour fruit they are injured; but let both sweet and sour grow in the orchard, and experience has determined that they will, of themselves, eat the due proportion of each. Cattle and hogs are as fond of variety in fruit as men are. In raising potatoes, pumpkins, apples, etc., for animals, it is frequently supposed that the larger and ranker the growth the better; that, at any rate, cattle fare as well on coarse-grained vegetables as on others. But a rank, coarse, watery vegetable is no better for an ox than for a man. The nutritious principle is the same to man or beast. A fine-fleshed, highly nutritious apple or potato is as much better for stock as it is for man. If a variety is not fit for men, it is not worth while to cultivate it at all. Cattle show themselves to be of this opinion when left to range; they avoid coarse, rough herbage, and pick the sweetest and highest flavored. Let the *best* sorts of apples be planted for stock. If one has a seedling orchard which it would be worth while to graft over for human use, let not its poor, miserable fruit be fed to hogs; let it be grafted over even if one means to use it for stock.

PULLING OFF POTATO FLOWERS.—The man who makes his potato-ground feed flowers, prevents it feeding his children. Every ounce of matter consumed by the flowers is so much taken from the consumption of the family.

To RESTORE an exhausted, or rather tired field, it should be sown in grass, and stock fed upon it during the winter months. Hogs fattened upon tired land enrich it very much.

THE FLOWER GARDEN.

SPRING FLOWERING-BULBS.—When crocus, hyacinths, narcissus, tulips, have done flowering, let the seed stalks be cut down, as the ripening of the seed severely taxes and exhausts the powers of a plant. Some persons are accustomed, after the bulbs have flowered, to cut off the tops, as if to do the most mischief possible. The success of the next year's flowering will depend very much on the care given to your beds now. Many bulbs, as the tulip, form entirely new bulbs; and others, as the hyacinth, form the flower bud for the next season. The *leaf* is the indispensable means of doing this; in it are perfected the juices which are returned and deposited in the root. If the bed is left to be choked with weeds, and your bulbs robbed of nutriment, or if the soil is left compact, or if there is too much moisture, or on the other hand, too little, the bud or bulb for the next year will be weakened. A very deep bed, or a sandy soil, will sufficiently prevent the effects of too much water.

The surface should be mellowed by the hand, and thoroughly weeded. The *most* careful cultivators raise their bulbs every year. The *careful* at least every third year. The *careless* let them alone and wonder, from year to year, why their bulbs do so poorly—"The moles must eat them, or, worms probably injure them;" but the worst worm in a flower-garden is careless indolence. When bulbs are raised, it should not be done until the leaves are dry.

GLADIOLUS.—We are surprised that this fine soldier-like plant is not more extensively employed to adorn gardens, yards, and lawns. A few varieties only are found in our gardens. Great attention has been given in Europe, especially in Belgium, to raising new varieties, and many magnificent kinds are now found in European collections which, so far as we know, are not to be had for love or money in

America. The bulb, or rather corm,* increases very rapidly, and by a little attention one may obtain from a few, a very large supply. They may be planted with good effect in rows, in clumps, and in beds, but not singly. A sandy loam, well mixed with leaf-mold, is their delight. We usually remove the top soil, and then take out and reject about twelve inches of the subsoil, making in all about twenty inches' depth; return the top earth, together with enough compost of leaf-mold, sand, and thoroughly decayed manure, to fill it; plant about four inches deep, measuring from the top of the corm. When your plants are growing, examine every day; if you see a sawdust-like matter about them, they need attention. On searching, a perforation will be found in the stem. With a penknife slit the stem down from the hole until you reach the worm which caused the mischief. If this course is not properly pursued, you will lose stem and root. With a thin strip of bass matting, or a bit of green ribbon, the stem may be tied and fastened to a rod for support. In door-yards, and in the scanty grounds of city yards, clumps of ten or fifteen gladioli would have a very beautiful appearance, especially if different varieties, instead of being mixed, should be planted in separate but contiguous patches.

TUBEROSE.—The beauty of its pure, white florets, but especially the delightful odor of this fragrant flower, has rendered it a favorite wherever it is known. It is very

---

* Bulbs are of two kinds: those which have a number of coats, or skins, one within the other, like the hyacinth, which are called tunicated bulbs; those which consist of a number of scales, only attached to the base, like the lily; but what are called corms, are only a solid mass of feculent matter, and which modern botanists do not allow to be bulbs but call underground stems. Corms do not require taking up so often as bulbs; and when they are intended to remain for several years in the ground, they should be planted from four to six inches deep at first; as every year a new corm will form above the old one; and thus, if planted too near the surface, the corm, in a few years, will be pushed out of the ground.—*Loudon.*

tender to frost, and must not be planted out until about the first of May. It is to be treated like the gladiolus. Its effect is heightened by being put in a half shade, where its pure white is relieved by a green background. The flower stem rises from two to three feet and requires a rod to sustain it. The fragrance is so powerful that a few plants will, at evening, scent a whole garden; a circumstance well known to owners of pleasure gardens, who render their grounds very delightful by dispersing these, and other odoriferous flowers, in various parts of their grounds, thus loading the dewy evening air with delicious perfume. They may be planted in ten-inch pots and sunk in the ground until they have begun to blossom, when the pots may be raised and conveyed to the parlor or veranda. A single plant will sometimes make a room disagreeable by its excessive odor.

The roots are imported to England from Italy, as that climate is too humid and cool too perfect them for flowering. But, in our soil and climate, we have found no difficulty in raising, from off-sets, the finest possible bulbs. No yard or garden should be without tuberoses.

PLANTS IN POTS.—It is better when one has ground at hand, to turn out plants which have been housed through the winter into the open garden. Roses, geraniums, azaleas, cape jasmins, fuchsias, etc., will be wonderfully invigorated by such treatment. The tea and Bengal roses can hardly be brought to perfection in pots, and those who have only seen the penurious growth and diminished and sparse blossoms in the parlor have no idea of the beauty of these roses. We usually excavate a place two feet square and two feet deep for each rose, filling it with sandy loam very highly enriched with leaf-mold and decayed manure. The trouble will be repaid four fold; for nature has never made a plant that forgets to be grateful for attention.

In turning out plants, put the left hand in such a way upon the top as that the stem shall come between the

second and third finger, then invert the pot and give the
bottom of it two or three sharp raps, when the pot will
come off. If the plant is in a lively, growing state, and the
outside of the ball of earth is covered with fine, white, new
roots, it will be best to put the ball into the ground without disturbing the roots at all. But if the plant is not growing, the earth may be carefully worked out from the roots
with the hands, taking care to break the fibres as little as
possible. Spread out the roots as much as possible in every
direction, and cover with fine earth.

Rose bushes will need attention soon, as worms and bugs
begin their depredations. When the number of bushes is
limited, hand-picking every day or two is best. For a
large collection one must resort to more general methods.
Drench your shrubs, which aphides and worms infest, with
soapsuds, made of two pounds of *whale-oil* soap to fifteen
gallons of water. This is by far the most efficacious—the
only efficacious—course for destroying insects.

As flower-seeds come up, see that they are well weeded,
and if crowded, thin them out. We would recommend the
cultivation of some old-fashioned flowers. Nothing is more
showy than a bed of poppies of mixed colors. Holyhocks
are becoming very great favorites, and we saw recently
flowers as magnificent, and as well worth having, as any
dahlia. The varieties of lupine should be sought for, and
for those who have seen nothing but the white and blue
lupines we make an extract from Mrs. Loudon's "Companion to the Flower Garden"—an admirable work, which,
though professedly written for ladies, may be used with
profit by everybody who cultivates a garden.

"Lupinus.—*Leguminosæ.*—The Lupine. A genus of
herbaceous annuals and perennials which contain some of
our most beautiful border flowers: yellow, blue, white, and
pink lupines are among the oldest border annuals; *L. nanus*
is a beautiful little annual, with dark blue flowers, a native
of California, and requiring the usual treatment of Cali-

fornia annuals. *L. mutabilis* and *Cruicshankii* are splendid plants, growing to the height of four or five feet, and branching like miniature trees. *L. Polyphyllus* and its varieties are perennials, and they are splendid and vigorous-growing plants, with spikes of flowers from one foot to eighteen inches in length; *L. nootkatensis* is a handsome dwarf perennial, and *L. arboreus*, when trained against a wall, will attain six feet in height, and in sheltered situations it will grow with equal vigor trained as a bush tied to a stake; *L. latifolius* is a perennial from California, with very long spikes of blue flowers. All the species will thrive in common garden soil; the annuals are propagated by seed sown in February or March, and the perennials by division of the roots."

PREPARATION OF SEED FOR SOWING.

MANY persons suppose that when seeds have been selected, nothing is necessary but to put them into the ground just as they are. A careful preparation of seed, both for field or garden use, will add much to the success of a planting.

1. ASSORTING SEEDS.—In every lot of seed there are many imperfect ones; some are insectiferous, some are unripe, some are the extreme terminal seeds, small and weak, some are very often a little moldy. In some way all defective seeds should be removed.

Then it should be remembered, that the soundest and largest seeds will produce plants of a corresponding vigor, and that by planting only the healthiest, the variety is kept pure—or even improved.

For garden use hand picking will suffice. We pour our corn on a table, and select only the kernels which are plump and large, rejecting any which show an intermixture of other varieties. Beet seed requires careful winnowing, nearly one-fourth, as they are usually sold, being unfit for planting. Peas are more uniform in size and quality, and require but little selection. Melons, squashes, and cucumbers should be culled, or better yet, be put into water; only those which sink promptly should be used, the swimming and floating ones being light and trashy. Beans are apt to be imperfect. We have usually found occasion to reject full one-third of every quart, for seedsmen are apt to put in every seed that grows, whether they will ever grow again or not. There is no dishonesty certainly in this; but if one would habitually screen or select, and put up only the very choicest, he would ultimately get a higher price, and secure for his seed a universal demand.

2. SOAKING SEEDS.—Some seeds will not germinate for a long period, unless they are artificially brought forward. Locust seeds are *scalded* before planting. Peas are scalded to kill the bug, when thus inhabited. The cypress vine seed require soaking to induce a quick germination. Celery seed is very sluggish unless soaked.

Seeds are often steeped in *prepared* liquids to force their growth. Old seeds, whose powers of germination are much diminished, are made to vegetate by being put into a weak solution of oxalic acid. Wheat is *pickled* in salt brine, then rolled in lime, as a preventive of *smut*.

Corn is protected from worms by copperas water; and peas are put into train oil to guard them from moles and mice. Tanner's oil, and a solution of saltpetre are often used; the first for turnip-seed, to protect them from a destructive insect; and the latter for all seeds, as a stimulant to their growth and to guard against worms and bugs.

Some excitement was made in Scotland, not long ago, by the great effects alleged to have been produced by so preparing seeds that they would contain in or on themselves all those fertilizing qualities usually looked for in the soil. It is possible, by employing chemical mixtures, or coatings, to make the seed germinate with great vigor, and to establish itself strongly; but we do not suppose any process can be made to reach beyond this. No mere soaking or coating can extend its influence through the whole growth of the crop.

When seeds are soaked they anticipate the weeds in coming up, especially seeds planted in May and June, and this is a very important object, as crops are, often, almost smothered with weeds before they are large enough to be weeded.

SOWING FLOWER SEEDS—TRANSPLANTING.

MANY flower-seeds require no more skill in planting than do peas or beans, for they are as large and as easily germinated. But very many are small, and some extremely small, and if planted too deeply, they will not shoot, or will shoot very feebly.

Select a free-working and rich piece of ground—a sandy loam is best, and a stiff clay the worst—let it be spaded deeply, incorporating very thoroughly-rotted manure, *i. e.* manure full two years old and which will crumble in the hand as fine as sand. With a fine-toothed rake reduce every lump and bring the surface to the finest state of pulverization. If the seed is very small, it had better be mixed with a little sand, or dry soil, to increase the bulk. The sowing will be easier and more equal. Scatter the seed upon the bed; then with the hands or a fine garden sieve, sift fresh and mellow earth upon it from a quarter to half an inch in depth. To bring the earth compactly about the seed, spat the bed with moderate strokes with the back of a spade. If the weather is very dry, water the bed at evening with a watering-pot—to pour it from a pail or cup would wash up the surface. Keep the plants from weeds, and when they are one or two inches high, they may be transplanted to the places where they are to stand. Balsams, larkspurs, poppies, and, indeed, most flowers do better by being transplanted. The operation checks the luxuriance of the plant, and increases its tendency to flower.

Sometimes seeds are planted where they are to remain; the treatment is precisely the same as before, except they are *thinned out* instead of transplanted. No mistake is more frequent, among inexperienced gardeners, than that of suffering too many plants to stand together. One is reluctant to pull up fine thriving plants; or he does not reflect that what may seem room enough while the plant is young, will be very scanty when it is grown.

There is much taste to be displayed in arranging flowers in a garden so that proper colors shall be contrasted. It is important that proper colors should be matched in a garden, as on a dress.

PARLOR-PLANTS AND FLOWERS IN WINTER.

THE treatment of house plants is very little understood, although the practice of keeping shrubs and flowers during the winter is almost universal. It is important that the physiological principles on which success depends should be familiarly understood; and then cultivators can apply them with success in all the varying circumstances in which they may be called to act.

Two objects are proposed in taking plants into the house —either simple protection, or the development of their foliage and flowers, during the winter. The same treatment will not do for both objects. Indeed, the greatest number of persons of our acquaintance, treat their winter plants, from which they desire flowers, as if they only wished to preserve them till spring; and the consequence is, that they have very little enjoyment in their favorites.

HOUSE PLANTS DESIGNED SIMPLY TO STAND OVER.

Tender roses, azaleas, cape jasmins, crape myrtles, oranges, lemons, figs, oleanders, may be kept in a *light* cellar if frost never penetrates it.

If kept in parlors, the following are the most essential points to be observed. The thermometer should never be permitted to rise above sixty degrees or sixty-five degrees; nor at night to sink below forty degrees. Although plants will not be frost-bitten until the mercury falls to thirty-two degrees, yet the chill of a temperature below forty degrees will often be as mischievous to tender plants as frost itself. Excessive heat, particularly a dry stove heat, will destroy the leaves almost as certainly as frost. We have seen plants languishing in a temperature of seventy degrees (it often rising ten degrees higher), while the owners wondered what could ail the plants, for they were sure that they kept the room warm enough!

Next, great care should be taken not to overwater. Plants which are not growing require *very little* water. If given, the roots become sogged, or rotten, and the whole plant is enfeebled. Water should never be suffered to stand in the saucers; nor be given, always, when the top-soil is dry. Let the earth be stirred, and when the *interior* of the ball is becoming dry, give it a *copious* supply; let it drain through thoroughly, and turn off what falls into the saucer.

PLANTS DESIGNED FOR WINTER FLOWERING.

It is to be remembered that the winter is naturally the season of *rest* for plants. All plants require to lie dormant during some portion of the year. You cannot cheat them out of it. If they are pushed the whole year they become exhausted and worthless. Here lies the most common error of plant-keepers. If you mean to have roses, blooming geraniums, etc., in winter, you must, *artificially*, *change*

their season of rest.   Plants which flower in summer must
rest in winter; those which are to flower in winter must
rest either in summer or autumn.   It is not, usually, worth
while to take into the house for flowering purposes any
shrub which has been in full bloom during the summer or
autumn.   Select and pot the wished-for flowers during summer; place them in a shaded position facing the north, give
very little water, and then keep them quiet.   Their energies will thus be saved for winter.   When taken into the
house, the four essential points of attention are light,
moisture, temperature, and cleanliness.

1. LIGHT.—The functions of the leaves cannot be health-
fully carried on without light.   If there be too little, the
sap is imperfectly elaborated, and returns from the leaves to
the body in a crude, undigested state.   The growth will be
coarse, watery, and brittle; and that ripeness which must
precede flowers and fruit cannot be attained.   The sprawling, spindling, white-colored, long-jointed, plants, of which
some persons are unwisely proud, are, often the result of
too little light and too much water.   The pots should be
turned around every day, unless when the light strikes
down from above, or from windows on each side; otherwise, they will grow out of shape by bending toward the
light.

2. MOISTURE.—Different species of plants require different quantities of water.   What are termed *aquatics*, of
which the *Calla Æthiopica*, is a specimen, require great
abundance of it.   Yet it should be often *changed* even in
the case of aquatics.   But roses, geraniums, etc., and the
common house plants require the soil to be *moist*, rather
than *wet*.   As a general rule it may be said that every pot
should have one-sixth part of its depth filled with coarse
pebbles, as a drainage, before the plants are potted.   This
gives all superfluous moisture a free passage out.   Plants
should be watered by *examination* and not by *time*.   They
require various quantities of moisture, according to their

activity, and the period of their growth. Let the earth be well stirred, and if it is becoming dry on the inside, give water. Never water by *dribblets*—a spoonful to-day, another to-morrow. In this way the outside will become bound, and the inside remain dry. Give a copious watering, so that the whole ball shall be soaked; then let it drain off, and that which comes into the saucer be poured off. But, in whatever way one prefers to give water, the thing to be gained is a full supply of moisture to every part of the roots, and yet not so much as to have it *stand* about them. Manure-water may be employed with great benefit every second or third watering. For this purpose we have never found anything of value equal to *guano*. Besides water to the root, plants are almost as much benefited by water on the leaf—but of this we shall speak under the head of *cleanliness*.

3. TEMPERATURE.—Sudden and violent *changes* of temperature are almost as trying to plants as to animals and men. At the same time, a moderate change of temperature is very desirable. Thus, in nature, there is a marked and uniform variation at night from the temperature of the day. At night, the room should be gradually lowered in temperature to from forty-five degrees to fifty degrees, while through the day it ranges from fifty-five degrees to seventy degrees. Too much, and too sudden heat will destroy tender leaves almost as surely as frost. It should also be remembered that the leaves of plants are constantly exhaling moisture during the day. If in too warm an atmosphere, or in one which is too dry, this perspiration becomes excessive and weakens the plant. If the room be stove-heated, a basin of water should be put on the stove to supply moisture to the air by evaporation. Sprinkling the leaves, a kind of artificial dew, is also beneficial, on this account. The air should be changed as often as possible. Every warm and sunny day should be improved to let in fresh air upon these vegetable breathers.

4. CLEANLINESS.—This is an important element of health as well as of beauty. *Animal-uncleanliness* is first to be removed. If ground-worms have been incorporated with the dirt, give a dose or two of lime-water to the soil. Next aphides or green-lice will appear upon the leaves and stems. Tobacco smoke will soon stupefy them and cause them to tumble upon the shelves or surface of the soil, whence they are to be carefully brushed, or crushed. If one has but a few plants, put them in a group on the floor; put four chairs around them and cover with an old blanket, forming a sort of tent. Set a dish of coals within, and throw on a handful of tobacco leaves. Fifteen minutes' smoking will destroy any decent aphis.

If a larger collection is on hand, let the dish or dishes be placed under the stands. When the destruction is completed, let the parlor be well ventilated, unless, fair lady, you have an inveterate smoker for a husband; in which case you may have become used to the nuisance.

The insects which infest large collections of green-houses, are fully treated of in horticultural books of directions.

Dust will settle every day upon the leaves, and choke up the perspiring pores. The leaves should be kept free by gentle wiping, or by washing.

———•••———

WHITE CLOVER is an important grass on flourishing old meadows. It grows very thick at the bottom of the other grass, although in a good season it will grow to the height of from twelve to sixteen inches. I have seen it in low spots completely covered for weeks together. Therefore land which produces abundant crops of grass, would require extensive draining for grain, and seeing that plowing such land destroys its life, it is far better to keep it in grass continually.

PARLOR FLOWERS AND PLANTS IN WINTER.—(*Art. 2.*)

THERE are so few who care enough for flowers to trouble themselves with them during the winter, that it seems almost unkind to criticise the imperfections of those who do. But it is very plain that, for the most part, skill and knowledge do not keep pace with good taste. *Not* to point out defects to those who are anxious to improve would be the real unkindness.

There are two objects for which plants are kept over.

Plants are housed for the sake of their verdure and bloom during the winter ; or, simply to protect them from the frosts. Our first criticism is, that these two separate objects are, to a great extent, improperly united. Tables and window-stands are crowded with plants which ought to be in the cellar or in a pit. Plants which have bloomed through the summer *will* rest during the winter. To remove them from the heat and dust of the parlor—to place them in a dry, light, warm cellar, will certainly conduce to their entire rest, and the parlor will lose no grace by the removal of ragged stems, falling leaves, and flowerless branches. When a large quantity of plants are to be protected, and cellar room is wanting, a pit may be prepared with little expense. Dig a place eight or ten feet square, in a dry exposure. The depth may be from five to six feet. Let the surface of this chamber be curbed about with a plank frame, the top of which should slope to the south at an inclination of about three inches to the foot. This may be covered with plank except in the middle, where two sash may be placed. The outside of the plank may be banked up with earth, and if light brush or haulm be placed upon the top, in severe weather, it will be all the better. The inside may be provided with shelves on every side for the pots, and thus hundreds of plants may be effectually protected. During severe freezing weather the sash should be covered with mats, old carpet, straw or anything of the

kind; and in *very* cold weather this should not be removed
during the daytime: for if the plants have been touched
with frost, the admission of light will destroy or maim them,
whereas, if kept in darkness, they will suffer little or no
injury. Several families may unite in the expense of forming a cold-pit and thus fill it with plants at a small expense
and very little inconvenience to each. *Very little* if any
water should be given to plants thus at rest.

Even where plants are wanted to bloom in the parlor late
in the winter, it is often better to let them spend the fore-
part of the winter in the cellar or pit.

Our second criticism respects the *character* of winter collections.

The most noticeable error is the strange crowd of plants
often huddled together, as if the excellence of a collection
consisted in the number of things brought together. Everything that the florist sees in other collections has been procured, as if it would be an unpardonable negligence not to
have what others have. Hence we sometimes see scores
of plants, very different in their habits, requiring widely
different conditions of growth, reduced to one regimen,
viz. a place near the window, so much water a day, and
one turning round. This summary procedure, of course,
soon results in a vegetable Falstaff's regiment; some plants
being long, sprawling, gangling, some dormant and dumpy;
some shedding their leaves and going to rest with unripe
wood, some mildewed, a few faintly struggling to show
here and there a bewildered blossom. In such a collection
the eye is pained by the entire want of sympathy arising
from jumbling together the most dissimilar kinds; from the
want of robust health, and from the entire disappearance
of that vivid freshness and sprightliness of growth, compact while it is rapid, which gives a charm to well managed plants.

All plants which are not growing, or for whose growth
your parlors are not suitable, should be put into the cellar

and should there be allowed to stand over in a state of rest. According to your accommodations, select a *few* vigorous, symmetrical, hearty, healthy plants for the window. *One plant* well tended, will afford you more pleasure than twenty, half-nurtured.

In our dwellings, one has to make his way between two extremes in the best manner that he can. Without a stove our thin-walled houses are cold as an ice-house, and a frosty night sends sad dismay among our favorites. Then, on the other hand, if we have a stove, the air is apt to be parched, and unwholesome, fit for salamanders, fat and torpid cats and dozing grandmothers. There is not much choice between an ice-house and an oven. *There can be no such thing as floral health without fresh air and enough of it.* This must be procured by frequent ventilation.

PROTECTING PLANTS IN WINTER.

VERY many shrubs, vines, roses, etc., usually regarded as tender, may yet be safely left standing in the garden if properly protected.

The neck of plants, i. e. that part at which the roots and stem come together, requires thorough protection; both because it is the most tender (as some say), and because it is at this point, that freezing and sudden thawing must occur. The black soil absorbing heat rapidly, the neck of a plant will be first and most affected by the morning sun; and this is the reason, we think, rather than any special tenderness of parts, why plants are killed at the crown of the root. Let the ground be well covered with leaves or with coarse manure, and let it come up three or four inches high on the stem. It is better to have the top strawy, rather than dark colored manure.

16

It is the sun, and not the frost, that, for the most part, kills the stems of half-hardy plants. Protection is often, therefore, only thorough shading. The Bengal tea, and noisette roses are left out at Philadelphia and at Cincinnati without detriment.

Drive a stake by the side of the plant, and drawing up the branches to it, cover them with straw, or bass-matting wrapped around them. Kegs, barrels, boxes, etc., may be turned over such as are not too high and will sufficiently protect them. Air-holes should be bored in barrels, etc., and the north side is the best for the purpose.

Grape vines which need protection should be loosened from the trellis or wall, pruned, laid down on the ground and earth thrown over them three or four inches deep. Isabella and Catawba grape vines will need no protection.

————•••————

TO PRESERVE DAHLIA ROOTS.

The least frost destroys these roots. In warm and damp cellars they rot. Very many persons have no cellars at all (a very frequent destitution at the West); others are so small and moist, as to be unfit (our own, for instance); and the extreme variations of temperature during the day and night make sitting-rooms and their closets very unsafe places for them. The labor of packing them in sand is not great to those who have it ready or men to procure it; but to ladies, and especially to many in towns and cities who are enthusiastic cultivators of flowers, but grievously vexed with poverty of pocket, this plan is inconvenient.

Why may not dahlias be kept in the soil? We think there is not the least doubt that they can be protected from *frost* and *heat.* Every one knows that in spading up in the spring the dahlia beds of the previous year, large sections of the tubers, which had broken off when the main roots were removed, are found in a fresh and sound condition.

Let a pit be dug say two feet deep, the roots carefully disposed in it, covered with soil, and the whole protected by coarse litter, straw, etc.   We do not advise any to adventure their whole stock in this manner; but we design to select the inferior sorts from our stock and treat them thus; and if successful, we shall, another year, try our whole stock.

———•••———

HEDGES.

1. WHERE a hedge is properly made and carefully trimmed, it is the most beautiful fence that can be made ; and, as an *object of beauty*, it may be well to form hedges in a wood country ; but as a mode of general fencing we deem it totally inappropriate to the condition of a country abounding in timber.   The labor of setting and tending it until it is established, is tenfold more than is required for a timber fence ; a hedge requires from five to eight years for its establishment ; and every year of this time it must be *well* tended ; when grown, it requires annual shearing ; which, on a long line of fence, is a labor to which few farmers will submit for the sake of *appearances*.   It is liable to get out of order by disease, or the death of particular parts ; and, if neglected a few years, it becomes ragged, a covert for vermin and mischievous animals.   In yards, gardens, and lawns, hedges should be grown for ornament, and to serve as screens, and backgrounds.

Upon the estates of the affluent where money is less valuable to the owner than decorations, hedges should be established.   Hedges may also be economical in a prairie country ; the labor and expense of making and keeping may be less than would be the cost of timber ; but on farms in a woodland district they are to be regarded as a *luxury;* and like all luxuries, they are expensive.

2. The white thorn will do very well for hedges if carefully tended. The usual materials for hedges, at the East, are the English white thorn (*cratægus oxycantha*), the buckthorn (*rhamnus catharticus*), Newcastle thorn (*cratægas crus-galli*), honey locust (*gleditschia triacanthos*), red cedar (*juniperus Virginiana*), the Washington or Virginia thorn (*cratægus cordata*).

The Osage orange (*maclura aurantiaca*) has been highly recommended; it is eminently beautiful, and if proved to be good for hedging, should be employed. Privet makes a sightly hedge, but is thornless. The Washington thorn is employed in this neighborhood by Aaron Aldredge; it is very beautiful; will require eight or ten years to give it maturity.

3. When the thorn is used, the berries should be gathered and mashed, in the fall, and the seed exposed, mixed with moist sand, to the frost of winter. In the spring they should be sown in nursery rows, and at a year old, they should be transplanted. A reserve of plants should be kept in the nursery to supply vacancies which may occur.

The ground should be thoroughly and deeply pulverized by plowing (spading would be much better) and the plants set about six inches apart. The ground should be kept entirely free from weeds; this may be done in a profitable manner by planting bush beans on each side, the tending of which will keep the hedge clean, the ground mellow, besides the profit of the crop. Dr. Shurtliff, of Boston, gives the following brief but excellent directions:

"Prepare your land in the best manner; use suitable plants of thrifty growth, the older the better; assort and accommodate to the different kinds of soil; preserve all the roots, but crop the tops, leaving only few buds; keep a few in your nursery; set them sloping to the north, and leave the ground a little concave about the roots; keep them clear of grass and weeds, and add a little earth to the roots at each hoeing; clear away the leaves at autumn; trim the side branches carefully, and leave the main stems to nature till they are six feet high, then crop off the tops to the height you mean to have your hedge. It will look like a wedge with the sharp end upwards, and will exhibit a most beautiful appearance."

WATERING TREES, ETC.

WE have observed many persons copiously watering young trees and garden plants.

1. In many cases much water is a positive injury. The roots draw up a larger supply of liquid than there is vigor in the tree to digest or appropriate. In such cases the tissue is enfeebled, the roots decay, and the tree perishes in the trying heats of July and August.

2. It often happens that wetting the tree itself is much better than watering the root. Take a watering-pot and drench the leaves, and limbs and trunk, several times in a day. In a small tree a large bunch of cotton or rags may be put in the crotch and saturated with water. It will gradually trickle down the stem, and also evaporate, keeping the leaves in a moist medium. This trouble is worth while in case of rare trees difficult to be obtained. A tree perspires as really as an animal or a man. Every leaf is furnished with *stomata* or pores, the number and size of which determine the amount of perspiration. Of course, as they vary in different plants, there is a corresponding difference in the amount which they perspire. Plants which grow in exposed situations, scorched by the sun, have a structure which admits but slight perspiration, while those which grow in the shade and in moist places perspire copiously.

It is upon this state of facts that watering the tree itself is beneficial. The exhalation from the leaf is diminished, and sap retained within the tree. Beside this, the leaf and young green bark absorb some moisture.

3. Where watering is resorted to it should not be upon the surface; especially is this injurious in clay soils. The moisture is immediately exhaled, and the sun hardens the wet earth into a crust, nearly as impervious to light, and air and moisture, as if it were sheet-iron. Let a slight trench be opened, and after the water has sunk away, replace the earth and pulverize it. In this way no baking will take place.

4. But the best method of watering by the root, is that which is technically denominated *mulching*. Cover the surface of the ground beneath the tree or shrub with three or four inches' thickness of coarse, strawy manure. If watered through this the earth will not bake; the moisture will not evaporate; the root will be shielded from the sun, and enriched by the infiltration of the juices of the manure.

LABELS FOR TREES.

IT is of *great* importance for every farmer to preserve the names of his fruit-trees; and no amateur cultivator should think himself worthy of a name whose garden and fruit ground is not registered and labelled.

It is best in every case to have a fruit-book, in which should be entered the name of each tree, its place, time of planting, from whom obtained, how old it was from the graft or bud, when set out, its size, condition, etc.

Such a book, kept in the house, is a sure and permanent record of the names of your fruit-trees. Beside this, each tree should have a *label* attached to it. For, in passing through an orchard or fruit garden, it is desirable to know

the names of trees without the inconvenience of carrying
your book under your arm.   The labels are for daily use;
the book keeps a permanent record, so that if a label be lost
the name of the tree does not go with it.   It is quite provoking to examine a friend's premises without being able to
learn the name of a single tree.   Beside, every cultivator
should know the names of his trees as well as of his cattle;
otherwise they will get local names, and the same fruit have
a new name in each orchard.

TRANSPLANTING EVERGREENS.

THE general impression that evergreens are very difficult
to transplant is not well founded if one will observe a few
directions.

The best time for transplanting is when the tips begin
to show fresh growth in spring.   This is exactly the
reverse of directions in English books, which denounce
spring, and enjoin fall transplanting—in the climate of England, doubtless with good reason; and it is a good illustra-
tion of the caution necessary before imitating, in our
climate, the most skillful foreign practices.

A friend informs us that he has always totally lost all
his fall transplantings; not saving ten in a hundred; and
other men say they have had similar experience, and *it is
a settled fact that fall transplanting of evergreens is bad
practice.*

The best method of removing is to lift the plant with as
many roots and fibres as possible.   More care should be
used in this respect than in the removal of fruit-trees;
indeed, there is little risk when good roots are obtained and
kept in a moist condition.   In planting, the most successful
operators that we have seen, mix about half and half com-

mon soil and old rotten wood from the forests, filling it in carefully about the roots and covering the surface with substances which will prevent too much evaporation of moisture, as litter, decayed wood, sods grass side down, etc., etc.

The old wood employed should be thoroughly decomposed; and that of the hackberry, maple, and beech are preferred. The decayed wood of the black walnut and oak do not seem congenial to plants.

When large trees are to be removed it is often done with success in the winter, by opening a trench about the tree and permitting the ball of earth to freeze pretty thoroughly. The tree is then undermined and upon a sledge easily removed to its destination. The hole for its reception should have been dug while the ground was unfrozen, and it will be necessary to wait until it thaws before it can again be filled in about the tree.

FLOWERS, LADIES, AND ANGELS.

If ladies wish to get into the very best company possible, we do not know of any pleasanter way than is detailed in this beautiful scrap from a German poet:

> A flower do but place near thy window glass,
> And through it no image of evil shall pass.
> Abroad must thou go? on thy white bosom wear
> A nosegay, and doubt not an angel is there;
> Forget not to water at break of the day
> The lilies, and thou shalt be fairer than they;
> Place a rose near thy bed nightly sentry to keep,
> And angels shall rock thee on roses to sleep.

And pray what will happen if a *gentleman* does all this? For one, we have a personal curiosity to know; for we do all these things and a good many more. If any other angels have hovered about us than angelic flowers, we make an especial request to them not, hereafter, to be so shy about it. Our natural eye would delight to behold in veritable substance all the flower-spirits which our ideality spies lurking in our garden-blossoms.

———•●•———

HORTICULTURAL CURIOSITIES.

MR. HOVEY, editor of the magazine which bears his name, had occasion during the year 1844 to visit Europe, for professional objects; "not the least was that of giving some account of the condition of gardening in that country, from whose works, whose practice, and experience, our own cultivators have derived so much knowledge."

We cull from the several numbers already published in his magazine, the most interesting facts.

RHODODENDRONS.—Speaking of the Liverpool botanical gardens, he says:

"The principal clumps were filled with rhododendrons of various kinds, which do remarkably well; the climate, from its humidity, seems to suit them, and most of the plants were clothed with branches from the base to the top. R. *altaclerense* we saw six feet high; how fine must be its numerous clusters of splendid rosy blossoms! From the time we entered this garden, where we first saw the rhododendrons in abundance, until we returned home, we were constantly impressed with the importance which this shrub is destined to hold in our gardens. Although a native of our woods and forests, it is scarcely known out of our native habitats; yet abroad we see it the first ornament of the garden. By hybridization, and the production of an immense number of seedlings, during the last fifteen years, it has been increased in splendor, until it now almost equals

16*

its tender, but gorgeous eastern sisters. How long shall our gardens be deficient in this great ornament?"

FUCHSIAS, OR LADIES' EARDROP.—Nothing will be more surprising to those who have cultivated this beautiful plant, and thought it well grown if a foot high, and brilliant if a dozen blossoms showed at once, than the magnificent size and flowering of *Fuchsias* as seen in England.

At the Sheffield Botanical Gardens Mr. Hovey saw the Fuchsias globosa major, upwards of *twenty feet* high, the stem, at the base, being two inches through! Its drooping branches were clothed with thousands of flowers; another variety, "called *Youngii grandiflora* was also twenty feet high, and equally strong, with innumerable flowers: this plant was only seven years old. It is almost impossible for those who have never seen specimens more than four or five feet high, to imagine the great beauty of such gigantic plants; notwithstanding their size they were well grown, being of symmetrical shape, and with vigorous and healthy foliage; they were planted in very large tubs, about two feet deep and two feet in diameter.

"The splendid *F. fulgens* and *corymbiflora* we also saw here upward of ten feet high, and full of their showy flowers."

The Regent's Park Garden occasions the following remarks:

"*Fuchsia globosa* was, perhaps, as beautiful as anything which we saw for this subject. There is an opinion prevalent that fuchsias in our climate do not do well in the open border; but we suspect such an idea has been prematurely formed without experience, for we recollect seeing in the garden of Mr. Johnson, of Lynn, three years ago, plants, which were then in profuse bloom, and had been so all summer, turned out of the pots into the soil; the probability is that the plants have not been abundant enough to give a fair trial. As they are easily propagated, and may be sold almost as cheap as verbenas, we hope to hear of experiments being tried to test their capability of enduring our warm sun."

At Chiswick Mr. Hovey saw the original tree of Williams' Bon Chrétien pear (the Bartlett of Boston gardens). It was hale and healthy.

Tulips.—Mr. H. visited Mr. Groom, at Clapham; "preparations were making for planting out the great collection of tulips in October. For this flower Mr. Groom is famous; he has raised several very splendid seedlings, some of which are priced as high as *five hundred dollars*, and a great number at *one hundred* dollars each (£21 sterling). It would seem to those who know little of the tulip that this was something of a tulip mania; but the tulip is a most gorgeous flower, and when once a love for it takes possession of the amateur, and he obtains a knowledge of its properties, there is scarce anything he would not sacrifice to obtain the choicest·kinds. In England, there are many collections valued at thousands of pounds. In this country the tulip is but little valued, and a bed of the most common kind attracts nearly as many admirers as one of the choicest and high-priced flowers."

Dwarf Pear-trees.—"The garden is laid out with numerous walks, and the borders of them were filled with bearing trees. They were from six to ten feet high, trained in pyramidal form, and many of them full of fruit. This mode of growing trees appears to be universally adopted around Paris; we scarcely saw a standard tree. The advantages of the pyramidal or quenouille form are, that, in gardens of moderate extent only, a collection of two or three hundred kinds may be cultivated; they occupy but little room, being placed about six feet apart, and being pruned in, they do not throw sufficient shade to injure anything growing near them. They afford greater facilities for examining the fruit while growing, and for picking it when ripe; the trees are not so much shaken by high winds, and the large kind of pears do not so easily blow off: the facilities for making observations upon the wood and leaves, are also greater; and, as regards appearance alone, they are, when well managed, far more beautiful than standards. To those who wish to plant out large quantities for orchard cultivation, they would not, of course, be recommended; but for the garden, the pyramidal form should be adopted."

ALPINE STRAWBERRY.—This variety is especially valuable from its propensity to bear all the summer. At the gardens of the Luxembourg, Paris, Mr. Hovey says:

"The Alpine strawberry is cultivated very extensively for the supply of the royal tables throughout the whole summer and autumn, and one-quarter was devoted to this fruit; the plants were set out in long rows, with alternate plantations of dahlias, which were now in most profuse bloom; a great many of them were the *fancy* sorts, which are greatly admired and extensively cultivated in and around Paris. One of the finest we saw was the Beauty of England, purple tipped with white; and every flower distinctly marked. The strawberries are set out in August or September, and the following season produce abundantly; or they may be raised from seed in the spring, and planted out to bear a crop in the autumn. A moist soil and half shady aspect is most favorable, and, in our climate, to expect success, such a locality should be selected if possible; an abundance of fruit may then be expected. The best berries were as large as the finest Woods we generally see in our market. We recommend all who love this delicious fruit to try the experiment of their cultivation. Such profusion as we saw them exposed for sale in the cafés of Paris, shows that there can be no great difficulty in the way of success."

THE CORN CROP.

THE valleys of the West are regarded as the corn-fields of the world, and the people seem to regard the crop of corn as the foundation crop. Lately wheat is becoming a rival, particularly in the northern part of Ohio, Indiana, Illinois, Iowa, and Wisconsin. Our real object, is, not to theorize,—to teach " book farming"—but to lay before practical men practical results, to inform them of *what has been done.* We give on page 382 the method of cultivating the potato as employed by eminent and successful cultivators. We here present the modes of cultivating corn which have produced the largest crops.

W. C. YOUNG'S METHOD.—Mr. Young is a Kentucky farmer, and raised 195 bushels of shelled corn to the acre. When this was first published it quite staggered the faith of eastern farmers. This roused the zeal of Kentucky, and the *Dollar Farmer* sets forth the manner, and adds a series of explanations, all of which we give. We must say, that such a depth, for seed on stiff soils—on any soil except the lightest and mellowest, and on these, in a cool or rainy spring, would not be proper. Neither could planting be done in March in the latitudes of Indiana unless in the southern part, and then only in early seasons. That Mr. Young did produce 195 bushels to the acre, we feel just as certain as that we now hold a pen in our hand. It was measured by as respectable gentlemen as any in Jessamine County—gentlemen appointed for the purpose by the Jessamine Agricultural Society. And let it be remembered that this was no first experiment on a single acre. The corn was planted and cultivated according to the method long adopted by Mr. Young, and his whole crop was pronounced equal to the five acres measured. This extraordinary crop was produced in 1840, a year very favorable to corn; but we are told by Mr. Young that in the dryest years he does not get less than 100 bushels to the acre.

Here then is not "book farming," but a method of cultivation *practised* for years by a plain, practical, but intelligent farmer. Here then is actual experience for a course of years, the very thing the farmer says he must have before he can be convinced! But, reader, are you convinced? No. You can not get round the experience, provided it *was* experience, and you will take a short way of evading the matter by simply saying that you don't believe a word of the whole story.

Strange as it may seem, these worthy farmers that go so strong for *facts* and *experience*, and who yet deny all facts and all experience that do not tally with their own notions—these very farmers are fond of arguing, and like mightily to have the reason or *rationale* of things explained; and many a one of them will yield to the *theory* who will not yield to a *fact*. Well, then, let us look into the theory of Mr. Y.'s practice. Hear him:

"My universal rule is, to plow my corn land the fall preceding the spring when I plant; and as early in the spring as possible, I cross-plow as deep as circumstances will permit; and as soon as this is done, I commence checking off— the first way with my large plows, and the second with my small ones; the checks three feet by three, admitting of working the land both ways. And then I plant my corn from the 20th to the 25th of March—a rule to which I adhere with scrupulous exactness; planting from eight to twelve grains in each hill, covering the same from *four to six inches deep*, greatly preferring the latter depth. So soon as my corn is up of sufficient height, I start the large harrow directly over the rows, allowing a horse to walk each side; harrowing the way the corn was planted; and on land prepared as above and harrowed as directed, the hoeing part will be so completely performed by this process, that it will satisfy the most skeptical. Then, allowing the corn thus harrowed, to remain a few days, I start my small plow with the bar next the corn; and so nicely will this be done, that when a row is thus plowed, so completely will the intermediate spaces, hills, etc., be lapped in by the loose earth, occasioned by this system of close plowing, as to render any other work useless for a time. I thin to four stalks upon a hill, never having to transplant, the second plowing being performed with the moldboard toward the rows of corn; and so rapid has been the growth of the corn between the first and second plowings, that this is performed with ease; and when in this stage, I consider my crop safe—my general rule being, never to plow my corn more than four times, and harrow once. My practice is, to put a field in corn two successive years, then grass it, and let it lie eight years—a rule from which I never deviate. Now, I do not pretend that the labor bestowed upon a sod-field to put it in a state of thorough cultivation, does not meet with a fair equivalent from one crop; but I presume no farmer will doubt when I say the second year's crop from sod land is better than the first, with not more than one half the labor. The best system of farming is to produce the greatest amount of profit from the smallest amount of labor."

Now what are the essentials of this method?

First—Fertility of soil, kept up by his system of manuring and grass, of which we shall not speak.

Second—Early planting. In consequence of this, the corn matures before the dry season commences, and every farmer knows that plenty of rain will make a good crop of corn in almost any soil. They all know that the essential thing for corn is rain, and there is generally plenty of rain till about the 1st of July. Mr. Young might plant his corn considerably later and have it come up as early, and grow off more rapidly, by soaking it in a solution of saltpetre. Thus would the effect of frost and chilly mornings be in a degree avoided, while we feel confident, from our own experience, all injury from the cut-worm would be avoided.

Third—Close planting. Every farmer must know that to produce the heaviest possible crop, a certain number of stalks must be upon the ground. It is often observed that the great sin of American agriculture is too thin sowing. Grass is nearly always sowed too thin, and the same is true of small grain.   In England they sow four and five and sometimes six bushels of oats to the acre; in this country generally not more than a bushel or a bushel and a half. Hence in England they yield three or four times as heavy as in this country; while in this country we never hear of an extraordinary crop where less than three or four bushels to the acre were sown.   Now, we venture to affirm that no very large corn crop was ever grown unless it was planted more than usually thick.   In the. crop of George W. Williams, of Bourbon county, Kentucky, the corn was planted in rows two feet apart, with a stalk every foot in the rows. This crop produced 167 bushels to the acre.   But there is another important advantage of close planting.   The corn very soon becomes so dense that the ground is shaded, and the growth of the grass is prevented, and the moisture retained in the soil.   By this method of cultivation, no grass is ever allowed to absorb the moisture from the earth, or to take up the nutritious gases which ought to be appropriated exclusively to the corn.

Fourth—Deep planting.   This probably operates favorably by giving the roots a bedding where the soil is always moist.   Another advantage may be that the roots are thus not so liable to be broken by the plow in cultivation.   But it must be here noted, that by Mr. Young's method, the corn is "laid by" before the roots are so extended as to be liable to much injury from the plow.

Fifth and last—It will be observed that, by Mr. Young's method, the soil is kept very friable and loose, and that to a considerable depth.   This may be considered the all-essential point in husbandry.   One of the chief advantages of all manures is, so to divide the soil that the atmosphere, from which plants derive their principal nutriment, may freely penetrate to the roots of the plants.   In such a loose soil, too, it is well known that much less rain is requisite than in a stiff, cold, close soil. For this reason, gravel, sand, or sawdust is often the best manure that can be put upon a stiff soil. In the fall of the year, Mr. Young turns down very deep a thick-rooted sod of eight years' standing. The vegetable matter in the sod will obviously keep the soil very loose for a year or two by mechanical division, as well as by the slow fermentation of this matter in the soil. But this is not all. The soil is deeply broken up before planting; it is harrowed thoroughly as soon as the corn comes up, and then there is a rapid succession of plowing, until the ground is shaded by the corn, and plowing is no longer possible or necessary. No doubt the plow is preferable to the hand-hoe or cultivator in the case of Mr. Young; for it makes the soil loose to a greater depth, and we have already explained that, according to his method, the roots of the corn are not exposed to injury from the plow..

We append to this account of Mr. Young's method, that of several other cultivators, and are indebted for them to the *Western Farmer and Guardian.* In Mr. Miller's account the reader will observe the *depth of planting* in a stiff clay.

MR. SUTTON'S METHOD.—Mr. James M. Sutton, of St. George, Delaware, who raised upon seventy-nine acres 6,284 bushels of corn, and who gives an accurate and detailed account of the condition and cultivation of each field, makes this remark in relation to the use of the plow:

"In order to test the advantage of the cultivator over the plow, for tilling corn, he had five rows in this field that he lapped the furrow to, with a plow, previous to going over it the last time with the cultivator. He soon discovered that the growth of these five rows fell short, in height, of those adjacent, and yielded one-fifth less corn.

"There is no doubt but the true mode of tilling corn, especially where sod-ground is used, is to plow deep, and use nothing but the fallow and flake-harrow for its cultivation. By not disturbing the sod plowed down, it remains

there as a reservoir of moisture, and an exhilarating principle throughout the season, to the growth of the corn."

Upon Mr. Sutton's report of his crop, Judge Buel adds
the following :

" The management which led to the extraordinary product of corn, should be deeply impressed upon the mind of
every corn-grower. 1, The ground was WELL dunged, with
LONG manure; 2, it was planted on a grass lay, one deep
plowing; 3, it was well pulverized with the harrow; 4,
the plow was not used in the after-culture, nor the corn
hilled, but the cultivator only, used; 5, the sod was not
disturbed, nor the manure turned to the surface; and 6,
the corn was cut at the ground when it was fit to top.
These are the points which we have repeatedly urged in
treating of the culture of this crop; and their correctness
is put beyond question by this notable result. The value of
lime and marl are well illustrated in the second experiment."

Mr. Charles H. Tomlinson, of Schenectady, N. Y., in giving an account of his experience says :

" The two last years' corn has been raised in the following manner, on the Mohawk Flats near this city. If in
grass, the land is plowed and well harrowed, lengthwise of
the furrow, without disturbing the sward.   The ground is
then prepared for planting, by being marked out two and a
half feet one way and three feet the other.   The last season,
the field was rolled after being planted, with evident benefit,
as it made it level.   When the corn is three inches high,
the cultivator is passed through both ways; and twice
afterward it is used in the same manner; no hills are made,
but the ground is kept level.   Neither hand-hoe nor plow
are used, after the corn is planted.   Fields manured with
coarse manure have been tilled in the same manner.   Corn
tilled in this way is as clean of weeds as when tilled in the
usual way : it is no more liable to be blown down, and the
produce equally good.   It saves a great deal of hard labor,
which is an expensive item in the usual culture of corn.

Last October, ten rods were measured out in two different places, in a corn-field, on grass land—the one yielding ten, the other nine, bushels of ears. In one corn-field, after the last dressing in July, timothy and clover-seed were sown, and in the fall the grass appeared to have taken as well as it has done in adjoining fields where it had been sown with oats."

Upon which Judge Buel again remarks: "All, or nearly all, the accounts we have published of great products of Indian corn, agree in two particulars, viz. in not using the plow in the culture, and in not earthing, or but very slightly, the hills. These results go to demonstrate, that the entire roots are essential to the vigor of the crops, and to enable them to perform their functions as nature designed, must be near the surface. If the roots are severed with the plow, in dressing the crop, the plants are deprived of a portion of their nourishment; and if they are buried deep by hilling, the plant is partially exhausted in throwing out a new set near the surface, where alone they can perform all their offices. There is another material advantage in this mode of cultivating the corn crop—it saves a vast deal of manual labor."

The preceding considerations justify us in recommending, that in the management of the Indian corn crop, the following rules be observed, or at least partially, so far as to test their correctness.

1. That the corn harrow and cultivator be substituted for the plow in the culture of the crop.

2. That the plants be not hilled, or but slightly so—this not to prevent the soil being often stirred and kept clean, and,

3. That in harvesting, the crop be cut at the ground as soon as the grain is glazed.

Again, in reference to the system of level cultivation of corn, Judge Buel remarks:

"The experience of the last two years has been sufficient to admonish us, that without due precaution, our crops of

Indian corn will not pay for the labor bestowed on the culture ; and yet, that where due attention has been paid to
soil, manure, seed and harvesting, the return has been
bountiful, notwithstanding bad seasons.   Having been uniformly successful in the culture of this crop, we feel
justified in repeating some leading directions for its management."

"AFTER-CULTURE.—In this the plow should not be used
if the corn harrow and cultivator can be had, and if used,
should not be suffered to penetrate the soil more than two
or three inches.   The plow tears the roots, turns up and
wastes the manure, and increases the injuries of drought.
The main object is to extirpate weeds, and to keep the
surface mellow and open, that the heat, air and moisture
may exert better their kind influences upon the vegetable
matter in the soil, in converting it into nutriment for the
crop.   At the first dressing with the hand-hoe, the plants
are reduced to four, or three, in a hill, the surface is broken
among the plants, the weeds carefully extirpated, and a little fresh mold gathered to the hill.   At the second dressing,
a like process is observed, taking care that the earthing
shall not exceed one inch and a half, that the hill be broad
and flat, and that the earth for this purpose be not taken
from one place, but gathered from the surface between the
rows, where it has been loosened by the cultivator."

MR. MILLER'S METHOD.

"GEORGETOWN × ROADS, *Kent Co., Md.*

"I have just finished measuring the corn that grew this
year on a lot of mine of five and a half acres, and have
measured 105½ barrels and one bushel of ears, making 103
bushels of corn per acre.   The following is the manner in
which I prepared the ground, etc.   The soil is a stiff clay:
and one and a half acres of said lot was in clover last year,

the balance in wheat. I put 265 two-horse cart loads of
barn-yard manure on it : the manure was coarse, made out of
straw, corn-tops and husks, hauled into the yard in January
and February, and hauled out in March and April, consequently was very little rotted. I spread it regularly and
plowed it down with a large concave plow, seven inches deep.
I then harrowed it twice the same way it was plowed. I then
had the rows marked out with a small plow, three 'feet ten
inches wide, and one and a half inches deep. I planted my
corn from eighteen to twenty-two inches apart, and covered
it with hoes : just drawing the furrows over the corn,
which covered it *one and a half inches below the surface.* When the corn was four inches high, I harrowed it,
and thinned it to two stalks in the hill : in about two weeks
after harrowing, I cultivated it : about the 15th of June I
cultivated it again, which was all the tillage I gave it. We
farmers of the eastern shore count our corn by the
thousand : I had 38,640 hills on my lot, and I think my corn
would have been better had I planted earlier : I did not
plant until the last of April. I think the planting of corn
shallow and working it with the cultivator is much the best
way, especially on clover lay.

MR. HOPKINS' METHOD.—"*Soil and Culture.*—The soil
is a warm sandy loam. It was plowed deep in the autumn.
About the first of May, I carried on, and spread all over
the ground, about thirty loads of stable and barn-yard
unfermented manure, then rolled and harrowed the ground
well, being careful not to disturb the sod, which was timothy, and mown the summer preceding ; and on the 9th and
10th of May planted the same, two and a half feet between
the rows, and fifteen inches between the hills. It was
dressed with ashes when it made its appearance above
ground. On the 10th June commenced weeding and thin-
ning, leaving from two to four of the best spears in each
hill, the whole averaging about three spears in a hill. After
this I ashed it again, using in all about ten bushels of good

unleached house ashes. On the 10th of July commenced hoeing, and at the same time took off all the suckers—put no more about the hills than we took from them, but carefully cleaned out all the weeds from the hills. The seed was prepared by simply wetting it with warm water, and rolling it in plaster.

"HARVESTING.—The corn was cut up on the 18th September at the ground, and shocked in small shocks; and on the 9th of October it was housed and husked, and subsequently threshed and measured.

"PRODUCT.—Ninety-nine bushels of first-rate corn, without even a nubbin of soft or poor grain, owing to the fact, probably, that there were no suckers on which to grow them."

POTATO CROP.

THE potato crop has never been as much attended to in this region as in New York, and New England. We believe, however, that its value is becoming apparent, and that potatoes will be produced to a much greater extent than hitherto. Reserving some remarks of our own to a future number, we insert the methods of cultivation, employed by eminent cultivators.

SPURRIER'S METHOD OF CULTIVATION.—"Be careful," says he, "to procure some good sets; that is, to pick a quantity of the best kind of potatoes perfectly sound and of a tolerably large size; these are to be prepared for planting by cutting each root into two, three or more pieces, minding particularly that each piece be furnished with at least one or two eyes, which is sufficient. Being thus prepared, they are to be planted in rows not less than eighteen inches distant: if they are to be plowed between, they must not be less than three feet, and if four feet apart the more eligible.

"The best method I have found by experience is to make a trench either with the spade or plow, about five inches deep, and put long dung or straw at the bottom, laying the sets on it at their proper distances, which is from 9 to 12 inches apart, covering them with mold. They must be kept clean from weeds."

MR. KNIGHT'S PLAN.—"He recommends the planting of whole potatoes, and those only which are of fine medium size—none to be of less weight than four ounces. The early sorts, and, indeed, all which seldom attain a greater height than two feet, are to be planted about four or five inches apart in the rows, centre from centre, the crown ends upward, the rows to be from 2 feet 6 inches to 3 feet asunder. The late potatoes, which produce a haulm above 3 feet in height, are to be planted 5 or 6 inches apart, centre from centre, in rows 4 or 5 feet asunder. The potatoes to point north and south and to be well manured."

MACKENZIE'S PLAN.—"Work the ground until it is completely reduced and free from root weeds. Three plowings, with frequent harrowings and rollings, are necessary in both cases, before the land is in a suitable condition. When this is accomplished, form the drills; place the manure in the drills, plant above it, reverse the drills for covering it and the seed, then harrow the drills in length.

"It is not advantageous to cut the seed into small slips; for the strength of the stem at the outset depends in direct proportion to the vigor and power of the seed-plant. The seed-plant, therefore, ought to be large, rarely smaller than the fourth part of the potato; and if the seed is of small size, one half of the potato may be profitably used. At all events, rather err in giving over large seed than in making it too small; because, by the first error, no great loss can ever be sustained; whereas, by the other, a feeble and late crop may be the consequence. When the seed is properly

cut, it requires from ten to twelve hundred weight of' potatoes, from 12½ to 15 bushels, where the rows are at 27 inches
distance; but this generally depends greatly upon the size
of the potatoes used; if they are large a greater weight
may be required; but the extra quality will be abundantly
repaid by the superiority of the crop, which large seed
usually produces.   Plant early in May."

BARNUM'S PLAN.—"Plow deep and pulverize well by
thoroughly harrowing; manure with compost, decomposed
vegetables or barnyard manure; the latter preferable.
When coarse or raw manure is used it must be spread and
plowed in immediately.   Stiff clay soil should always be
plowed the fall previous.   Lay your land in drills 27 inches
apart, with a small plow, calculated for turning a deep, narrow furrow running north and south; lay on the bottom of
the drills 2 inches of well-rotted barnyard manure, or its
equivalent, then drop your potatoes, if of the common size,
or what is more important, if they retain the usual quantity of eyes—if more, they should be cut to prevent too
many stalks shooting up together: put a single potato in
the drills or trenches 10 inches apart, the first should remain
uncovered until the second one is deposited, to place them
diagonally in the drills, which will afford more space
between the potatoes one way, than if laid at right angles
in the rows.   The covering may be performed with a hoe,
first hauling in the furrow raised on each side the drill,
then carefully take from the centre of the space the soil to
finish the covering to the depth of 3½ or 4 inches; by taking
the earth from the centre of the space on either side to the
width of 3 inches, it will leave a drain of 6 inches in the
centre of the space and a hill of 14 inches in width gently
descending from the drill to the drain; the width and depth
of the drill will be sufficient to protect the plant against any
injurious effects of a scorching sun or drenching rain.   The
drains in the centre will at all times be found sufficient to
pass off the surplus water.

"When the plant makes its appearance above the surface, the following mixture may be used: for each acre take 1 bushel of plaster and 2 bushels of good ashes, and sow it broadcast as even as possible; a moist day is preferable for this operation—for want of it, a still evening will do.

"The operation of hilling should be performed *once* and *once only* during the season; if repeated after the potatoe is formed it will cause young shoots to spring up, which retards the growth of the potatoe and diminishes its size. If weeds spring up at any time they should be kept down by the hand or hoe, which can be done without disturbing the growth of the stalk.

"My manner of *hoeing* or *hilling* is not to haul in the earth from the space between the hills or rows, but to bring on fresh earth sufficient to raise the hill around the plant 1½ or 2 inches; in a wet season the lesser quantity will be sufficient, in a dry one the larger will not be found too much. The substance for this purpose may consist of the scrapings of ditches or filthy streets, or the earth from a barnyard that requires levelling: where convenient, it may be taken from swamps, marshes, the beds and banks of rivers or small sluggish streams at low water. If planted on a clay soil, fresh loam taken at any depth from the surface, even if it partakes largely of fine sand, will be found an excellent top-dressing. If planted on a loamy soil, the earth taken from clay pits, clay or slaty soil will answer a valuable purpose; in fact, there are but few farms in the country but what may be furnished with some suitable substance for top-dressing, if sought for. The hoeing and hilling may be performed with facility by the aid of a horse and cart, the horse travelling in the centre of a space between the drills, the cart-wheels occupying the two adjoining ones, thereby avoiding any disturbance or injury to the growing plants."

Mr. Barnum's method has attracted great attention, from the fact that he actually raised from 1,000 to 1,500 bushels

17

of potatoes to the acre! When this was first published it was received with great incredulity; calls were made for the method of cultivation, which drew forth an elaborate article from Mr. B., of which the above is but a morsel. It afterward was stated, and the most authentic and unquestionable evidence adduced in proof, that Mr. Barnum raised, upon experiment, *at the rate* of more than 3,000 bushels to the acre. Now, although the labor and the great amount of seed required would prevent the cultivation of many acres of land thus, yet it is worth a trial in a small way; and if one acre can be made to produce 1,000 bushels, it will be as much as is usually dug from *five* acres; and it is questionable whether the labor and seed for five acres are not more than that required by Mr. B.'s method for one.

MR. A. ROBINSON'S PLAN.—He says: "If I plant low ground, I plow my ground in beds in a different direction for the water to drain off, then harrow lengthwise of the furrows and small lands; having a number of them, side and side, I take a light, sharp horse-harrow, and harrow crosswise of the beds, which pulverizes the ground and fits it well for planting, leaving a small space between the rows, which answers for two purposes, one for a guide for the rows for dropping: this is done by dropping in the middle of the tracks of the harrow, which is easily and correctly performed, by any small boy. It also serves completely to fill up all cracks or holes, the seed lying fair and easy. I then drop my manure directly over the seed potatoes, and when covered up, the seed is safe from inundation, by being some inches above the surrounding surface: the seed lies warm under this manure, the rains drain into the middle furrows; I plant three feet distance; it takes the most of the surface that is pulverized to cover the potatoes, and by the time they are twice well hoed, my hills are as I want them to be. They naturally rise high above the surface in the form of a sugar-loaf: this hill is to turn off heavy rains, and it naturally keeps the potatoes from being too moist, and they are often injured thereby. I have found that three feet each way is the most proper distance to insure a good crop; I plant three common sized potatoes in the hill; it is no use to cut them: if cut small, the vines come up small and weak, grow fast and fall down."

The following method we take from an able writer in the *Louisville Journal,* signing himself "Grazier :"

"The ground selected for potatoes should be dry, where no surface-water will rest. It should be rich; if not naturally so, it must be made so by a sufficient quantity of good manure. It should be plowed twice, and at least twelve inches deep. After the first plowing, it should be harrowed and cross harrowed; and after the second plowing, harrowed again, and if not very friable and free from clods it should then be rolled. The mold cannot be too fine, as on the depth of the plowing, and fineness of the earth, depend the *retention of that moisture* so indispensable to the health and maturing of all bulbous roots in particular. The ground thus prepared, should then be opened off in *drills,* three feet from the centre of one to the centre of the other, and, if practicable, running north and south. When opened, if manure is to be applied, it must then be hauled in carts; the horse going down between the drills, the bed of the cart will cover two drills, where the manure can be pulled out at intervals, in quantity sufficient, not only for the two drills described, but for one on each side in addition; all of which one hand, following with a fork, can easily distribute and spread in the four drills.

"This done, the ground is ready for the seed. I shall first describe the whole of the cultivation and harvesting necessary, and then speak of the seed and its preparation separately. The seed should be dropped in the manure, twelve inches apart, and as quickly as a drill is planted, the plow should follow and cover it in. The *double mold-board* plow, which is the proper implement for the business, will cover two drills by going once up and once down the field; if the single mold-board plow is used, it will of course cover but one drill by the same operation. When your ground is thus gone over, your land will all be in high drills, and can rest so for about one week, when you must take a two-horse harrow, and harrow your drills *across*, leaving your field as level as before your drills were opened. There is no danger, as some would suppose, of disturbing your seed.

"In a few days, when you can see your plants distinctly above ground, from one end of your drills to the other, you must take your one-horse plow, and go up and down each drill, running the *land side* of your plow as close to the plant on each side as you safely can, throwing the earth *away* from it, which operation will leave your field in raised drills between your plants. In a few days after this you take your *double mold-board* plow, and go down the centre of the blank drills, covering all your plants nearly out of sight, observing as you go along that the weight of earth is thrown *against*, and not *on*, the plants. Then, in some days after, when your plants are well over the top of your drills, take your scuffle, an implement not unlike your cultivator in this country, and for which the cultivator can be substituted, and go over your whole field between the drills, giving the earth a good stirring, and not be afraid of encroaching a little at each side on the drill. At this stage, a boy should follow the scuffle, and pull up any weeds that appear on the top or sides of the drills. In a few days after this, when your plants are strong and well up, you go down the centre between the drills, with your *double mold-board* plow, the wings well apart, and throw the earth well up to the plants. This must sometimes finish the cultivation, if the vines have spread and are closed too much, but *generally* the vines will allow it, and the crop be much benefited by one more scuffling; but this time take *particular care not to disturb the drill at the bottom*, as the bulbs are now forming and spreading; then gently run your *double mold-board plow* through the whole field again, *narrowing the wings of it*, which will have the effect of adding the earth, and compressing it to the *bottom* of the drill, where the bulbs are forming, rather than throwing it up to the stalk at top, where there is sufficient already. This finishes the cultivation.

" To prepare the seed you must select well-shaped, even potatoes, not too small nor too large. Cut them, leaving one good eye at least to every set; prepare them from two to three weeks *at least*, before you plant; and each day, as you cut, roll your sets in pulverized lime, and spread them on the barn floor to dry: when dry, heap them in a corner till taken out to plant. If this plan is pursued, and the ground selected and prepared as directed, you may rest satisfied that so sure as the laws of nature are invariable, and that like effects follow like causes, as sure will a *good* and *sound* crop of potatoes be produced in this climate with no variation in the result, except what may be occasioned by the vicissitudes of the season.

"Ten tons of potatoes, two thousand two hundred and forty pounds to the ton, is considered a *fair* crop in Ireland. Twelve tons an *extra* one—equal to three hundred and seventy bushels the first, and four hundred and forty-four bushels the second, allowing sixty pounds to the bushel, which I have found to be about the average weight of a bushel here. I have grown four crops of potatoes in this country, in two different situations and latitudes (six acres the smallest quantity cultivated any season). Each crop was treated in every particular as here described, and in three instances out of the four, I got a little over four hundred measured bushels to the acre. The fourth crop was only about three hundred and fifty bushels to the acre, caused by the peculiarity of the season, which produced an almost entire failure with my neighbors, under their management."

POTTING GARDEN PLANTS FOR WINTER USE.

ROSES, geraniums, chrysanthemums, Cape jasmins, etc., which have been put into the garden borders, should be prepared for removal to the parlor for winter, before frost, else the plants will not be established in the pots when removed to the parlor, and will thrive but poorly.

Select the pot which is to receive each plant, draw a circle about the plant of the size of the pot, then thrust a sharp spade down so as to cut all the roots at the line of the circle described. Let the plant remain, watering it *thoroughly ;* and if it droops, let it be sheltered from the sun. In a few days new roots will begin to form within the ball of earth described by the circle, and in three or four weeks that ball may be carefully lifted, placed in the pot for which it was measured, and it will go on growing as if nothing had happened to it. If one waits till frost, then digs up the plant without a previous preparation of its roots, it will oftentimes not recover from the violence during the winter. But by the method suggested above, roses, etc., will go on growing and blooming through the winter.

———•••———

THERE are many who suppose it necessary to leave the second growth of grass undisturbed, to rot on the ground, in order to preserve the fertility of old meadows in grass where top dressing with manure is not resorted to. But such management is oftentimes extremely hurtful, and the injury is proportioned to the amount left untrodden and unfed. If the amount left standing, or laying loose upon the surface, be considerable, it makes a harbor for mice, which will, under cover of the old grass, intersect the surface of the land with paths innumerable, from which they cut all the grass that comes in their way.

MARY HOWITT'S USE OF FLOWERS.

HERE is another of those beautiful gems which can never be brought to the light too often.   And when more appropriately than in the middle of our spring-time, while bursting buds and fragrant blossoms are delighting every sense ?

> God might have made the earth bring forth
>   Enough for great and small,
> The oak-tree and the cedar-tree,
>   Without a flower at all.
>
> We might have had enough, enough
>   For every want of ours,
> For luxury, medicine, and toil,
>   And yet have had no flowers.
>
> The ore within the mountain mine
>   Requireth none to grow,
> Nor does it need the lotus flower
>   To make the river flow.
>
> The clouds might give abundant rain,
>   The nightly dews might fall,
> And the herb that keepeth life in man,
>   Might yet have drunk them all.
>
> Then wherefore, wherefore were they made,
>   And dyed with rainbow light,
> All fashioned with supremest grace,
>   Upspringing day and night?
>
> Springing in valleys green and low,
>   And on the mountains high,
> And in the silent wilderness,
>   Where no man passeth by ?
>
> Our outward life requires them not,
>   Then wherefore had they birth ?
> To minister delight to man—
>   To beautify the earth.

To comfort man, to whisper hope
Whene'er his faith is dim,
For whoso.careth for the flowers,
Will much more care for Him.

————•••————

WHAT ARE FLOWERS GOOD FOR?

"I HAVE said and written a great deal to my countrymen about the cultivation of flowers, ornamental gardening, and rural embellishments; and I would read them a homily on the subject every day of every remaining . year of my life, if I thought it would induce them to make this a matter of particular attention and care. When a man asks me, what is the use of shrubs and flowers, my first impulse is always, *to look under his hat and see the length of his ears.* I am heartily sick of measuring everything by a standard of mere utility and profit; and as heartily do I pity the man, who can see no good in life but in the pecuniary gain, or in the mere animal indulgences of eating and drinking."— *Colman's Agricultural Tour.*

We protest against the sauciness of the italicized line. Mr. Colman never feels any such impulse; and if he does, he ought to suspect his own ears. Nothing is more preposterous than interflagellations among men on the matter of likes and dislikes. Every man selects *his* ruling passion, and scoffs at such as do not grow enthusiastic with him. A market gardener rails at a florist for fol-de-rol trifles; and the florist looks at the length of the fellow's ears who has nothing but turnips, onions, and cabages; while a big Miami farmer, who puts in his five-hundred-acre corn-patch, by way of summer amusement, regards both as small affairs. We find no fault with those who possess a super-ardent enthusiasm for flowers; but when they throw it in other people's faces, and call them brutes and asses, for not liking pretty flowers, we think the thing has been carried quite far enough. We love good manners *along* with pretty flowers.

THE BLIGHT IN THE PEAR-TREE.*

ITS CAUSE AND A REMEDY FOR IT.

THE year 1844 will long be remembered for the extensive ravages of that disease hitherto denominated *fire-blight*. Beginning at the Atlantic coast, we have heard of it in Pennsylvania, Maryland, Virginia, Ohio, Kentucky, Indiana, and as far as Tennessee; and it is probable that it has been felt in every fruit-growing State in the Union where the season of 1843 was the same as that west of the Alleghany range, namely, cold in spring, dry throughout the summer, and a wet and warm fall, with early and sudden winter.

In Indiana and Ohio the *blight* has prevailed to such an extent as to spread dismay among cultivators; destroying entire collections—taking half the trees in large orchards—affecting both young and old trees, whether grafted or seedings in soils of every kind. Many have seen the labor and fond hope of years cut off, in one season, by an invisible destroyer, against which none could guard; because, in the conflicting opinions, none were certain whether the disease was atmospheric, insect or chemical.

I shall now proceed to describe that blight known in the western States (without pretending to identify it with the blight known in New York and New England), to examine the theories proposed for its causation, and to present what now seems to me the true cause.

I. DESCRIPTION.—Although the signs of it, as will appear in the sequel, may be detected long before the leaves put out in the spring, yet its full effects do not begin to appear until May, or if the spring be backward, until June. On the wood of the last year will be found a point where the

---

* Read before the Indiana Horticultural Society, and communicated by Mr. Beecher to Hovey's Magazine of Horticulture, December, 1844.

bark is either dead and dry, or else at the same point the bark will be puffed, softened, or sappy with thickened sap —these two appearances indicating only different degrees of the same blight. Wherever the bark is dead and dry, the limb will flourish above it, make new wood, ripen its fruit, but perish the ensuing winter. In the other case, as soon as the circulation of the sap becomes active, the point described shows signs of disease, the leaf turns to a darker brown than is natural to its ordinary decay, being nearly black, and the wood perishes.

The disease, at first, blights the terminal portions of the branch; but the affection spreads gradually downward, and sometimes affects the whole trunk. The time from the first appearance of the blight to that in which any affected part dies, is various; sometimes two or three weeks—sometimes a day only; and sometimes, but rarely, even a few hours consummate the disease.

On dissecting the branch, the wood is of a dirty, brownish, yellow color; the sap thick and unctuous, of a sour disagreeable odor, like that of a fermented watermelon, on the tops of potato vines after they have been frosted. In still, moist days, where the blight is extensive in an orchard, this odor fills the air, and is disagreeably perceptible at some distance from the trees.

Sometimes the bark bursts, the sap exudes, and runs down, turning black; and its acridity will destroy vegetation on which it may drop, and shoots, at a distance from the trunk, upon which the rain washes this ichor, will soon perish. When we come to treat of the *cause* of this disease, it will be important to remember this malignancy of the fluids.

We are carefully to distinguish these appearances, peculiar to what I suppose ought to be called *winter-blight*, from another and a *summer-blight*. In this last, the leaf is affected at first in spots; gradually the whole leaf turns russet color and drops. Along the wood may be seen the hardened trail as of a slimy insect, of an ash color. The *wood* suffers very little by this summer-blight, and sometimes none. The winter-blight is found on almost all kinds of trees. This summer it has affected the apple, the pear, the peach, the quince, the English hawthorn, privet, black birch, Spanish chestnut, elder, and calycanthus. I enumerate the most of these kinds on the authority of J. H. James, of Urbana, Ohio, and C. W. Elliott, of Cincinnati, having observed it myself only on fruit-trees.

II. THEORIES.—A variety of theories exist as to the causes of this disease. Some are mere imaginations; some are only ingenious; and some so near to what I suppose to be the truth, that it is hardly possible to imagine how the discovery was not made.

The injury is done in the fall, but is not seen till spring or summer, or even the next fall. Thus, six months or a year intervene between the *cause* and the *effect*—a sufficient reason for the difficulty of detecting the origin of the evil.

1. Some have alleged that the rays of the sun, passing through vapors which arise about the trees, concentrate upon the branches, and destroy them by the literal energy of fire. Were this true, the young and tender shoots would suffer first and most; all pear-trees would suffer alike; all moist and hot summers would be affected with blight; herbaceous plants would suffer more than ligneous: all of which results are contrary to facts.

2. Some have supposed the soil to contain deleterious substances, or to be wanting in properties necessary to health. But in either case such a cause of the blight appears untrue, when we consider that trees suffer in all soils, rich or poor; that, in the same soil, one tree is blighted and the next tree escapes; that they will flourish for twenty years and then blight; that a tree partially diseased recovers, and thrives for ten or more years without recurrence of blight.

3. It has been attributed to violent and sudden changes

of temperature in the air and of moisture in the earth; to sudden change from sward to high tillage; and the result is stated to be an "overplus" of sap, or a "surfeit." All these causes occur every year; but the blight does not every year follow them. Changes of temperature, and violent changes in the condition of the soil, may be *allied* with the true cause. But when *only* these things exist, no blight follows.

4. Others have attributed the disease to over-stimulation by high manuring, or constant tillage; and it has been said that covering the roots with stones and rubbish, or laying the orchard down to grass, would prevent the evil. Facts warrant no such conclusions. Pear-trees in Gibson County, Indiana, on a clay soil, with blue slaty subsoil, were affected this year more severely than any of which we have heard. Pears in southern parts of this State, on red clay, where the ground had long been neglected, suffered as much as along the rich bottom lands of the Wabash about Vincennes. If there was any difference it was in favor of the richest land. About Mooresville, Morgan County, Indiana, pears have been generally affected, and those in grass lands *as much* as those in open soils. Aside from these facts, it is well known that pear-trees do not blight in those seasons when they make the rankest growth more than in others. They will thrive rampantly for years, no evil arising from their luxuriance, and then suddenly die of blight.

5. It has been supposed by a few to be the effect of *age*, the disease beginning on old varieties, and propagated upon new varieties by contagion. Were this the true cause, we should expect it to be most frequently developed in those pear regions where old varieties most abound. But this disease seems to be so little known in England, that Loudon, in his elaborate *Encyclopedia of Gardening*, does not even mention it. Mr. Manning's statement will be given further on, to the same purport.

6. Insect theory: The confidence with which eastern cultivators pronounce the cause to be an *insect*, has in part served to cover up singular discrepancies in the separate statements in respect to the ravages, and even the species of this destroyer. The *Genesee Farmer* of July, 1843, says, " the cause of the disease was for many years a matter of dispute, and is so still by some persons; but the majority are now fully convinced that it is the work of an insect (*scolytus pyri*). T. W. Harris, in his work on insects, speaks of the minuteness and obscure habits of this insect, as " reasons why it has eluded the researches of those persons who disbelieve in its existence as the cause of the blasting of the limbs of the *pear-tree*." Dr. Harris evidently supposed, until so late as 1843, that this insect infested only the *pear-tree;* for he says, " the discovery of the blight-beetle in the limbs of the apple-tree, is a new fact in natural history; but it is easily accounted for, because this tree belongs not only to the same natural group, but also to the same genus as the pear-tree. It is not, therefore, surprising, that both the pear and the apple-tree should occasionally be attacked by the same insect." [See an article in the *Massachusetts Ploughman*, summer of 1843, quoted in *Genesee Farmer*, July, 1843.]

This insect is said to eat through the *alburnum*, the hard wood, and even a part of the pith, and to destroy the branch by separation of part from part, as a saw would. On these facts, which there is no room to question, we make two remarks.

1st. That the blight thus produced is *limited*, and probably sectional or local. No account has met my eye which leads me to suppose that any considerable injury has been done by it. Mr. Manning, of Salem, Mass., in the second edition of his " Book of Flowers," states that he has never " *had any trees affected by it*"—the blight. Yet his garden and nursery has existed for twenty years, and contained immense numbers of trees.

2d. It is very plain that neither Mr. Lowell, originally, nor Dr. Harris, nor any who describe the blight as caused by the blight-beetle, had any notion of that disease which passes by the same name in the middle and western States. The blight of the *scolytus pyri* is a mere *girdling* of the branches—a mechanical separation of parts; and no mention is made of the most striking facts incident to the great blight—the viscid unctuous sap; the bursting of the bark, through which it issues; and its poisonous effects on the young shoots upon which it drops.

We do not doubt the insect-blight; but we are sure that it is not *our* blight. We feel very confident, also, that this blight, which from its devastations may be called the great blight, has been felt in New England, in connection with the insect-blight, and confounded with it, and the effects of two different causes happening to appear in conjunction, have been attributed to one, and the least influential cause. The writer in Fessenden's *American Gardener* (Mr. Lowell ?) says of the blight, "it is sometimes so rapid in its progress, that in a few hours from its first appearance the whole tree will appear to be mortally diseased." This is not insect-blight; for did the blight-beetle eat so *suddenly* around the whole *trunk ?* Now here is a striking appearance of the great blight, confounded with the minor blight, as we think will appear in the sequel.

This theory has stood in the way of a discovery of the true cause of the great blight; for every cultivator has gone in search of insects; they have been found in great plenty, and in great variety of species, and their harmless presence accused with all the mischief of the season. A writer in the *Farmer's Advocate*, Jamestown, N. C., discerned the fire-blight, and traced it to "small, *red*, pellucid insects, briskly moving from place to place on the branches." This is not the *scolytus pyri* of Prof. Peck and Dr. Harris.

Dr. Mosher, of Cincinnati, in a letter published in the *Farmer and Gardener* for June, 1844, describes a third insect—"*very minute brown-colored aphides,* snugly secreted in the axilla of every leaf on several small branches; . . . most of them were busily engaged with their proboscis inserted through the tender cuticle of this part of the *petiole* of the leaf, feasting upon the *vital juices* of the tree. The leaves being thus deprived of the necessary sap for nourishment and elaboration soon perished, . . . while all that part of the branch and trunk below, dependent upon the elaborated sap of the deadened leaves above, shrunk, turned black, and dried up," p. 261.

Lindley, in his work on *Horticulture,* p. 42–46, has detailed experiments illustrating vegetable *perspiration,* from which we may form an idea of the amount of fluid which these " very minute brown-colored aphides " would have to drink. A sunflower, three and a half feet high, perspired in a very warm day thirty ounces—nearly two pounds; on another day, twenty ounces. Taking the old rule, " a pint a pound," nearly a quart of fluid was exhaled by a sunflower in twelve hours; and the vessels were still inflated with a fresh supply drawn from the roots. Admitting that the leaves of a fruit-tree have a less current of sap than a sunflower or a grape-vine, yet in the months of May and June, the amount of sap to be exhausted by these very minute brown aphides, would be so great, that if they drank it so suddenly as to cause a tree to die in a day, they would surely augment in bulk enough to be discovered without a lens. If some one had accounted for the low water in the Mississippi, in the summer of 1843, by saying that buffaloes had drank up all the upper Missouri, and cut off the supply, we should be at a loss which most to pity, the faith of the narrator, or the probable condition of the buffaloes after their feat of imbibition. ·

But the most curious results *follow* these feats of suction. The limbs and trunk *below* shrink and turn black, for want of that elaborated sap extracted by the aphides. And yet every year we perform artificially this very operation in *ringing* or *decortication* of branches, for the purpose of accelerating maturation or improving the fruit. Every year the *saw* takes off a third, a half, and sometimes more, of a living tree; and the effect is to produce new shoots, not death. Is an operation which can be safely performed by man, *deadly* when performed by an insect? Dr. Masher did not detect the insects without extreme search, and then only· in colonies, on healthy branches. Do whole trees wither in a day by the mere suction of such insects? Had they been supposed to *poison* the fluids, the theory would be less exceptionable, since poisons in minute quantities may be very malignant.

While we admit a limited mischief of insects, they can never be the cause of the prevalent blight of .the middle and western States—such a blight as prevailed in and around Cincinnati in the summer of 1844—nor of that blight which prevailed in 1832. The *blight-beetle*, after most careful search and dissection, has not been found, nor any trace or passage of it. Dr. Mosher's insect may be set aside without further remark.

I think that further observation will confirm the following conclusions:

1. Insects are frequently found feeding in various ways upon blighted trees, or on trees which afterward become so.

2. Trees are fatally blighted on which no insects are discerned feeding—neither aphides nor *scolytus pyri*.

3. Multitudes of trees have such insects on them as are in other cases supposed to cause the blight, without a sign of blight following. This has been the case in our own garden.

III. CAUSE OF THE BLIGHT.—The Indiana Horticultural Society, early in the summer of 1844, appointed a committee to collect and investigate facts on the Fire-Blight. While serving on this committee, and inquiring in all the pear-growing regions, we learned that Reuben Reagan, of Putnam County, Ind., was in possession of much information, and supposed himself to have discovered the cause of this evil; and to him we are indebted for a first suggestion of the cause. Mr. Reagan has for more than twelve years past suspected that this disease originated in the fall previous to the summer on which it declares itself. During the last winter Mr. Reagan predicted the blight, and in his pear-orchards he marked the trees that would suffer, and pointed to the spot which would be the seat of the disease; and his prognostications were strictly verified. After gathering from him all the information which a limited time would allow, we obtained from Aaron Alldredge, of Indianapolis, a nurseryman of great skill, and possessed of careful, cautious habits of observation, much corroborative information; and particularly a tabular account of the blight for nine years past in his nursery and orchard.

The spring of 1843 opened early, but cold and wet, until the last of May. The summer was both dry and cool, and trees made very little growth of new wood. Toward autumn, however, the drought ceased, copious rains saturated the ground, and warm weather started all trees into vigorous, though late, growth. At this time, while we hoped for a long fall and a late winter, on the contrary we were surprised by an early and sudden winter, and with unusual severity at the very beginning. In the West, much corn was ruined and more damaged; and hundreds of bushels of apples were caught on the trees and spoiled—one cultivator alone losing five hundred bushels. Caught in this early winter, what was the condition of fruit-trees? They were making rapid growth, every part in a state of excitement, the wood unripe, the passages of ascent and descent impleted with sap. In this condition, the fluids were suddenly frozen—the growth instantly checked; and the whole tree, from a state of great excitability, was, by one shock, rudely forced into a state of rest. Warm suns, for a time, followed severe nights. What would be the effect of this freezing and sudden thawing upon the fluids and their vessels? We have been able to find so little written upon vegetable morbid anatomy (probably from the want of access to books), that we can give but an imperfect account of the derangement produced upon the circulating fluids by congelation. We cannot state the specific changes produced by cold upon the ascending sap, or on the cambium, nor upon the elaborated descending current. There is reason to suppose that the two latter only suffer, and probably only the last. That freezing and thawing decompose the coloring matter of plants is known; but what other decomposition, if any, is effected, we know not. The effect of congelation upon the descending sap of pear and apple-trees, is to turn it to a viscid, unctuous state. It assumes a reddish brown color; becomes black by exposure to the air; is poisonous to vegetables even when applied upon the leaf. Whether in some measure this follows all degrees of congelation, or only under certain conditions, we have no means of knowing.

The effect of freezing and thawing upon the tissues and sap-vessels is better known. Congelation is accompanied with expansion; the tender vessels are either burst or lacerated; the excitability of the parts is impaired or destroyed; the air is expelled from the aëriferous cavities, and forced into the passages for fluids; and lastly, the tubes for the conveyance of fluids are obstructing by a thickening of their sides.* The fruit-trees, in the fall of 1843, were then brought into a morbid state—the sap thickened and diseased; the passages lacerated, obstructed, and probably, in many instances burst. The sap elaborated, and now passing down in an injured state, would descend slowly, by reason of its inspissation, the torpidity of the parts, and the injured condition of the vessels. The grosser parts, naturally the most sluggish, would tend to lodge and gradually collect at the junction of fruit-spurs, the forks of branches,

* Lindley's Horticulture, p. 81–82.

or wherever the condition of the sap-vessels favored a lodgment. In some cases the passages are wholly obstructed; in others, only in part.

At length the spring approaches. In early pruning, the cultivator will find, in those trees which will ere long develop blight, that the knife is followed by an unctuous sap, and that the liber is of a greenish yellow color. These will be the first signs, and the practised eye may detect them long before a leaf is put forth.

When the season is advanced sufficiently to excite the tree to action, the sap will, as usual, ascend by the alburnum, which has probably been but little injured; the leaf puts out, and no outward sign of disease appears; nor will it appear until the leaf prepares the downward current. May, June and July, are the months when the growth is most rapid, and when the tree requires the most elaborate sap; and in these months the blight is fully developed. When the descending fluid reaches the point where, in the previous fall, a total obstruction had taken place, it is as effectually stopped as if the branch were girdled. For the sap which had lodged there would, by the winds and sun, be entirely dried. This would not be the case if the sap was good and the vitality of the wood unimpaired; but where the sap and vessels are both diseased, the sun affects the branch on the tree just as it would if severed and lying on the ground. There will, therefore, be found on the tree, branches with spots where the bark is dead and shrunk away below the level of the surrounding bark; and at these points the current downward is wholly stopped. Only the *outward* part, however, is dead, while the *alburnum*, or sap-wood, is but partially injured. Through the alburnum, then, the sap from the roots passes up, enters the leaf, and men are astonished to see a branch, seemingly dead in the middle, growing thriftily at its extremity. No insect-theory can account for this case; yet it is perfectly plain and simple when we consider that there are two currents of sap, one of which may be destroyed, and the other for a *limited time* go on. The blight, under this aspect, is nothing but *ringing* or *decortication*, effected by diseased sap, destroying the parts in which it lodges, and then itself drying up. The branch will grow, fruit will set, and frequently become larger and finer flavored than usual.

But in a second class of cases, the downward current comes to a point where the diseased sap had effected only a partial lodgment. The vitality of the neighboring parts was preserved, and the diseased fluids have been undried by wind or sun, and remain more or less inspissated. The descending current meets and takes up more or less of this diseased matter, according to the particular condition of the sap. Wherever the elaborated sap passes, after touching this diseased region, it will carry its poison along with it down the trunk, and, by the lateral vessels, in toward the pith. We may suppose that a violence which would destroy the health of the outer parts, would, to some degree, rupture the inner sap-vessels. By this, or by some unknown way, the diseased sap is taken into the inner,* upward current, and goes into the general circulation. If it be in a diluted state, or in small quantities, languor and decline will be the result; if in large quantities, and concentrated, the branch will die suddenly, and the odor of it will be that of frost-bitten vegetation. All the different degrees of mortality result from the quantity and quality of the diseased sap which is taken into circulation. In conclusion, then, where, in one class of cases, the feculent matter was, in the fall, so virulent as to destroy the parts where it lodged, and was then dried by exposure to wind and sun, the branch above will live, even through the summer, but perish the next winter; and the spring afterward, standing bare amid green branches, the cultivator may suppose the branch to

* See Lindley, p. 82.

have blighted that spring, although the cause of death was seated eighteen months before. When, in the other class of cases, the diseased sap is less virulent in the fall, but probably growing worse through the spring, a worse blight ensues, and a more sudden mortality.

We will mention some proofs of the truth of this explanation.

1. The two great blight years throughout the region of Indianapolis, 1832 and 1844, were preceded by a summer and fall such as we have described. In the autumns of both 1831 and 1843, the orchards were overtaken by a sudden freeze while in a fresh-growing state; and in both cases the consequence was excessive destruction the ensuing spring and summer.

2. In consequence of this diagnosis, it has been found practicable to predict the blight six months before its development. The statement of this fact, on paper, may seem a small measure of proof; but it would weigh much with any candid man to be told, by an experienced nurseryman, this is such a fall as will make blight; to be taken, during the winter into the orchard, and told, this tree has been struck at the junction of these branches; that tree is not at all affected; this tree will die entirely the next season; this tree will go first on this side, etc., and to find, afterward, the prediction verified.

3. This leads us to state separately, the fact, that, after such a fall, blighted-trees may be ascertained during the process of late winter or early spring pruning.

In pruning before the sap begins to rise freely, no sap should follow the knife in a healthy tree. But in trees which have been affected with blight, a sticky, viscid sap exudes from the wound.

4. Trees which ripen their wood and leaves early, are seldom affected. This ought to elicit careful observation; for, if found true, it will be an important element in determining the value of varieties of the pear in the middle and

western States, where the late and warm autumns render
orchards more liable to winter blight than New England
orchards. An Orange Bergamot, grafted upon an apple
stock, had about run out; it made a small and feeble growth,
and cast its leaves in the summer of 1843, long before frost.
It escaped the blight entirely; while young trees, and of the
same kind (we believe), standing about it, and growing vigorously till the freeze, perished the next season. I have
before me a list of more than fifty varieties, growing in the
orchard of Aaron Alldredge, of Indianapolis, and their history
since 1836; and so far as it can be ascertained, late-grow-
ing varieties are the ones, in every case, subject to blight;
and of those which have always escaped, the most part are
known to ripen leaf and wood early.

5. Wherever artificial causes have either *produced* or
prevented a growth so late as to be overtaken by a freeze,
blight has, respectively, been *felt* or *avoided*. Out of 200
pear-trees, only four escaped in 1832, in the orchard of Mr.
Reagan. These four had, the previous spring, been *transplanted*, and had made little or no growth during summer
or fall. If, however, they had recovered themselves, during the summer, so as to grow in the autumn, transplanting would have had just the other effect; as was the case
in a row of pear-trees, transplanted by Mr. Alldredge in
1843. They stood still through the summer and made
growth in the fall—were frozen—and in 1844 manifested
severe blight. Mr. Alldredge's orchard affords another
instructive fact. Having a row of the St. Michael pear (of
which any cultivator might have been proud), standing
close by his stable, he was accustomed, in the summer of
1843, to throw out, now and then, manure about them, to
force their growth. Under this stimulus they were making
excessive growth when winter-struck. Of all his orchard,
they suffered, the ensuing summer, the most severely. Of
twenty-two trees *twelve* were affected by the blight, and
eight entirely killed. Of seventeen trees of the Bell pear,

eleven suffered, but none were killed. All in this region know the vigorous habit of this tree. Of eight Crassane Bergamot (a late grower), five were affected and two killed. In an orchard of 325 trees of 79 varieties, one in seven blighted, 25 were totally destroyed. Although a minute observation was not made on each tree, yet, as a general fact, those which suffered were trees of a full habit and of a late growth.

6. Mr. White, a nurseryman near Mooresville, Morgan County, Indiana, in an orchard of from 150 to 200 trees, had not a single case of the blight in the year 1844, though all around him its ravages were felt. What were the facts in this case? His orchard is planted on a mound-like piece of ground; is high, of a sandy, gravelly soil: earlier by a week than nursery soils in this county; and in the summer of 1843 his trees grew through the summer; wound up and shed their leaves early in the fall, and during the warm spell made no *second growth*. The orchard, then, that escaped, was one on such a soil as insured an *early* growth, so that the winter fell upon ripened wood.

7. It may be objected, that if the blight *began* in the new and growing wood, it would appear there; whereas the seat of the evil, *i. e.* the place where the bark is diseased or dead, is lower down and on old wood. Certainly, it should be; for the returning sap falls some ways down before it effects a lodgment.

8. It might be said that *spring-frosts* might produce this disease. But in the spring of 1834, in the last of May, after the forest-trees were in full leaf, there came frost so severe as to cut every leaf; and to this day the dead tops of the beech attest the power of the frost. But no *blight* occurred that year in orchard, garden or nursery.

9. It may be asked why forest-trees do not suffer. To some extent they do. But usually the dense shade preserves the moisture of the soil, and favors an equal growth during the spring and summer; so that the excitability of

the tree is spent before autumn, and it is going to rest when frost strikes it.

10. It may be inquired why fall-growing shrubs are not always blighted, since many kinds are invariably caught by the frost in a growing state.

We reply, first, that we are not to say that *every* tree or shrub suffers from cold in the same manner. We assert it of fruit-trees because it has been observed; it must be asserted of other trees only when ascertained.

We reply more particularly, that a *mere frost* is not supposed to do the injury. The conditions under which blight is supposed to originate are, a growing state of the tree, a sudden *freeze*, and sudden thawing.

We would here add, that many things are yet to be ascertained before this theory can be considered as settled; as the actual state of the sap after congelation, ascertained by experiment; the condition of sap-vessels, as ascertained by dissection; whether the congelation, or the thawing, or both, produce the mischief; whether the character of the season *following* the fall-injury may not materially modify the malignancy of the disease; seasons that are hot, moist and cloudy, propagating the evil; and others dry, and cool, restraining growth and the dsease. It is to be hoped that these points will be carefully investigated, not by conjecture, but by scientific processes.

11. We have heard it objected, that trees grafted in the spring blight in the graft during the summer. If the *stock* had been affected in the fall, blight would arise from *it;* if the scion had, in common with the tree from which it was cut, been injured, blight must arise from *it*.

Blight is frequently caused in the nursery; and the cultivator, who has brought trees from a distance, and with much expense, has scarcely planted them before they show blight and die.

12. It is objected, that while only a single branch is at first affected, the evil is imparted to the whole tree; not

only to the wood of the last year, but to the old branches.
We reply, that if a single branch only should be affected by
fall-frost, and be so severely affected as to become a reposi-
tory of much malignant fluid, it might gradually enter the
system of the whole tree, through the circulation. This
fact shows, why *cutting* is a partial remedy; every diseased
branch removed, removes so much poison; it shows also
why cutting from *below* the seat of the disease (as if to fall
below the haunt of a supposed insect), is beneficial. The
further the cut is made from that point where the sap has
clogged the passages, the less of it will remain to enter the
circulation.

13. Trees of great vigor of constitution, in whose system
but little poison exists, may succeed after a while in rejecting the evil, and recover. Where much enters the system,
the tree must die; and with a suddenness proportioned to
the amount of poison circulated.

14. A rich and *dry* soil would be likely to promote early
growth, and the tree would finish its work in time; but a
rich and *moist* soil, by forcing the growth, would prepare
the tree for blight; so that rich soils may prevent or prepare for the blight, and the difference will be the difference
of the respective soils in producing an early instead of a late
growth.

IV. REMEDY.—So long as the blight was believed to be
of insect origin, it appeared totally irremediable. If the foregoing reasoning be found correct, it will be plain that the
scourge can only be occasional; that it may be in a degree
prevented; and to some extent remedied where it exists.

1. We should begin by selecting for pear orchards a
warm, light, rich, dry and early soil. This will secure an
early growth and ripe wood before winter sets in.

2. So soon as observation has determined what kinds are
naturally early growers and early ripeners of wood, such
should be selected; as they will be least likely to come
under those conditions in which blight occurs.

3. Wherever orchards are already planted; or where a choice in soils cannot be had, the cultivator may know by the last of August or September, whether a fall-growth is to be expected. To prevent it, we suggest immediate *root-pruning*. This will benefit the tree at any rate, and will probably, by immediately restraining growth, prevent blight.

4. Whenever blight has occurred, we know of no remedy but free and early *cutting*. In some cases it will remove all diseased matter; in some it will alleviate only; but in bad blight, there is neither in this, nor in anything else that we are aware of, any remedy.

There are two additional subjects, with which we shall close this paper.

1. This blight is not to be confounded with *winter-killing*. In the winter of either 1837 or 1838, in March a deep snow fell (in the region of Indianapolis) and was immediately followed by brilliant sun. Thousands of nursery-trees perished in consequence, but without putting out leaves, or lingering. It is a familiar fact to orchardists, that severe cold, followed by warm suns, produce a bursting of the bark along the trunk; but usually at the surface of the ground.

2. We call the attention of cultivators to the disease of the peach-tree, called "The Yellows." We have not spoken of it as the same disease as the *blight* in the pear and the apple, only because we did not wish to embarrass this subject by too many issues. We will only say, that it is the opinion of the most intelligent cultivators among us, that the yellows are nothing but the development of the blight according to the peculiar habits of the peach-tree. We mention it, that observation may be directed to the facts.

PROGRESS OF HORTICULTURE IN INDIANA.*

I AM induced to send you some remarks upon Horticultural matters, from observing your disposition to make your magazine not merely a record of specific processes, and a register of plants and fruits, but also a chronicle of the yearly progress and condition of the Horticultural art. I should be glad if I could in any degree thus repay the pleasure which others have given me through your numbers, by reciprocal efforts.

The Indiana Horticultural State fair is held annually, on the 4th and 5th of October. Experience has shown that it should be earlier; for, although a better assortment of late fruits, in which, hitherto, we have chiefly excelled, is secured, it is at the expense of small fruits and flowers. The floral exhibition was meagre—the frost having already visited and despoiled our gardens. The chief attraction, as, in an agricultural community, it must long continue to be, was the exhibition of fruit. My recollection of New England fruits, after an absence of more than ten years, is not distinct; but my impression is, that so fine a collection of fruits could scarcely be shown there. The luxuriance of the peach, the plum, the pear and the apple, is such, in this region, as to afford the most perfect possible specimens. The vigor of fruit-trees, in such a soil and under a heaven so congenial, produces fruits which are very large without being coarse-fleshed; the flavor concentrated, and the color very high. It is the constant remark of emigrants from the East, that our apples surpass those to which they have been accustomed. Many fruits which I remember in Connecticut as light-colored, appear with us almost refulgent. All summer and early fall apples were gone before our exhibition; but between seventy and a hundred varieties of winter ap-

* A letter published in Hovey's Magazine of Horticulture, February, 1845.

ples were exhibited. We never expect to see finer. Our most popular winter apples are : Yellow Bellflower ; White Bellflower (called *Detroit* by the gentlemen of Cincinnati Horticultural Society—but for reasons which are not satisfactory to my mind. What has become of the White Bellflower of *Coxe*, if this is not it?) Newtown Spitzenberg, exceedingly fine with us ; Canfield, Jennetting or Neverfail, escaping spring frosts by late blossoming, very hardy, a great bearer every year ; the fruit comes into eating in February, is tender, juicy, mild and sprightly, and preferred with us to the Green Newtown pippin—keeping full as well, bearing better, the pulp much more *manageable* in the mouth, and the apple has the peculiar property of bearing frosts, and even freezing, without material injury ; Green Newtown pippin ; Michael Henry pippin (very fine) ; Pryor's Red, in flavor resembling the New England Seek-no-further ; Golden Russet, the prince of small apples, and resembling a fine butter-pear more nearly than any apple in our orchards —an enormous bearer ; some limbs exhibited were clustered with fruit, more like bunches of grapes than apples ; Milam, favorite early winter ; Rambo, the same. But the apple most universally cultivated is the Vandervere pippin, only a second or third-rate table apple, but having other qualities which quite ravish the hearts of our farmers. The tree is remarkably vigorous and healthy ; it almost never fails in a crop ; when all others *miss*, the Vandervere pippin *hits;* the fruit, which is very large and comely, is a late winter fruit— yet swells so quickly as to be the first and best summer cooking apple. If its flesh (which is coarse) were fine, and its (too sharp) flavor equalled that of the Golden Russet, it would stand without a rival, or near neighbor, at the very head of the list of winter apples. As it is, it is a *first-rate* tree, bearing a *second-rate* apple. A hybrid between it and the Golden Russet, or Newtown Spitzenberg, appropriating the virtues of both, would leave little more to be hoped for or wished. The *Baldwin* has never come up to its eastern reputation with us; the Rhode Island Greening is eaten for the sake of "auld lang syne;" the Roxbury russet is not yet in bearing—instead of it several false varieties have been presented at our exhibitions. All the classic apples of your orchards are planted here, but are yet on probation.

Nothing can exhibit better the folly of trusting to *seedling* orchards for fruit, for a main supply, than our experience in this matter. The early settlers could not bring trees from Kentucky, Virginia or Pennsylvania—and, as the next resort, brought and planted seeds of popular apples. A later population found no nurseries to supply the awakening demand for fruit-trees, and resorted also to planting seed. That which, at first, sprang from necessity, has been continued from habit, and from an erroneous opinion that seedling fruit was better than grafted. An immense number of seedling trees are found in our State. Since the Indiana Horticultural Society began to collect specimens of these, more than one hundred and fifty varieties have been sent up for inspection. Our rule is to reject every apple which, the habits of the tree and the quality of its fruit being considered, has a superior or equal already in cultivation. Of all the number presented, not six have vindicated their claims to a name or a place—and not more than *three* will probably be known ten years hence. While, then, we encourage cultivators to raise seedlings experimentally, it is the clearest folly to reject the established varieties and trust to inferior seedling orchards. From facts which I have collected there has been planted, during the past year, in this State, at least one hundred thousand apple-trees. Every year the demand increases. It is supposed that the next year will surpass this by at least twenty-five thousand.

In connection with apple orchards, our farmers are increasingly zealous in pear cultivation. We are fortunate in having secured to our nurseries not only the most approved old varieties, but the choicest new pears of British,

Continental or American origin. A few years ago to each
one hundred apple-trees, our nurseries sold, perhaps, two
pear-trees; now they sell at least twenty to a hundred.
Very large pear *orchards* are established, and in some instances are now beginning to bear. I purchased Williams's
Bon Chrétien in our market last fall for seventy-five cents
the bushel. This pear, with the St. Michael's, Beurré Diel,
Beurré d'Aremberg, Passe Colmar, Duchesse d'Angoulême,
Seckel, and Marie Louise, are the most widely diffused, and
all of them regularly at our exhibitions. Every year enables us to test other varieties. The Passe Colmar and
Beurré d'Aremberg have done exceedingly well—a branch
of the latter, about eighteen inches in length, was exhibited at our Fair, bearing over twenty pears, none of which
were smaller than a turkey's egg. The demand for pear-
trees, this year, has been such that our nurseries have not
been able to answer it—and they are swept almost entirely
clean. I may as well mention here that, beside many more
neighborhood nurseries, there are in this State eighteen
which are large and skillfully conducted.

The extraordinary cheapness of trees favors their general
cultivation. Apple-trees, not under ten feet high, and finely
grown, sell at *ten*, and pears at *twenty* cents; and in some
nurseries, apples may be had at *six* cents. This price, it
should be recollected, is in a community where corn brings
from twelve to twenty cents only, a bushel; wheat sells
from forty-five to fifty; hay at five dollars the ton. During
the season of 1843–'44, apples of the finest sorts (Jennetting,
green Newtown pippin, etc.), sold at my door, as late as
April, for *twenty-five* cents a bushel—and dull at that. This
winter they command *thirty-seven* cents. Attention is increasingly turned to the cultivation of apples for exportation. Our inland orchards will soon find an outlet, both to
the Ohio River by railroad, and the Lakes by canal. The
effects of such a deluge of fruit is worthy of some speculation. It will diminish the price but increase the *profit* of

fruit. An analogous case is seen in the penny-postage system of England. Fruit will become more generally and largely an article, not of luxury, but of daily and ordinary diet. It will find its way down to the poorest table—and the *quantity* consumed will make up in profit to the dealer, what is lost in lessening its price. A few years and the apple crop will be a matter of reckoning by farmers and speculators, just as is now, the potato crop, the wheat crop, the pork, etc. Nor will it create a home market alone. By care it may be exported with such facility, that the world will receive it as a part of its diet. It will, in this respect, follow the history of grains and edible roots, and from a local and limited use, the apple and the pear will become articles of universal demand. The reasons of such an opinion are few and simple. It is a fruit always palatable—and as such, will be welcome to mankind whatever their tastes, if it can be brought within their reach. The western States will, before many years, be *forested* with orchards. The fruit bears exportation kindly. Thus there will be a *supply;* a possibility of distributing it by commerce, to meet a taste already existing. These views may seem fanciful—may prove so; but they are analogical. Nor, if I inherit my three score years and ten, do I expect to die, until the apple crop of the United States shall surpass the potato crop in value, both for man and beast. It has the double quality of palatableness, raw or cooked—it is a *permanent* crop, not requiring annual planting—and it produces more bushels to the acre than corn, wheat, or, on an average, than potatoes. The calculations may be made, allowing an average of fifteen bushels to a tree. The same reasoning is true of the pear; it and the apple, are to hold a place yet, as universal eatables—a *fruit-grain*, not known in their past history. If not another tree should be set in this county (Marion County), in ten years the annual crop of apples will be 200,000 bushels. But Wayne County has double our number of trees; suppose, however, the ninety counties of Indiana to have only 25 trees to a quarter section of land, *i. e.* to each 160 acres, the crop, of fifteen bushels a tree, would be nearly *two millions.*

The past year has greatly increased the cultivation of small fruits in the State. Strawberries are found in almost every garden, and of select sorts. None among them all is more popular—or more deservedly so—than Hovey's Seedling. We have a native white strawberry, removed from our meadows to our gardens, which produces fruit of superior fragrance and flavor. The crop is not large—but continues gradually ripening for many weeks. The blackberry is introduced to the garden among us. The fruit sells at our market for from three to five cents—profit is not therefore the motive for cultivating it, but improvement. I have a *white* variety. "What color is a *black*-berry when it is *green ?* " We used to say *red,* but now we have ripe *black*-berries which are *white,* and *green black*-berries which are *red.* Assorted gooseberries and the new raspberries, Franconia and Fastolff are finding their way into our gardens. The Antwerps we have long had in abundance. If next spring I can produce rhubarb weighing two pounds to the stalk, shall I have surpassed you ? I have a *seedling* which last year, without good cultivation, produced petioles weighing from eighteen to twenty ounces. My wrist is not very delicate, and yet it is much smaller in girth than they were.

In no department is there more decided advance among our citizens than in floriculture. In all our rising towns, yards and gardens are to be found choicely stocked. All hardy bulbs are now sought after. Ornamental shrubs are taken from our forests, or imported from abroad, in great variety. Altheas, rose acacia, jasmin, calycanthus, snowberry, snowball, sumach, syringas, spicewood, shepherdia, dogwood, redwood, and other hardy shrubs abound. The rose is an especial favorite. The Bengal, Tea and Noisettes bear our winters in the open garden with but slight protection. The Bourbon and Remontantes will, however, drive

2222222222222

out all old and ordinary varieties. The gardens of this town would afford about *sixty* varieties of roses, which would be reckoned first rate in Boston or Philadelphia.

While New England suffered under a season of drought, on this side of the mountains the season was uncommonly fine—scarcely a week elapsed without copious showers, and gardens remained moist the whole season. Fruits ripened from two to three weeks earlier than usual. In consequence of this, winter fruits are rapidly decaying. To-day is Christmas, the weather is spring-like—no snow—the thermometer this morning, forty degrees. My Noisettes retain their terminal leaves green; and in the southward-looking dells of the woods, grasses and herbs are yet of a vivid green. Birds are still here—three this morning were singing on the trees in my yard. There are some curious facts in the early history of horticulture in this region, which I meant to have included in this communication; but insensibly I have, already, prolonged it beyond, I fear, a convenient space for your magazine. I yield it to you for cutting, carving, suppressing, or whatever other operation will fit it for your purpose.

BROWNE'S AMERICAN POULTRY YARD.*

LET no man turn up his contemptuous nose at this Treatise until he has traced the manifold relations of eggs and capons to cake, company, and civilization. Banish the barnyard, and the universal aldermanhood would shrink and grow lean; cup-cakes and sponge-cakes, omelets, whips and legionary confections, would become mere dreams of remembrance.

Every friend of the trencher, every notable housewife,

* Published by A. O. Moore & Co., New York. Price $1 00.

complacently glorious amidst stacks of praised and devoured cake, has an interest in this book. There is, therefore, a certain interest which every civilized community should take in the progress of the great art of fowl-breeding.

There are striking analogies, also, which should be noticed by every comparative psychologist. The doctrine of trans-migration has some of its strongest proofs in the Kingdom of Poultry. The glowing comb, the haughty carriage, the resplendent tail-feathers, and ostentatious crowing of the lord of the barn-yard creation, reveals to the sagacious reasoner either the origin or destination of many other "lords of creation."

Nor can one mistake the resemblances traceable in the gentler sex of hens. Some there are industrious only in scratching and cackling, but nervous, gadding, restless; never content at home, never so happy as when at work in a new-made garden, and sagacious always of the very spots which are most precious in the owner's eyes. Are these the types of human busybodies, or are these resemblances only accidental? Others are discreet, domestic, prolific, useful and happy hens, human and feathered. Many there are neglectful. Some fowls are laborious egg-layers, but poor setters; others disdain the pains of laying, but are quite willing of a leisure summer's month to set awhile upon other eggs.

In the management, too, of their families, can any candid man resist the evidence of resemblances and affiliations between hens and humanity? Here a hen walks forth from her nest with but a single chick; the whole farm is too small for her anxious spirit. On this one precious pledge she bestows more clucking, more research and scratching, than a discreet old matron of many broods would upon five annual generations! And after all, what is the little brat good for—lazy and worked for, but never taught to work, it lives a few months petted and spoiled— dies of neglect, or is anatomized by some science-loving weasel! Other, and unnatural hens there are, to whom the vast brood of peeping, chirping chicks is but a burden. They seem to have thoughts of their own, and are perplexed and interrupted by the cares needful for their household. Could we pry into the secrets of this race, doubtless there would be found to be literary mothers, too busy for the general good to have much time for special duties. We cannot stop now to draw out these analogies, so well worthy the study of mental philosophers; else we should exhibit the distinctions of rank, race, and culture, in this interesting kingdom. There are nice questions of pedigree, there are points in relation to feathers and top-knots, combs and spurs, tail-feathers and wing-feathers, neck-hackles and toes, which are worthy the attention of any Calhoun of the barn-yard. The more savory but homely considerations of fattening, slaying, dressing, selling, stuffing, cooking, carving, distributing, eating and digestion, must be left to our readers' own reflections. Meanwhile, any man that owns a hen, or has a coop in prospect, may buy this book, certain of his money's worth. Book-farming and book-fowling are better than nothing.

REFLECTIONS ON THE CLOSE OF THE YEAR.*

THE labor of another year has passed beyond our reach. We can alter nothing, and the past is of no use to us except as a lesson for the future. The soil that the plow ripped up, in the spring, has yielded its harvest, its work is closed, its fruits garnered. The tree whose boughs grew green when the singing of birds proclaimed that spring was come, has ripened its fruit, perfected its growth, its store is gathered, and its leaves are lying beneath it, and slowly

* A.D. 1845.

returning to the earth from which they sprang. Only here and there, on a bright morning, do we see one of those birds which, a few months ago, builded their nest, watched their young, or taught the nestlings how to fly—young and old, with their grace of motion and sweet notes, are gone to a fairer clime. These changes one cannot help noticing; and no meditative mind can avoid many thoughts which flow out of them. Where are the harvests garnered which grew in the soil of the human heart? What thoughts and generous purposes have been ripened and stored up like fruit, and what ones have fallen and perished like leaves? Our vernal orchards never stood, within our remembrance, in such a glory of bloom; yet when the fruit should have set, most of the blossoms proved vain. And how many good purposes and fair resolutions have so perished within us! Have we, like the trees which we love and care for, made growth, of root and branch? Everything in nature has gradually assumed a preparation for winter. Those frosts and that ice which would have sent such mischief upon the leaves of summer, now lie, without harm, upon orchard and garden. Are we ripe and ready, too, for such a winter as adversity brings upon men?

THE END.

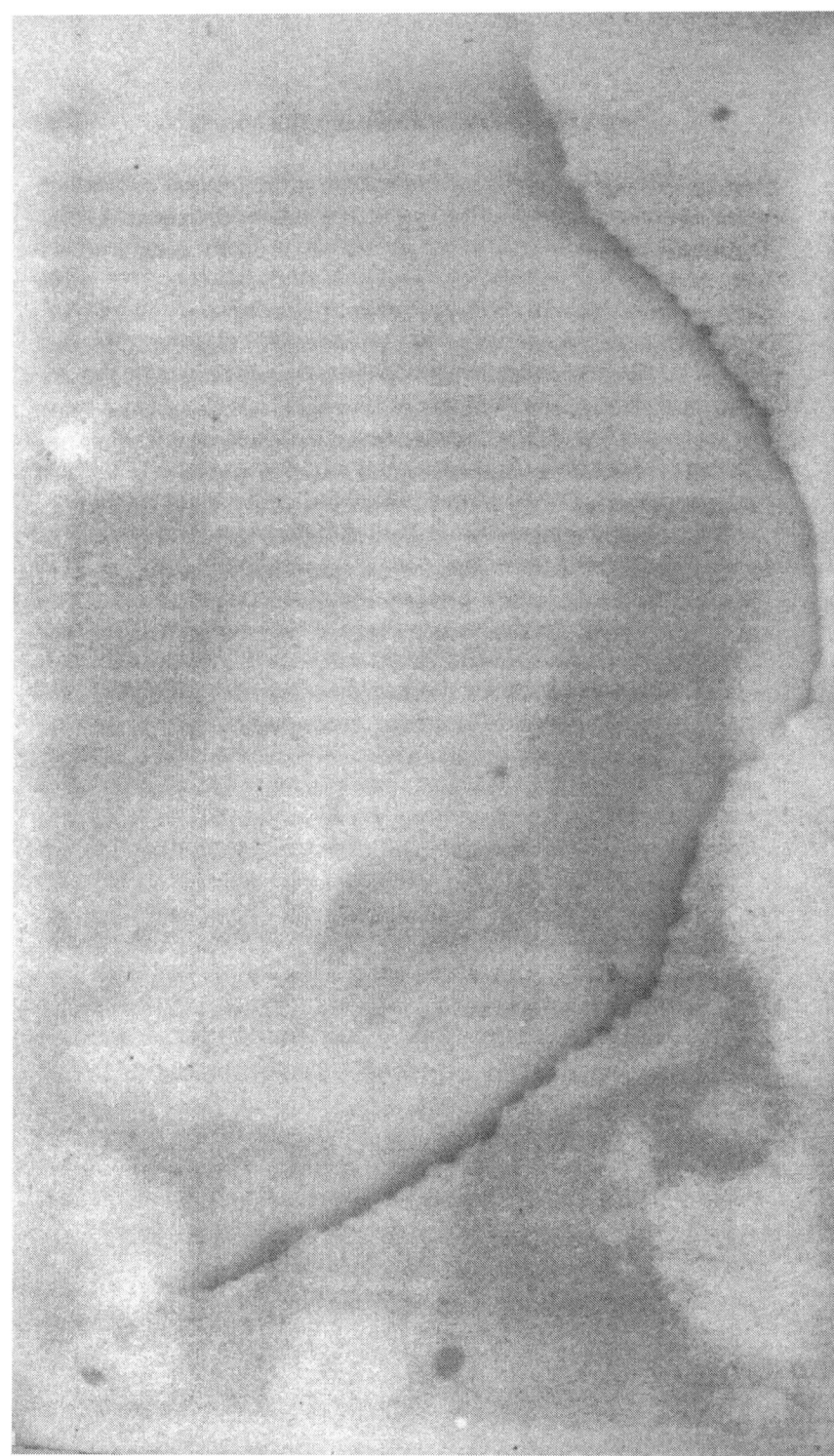

CPSIA information can be obtained
at www.ICGtesting.com
Printed in the USA
LVHW010735071222
734685LV00004B/270